PETER PARKER: THE SPECTACULAR

SPIDER-MAN

INTO THE
TWILIGHT

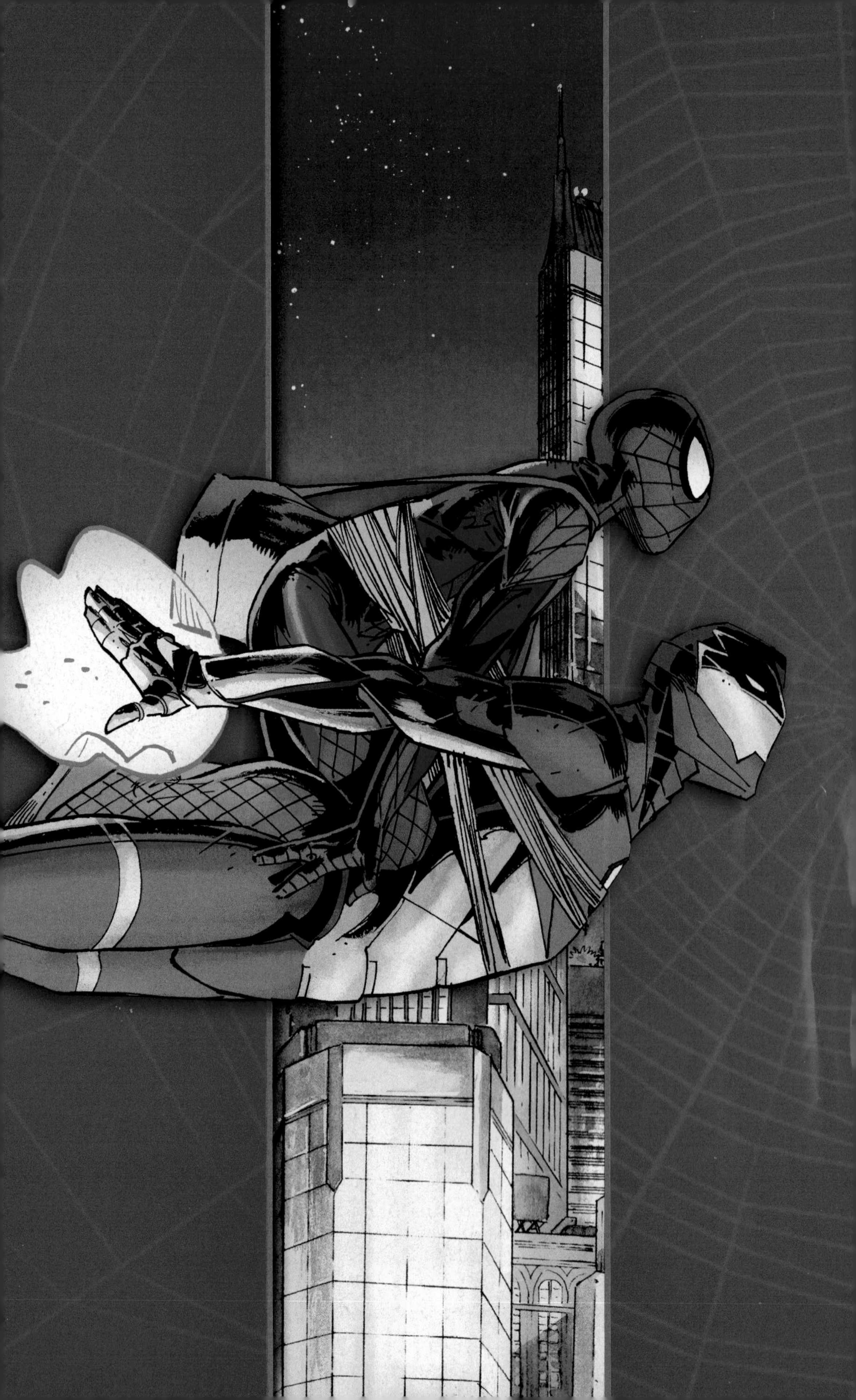

PETER PARKER: THE SPECTACULAR SPIDER-MAN

INTO THE TWILIGHT

CHIP ZDARSKY
WRITER

ADAM KUBERT & MICHAEL WALSH (#6)
ARTISTS

JORDIE BELLAIRE & IAN HERRING (#6)
COLORISTS

"TIME FLIES"
FROM *FREE COMIC BOOK DAY 2017*

PAULO SIQUEIRA
PENCILER

WALDEN WONG, CAM SMITH, JAY LEISTEN & PAULO SIQUEIRA
INKERS

FRANK D'ARMATA
COLORIST

"SPIDER-FIGHT"
FROM *PETER PARKER: THE SPECTACULAR SPIDER-MAN #1*

GORAN PARLOV
ARTIST

NATHAN FAIRBAIRN
COLORIST

VC's TRAVIS LANHAM
LETTERER

ADAM KUBERT & MORRY HOLLOWELL (#1), ADAM KUBERT & RICHARD ISANOVE (#2)
ADAM KUBERT & JORDIE BELLAIRE (#3-5) AND PAULO SIQUEIRA & RACHELLE ROSENBERG (#6)
COVER ART

ALLISON STOCK
ASSISTANT EDITOR

DEVIN LEWIS
ASSOCIATE EDITOR

NICK LOWE
EDITOR

COLLECTION EDITOR: MARK D. BEAZLEY
ASSISTANT EDITOR: CAITLIN O'CONNELL
ASSOCIATE MANAGING EDITOR: KATERI WOODY
SENIOR EDITOR, SPECIAL PROJECTS: JENNIFER GRÜNWALD
VP PRODUCTION & SPECIAL PROJECTS: JEFF YOUNGQUIST
SVP PRINT, SALES & MARKETING: DAVID GABRIEL
BOOK DESIGNER: ADAM DEL RE

EDITOR IN CHIEF: AXEL ALONSO
CHIEF CREATIVE OFFICER: JOE QUESADA
PRESIDENT: DAN BUCKLEY
EXECUTIVE PRODUCER: ALAN FINE

SPIDER-MAN CREATED BY STAN LEE & STEVE DITKO

PETER PARKER: THE SPECTACULAR SPIDER-MAN VOL. 1 — INTO THE TWILIGHT. Contains material originally published in magazine form as PETER PARKER: THE SPECTACULAR SPIDER-MAN #1-6 and FREE COMIC BOOK DAY 2017 (SECRET EMPIRE) #1. First printing 2017. ISBN# 978-1-302-90756-3. Published by MARVEL WORLDWIDE, INC., a subsidiary of MARVEL ENTERTAINMENT, LLC. OFFICE OF PUBLICATION: 135 West 50th Street, New York, NY 10020. Printed in the U.S.A. DAN BUCKLEY, President, Marvel Entertainment; JOE QUESADA, Chief Creative Officer; TOM BREVOORT, SVP of Publishing; DAVID BOGART, SVP of Business Affairs & Operations, Publishing & Partnership; C.B. CEBULSKI, VP of Brand Management & Development, Asia; DAVID GABRIEL, SVP of Sales & Marketing, Publishing; JEFF YOUNGQUIST, VP of Production & Special Projects; DAN CARR, Executive Director of Publishing Technology; ALEX MORALES, Director of Publishing Operations; SUSAN CRESPI, Production Manager; STAN LEE, Chairman Emeritus. For information regarding advertising in Marvel Comics or on Marvel.com, please contact Vit DeBellis, Integrated Sales Manager, at vdebellis@marvel.com. For Marvel subscription inquiries, please call 888-511-5480. Manufactured between 10/20/2017 and 11/20/2017 by QUAD/GRAPHICS WASECA, WASECA, MN, USA.

10 9 8 7 6 5 4 3 2 1

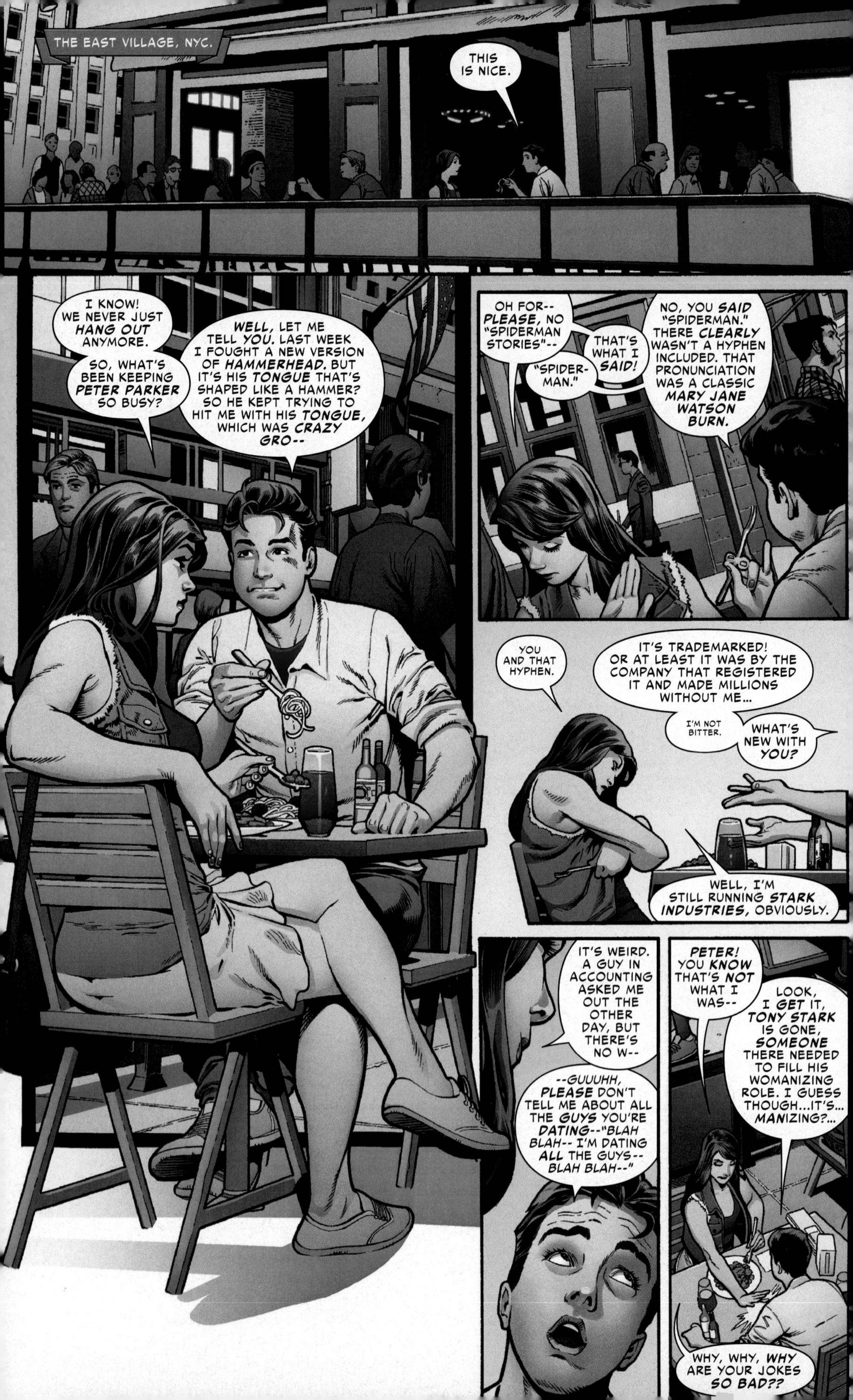
THE EAST VILLAGE, NYC.
THIS IS NICE.
I KNOW! WE NEVER JUST HANG OUT ANYMORE.
SO, WHAT'S BEEN KEEPING PETER PARKER SO BUSY?
WELL, LET ME TELL YOU. LAST WEEK I FOUGHT A NEW VERSION OF HAMMERHEAD. BUT IT'S HIS TONGUE THAT'S SHAPED LIKE A HAMMER? SO HE KEPT TRYING TO HIT ME WITH HIS TONGUE, WHICH WAS CRAZY GRO--
OH FOR-- PLEASE, NO "SPIDERMAN STORIES"--
"SPIDER-MAN."
THAT'S WHAT I SAID!
NO, YOU SAID "SPIDERMAN." THERE CLEARLY WASN'T A HYPHEN INCLUDED. THAT PRONUNCIATION WAS A CLASSIC MARY JANE WATSON BURN.
YOU AND THAT HYPHEN.
IT'S TRADEMARKED! OR AT LEAST IT WAS BY THE COMPANY THAT REGISTERED IT AND MADE MILLIONS WITHOUT ME...
I'M NOT BITTER.
WHAT'S NEW WITH YOU?
WELL, I'M STILL RUNNING STARK INDUSTRIES, OBVIOUSLY.
IT'S WEIRD. A GUY IN ACCOUNTING ASKED ME OUT THE OTHER DAY, BUT THERE'S NO W--
--GUUUHH, PLEASE DON'T TELL ME ABOUT ALL THE GUYS YOU'RE DATING--"BLAH BLAH-- I'M DATING ALL THE GUYS-- BLAH BLAH--"
PETER! YOU KNOW THAT'S NOT WHAT I WAS--
LOOK, I GET IT, TONY STARK IS GONE, SOMEONE THERE NEEDED TO FILL HIS WOMANIZING ROLE. I GUESS THOUGH...IT'S... MANIZING?...
WHY, WHY, WHY ARE YOUR JOKES SO BAD??

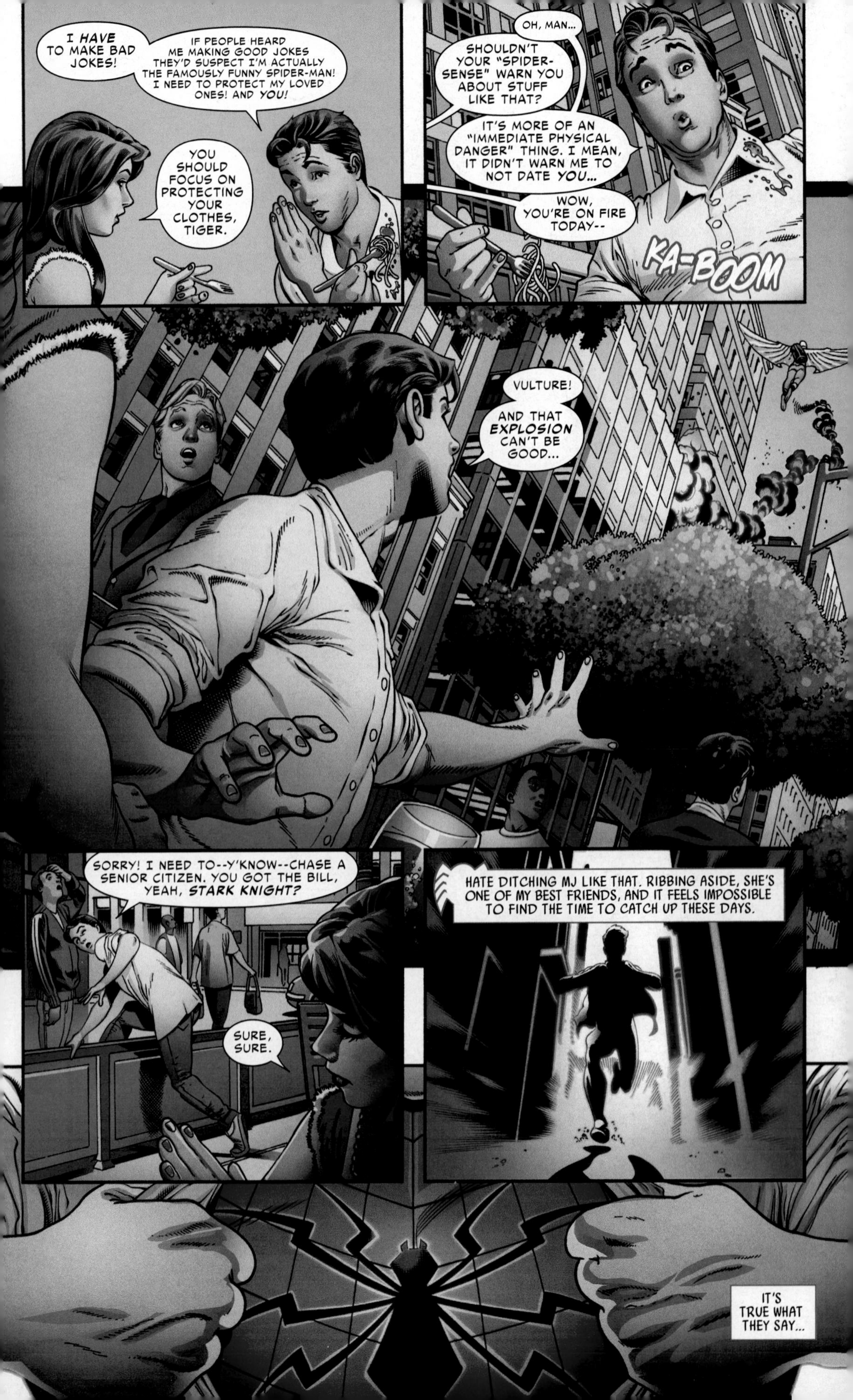

I HAVE TO MAKE BAD JOKES!
IF PEOPLE HEARD ME MAKING GOOD JOKES THEY'D SUSPECT I'M ACTUALLY THE FAMOUSLY FUNNY SPIDER-MAN! I NEED TO PROTECT MY LOVED ONES! AND YOU!
YOU SHOULD FOCUS ON PROTECTING YOUR CLOTHES, TIGER.
OH, MAN...
SHOULDN'T YOUR "SPIDER-SENSE" WARN YOU ABOUT STUFF LIKE THAT?
IT'S MORE OF AN "IMMEDIATE PHYSICAL DANGER" THING. I MEAN, IT DIDN'T WARN ME TO NOT DATE YOU...
WOW, YOU'RE ON FIRE TODAY--
KA-BOOM
VULTURE!
AND THAT EXPLOSION CAN'T BE GOOD...
SORRY! I NEED TO--Y'KNOW--CHASE A SENIOR CITIZEN. YOU GOT THE BILL, YEAH, STARK KNIGHT?
SURE, SURE.
HATE DITCHING MJ LIKE THAT. RIBBING ASIDE, SHE'S ONE OF MY BEST FRIENDS, AND IT FEELS IMPOSSIBLE TO FIND THE TIME TO CATCH UP THESE DAYS.
IT'S TRUE WHAT THEY SAY...

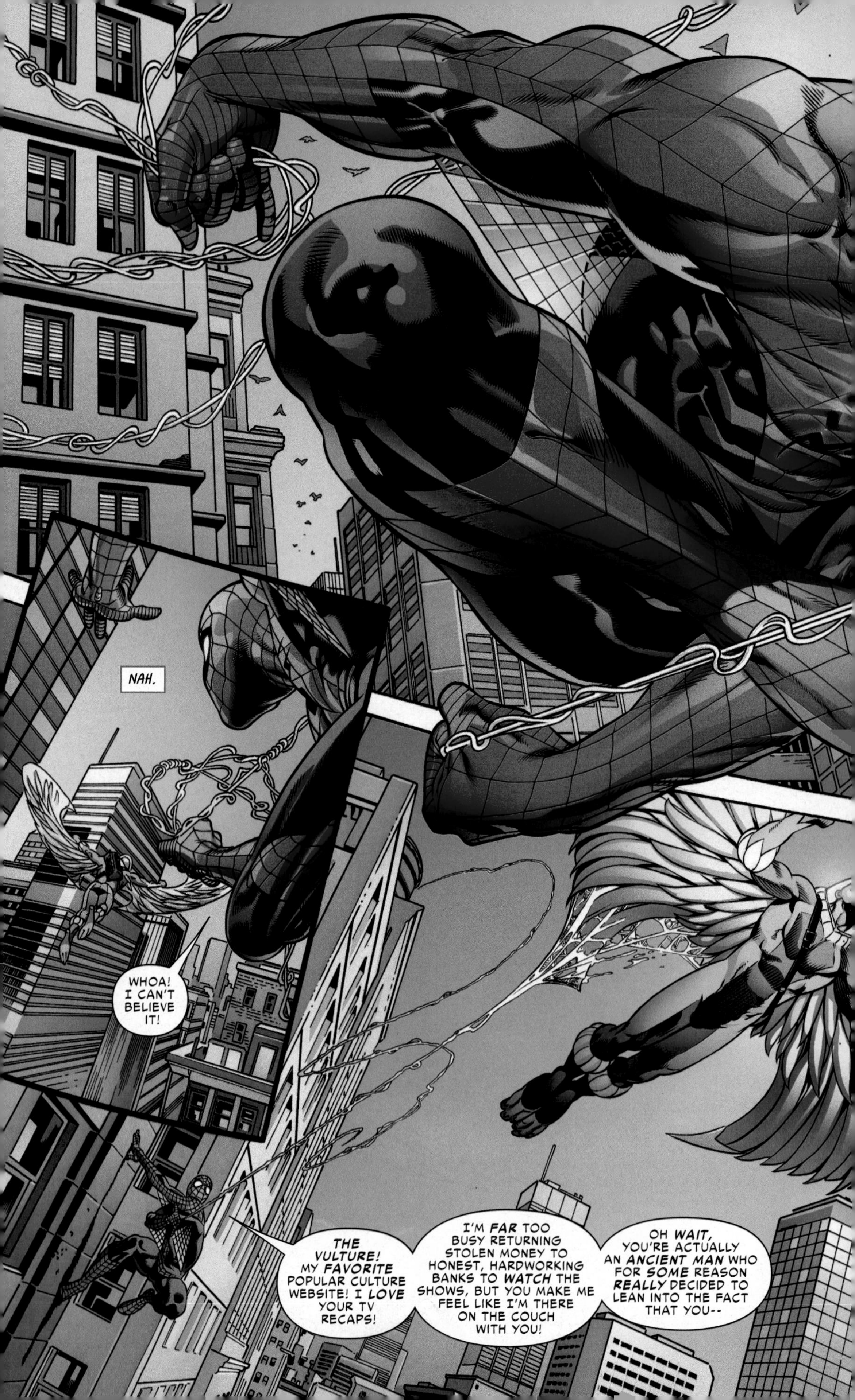
NAH.
WHOA! I CAN'T BELIEVE IT!
THE VULTURE! MY FAVORITE POPULAR CULTURE WEBSITE! I LOVE YOUR TV RECAPS!
I'M FAR TOO BUSY RETURNING STOLEN MONEY TO HONEST, HARDWORKING BANKS TO WATCH THE SHOWS, BUT YOU MAKE ME FEEL LIKE I'M THERE ON THE COUCH WITH YOU!
OH WAIT, YOU'RE ACTUALLY AN ANCIENT MAN WHO FOR SOME REASON REALLY DECIDED TO LEAN INTO THE FACT THAT YOU--

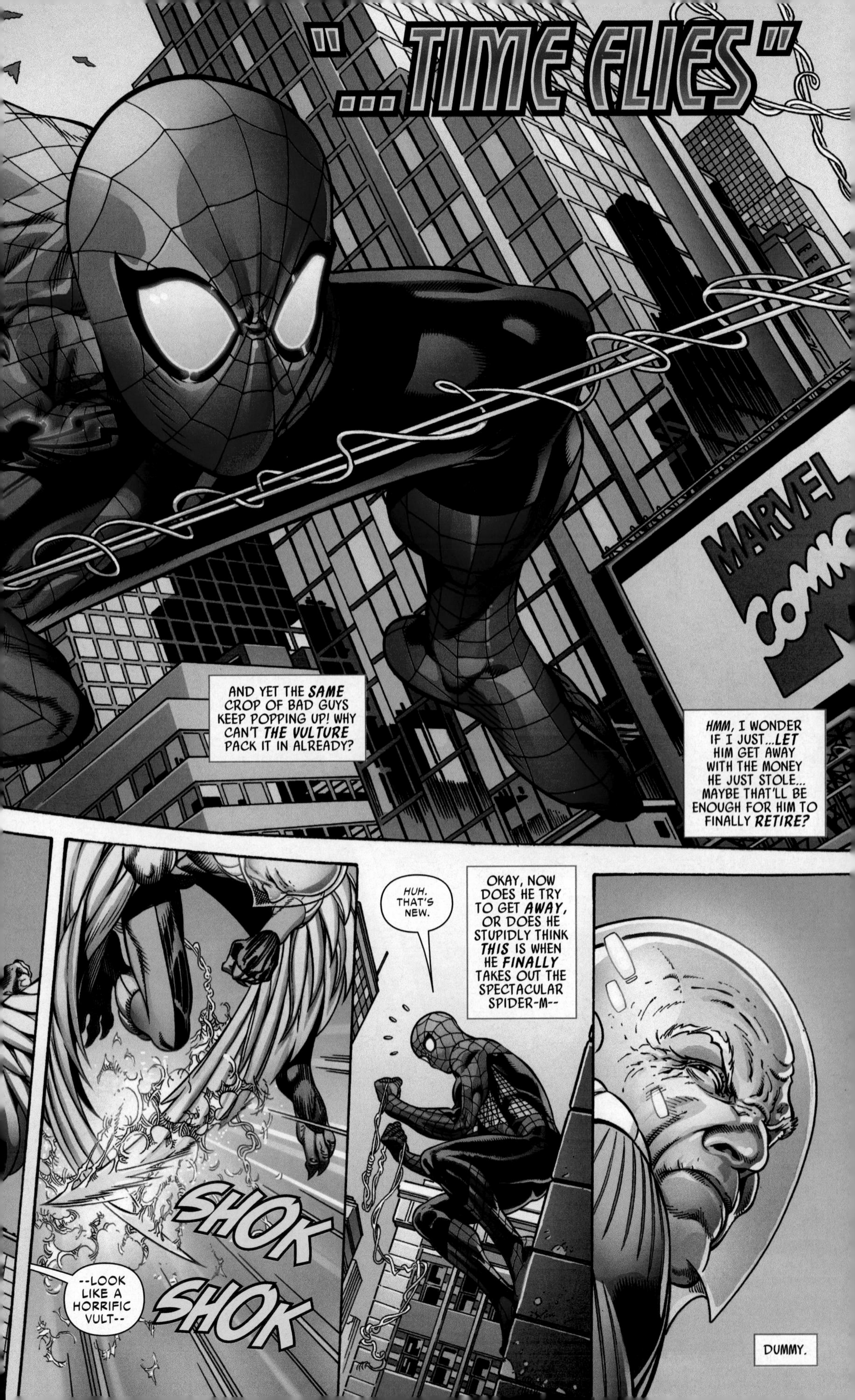
"...TIME FLIES"
MARVEL COMICS
AND YET THE SAME CROP OF BAD GUYS KEEP POPPING UP! WHY CAN'T THE VULTURE PACK IT IN ALREADY?
HMM, I WONDER IF I JUST...LET HIM GET AWAY WITH THE MONEY HE JUST STOLE... MAYBE THAT'LL BE ENOUGH FOR HIM TO FINALLY RETIRE?
HUH. THAT'S NEW.
OKAY, NOW DOES HE TRY TO GET AWAY, OR DOES HE STUPIDLY THINK THIS IS WHEN HE FINALLY TAKES OUT THE SPECTACULAR SPIDER-M--
SHOK
SHOK
--LOOK LIKE A HORRIFIC VULT--
DUMMY.

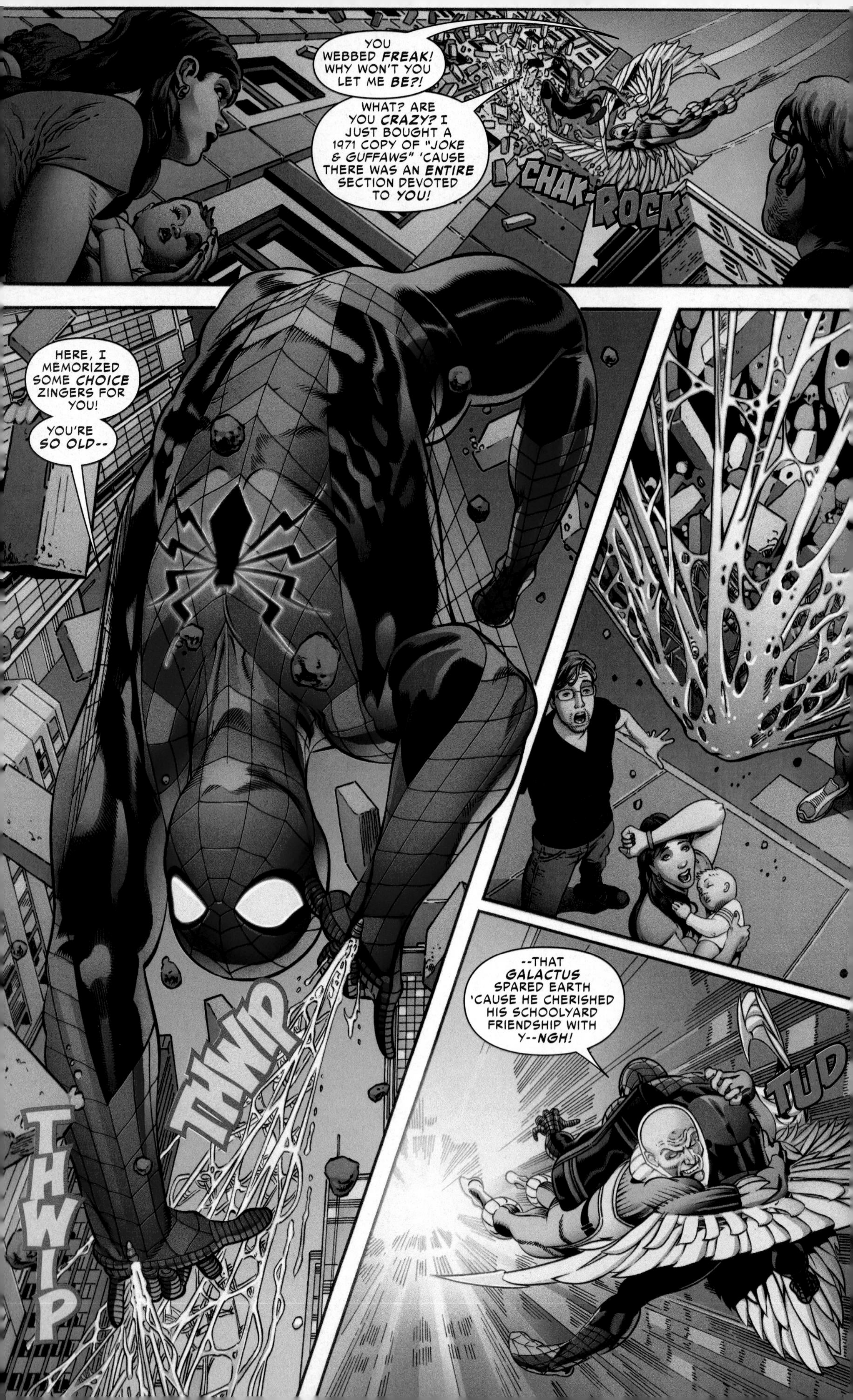
YOU WEBBED FREAK! WHY WON'T YOU LET ME BE?!
WHAT? ARE YOU CRAZY? I JUST BOUGHT A 1971 COPY OF "JOKE & GUFFAWS" 'CAUSE THERE WAS AN ENTIRE SECTION DEVOTED TO YOU!
CHAK-ROCK
HERE, I MEMORIZED SOME CHOICE ZINGERS FOR YOU!
YOU'RE SO OLD--
THWIP
THWIP
--THAT GALACTUS SPARED EARTH 'CAUSE HE CHERISHED HIS SCHOOLYARD FRIENDSHIP WITH Y--NGH!
TUD

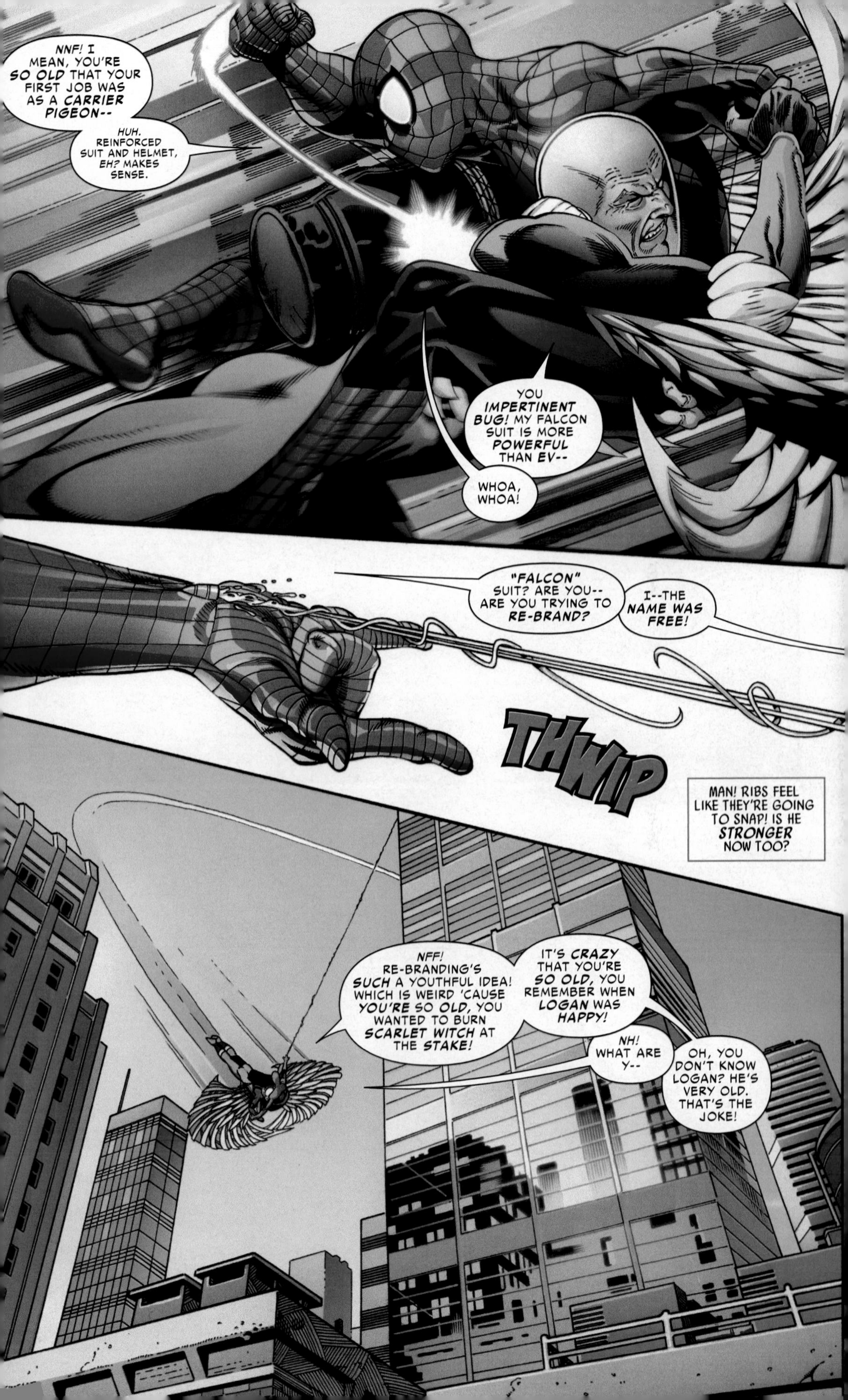
NNF! I MEAN, YOU'RE SO OLD THAT YOUR FIRST JOB WAS AS A CARRIER PIGEON--
HUH. REINFORCED SUIT AND HELMET, EH? MAKES SENSE.
YOU IMPERTINENT BUG! MY FALCON SUIT IS MORE POWERFUL THAN EV--
WHOA, WHOA!
"FALCON" SUIT? ARE YOU-- ARE YOU TRYING TO RE-BRAND?
I--THE NAME WAS FREE!
THWIP
MAN! RIBS FEEL LIKE THEY'RE GOING TO SNAP! IS HE STRONGER NOW TOO?
NFF! RE-BRANDING'S SUCH A YOUTHFUL IDEA! WHICH IS WEIRD 'CAUSE YOU'RE SO OLD, YOU WANTED TO BURN SCARLET WITCH AT THE STAKE!
IT'S CRAZY THAT YOU'RE SO OLD, YOU REMEMBER WHEN LOGAN WAS HAPPY!
NH! WHAT ARE Y--
OH, YOU DON'T KNOW LOGAN? HE'S VERY OLD. THAT'S THE JOKE!

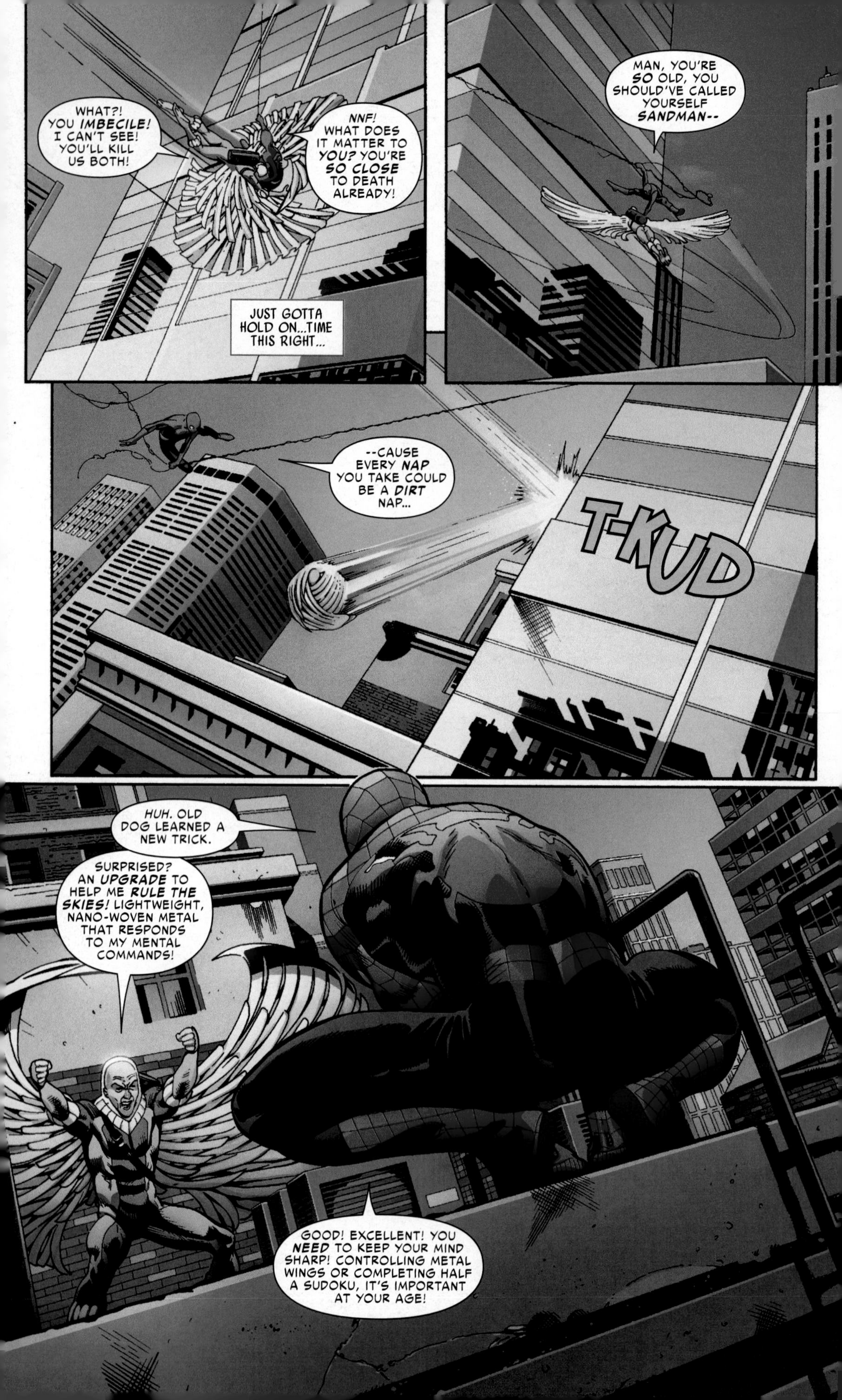
WHAT?! YOU IMBECILE! I CAN'T SEE! YOU'LL KILL US BOTH!
NNF! WHAT DOES IT MATTER TO YOU? YOU'RE SO CLOSE TO DEATH ALREADY!
JUST GOTTA HOLD ON...TIME THIS RIGHT...
MAN, YOU'RE SO OLD, YOU SHOULD'VE CALLED YOURSELF SANDMAN--
--CAUSE EVERY NAP YOU TAKE COULD BE A DIRT NAP...
T-KUD
HUH. OLD DOG LEARNED A NEW TRICK.
SURPRISED? AN UPGRADE TO HELP ME RULE THE SKIES! LIGHTWEIGHT, NANO-WOVEN METAL THAT RESPONDS TO MY MENTAL COMMANDS!
GOOD! EXCELLENT! YOU NEED TO KEEP YOUR MIND SHARP! CONTROLLING METAL WINGS OR COMPLETING HALF A SUDOKU, IT'S IMPORTANT AT YOUR AGE!

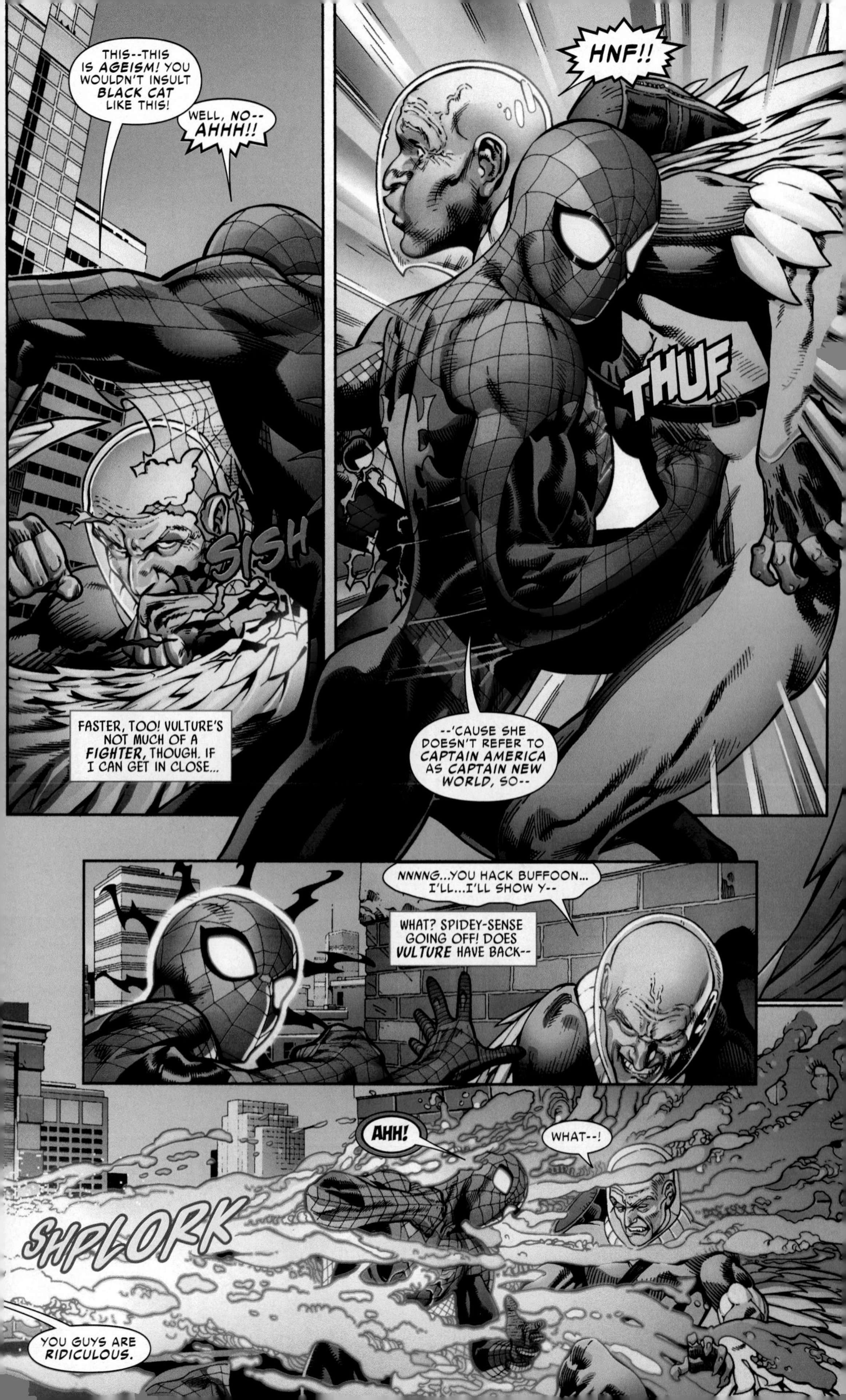
THIS--THIS IS AGEISM! YOU WOULDN'T INSULT BLACK CAT LIKE THIS!
WELL, NO--AHHH!!
HNF!!
THUF
SISH
FASTER, TOO! VULTURE'S NOT MUCH OF A FIGHTER, THOUGH. IF I CAN GET IN CLOSE...
--'CAUSE SHE DOESN'T REFER TO CAPTAIN AMERICA AS CAPTAIN NEW WORLD, SO--
NNNNG...YOU HACK BUFFOON... I'LL...I'LL SHOW Y--
WHAT? SPIDEY-SENSE GOING OFF! DOES VULTURE HAVE BACK--
AHH!
WHAT--!
SHPLORK
YOU GUYS ARE RIDICULOUS.

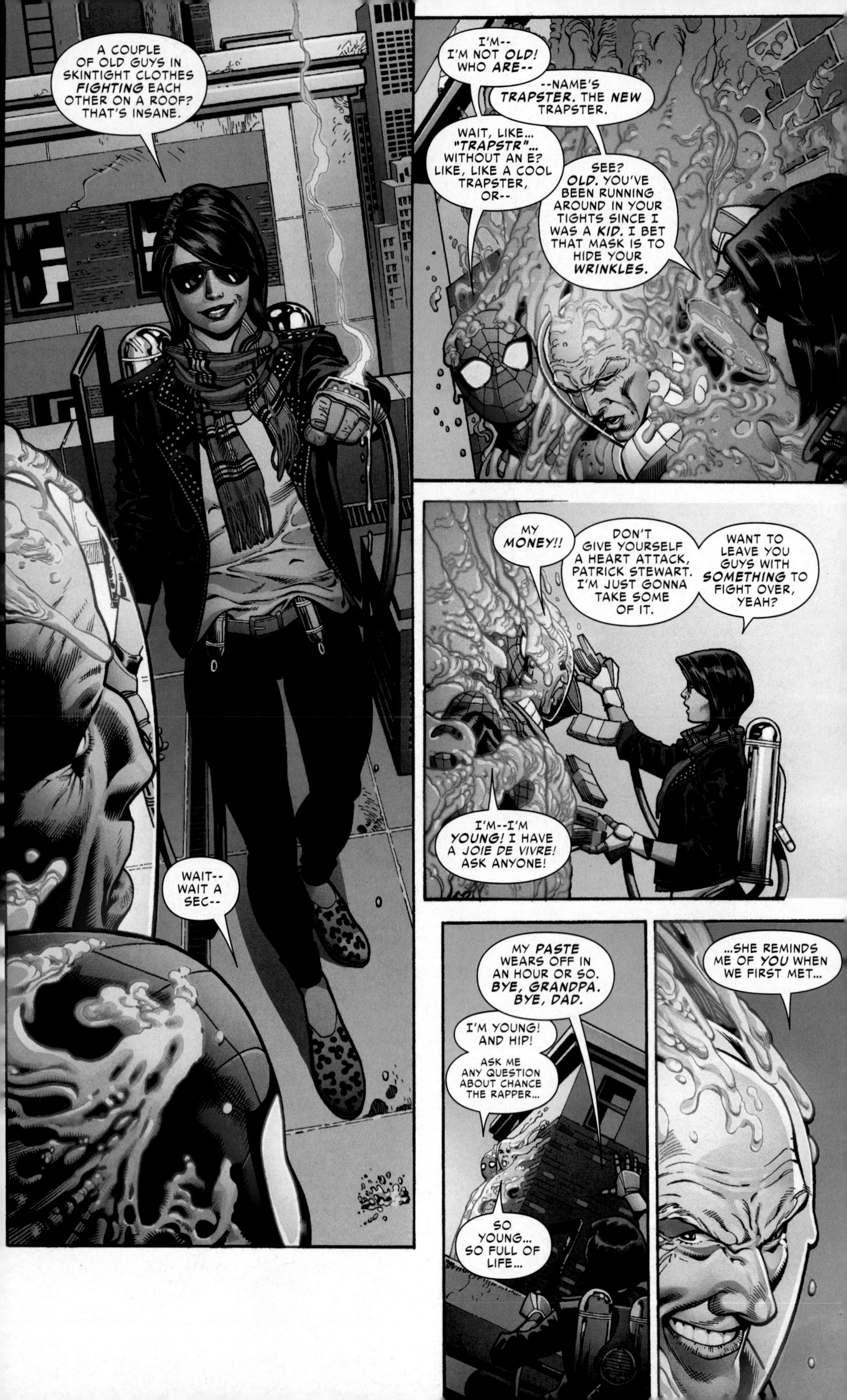

A COUPLE OF OLD GUYS IN SKINTIGHT CLOTHES *FIGHTING* EACH OTHER ON A ROOF? THAT'S INSANE.
WAIT-- WAIT A SEC--
I'M-- I'M NOT *OLD!* WHO *ARE--*
--NAME'S *TRAPSTER.* THE *NEW* TRAPSTER.
WAIT, LIKE... *"TRAPSTR"...* WITHOUT AN E? LIKE, LIKE A COOL TRAPSTER, OR--
SEE? *OLD.* YOU'VE BEEN RUNNING AROUND IN YOUR TIGHTS SINCE I WAS A *KID.* I BET THAT MASK IS TO HIDE YOUR *WRINKLES.*
MY *MONEY!!*
DON'T GIVE YOURSELF A HEART ATTACK, PATRICK STEWART. I'M JUST GONNA TAKE SOME OF IT.
WANT TO LEAVE YOU GUYS WITH *SOMETHING* TO FIGHT OVER, YEAH?
I'M--I'M *YOUNG!* I HAVE A *JOIE DE VIVRE!* ASK ANYONE!
MY *PASTE* WEARS OFF IN AN HOUR OR SO. *BYE, GRANDPA. BYE, DAD.*
I'M YOUNG! AND HIP!
ASK ME ANY QUESTION ABOUT CHANCE THE RAPPER...
SO YOUNG... SO FULL OF LIFE...
...SHE REMINDS ME OF *YOU* WHEN WE FIRST MET...

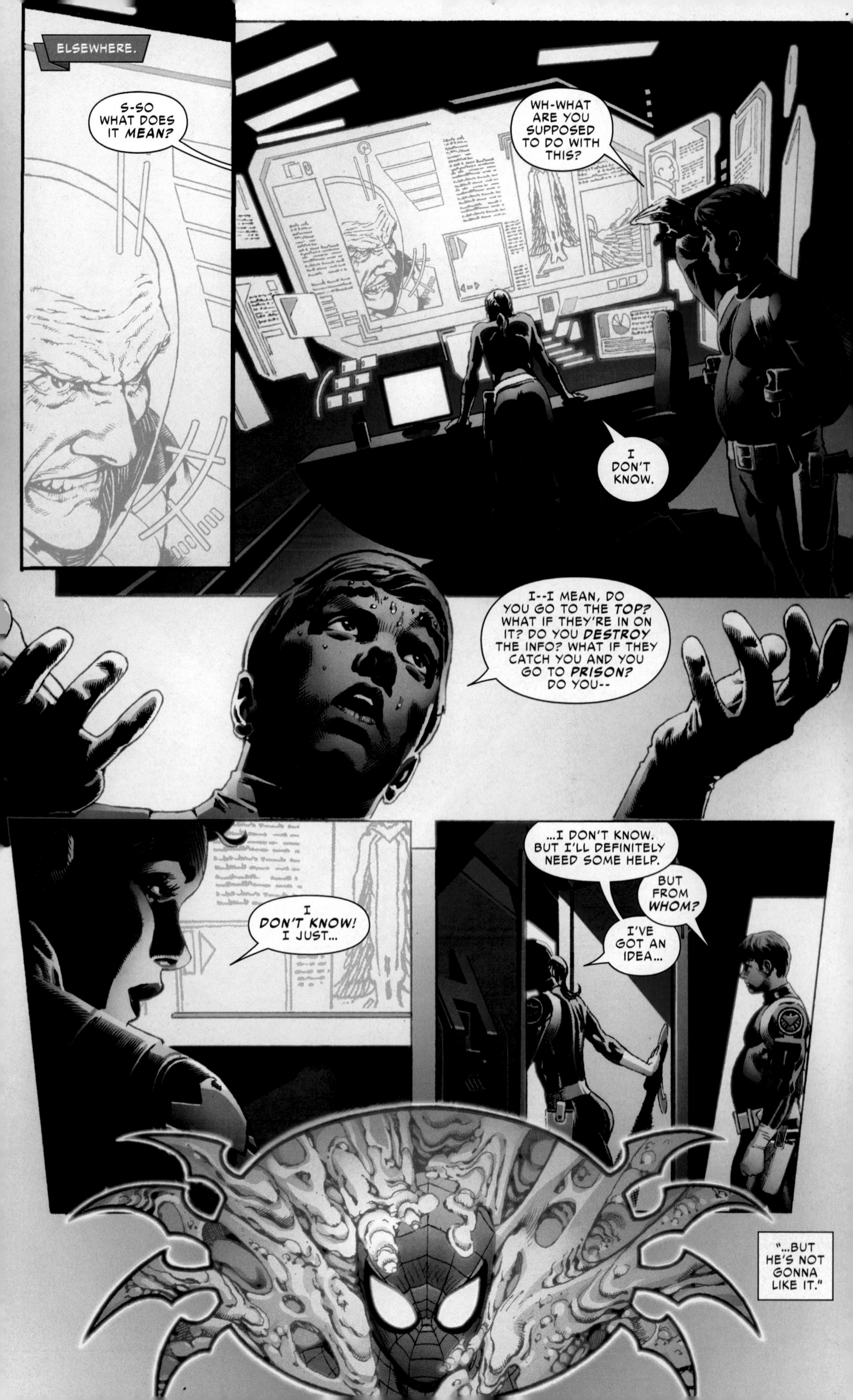
ELSEWHERE.
S-SO WHAT DOES IT *MEAN?*
WH-WHAT ARE YOU SUPPOSED TO DO WITH THIS?
I DON'T KNOW.
I--I MEAN, DO YOU GO TO THE *TOP?* WHAT IF THEY'RE IN ON IT? DO YOU *DESTROY* THE INFO? WHAT IF THEY CATCH YOU AND YOU GO TO *PRISON?* DO YOU--
I *DON'T KNOW!* I JUST...
...I DON'T KNOW. BUT I'LL DEFINITELY NEED SOME HELP.
BUT FROM *WHOM?*
I'VE GOT AN IDEA...
"...BUT HE'S NOT GONNA LIKE IT."

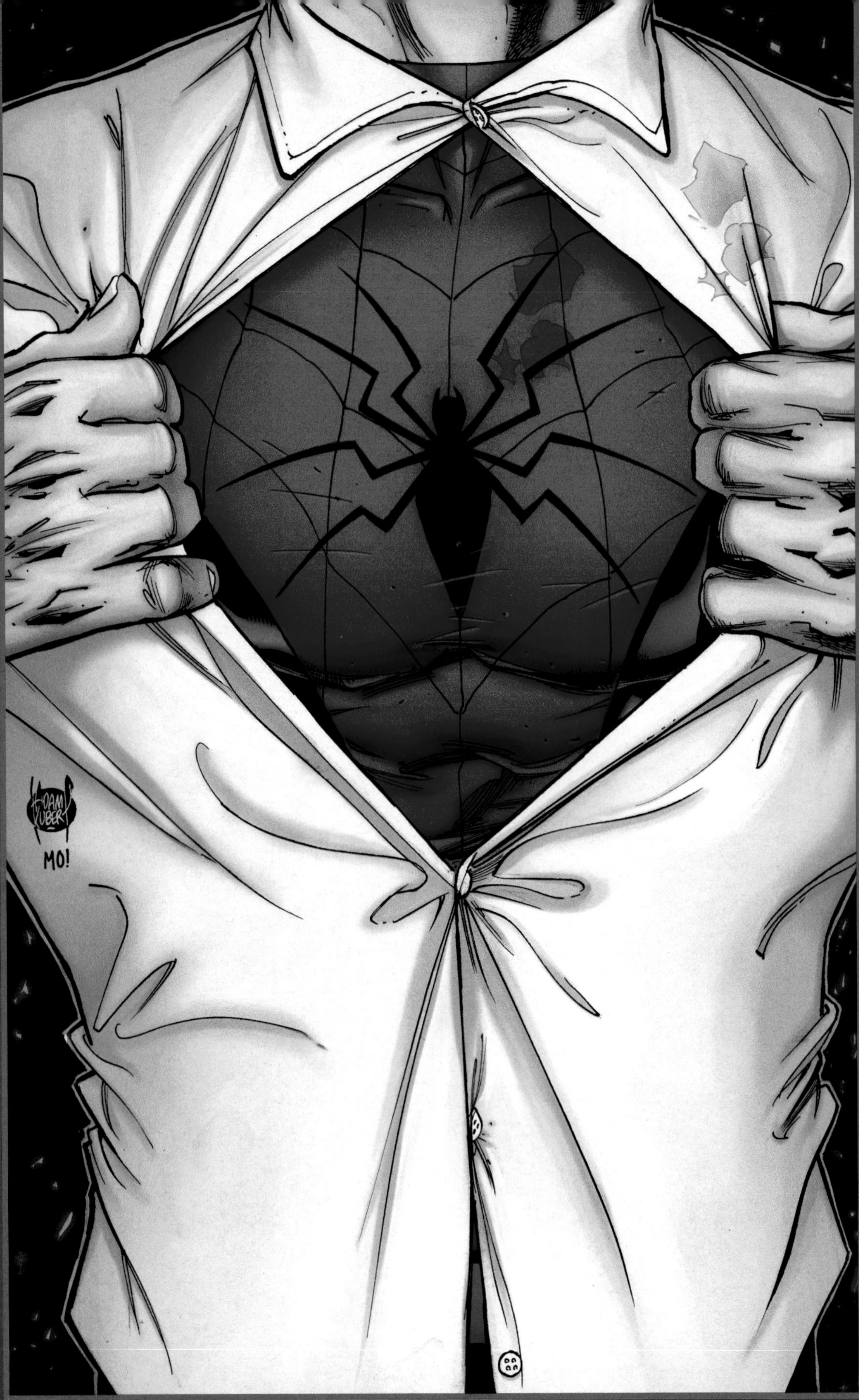
ADAM KUBERT
MO!

1

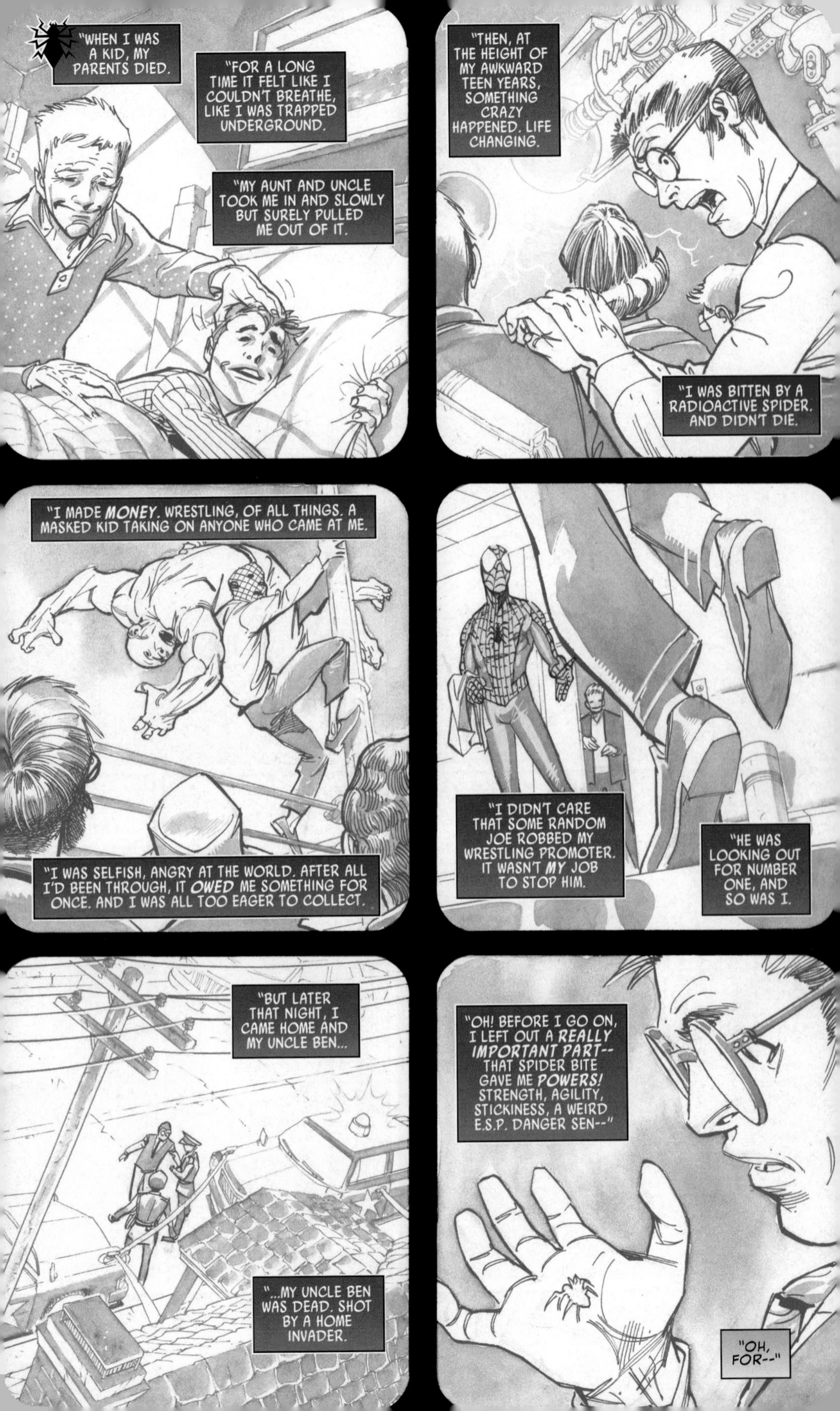
"WHEN I WAS A KID, MY PARENTS DIED.
"FOR A LONG TIME IT FELT LIKE I COULDN'T BREATHE, LIKE I WAS TRAPPED UNDERGROUND.
"MY AUNT AND UNCLE TOOK ME IN AND SLOWLY BUT SURELY PULLED ME OUT OF IT.
"THEN, AT THE HEIGHT OF MY AWKWARD TEEN YEARS, SOMETHING CRAZY HAPPENED. LIFE CHANGING.
"I WAS BITTEN BY A RADIOACTIVE SPIDER. AND DIDN'T DIE.
"I MADE *MONEY*. WRESTLING, OF ALL THINGS. A MASKED KID TAKING ON ANYONE WHO CAME AT ME.
"I WAS SELFISH, ANGRY AT THE WORLD. AFTER ALL I'D BEEN THROUGH, IT *OWED* ME SOMETHING FOR ONCE. AND I WAS ALL TOO EAGER TO COLLECT.
"I DIDN'T CARE THAT SOME RANDOM JOE ROBBED MY WRESTLING PROMOTER. IT WASN'T *MY* JOB TO STOP HIM.
"HE WAS LOOKING OUT FOR NUMBER ONE, AND SO WAS I.
"BUT LATER THAT NIGHT, I CAME HOME AND MY UNCLE BEN...
"...MY UNCLE BEN WAS DEAD. SHOT BY A HOME INVADER.
"OH! BEFORE I GO ON, I LEFT OUT A *REALLY IMPORTANT PART*-- THAT SPIDER BITE GAVE ME *POWERS!* STRENGTH, AGILITY, STICKINESS, A WEIRD E.S.P. DANGER SEN--"
"OH, FOR--"

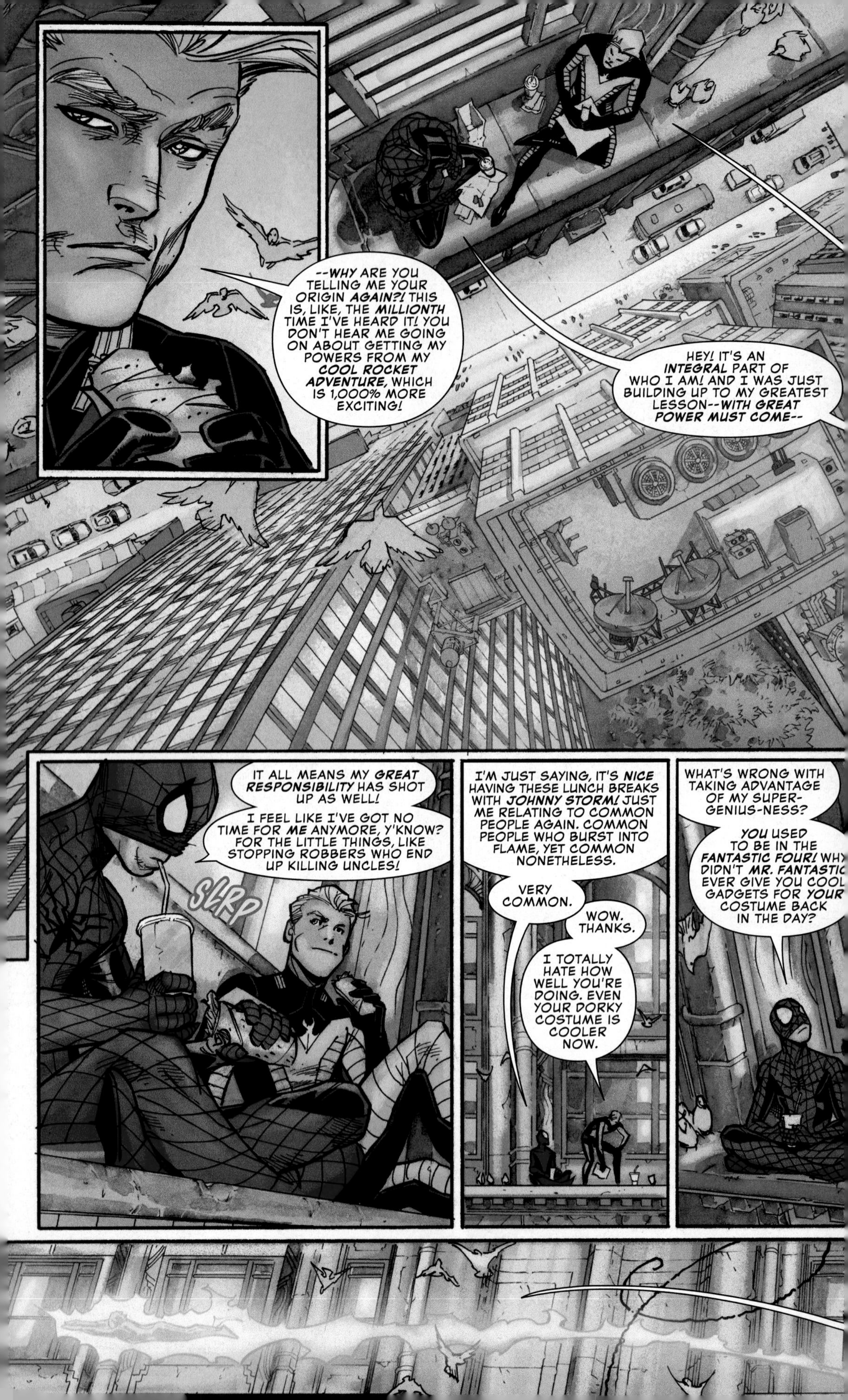
--WHY ARE YOU TELLING ME YOUR ORIGIN AGAIN?! THIS IS, LIKE, THE MILLIONTH TIME I'VE HEARD IT! YOU DON'T HEAR ME GOING ON ABOUT GETTING MY POWERS FROM MY COOL ROCKET ADVENTURE, WHICH IS 1,000% MORE EXCITING!
HEY! IT'S AN INTEGRAL PART OF WHO I AM! AND I WAS JUST BUILDING UP TO MY GREATEST LESSON--WITH GREAT POWER MUST COME--
IT ALL MEANS MY GREAT RESPONSIBILITY HAS SHOT UP AS WELL!
I FEEL LIKE I'VE GOT NO TIME FOR ME ANYMORE, Y'KNOW? FOR THE LITTLE THINGS, LIKE STOPPING ROBBERS WHO END UP KILLING UNCLES!
SLRP
I'M JUST SAYING, IT'S NICE HAVING THESE LUNCH BREAKS WITH JOHNNY STORM! JUST ME RELATING TO COMMON PEOPLE AGAIN. COMMON PEOPLE WHO BURST INTO FLAME, YET COMMON NONETHELESS.
VERY COMMON.
WOW. THANKS.
I TOTALLY HATE HOW WELL YOU'RE DOING. EVEN YOUR DORKY COSTUME IS COOLER NOW.
WHAT'S WRONG WITH TAKING ADVANTAGE OF MY SUPER-GENIUS-NESS?
YOU USED TO BE IN THE FANTASTIC FOUR! WHY DIDN'T MR. FANTASTIC EVER GIVE YOU COOL GADGETS FOR YOUR COSTUME BACK IN THE DAY?

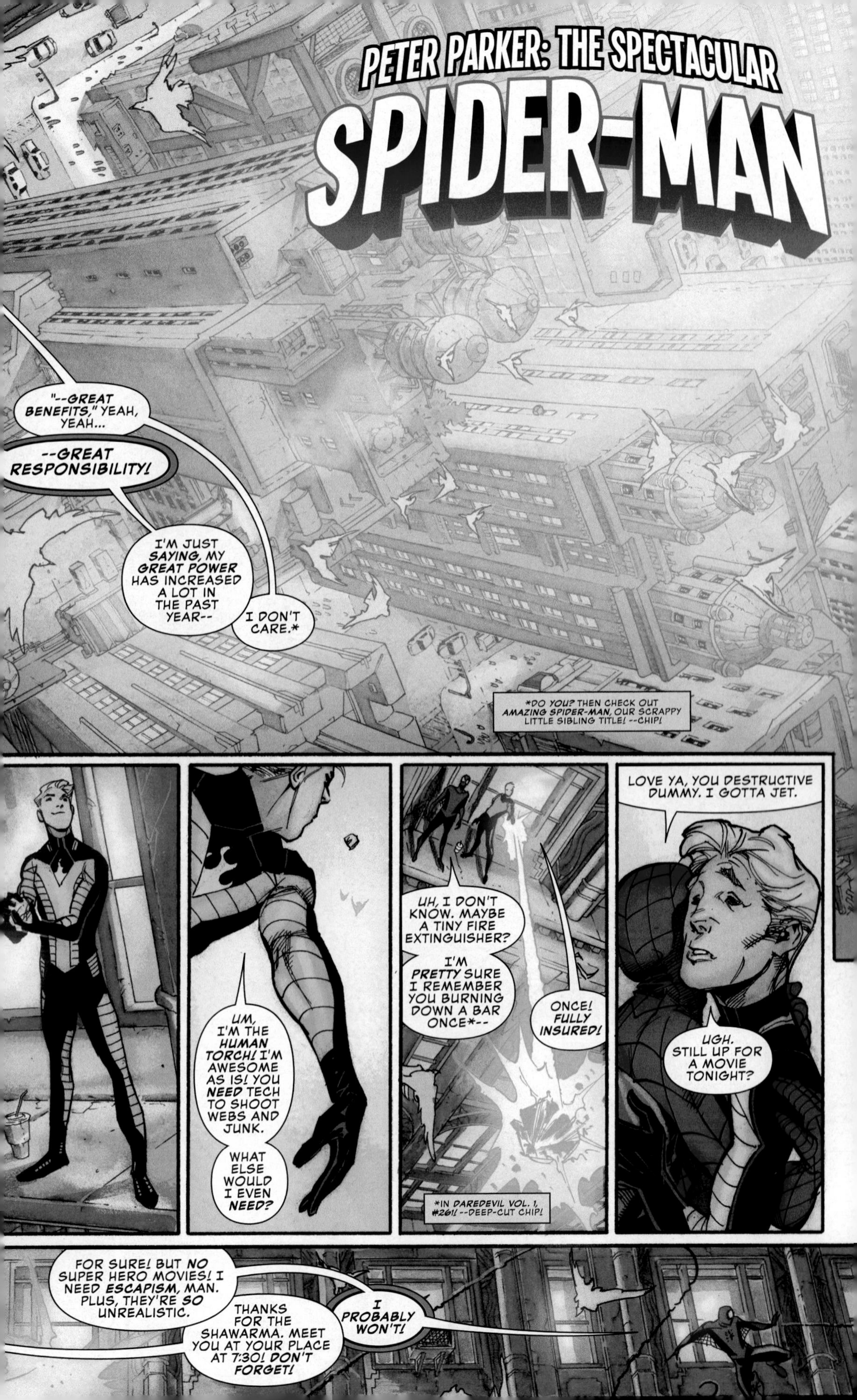

PETER PARKER: THE SPECTACULAR SPIDER-MAN
"--GREAT BENEFITS," YEAH, YEAH...
--GREAT RESPONSIBILITY!
I'M JUST SAYING, MY GREAT POWER HAS INCREASED A LOT IN THE PAST YEAR--
I DON'T CARE.*
*DO YOU? THEN CHECK OUT AMAZING SPIDER-MAN, OUR SCRAPPY LITTLE SIBLING TITLE! --CHIP!
UM, I'M THE HUMAN TORCH! I'M AWESOME AS IS! YOU NEED TECH TO SHOOT WEBS AND JUNK.
WHAT ELSE WOULD I EVEN NEED?
UH, I DON'T KNOW. MAYBE A TINY FIRE EXTINGUISHER?
I'M PRETTY SURE I REMEMBER YOU BURNING DOWN A BAR ONCE*--
ONCE! FULLY INSURED!
*IN DAREDEVIL VOL. 1, #261! --DEEP-CUT CHIP!
LOVE YA, YOU DESTRUCTIVE DUMMY. I GOTTA JET.
UGH. STILL UP FOR A MOVIE TONIGHT?
FOR SURE! BUT NO SUPER HERO MOVIES! I NEED ESCAPISM, MAN. PLUS, THEY'RE SO UNREALISTIC.
THANKS FOR THE SHAWARMA. MEET YOU AT YOUR PLACE AT 7:30! DON'T FORGET!
I PROBABLY WON'T!

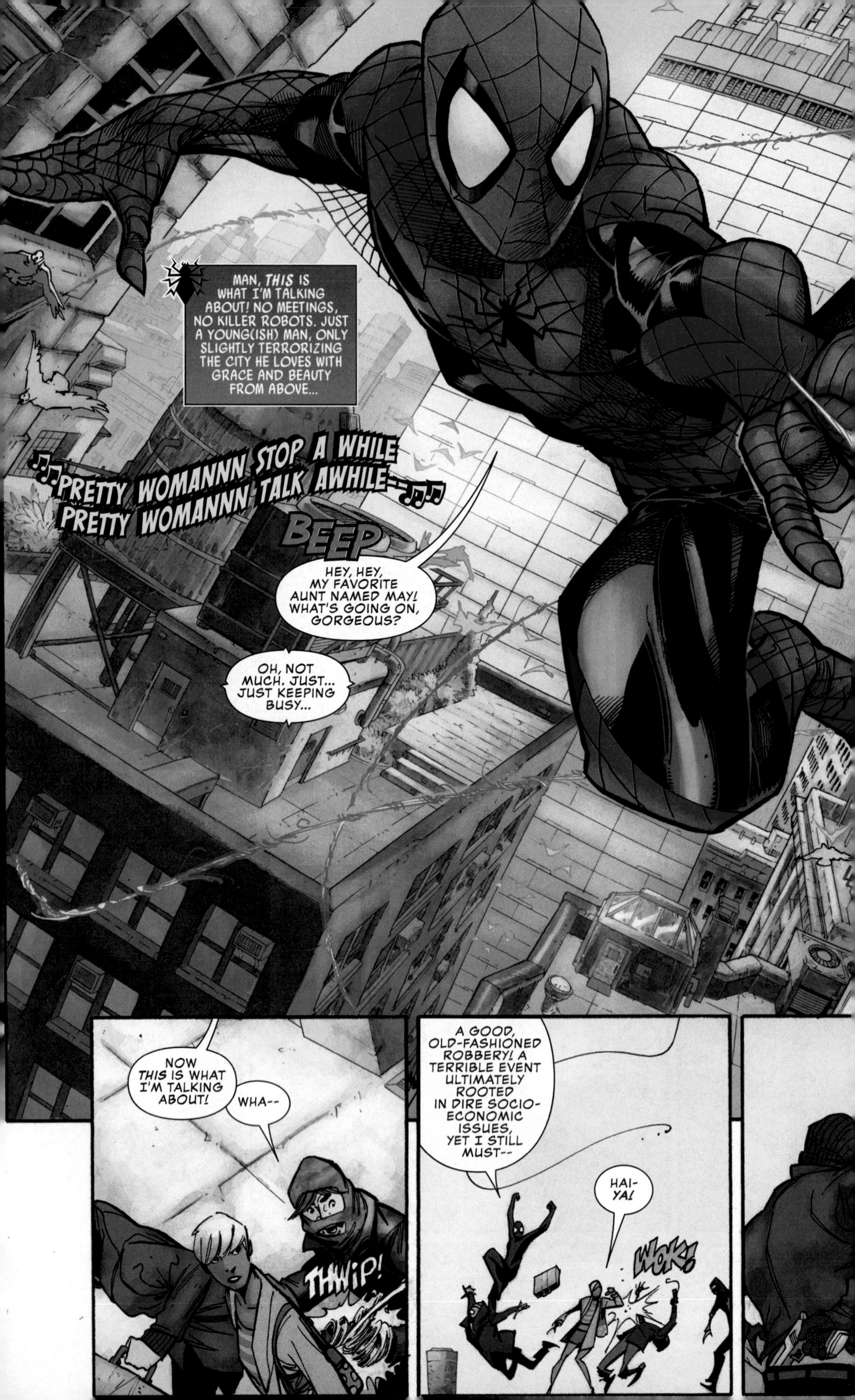
MAN, THIS IS WHAT I'M TALKING ABOUT! NO MEETINGS, NO KILLER ROBOTS. JUST A YOUNG(ISH) MAN, ONLY SLIGHTLY TERRORIZING THE CITY HE LOVES WITH GRACE AND BEAUTY FROM ABOVE...
PRETTY WOMANNN STOP A WHILE
PRETTY WOMANNN TALK AWHILE--
BEEP
HEY, HEY, MY FAVORITE AUNT NAMED MAY! WHAT'S GOING ON, GORGEOUS?
OH, NOT MUCH. JUST... JUST KEEPING BUSY...
NOW THIS IS WHAT I'M TALKING ABOUT!
WHA--
THWIP!
A GOOD, OLD-FASHIONED ROBBERY! A TERRIBLE EVENT ULTIMATELY ROOTED IN DIRE SOCIO-ECONOMIC ISSUES, YET I STILL MUST--
HAI-YA!
WOK!

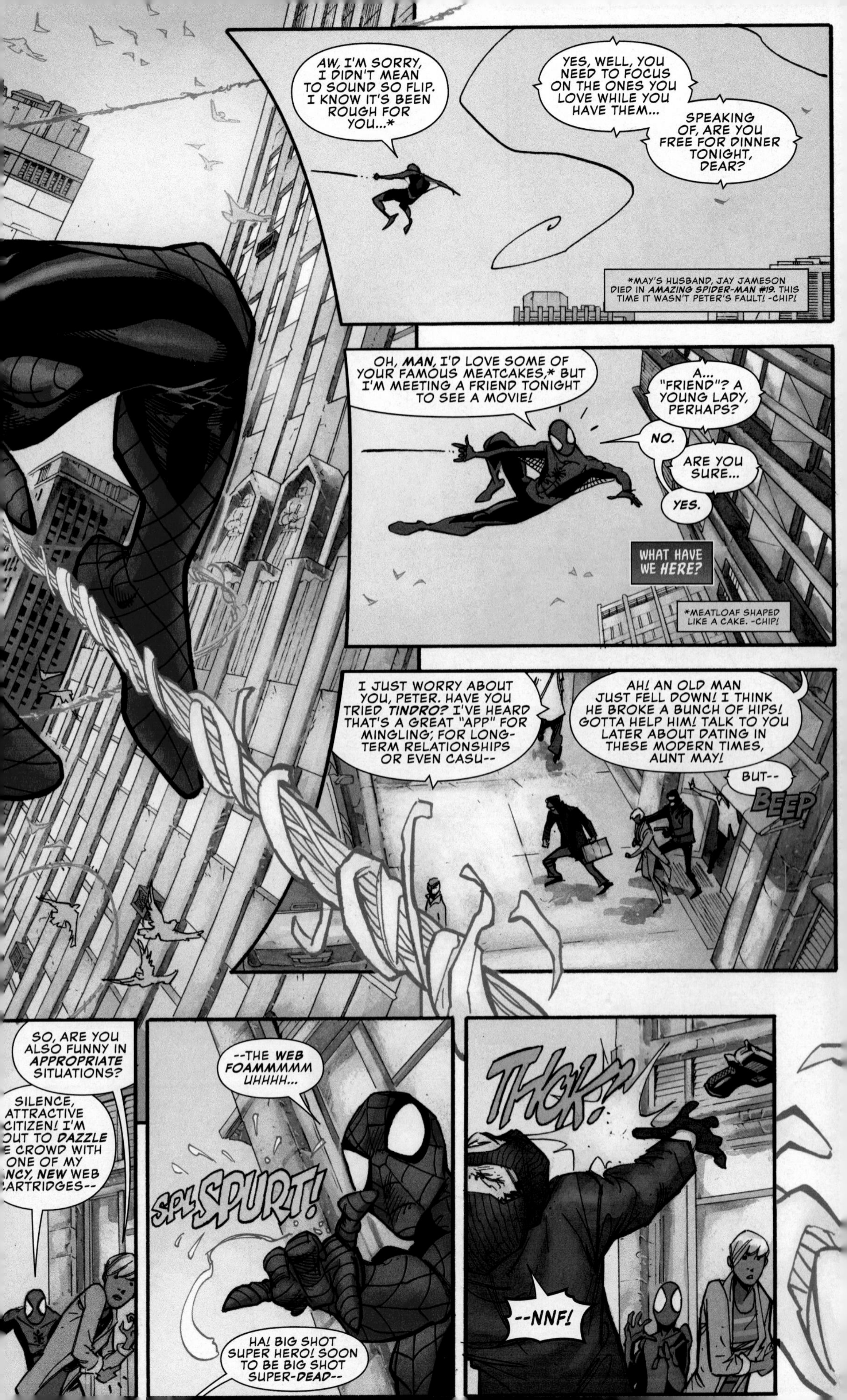
AW, I'M SORRY, I DIDN'T MEAN TO SOUND SO FLIP. I KNOW IT'S BEEN ROUGH FOR YOU...*
YES, WELL, YOU NEED TO FOCUS ON THE ONES YOU LOVE WHILE YOU HAVE THEM...
SPEAKING OF, ARE YOU FREE FOR DINNER TONIGHT, DEAR?
*MAY'S HUSBAND, JAY JAMESON DIED IN AMAZING SPIDER-MAN #19. THIS TIME IT WASN'T PETER'S FAULT! -CHIP!
OH, MAN, I'D LOVE SOME OF YOUR FAMOUS MEATCAKES,* BUT I'M MEETING A FRIEND TONIGHT TO SEE A MOVIE!
A... "FRIEND"? A YOUNG LADY, PERHAPS?
NO.
ARE YOU SURE...
YES.
WHAT HAVE WE HERE?
*MEATLOAF SHAPED LIKE A CAKE. -CHIP!
I JUST WORRY ABOUT YOU, PETER. HAVE YOU TRIED TINDRO? I'VE HEARD THAT'S A GREAT "APP" FOR MINGLING; FOR LONG-TERM RELATIONSHIPS OR EVEN CASU--
AH! AN OLD MAN JUST FELL DOWN! I THINK HE BROKE A BUNCH OF HIPS! GOTTA HELP HIM! TALK TO YOU LATER ABOUT DATING IN THESE MODERN TIMES, AUNT MAY!
BUT--
BEEP
SO, ARE YOU ALSO FUNNY IN APPROPRIATE SITUATIONS?
SILENCE, ATTRACTIVE CITIZEN! I'M OUT TO DAZZLE THE CROWD WITH ONE OF MY FANCY, NEW WEB CARTRIDGES--
--THE WEB FOAMMMMM UHHHH...
SPL SPURT!
HA! BIG SHOT SUPER HERO! SOON TO BE BIG SHOT SUPER-DEAD--
THCK!
--NNF!

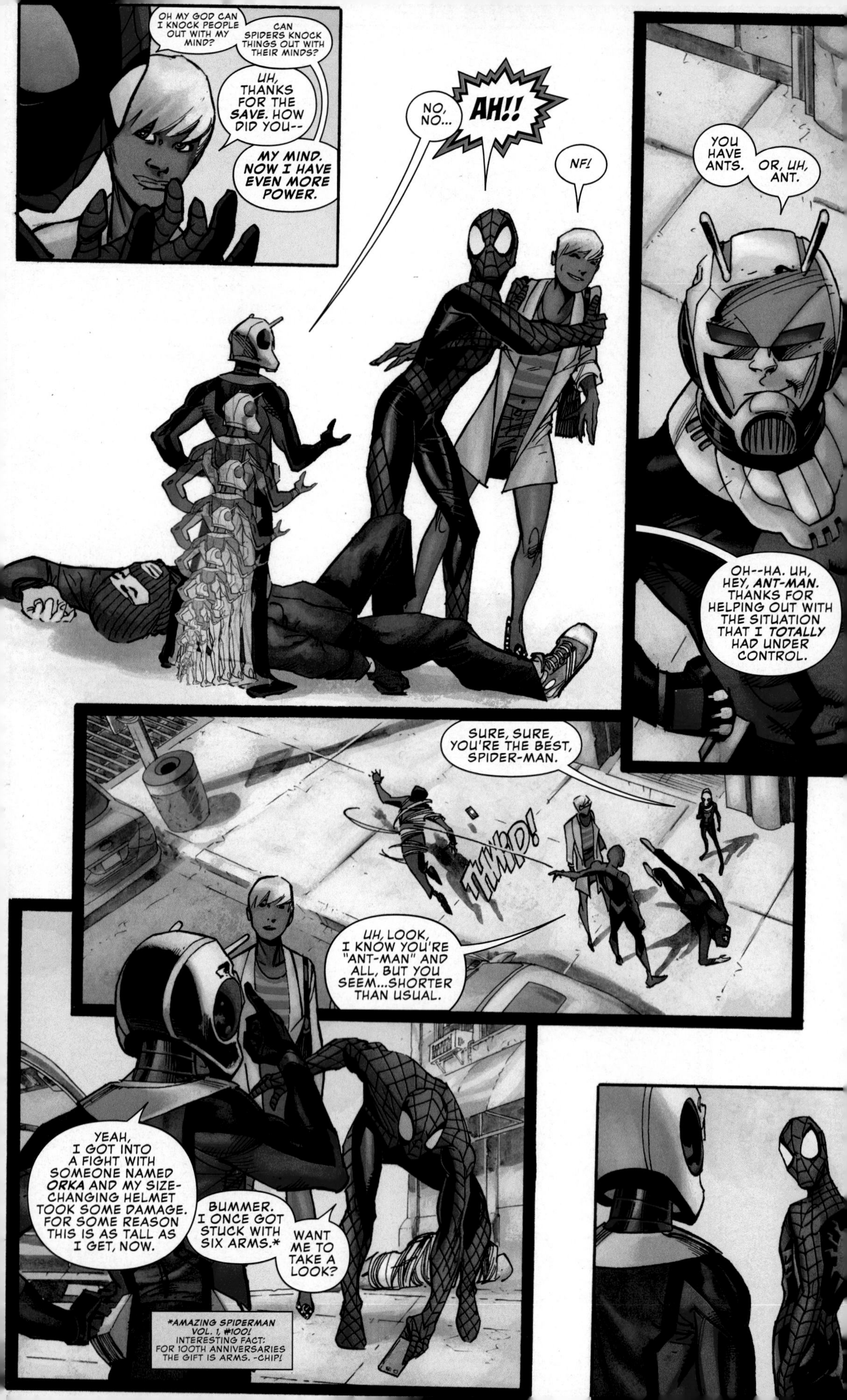
OH MY GOD CAN I KNOCK PEOPLE OUT WITH MY MIND?
CAN SPIDERS KNOCK THINGS OUT WITH THEIR MINDS?
UH, THANKS FOR THE SAVE. HOW DID YOU--
MY MIND. NOW I HAVE EVEN MORE POWER.
NO, NO...
AH!!
NF!
YOU HAVE ANTS.
OR, UH, ANT.
OH--HA. UH, HEY, ANT-MAN. THANKS FOR HELPING OUT WITH THE SITUATION THAT I TOTALLY HAD UNDER CONTROL.
SURE, SURE, YOU'RE THE BEST, SPIDER-MAN.
THWIP!
UH, LOOK, I KNOW YOU'RE "ANT-MAN" AND ALL, BUT YOU SEEM...SHORTER THAN USUAL.
YEAH, I GOT INTO A FIGHT WITH SOMEONE NAMED ORKA AND MY SIZE-CHANGING HELMET TOOK SOME DAMAGE. FOR SOME REASON THIS IS AS TALL AS I GET, NOW.
BUMMER. I ONCE GOT STUCK WITH SIX ARMS.*
WANT ME TO TAKE A LOOK?
*AMAZING SPIDERMAN VOL. 1, #100! INTERESTING FACT: FOR 100TH ANNIVERSARIES THE GIFT IS ARMS. -CHIP!

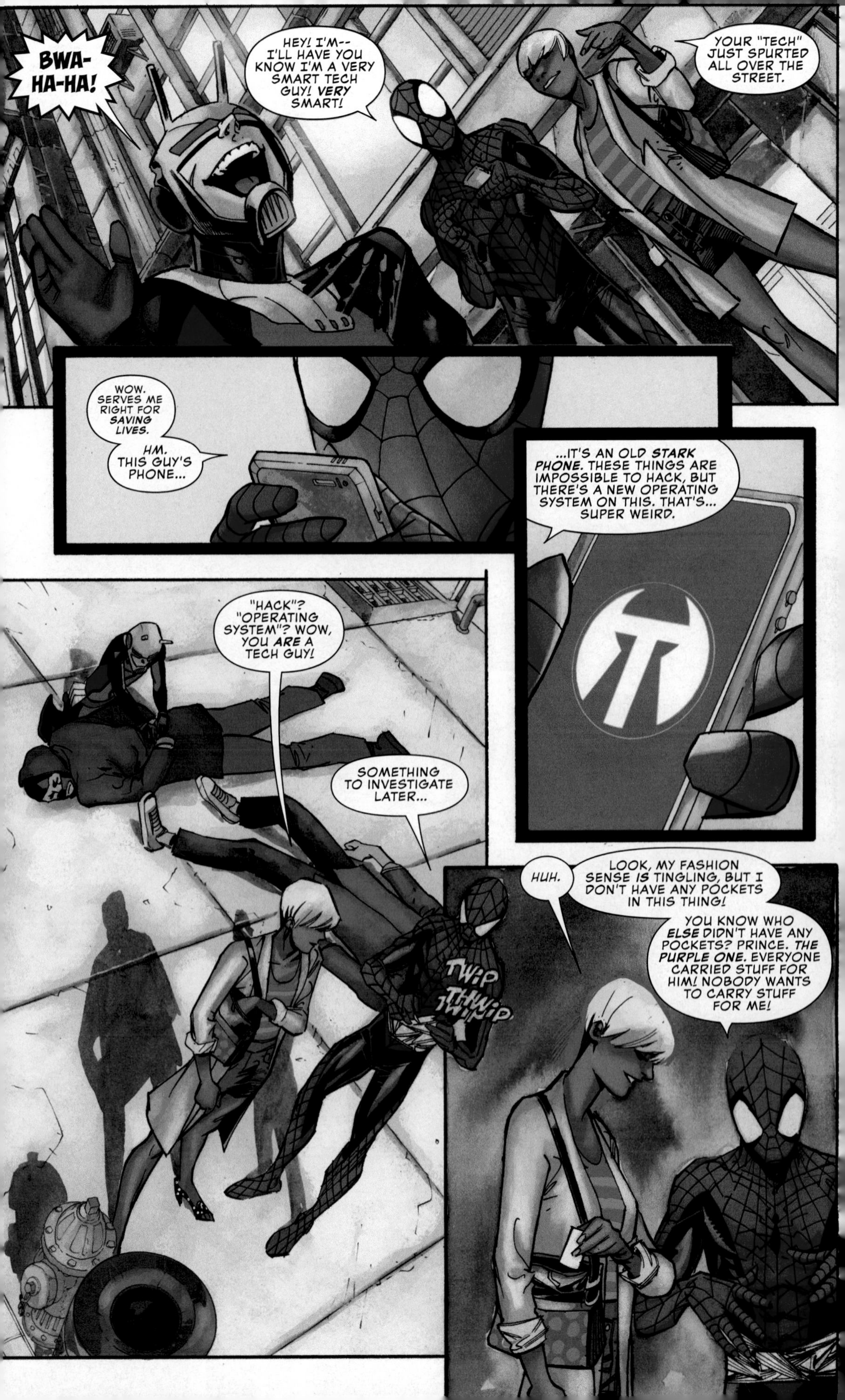
BWA-HA-HA!
HEY! I'M-- I'LL HAVE YOU KNOW I'M A VERY SMART TECH GUY! VERY SMART!
YOUR "TECH" JUST SPURTED ALL OVER THE STREET.
WOW. SERVES ME RIGHT FOR SAVING LIVES.
HM. THIS GUY'S PHONE...
...IT'S AN OLD STARK PHONE. THESE THINGS ARE IMPOSSIBLE TO HACK, BUT THERE'S A NEW OPERATING SYSTEM ON THIS. THAT'S... SUPER WEIRD.
"HACK"? "OPERATING SYSTEM"? WOW, YOU ARE A TECH GUY!
SOMETHING TO INVESTIGATE LATER...
THWIP THWIP THWIP
HUH.
LOOK, MY FASHION SENSE IS TINGLING, BUT I DON'T HAVE ANY POCKETS IN THIS THING!
YOU KNOW WHO ELSE DIDN'T HAVE ANY POCKETS? PRINCE. THE PURPLE ONE. EVERYONE CARRIED STUFF FOR HIM! NOBODY WANTS TO CARRY STUFF FOR ME!

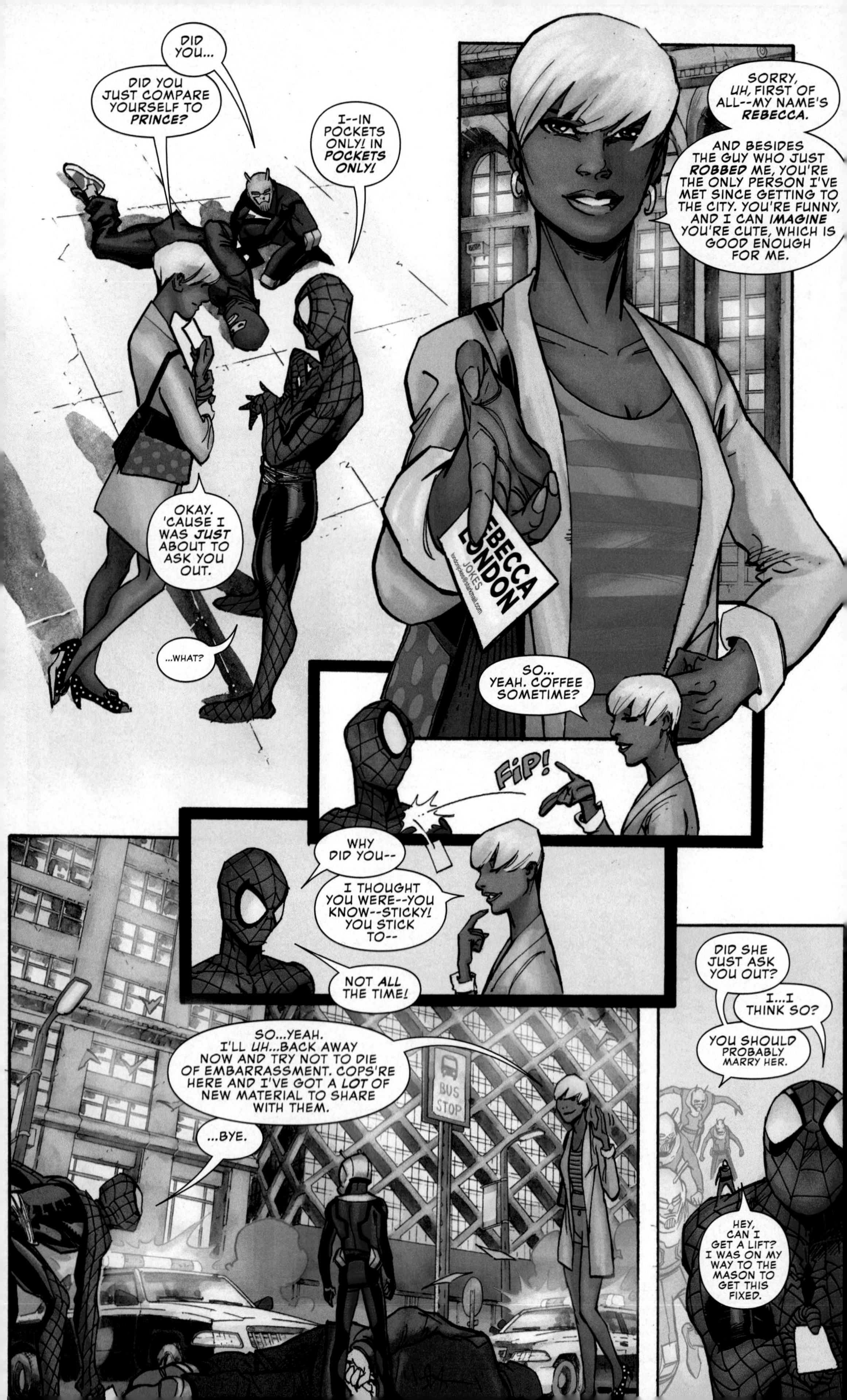
DID YOU...
DID YOU JUST COMPARE YOURSELF TO PRINCE?
I--IN POCKETS ONLY! IN POCKETS ONLY!
OKAY. 'CAUSE I WAS JUST ABOUT TO ASK YOU OUT.
...WHAT?
SORRY, UH, FIRST OF ALL--MY NAME'S REBECCA.
AND BESIDES THE GUY WHO JUST ROBBED ME, YOU'RE THE ONLY PERSON I'VE MET SINCE GETTING TO THE CITY. YOU'RE FUNNY, AND I CAN IMAGINE YOU'RE CUTE, WHICH IS GOOD ENOUGH FOR ME.
REBECCA LONDON
JOKES
SO... YEAH. COFFEE SOMETIME?
FIP!
WHY DID YOU--
I THOUGHT YOU WERE--YOU KNOW--STICKY! YOU STICK TO--
NOT ALL THE TIME!
SO...YEAH. I'LL UH...BACK AWAY NOW AND TRY NOT TO DIE OF EMBARRASSMENT. COP'S'RE HERE AND I'VE GOT A LOT OF NEW MATERIAL TO SHARE WITH THEM.
BUS STOP
...BYE.
DID SHE JUST ASK YOU OUT?
I...I THINK SO?
YOU SHOULD PROBABLY MARRY HER.
HEY, CAN I GET A LIFT? I WAS ON MY WAY TO THE MASON TO GET THIS FIXED.

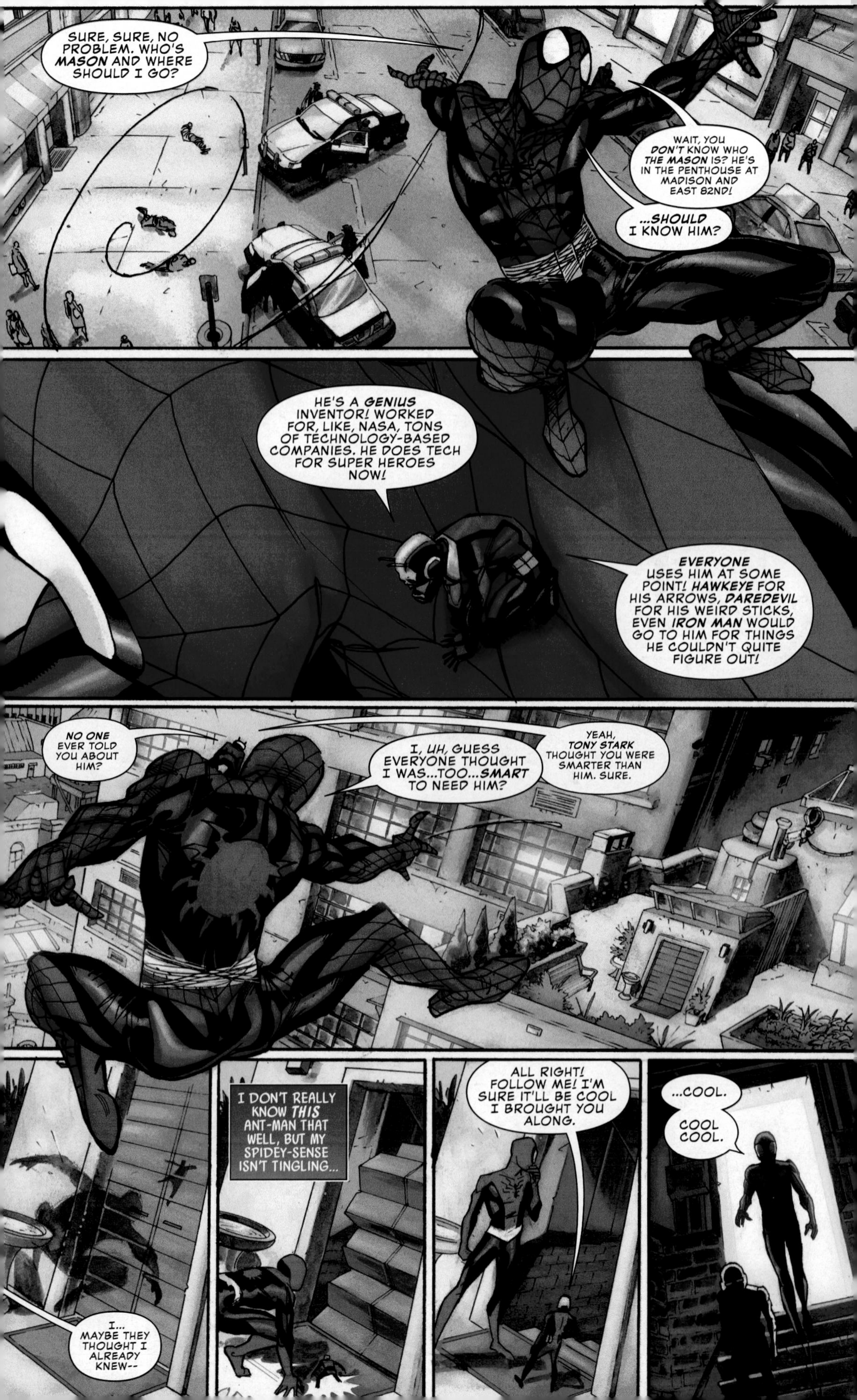
SURE, SURE, NO PROBLEM. WHO'S MASON AND WHERE SHOULD I GO?
WAIT, YOU DON'T KNOW WHO THE MASON IS? HE'S IN THE PENTHOUSE AT MADISON AND EAST 82ND!
...SHOULD I KNOW HIM?
HE'S A GENIUS INVENTOR! WORKED FOR, LIKE, NASA, TONS OF TECHNOLOGY-BASED COMPANIES. HE DOES TECH FOR SUPER HEROES NOW!
EVERYONE USES HIM AT SOME POINT! HAWKEYE FOR HIS ARROWS, DAREDEVIL FOR HIS WEIRD STICKS, EVEN IRON MAN WOULD GO TO HIM FOR THINGS HE COULDN'T QUITE FIGURE OUT!
NO ONE EVER TOLD YOU ABOUT HIM?
I, UH, GUESS EVERYONE THOUGHT I WAS...TOO...SMART TO NEED HIM?
YEAH, TONY STARK THOUGHT YOU WERE SMARTER THAN HIM. SURE.
I... MAYBE THEY THOUGHT I ALREADY KNEW--
I DON'T REALLY KNOW THIS ANT-MAN THAT WELL, BUT MY SPIDEY-SENSE ISN'T TINGLING...
ALL RIGHT! FOLLOW ME! I'M SURE IT'LL BE COOL I BROUGHT YOU ALONG.
...COOL.
COOL COOL.

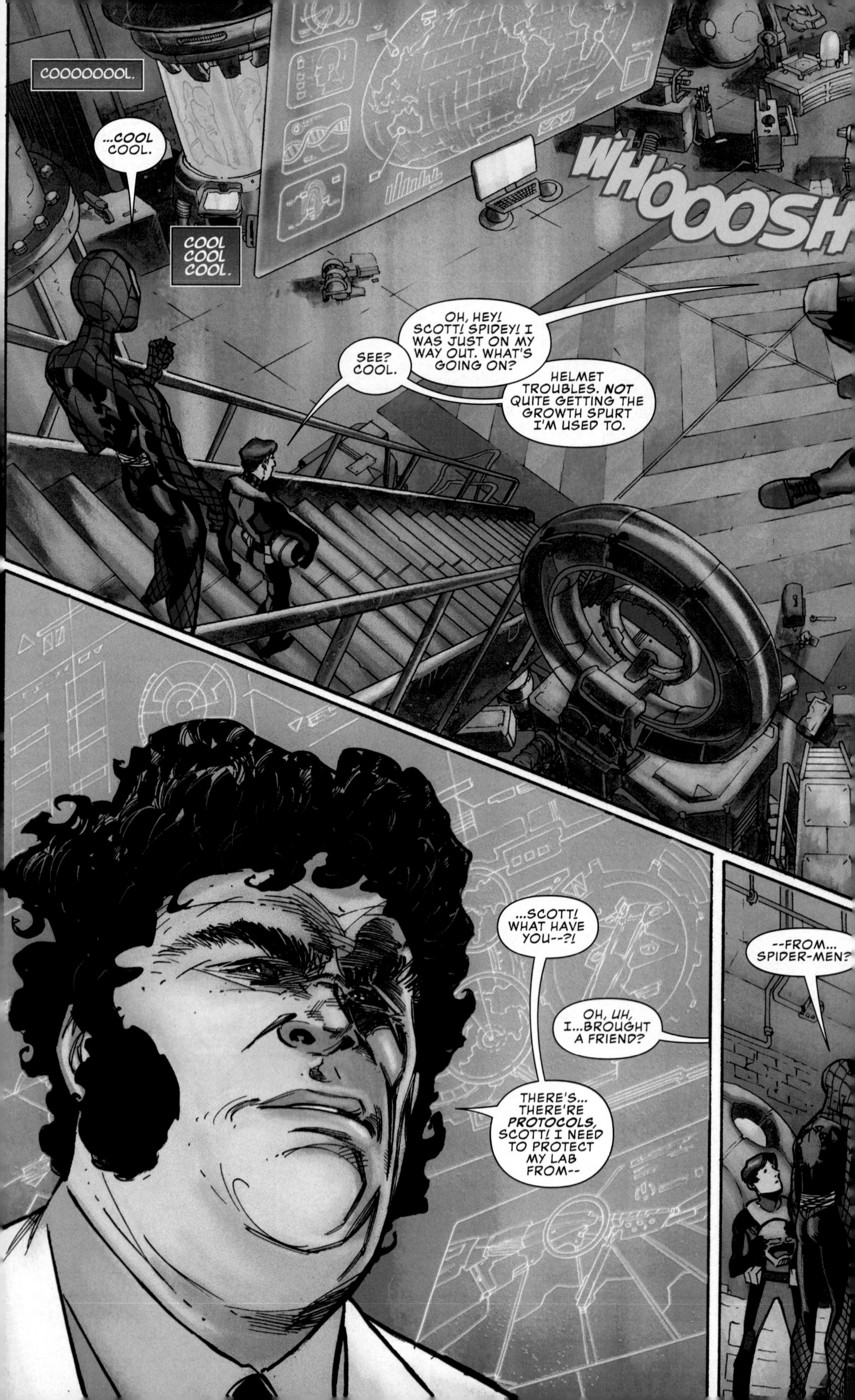

COOOOOOOL.
...COOL COOL.
COOL COOL COOL.
WHOOOOSH
OH, HEY! SCOTT! SPIDEY! I WAS JUST ON MY WAY OUT. WHAT'S GOING ON?
SEE? COOL.
HELMET TROUBLES. NOT QUITE GETTING THE GROWTH SPURT I'M USED TO.
...SCOTT! WHAT HAVE YOU--?!
OH, UH, I...BROUGHT A FRIEND?
THERE'S... THERE'RE PROTOCOLS, SCOTT! I NEED TO PROTECT MY LAB FROM--
--FROM... SPIDER-MEN?

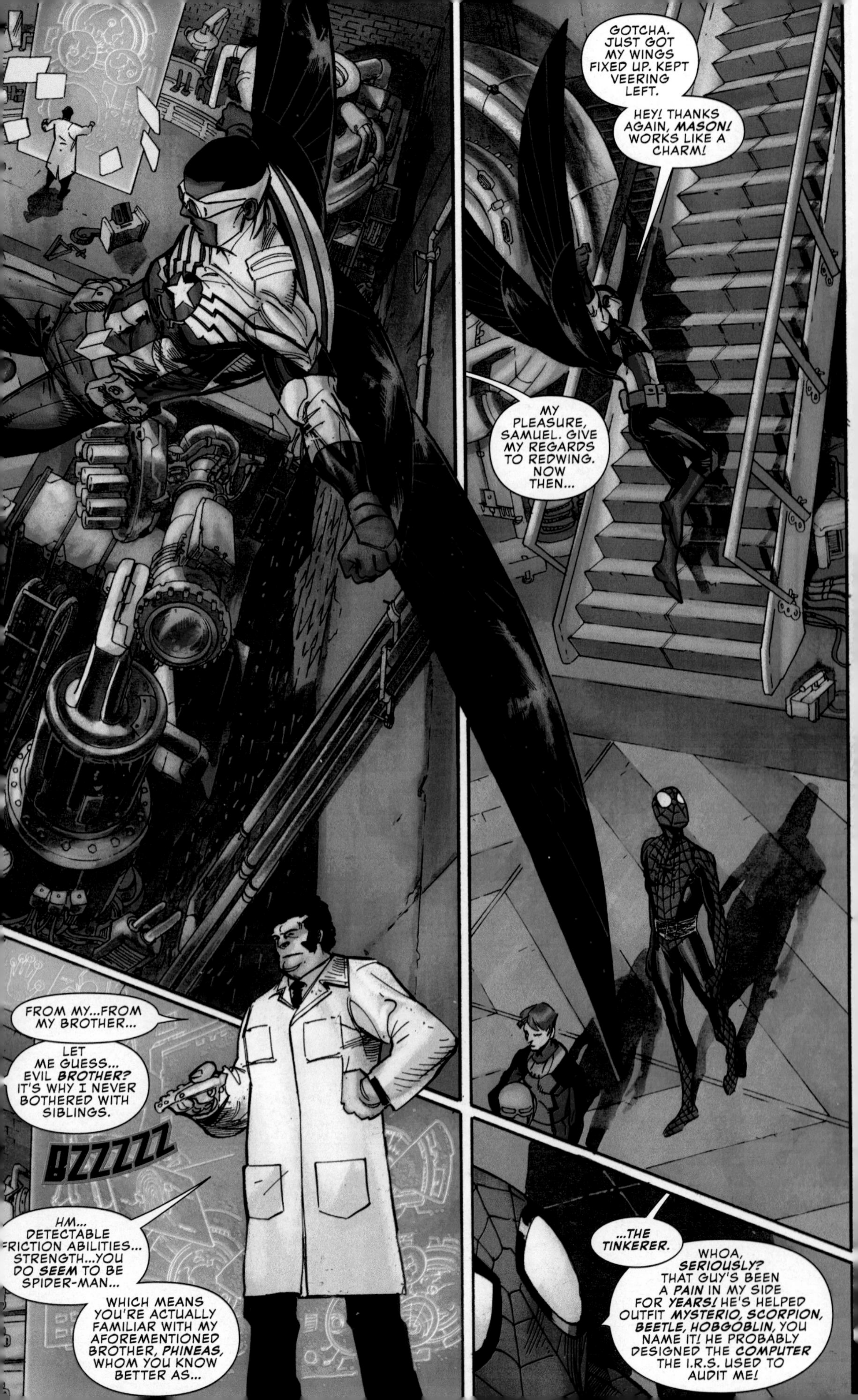
GOTCHA. JUST GOT MY WINGS FIXED UP. KEPT VEERING LEFT.
HEY! THANKS AGAIN, MASON! WORKS LIKE A CHARM!
MY PLEASURE, SAMUEL. GIVE MY REGARDS TO REDWING. NOW THEN...
FROM MY...FROM MY BROTHER...
LET ME GUESS... EVIL BROTHER? IT'S WHY I NEVER BOTHERED WITH SIBLINGS.
BZZZZZ
HM... DETECTABLE FRICTION ABILITIES... STRENGTH...YOU DO SEEM TO BE SPIDER-MAN...
WHICH MEANS YOU'RE ACTUALLY FAMILIAR WITH MY AFOREMENTIONED BROTHER, PHINEAS, WHOM YOU KNOW BETTER AS...
...THE TINKERER.
WHOA, SERIOUSLY? THAT GUY'S BEEN A PAIN IN MY SIDE FOR YEARS! HE'S HELPED OUTFIT MYSTERIO, SCORPION, BEETLE, HOBGOBLIN, YOU NAME IT! HE PROBABLY DESIGNED THE COMPUTER THE I.R.S. USED TO AUDIT ME!

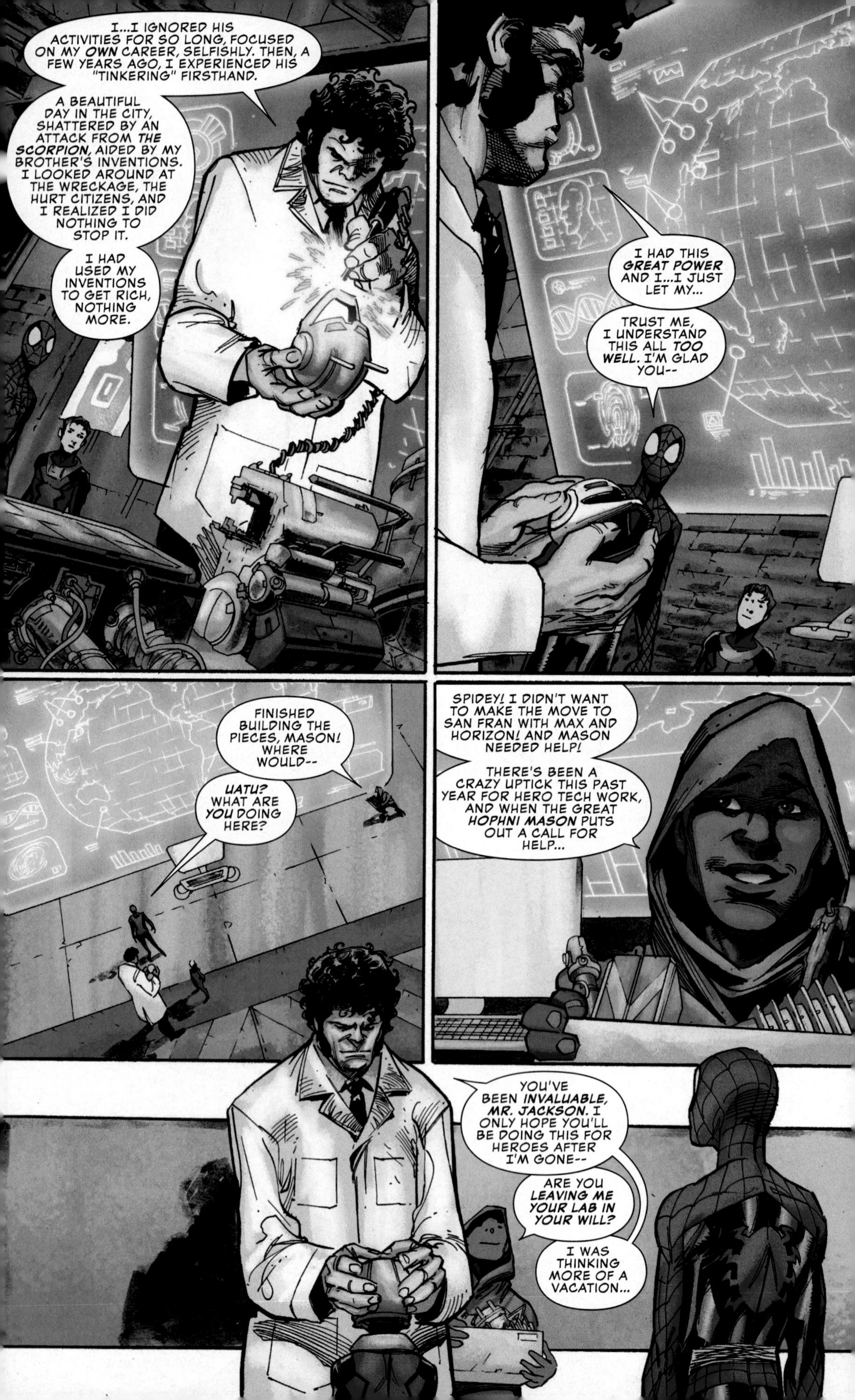
I...I IGNORED HIS ACTIVITIES FOR SO LONG, FOCUSED ON MY OWN CAREER, SELFISHLY. THEN, A FEW YEARS AGO, I EXPERIENCED HIS "TINKERING" FIRSTHAND.
A BEAUTIFUL DAY IN THE CITY, SHATTERED BY AN ATTACK FROM THE SCORPION, AIDED BY MY BROTHER'S INVENTIONS. I LOOKED AROUND AT THE WRECKAGE, THE HURT CITIZENS, AND I REALIZED I DID NOTHING TO STOP IT.
I HAD USED MY INVENTIONS TO GET RICH, NOTHING MORE.
I HAD THIS GREAT POWER AND I...I JUST LET MY...
TRUST ME, I UNDERSTAND THIS ALL TOO WELL. I'M GLAD YOU--
FINISHED BUILDING THE PIECES, MASON! WHERE WOULD--
UATU? WHAT ARE YOU DOING HERE?
SPIDEY! I DIDN'T WANT TO MAKE THE MOVE TO SAN FRAN WITH MAX AND HORIZON! AND MASON NEEDED HELP!
THERE'S BEEN A CRAZY UPTICK THIS PAST YEAR FOR HERO TECH WORK, AND WHEN THE GREAT HOPHNI MASON PUTS OUT A CALL FOR HELP...
YOU'VE BEEN INVALUABLE, MR. JACKSON. I ONLY HOPE YOU'LL BE DOING THIS FOR HEROES AFTER I'M GONE--
ARE YOU LEAVING ME YOUR LAB IN YOUR WILL?
I WAS THINKING MORE OF A VACATION...

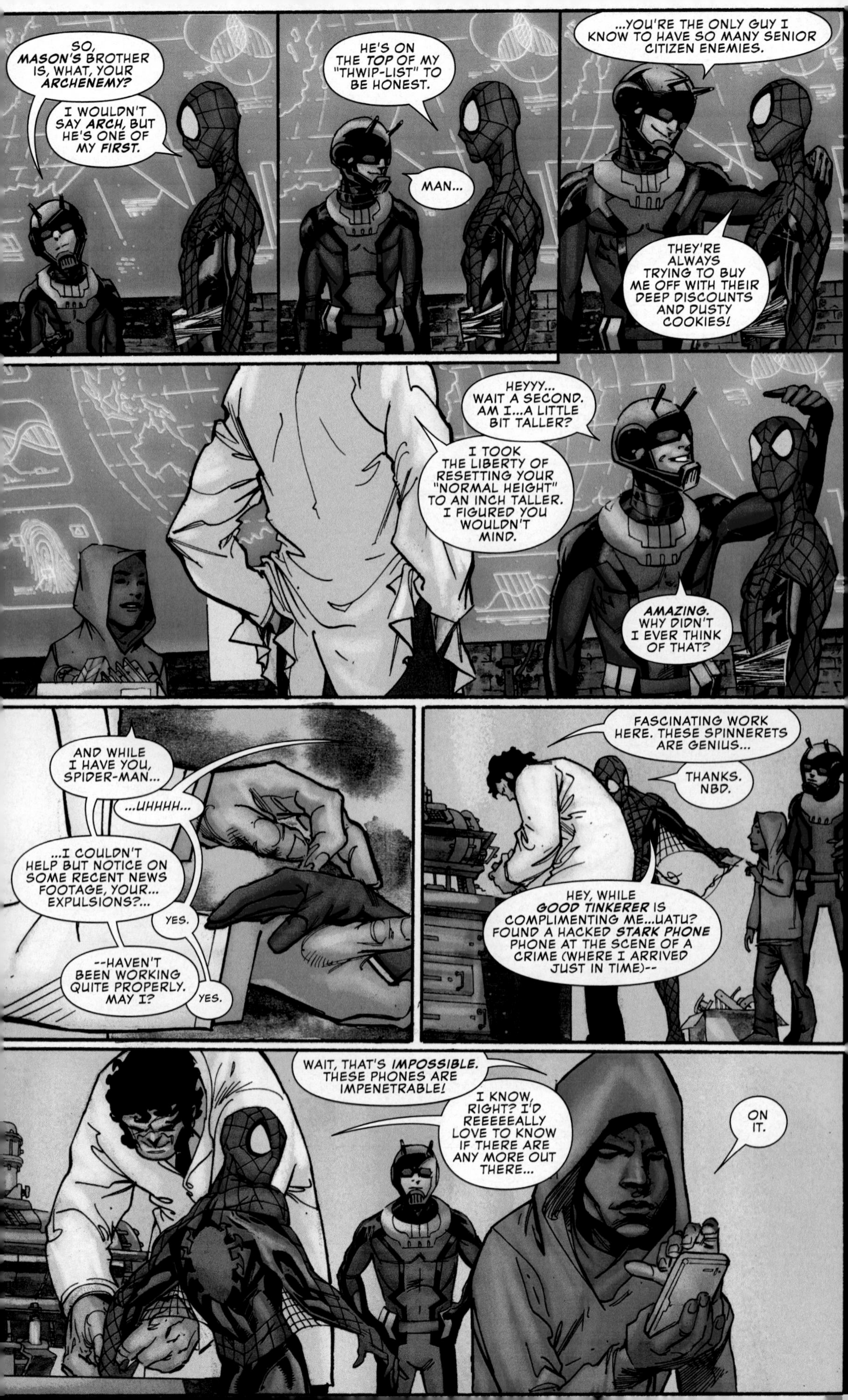
SO, MASON'S BROTHER IS, WHAT, YOUR ARCHENEMY?
I WOULDN'T SAY ARCH, BUT HE'S ONE OF MY FIRST.
HE'S ON THE TOP OF MY "THWIP-LIST" TO BE HONEST.
MAN...
...YOU'RE THE ONLY GUY I KNOW TO HAVE SO MANY SENIOR CITIZEN ENEMIES.
THEY'RE ALWAYS TRYING TO BUY ME OFF WITH THEIR DEEP DISCOUNTS AND DUSTY COOKIES!
HEYYY... WAIT A SECOND. AM I...A LITTLE BIT TALLER?
I TOOK THE LIBERTY OF RESETTING YOUR "NORMAL HEIGHT" TO AN INCH TALLER. I FIGURED YOU WOULDN'T MIND.
AMAZING. WHY DIDN'T I EVER THINK OF THAT?
AND WHILE I HAVE YOU, SPIDER-MAN...
...UHHHH...
...I COULDN'T HELP BUT NOTICE ON SOME RECENT NEWS FOOTAGE, YOUR... EXPULSIONS?...
YES.
--HAVEN'T BEEN WORKING QUITE PROPERLY. MAY I?
YES.
FASCINATING WORK HERE. THESE SPINNERETS ARE GENIUS...
THANKS. NBD.
HEY, WHILE GOOD TINKERER IS COMPLIMENTING ME...UATU? FOUND A HACKED STARK PHONE PHONE AT THE SCENE OF A CRIME (WHERE I ARRIVED JUST IN TIME)--
WAIT, THAT'S IMPOSSIBLE. THESE PHONES ARE IMPENETRABLE!
I KNOW, RIGHT? I'D REEEEEALLY LOVE TO KNOW IF THERE ARE ANY MORE OUT THERE...
ON IT.

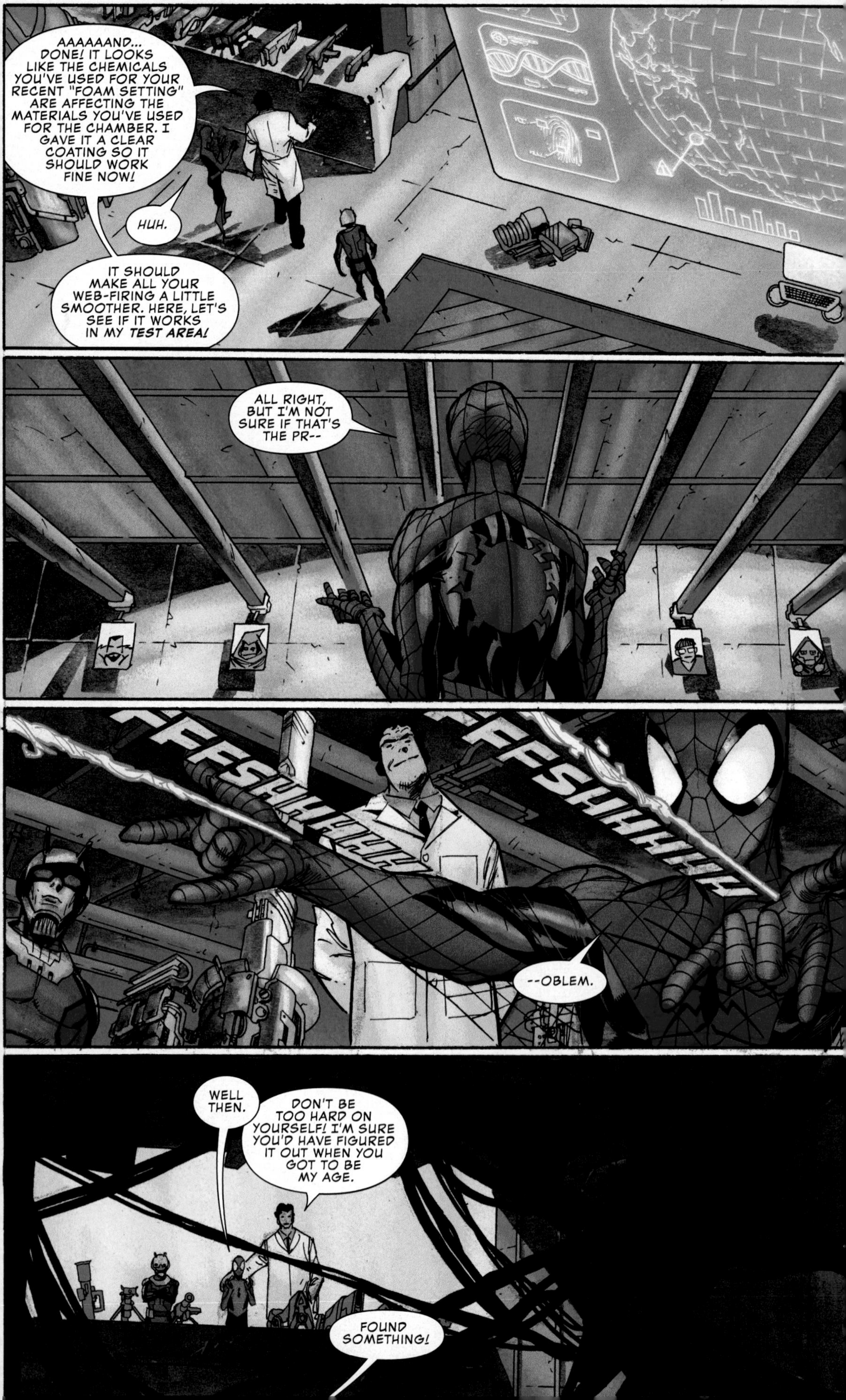
AAAAAAAND... DONE! IT LOOKS LIKE THE CHEMICALS YOU'VE USED FOR YOUR RECENT "FOAM SETTING" ARE AFFECTING THE MATERIALS YOU'VE USED FOR THE CHAMBER. I GAVE IT A CLEAR COATING SO IT SHOULD WORK FINE NOW!
HUH.
IT SHOULD MAKE ALL YOUR WEB-FIRING A LITTLE SMOOTHER. HERE, LET'S SEE IF IT WORKS IN MY TEST AREA!
ALL RIGHT, BUT I'M NOT SURE IF THAT'S THE PR--
--OBLEM.
WELL THEN.
DON'T BE TOO HARD ON YOURSELF! I'M SURE YOU'D HAVE FIGURED IT OUT WHEN YOU GOT TO BE MY AGE.
FOUND SOMETHING!

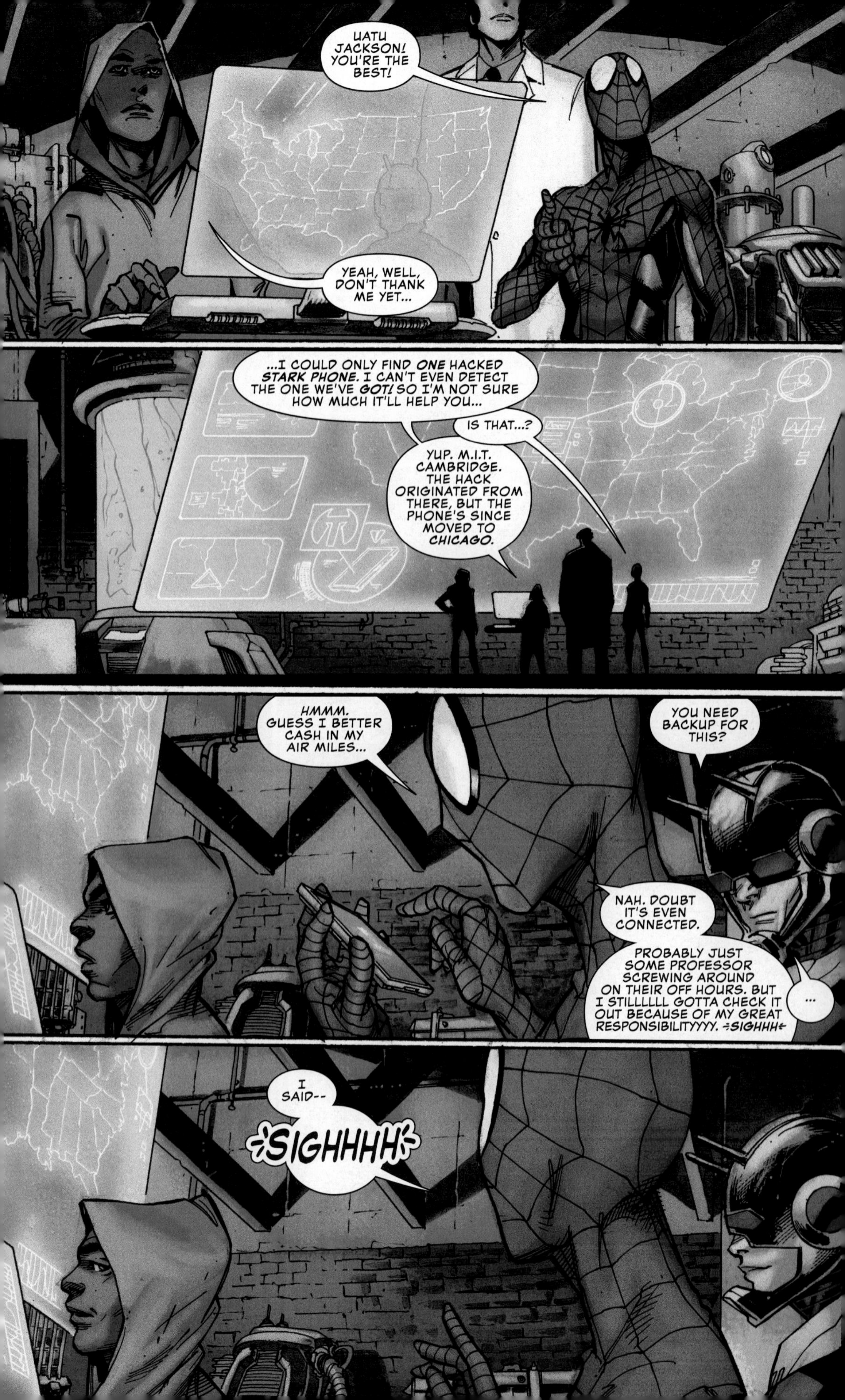
UATU JACKSON! YOU'RE THE BEST!
YEAH, WELL, DON'T THANK ME YET...
...I COULD ONLY FIND ONE HACKED STARK PHONE. I CAN'T EVEN DETECT THE ONE WE'VE GOT! SO I'M NOT SURE HOW MUCH IT'LL HELP YOU...
IS THAT...?
YUP. M.I.T. CAMBRIDGE. THE HACK ORIGINATED FROM THERE, BUT THE PHONE'S SINCE MOVED TO CHICAGO.
HMMM. GUESS I BETTER CASH IN MY AIR MILES...
YOU NEED BACKUP FOR THIS?
NAH. DOUBT IT'S EVEN CONNECTED.
PROBABLY JUST SOME PROFESSOR SCREWING AROUND ON THEIR OFF HOURS. BUT I STILLLLLL GOTTA CHECK IT OUT BECAUSE OF MY GREAT RESPONSIBILITYYYY. *SIGHHH*
...
I SAID--
SIGHHHH

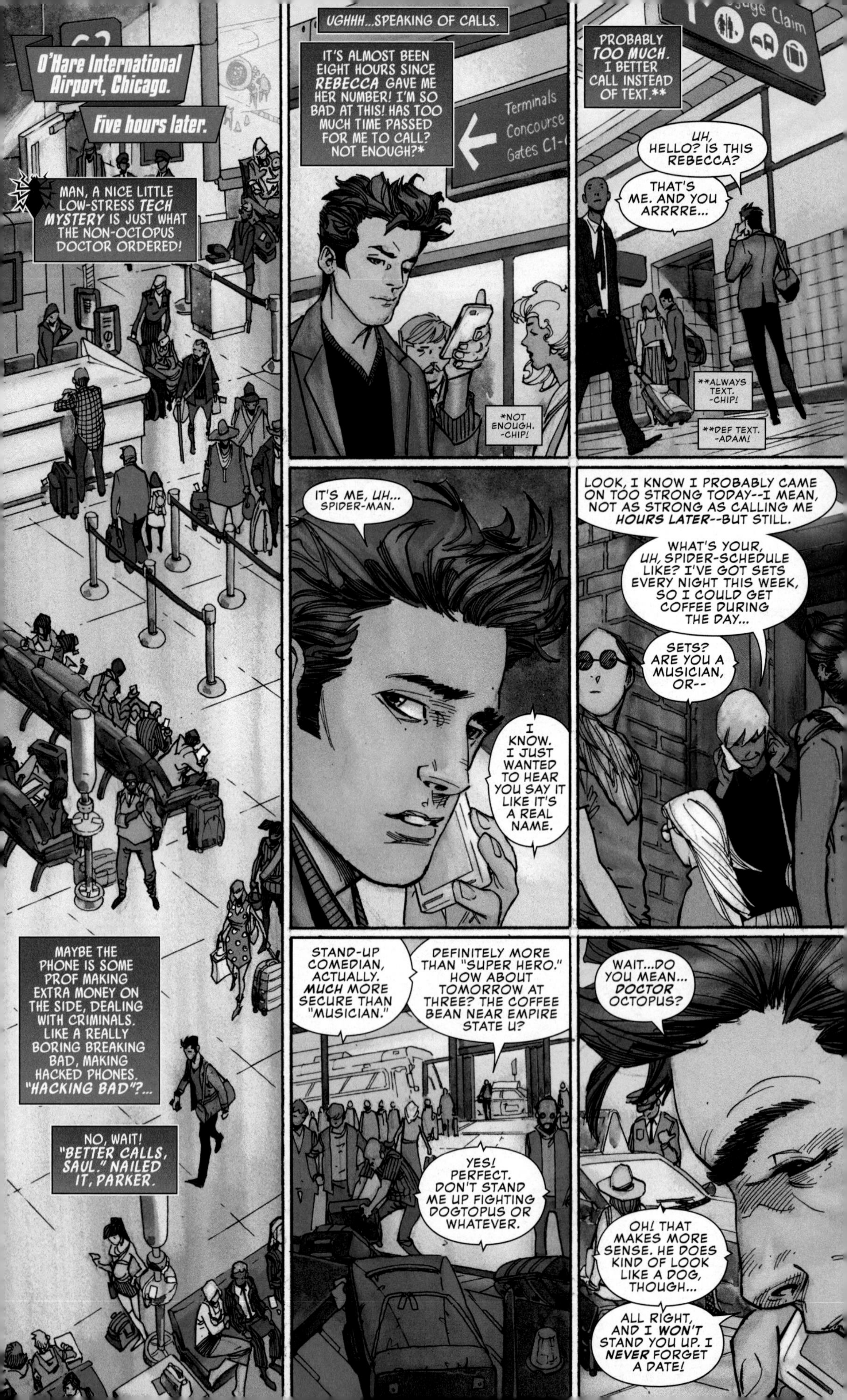
O'Hare International Airport, Chicago.
Five hours later.
MAN, A NICE LITTLE LOW-STRESS TECH MYSTERY IS JUST WHAT THE NON-OCTOPUS DOCTOR ORDERED!
MAYBE THE PHONE IS SOME PROF MAKING EXTRA MONEY ON THE SIDE, DEALING WITH CRIMINALS. LIKE A REALLY BORING BREAKING BAD, MAKING HACKED PHONES. "HACKING BAD"?...
NO, WAIT! "BETTER CALLS, SAUL." NAILED IT, PARKER.
UGHHH...SPEAKING OF CALLS.
IT'S ALMOST BEEN EIGHT HOURS SINCE REBECCA GAVE ME HER NUMBER! I'M SO BAD AT THIS! HAS TOO MUCH TIME PASSED FOR ME TO CALL? NOT ENOUGH?*
Terminals
Concourse
Gates C1-
*NOT ENOUGH. -CHIP!
PROBABLY TOO MUCH. I BETTER CALL INSTEAD OF TEXT.**
Claim
UH, HELLO? IS THIS REBECCA?
THAT'S ME. AND YOU ARRRRE...
**ALWAYS TEXT. -CHIP!
**DEF TEXT. -ADAM!
IT'S ME, UH... SPIDER-MAN.
I KNOW. I JUST WANTED TO HEAR YOU SAY IT LIKE IT'S A REAL NAME.
LOOK, I KNOW I PROBABLY CAME ON TOO STRONG TODAY--I MEAN, NOT AS STRONG AS CALLING ME HOURS LATER--BUT STILL.
WHAT'S YOUR, UH, SPIDER-SCHEDULE LIKE? I'VE GOT SETS EVERY NIGHT THIS WEEK, SO I COULD GET COFFEE DURING THE DAY...
SETS? ARE YOU A MUSICIAN, OR--
STAND-UP COMEDIAN, ACTUALLY. MUCH MORE SECURE THAN "MUSICIAN."
DEFINITELY MORE THAN "SUPER HERO." HOW ABOUT TOMORROW AT THREE? THE COFFEE BEAN NEAR EMPIRE STATE U?
YES! PERFECT. DON'T STAND ME UP FIGHTING DOGTOPUS OR WHATEVER.
WAIT...DO YOU MEAN... DOCTOR OCTOPUS?
OH! THAT MAKES MORE SENSE. HE DOES KIND OF LOOK LIKE A DOG, THOUGH...
ALL RIGHT, AND I WON'T STAND YOU UP. I NEVER FORGET A DATE!

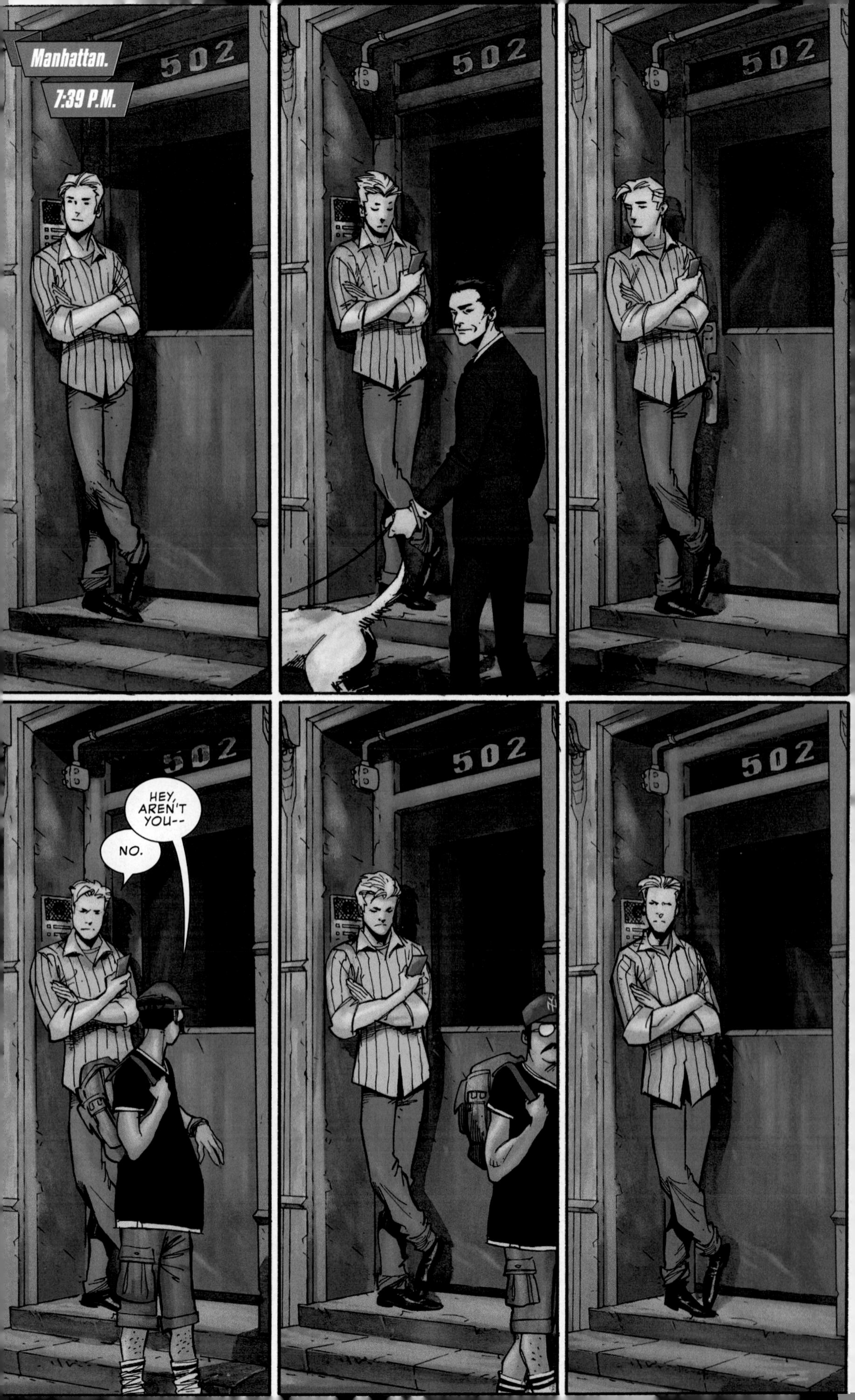
Manhattan.
7:39 P.M.
502
502
502
502
HEY, AREN'T YOU--
NO.
502
502

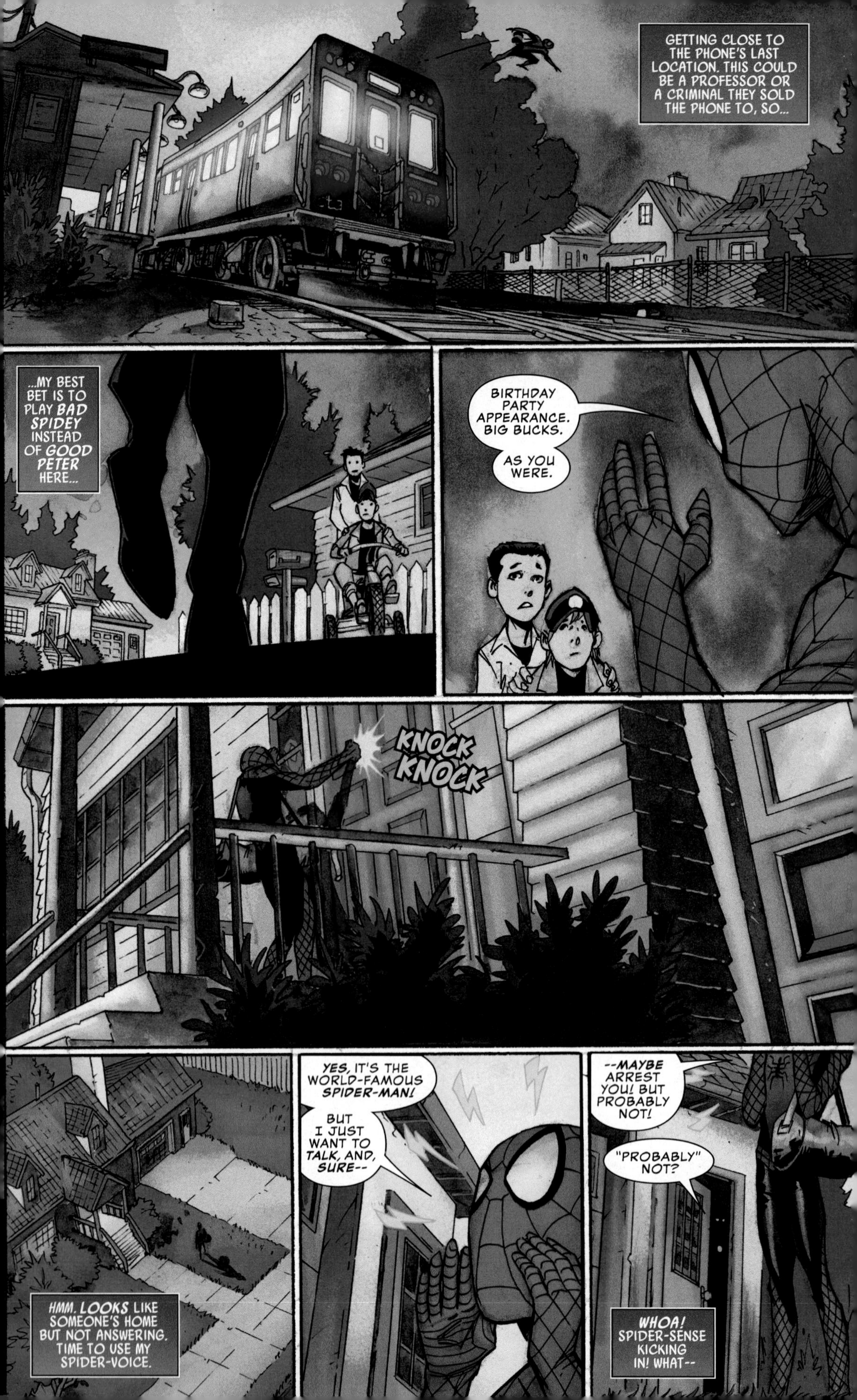
GETTING CLOSE TO THE PHONE'S LAST LOCATION. THIS COULD BE A PROFESSOR OR A CRIMINAL THEY SOLD THE PHONE TO, SO...
...MY BEST BET IS TO PLAY BAD SPIDEY INSTEAD OF GOOD PETER HERE...
BIRTHDAY PARTY APPEARANCE. BIG BUCKS.
AS YOU WERE.
KNOCK KNOCK
HMM. LOOKS LIKE SOMEONE'S HOME BUT NOT ANSWERING. TIME TO USE MY SPIDER-VOICE.
YES, IT'S THE WORLD-FAMOUS SPIDER-MAN!
BUT I JUST WANT TO TALK, AND, SURE--
--MAYBE ARREST YOU! BUT PROBABLY NOT!
"PROBABLY" NOT?
WHOA! SPIDER-SENSE KICKING IN! WHAT--

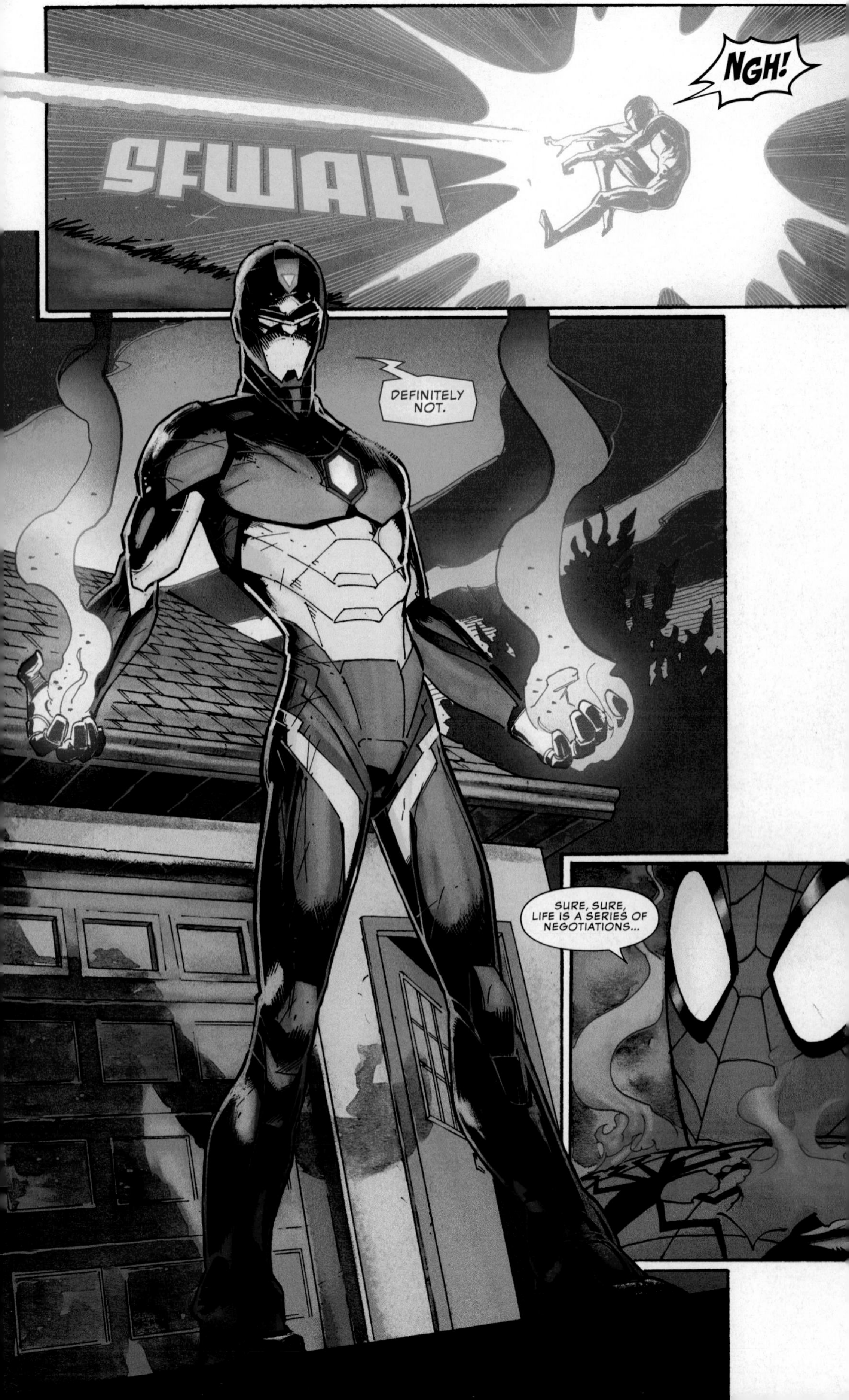
SFWAH
NGH!
DEFINITELY NOT.
SURE, SURE, LIFE IS A SERIES OF NEGOTIATIONS...

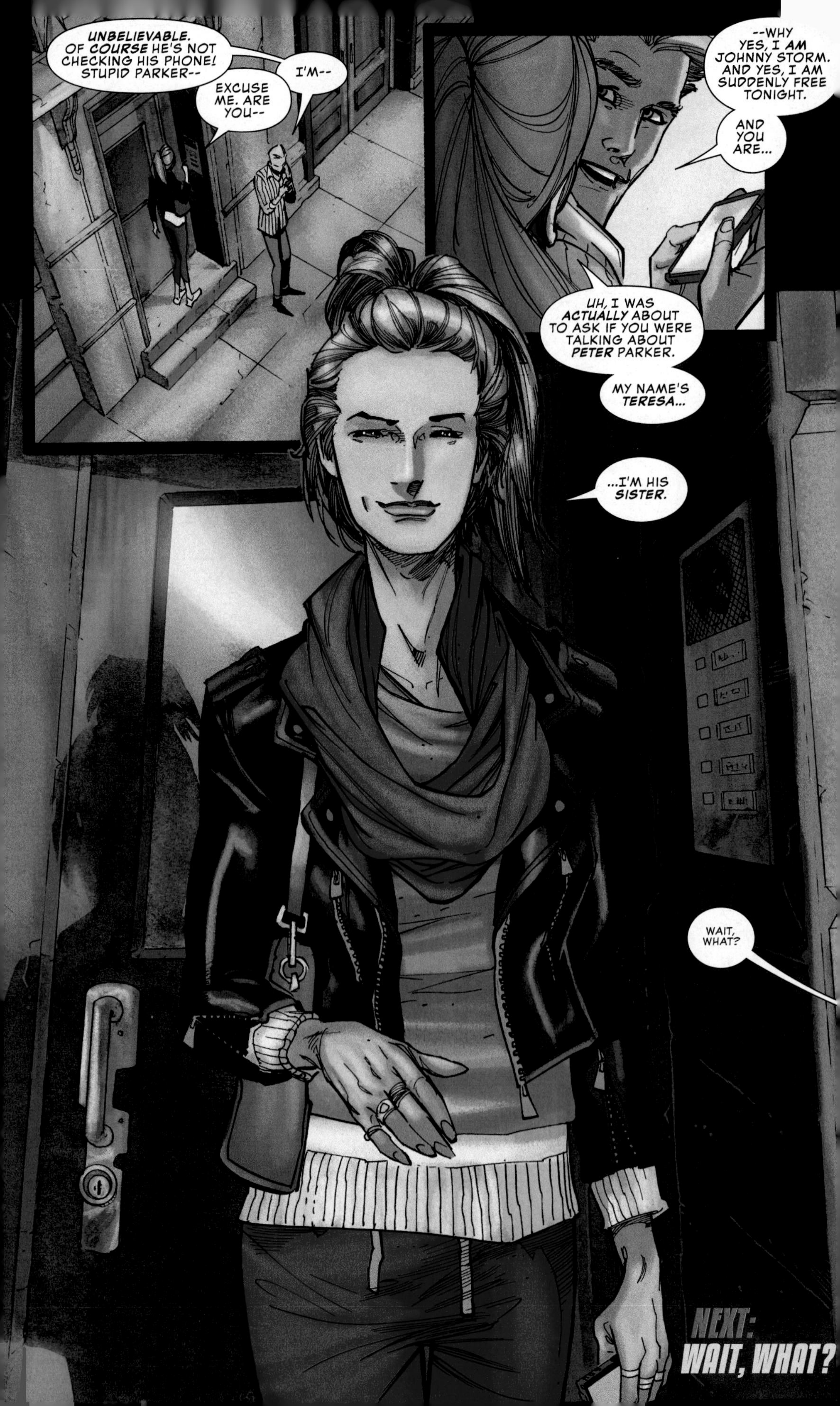
UNBELIEVABLE. OF COURSE HE'S NOT CHECKING HIS PHONE! STUPID PARKER--
EXCUSE ME. ARE YOU--
I'M--
--WHY YES, I AM JOHNNY STORM. AND YES, I AM SUDDENLY FREE TONIGHT.
AND YOU ARE...
UH, I WAS ACTUALLY ABOUT TO ASK IF YOU WERE TALKING ABOUT PETER PARKER.
MY NAME'S TERESA...
...I'M HIS SISTER.
WAIT, WHAT?
NEXT: WAIT, WHAT?

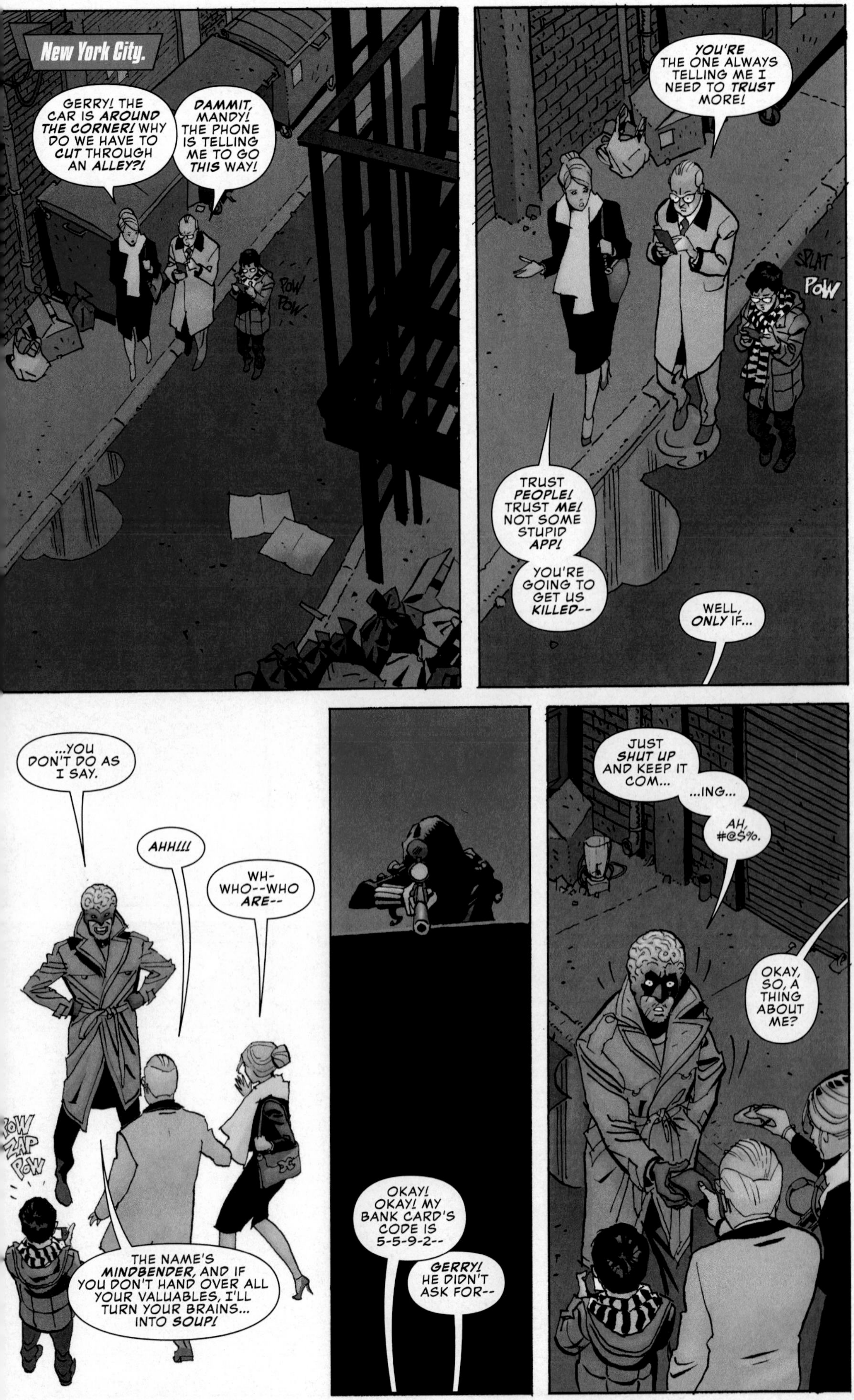
New York City.
GERRY! THE CAR IS AROUND THE CORNER! WHY DO WE HAVE TO CUT THROUGH AN ALLEY?!
DAMMIT, MANDY! THE PHONE IS TELLING ME TO GO THIS WAY!
POW
POW
YOU'RE THE ONE ALWAYS TELLING ME I NEED TO TRUST MORE!
SPLAT
POW
TRUST PEOPLE! TRUST ME! NOT SOME STUPID APP!
YOU'RE GOING TO GET US KILLED--
WELL, ONLY IF...
...YOU DON'T DO AS I SAY.
AHH!!!
WH-WHO--WHO ARE--
POW
ZAP
POW
THE NAME'S MINDBENDER, AND IF YOU DON'T HAND OVER ALL YOUR VALUABLES, I'LL TURN YOUR BRAINS... INTO SOUP!
OKAY! OKAY! MY BANK CARD'S CODE IS 5-5-9-2--
GERRY! HE DIDN'T ASK FOR--
JUST SHUT UP AND KEEP IT COM...
...ING...
AH, #@$%.
OKAY, SO, A THING ABOUT ME?

...I HAVE A POWER CALLED "SPIDER-SENSE"! VERY HANDY! TINGLES IN MY NOGGIN TO WARN ME OF DANGER!

OH GOD OH GOD SPIDER-MAN I DIDN'T I WASN'T--

BUT THE FUNNY THING IS, RIGHT NOW I HAVE SOMETHING I'VE NEVER HAD BEFORE! IT'S LIKE--LIKE--LIKE A REVERSE-SPIDER-SENSE!

MY NOGGIN IS REWARDING ME WITH SOOTHING, WARM KISSES FOR BEING SO COMPLETELY SAFE!

I JUST THOUGHT... I JUST...

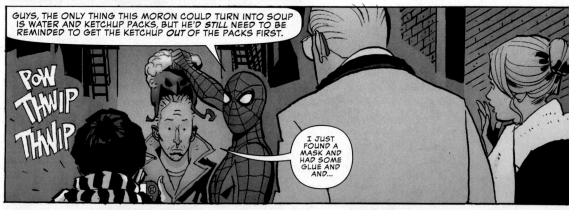

GUYS, THE ONLY THING THIS MORON COULD TURN INTO SOUP IS WATER AND KETCHUP PACKS, BUT HE'D STILL NEED TO BE REMINDED TO GET THE KETCHUP OUT OF THE PACKS FIRST.

POW THWIP THWIP

I JUST FOUND A MASK AND HAD SOME GLUE AND AND...

WAIT, "THWIP"? IS THAT...

IT'S IRON MAN 7: SECRET ARMOR WARS. SPIDER-MAN IS AN NPC.

THWIP POW

≠SNIFF SNIFF≠ HELP ME, IRON MAN! HELP ME!

...AM I CRYING?...

UHHHH--

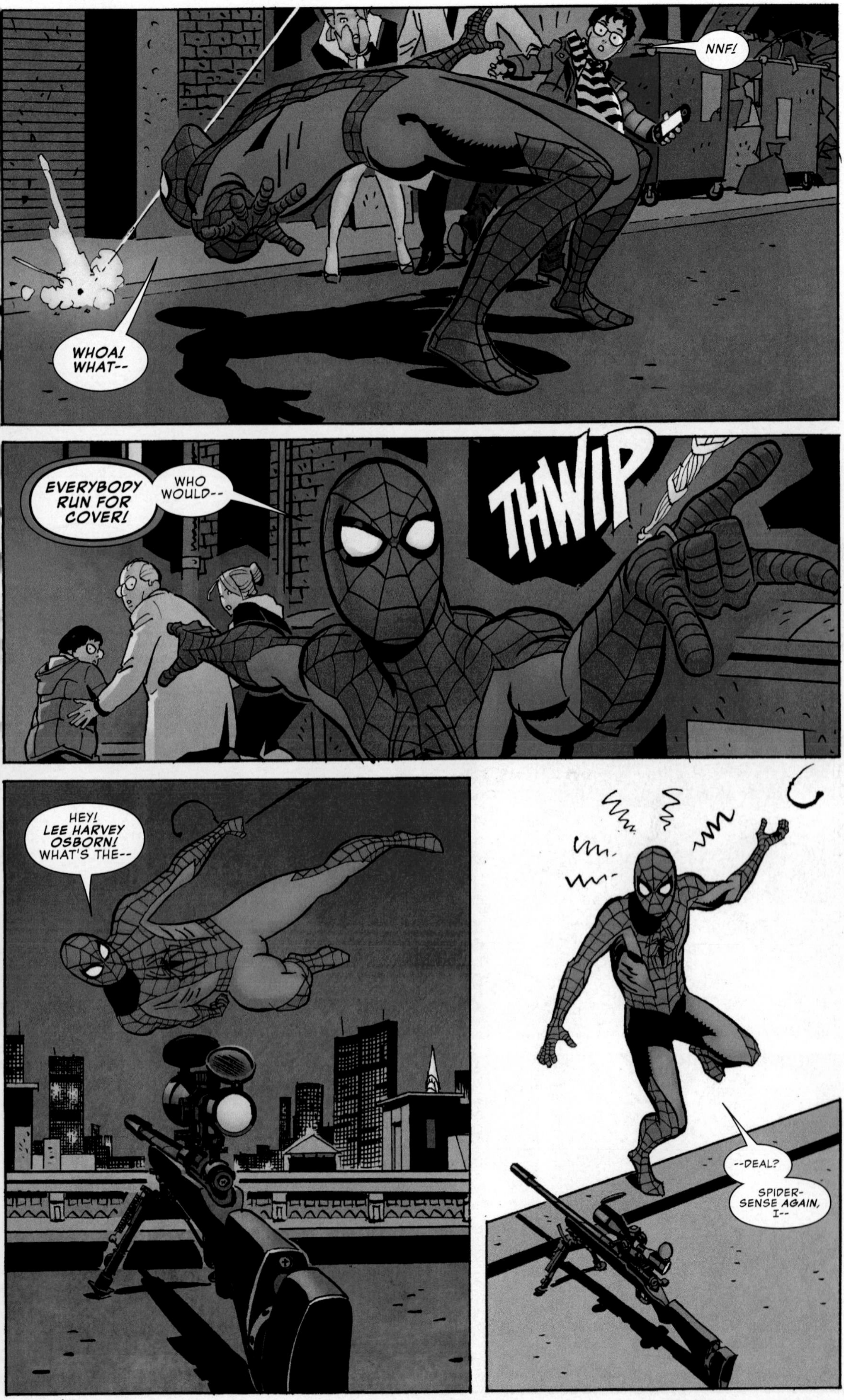
NNF!
WHOA! WHAT--
EVERYBODY RUN FOR COVER!
WHO WOULD--
THWIP
HEY! LEE HARVEY OSBORN! WHAT'S THE--
--DEAL?
SPIDER-SENSE AGAIN, I--

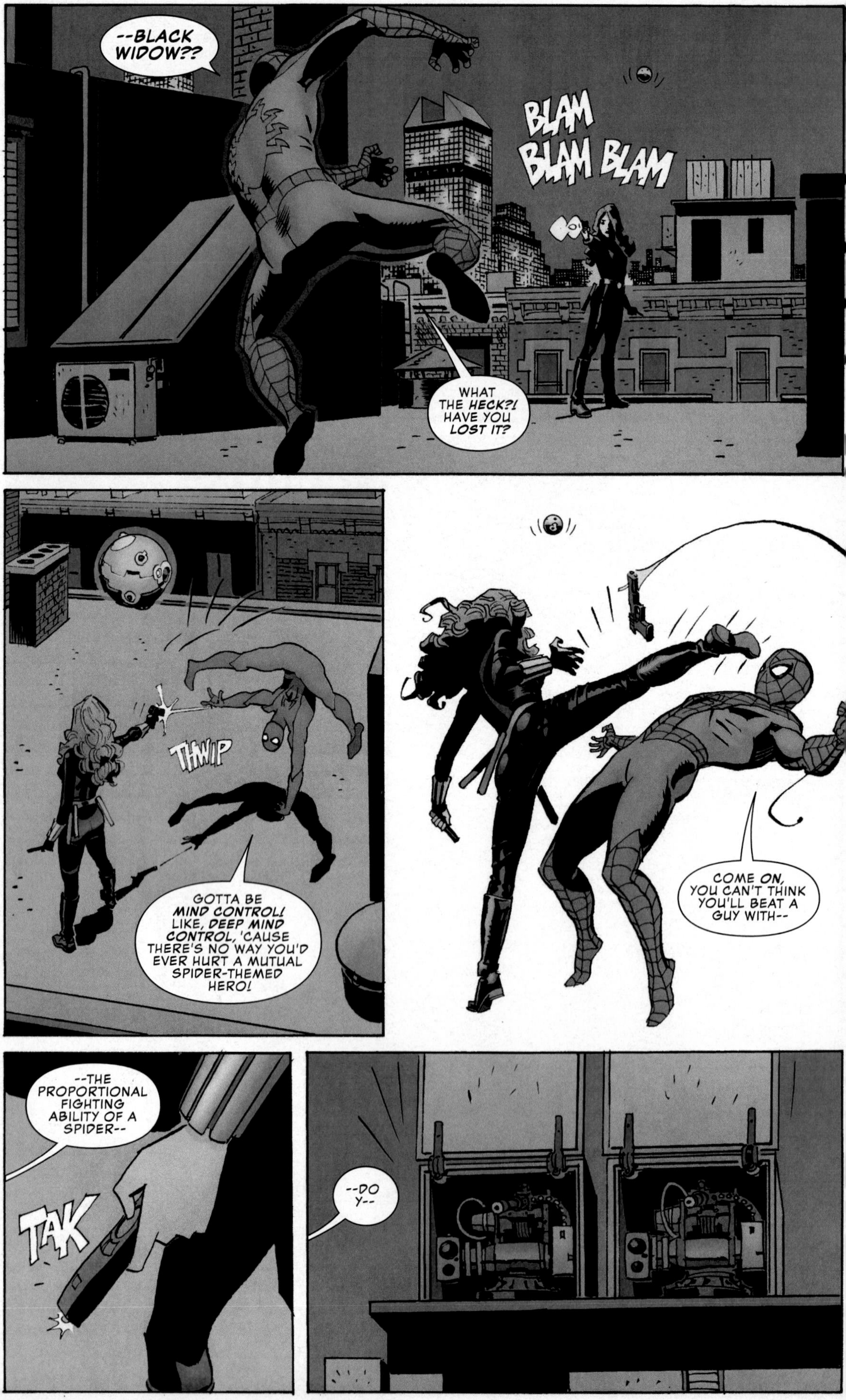

--BLACK WIDOW??
BLAM BLAM BLAM
WHAT THE HECK?! HAVE YOU LOST IT?
THWIP
GOTTA BE MIND CONTROL! LIKE, DEEP MIND CONTROL, 'CAUSE THERE'S NO WAY YOU'D EVER HURT A MUTUAL SPIDER-THEMED HERO!
COME ON, YOU CAN'T THINK YOU'LL BEAT A GUY WITH--
--THE PROPORTIONAL FIGHTING ABILITY OF A SPIDER--
TAK
--DO Y--

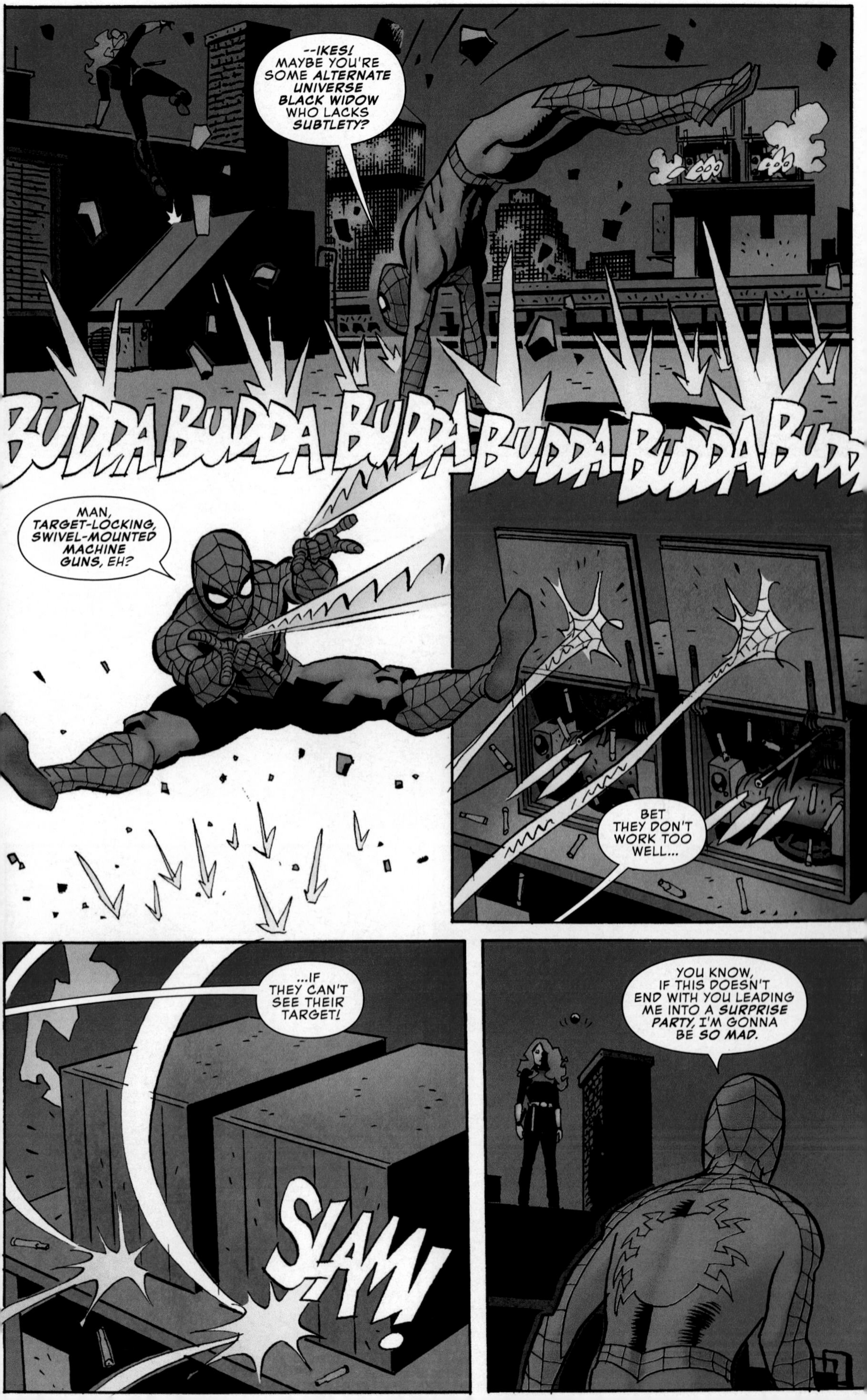
--IKES! MAYBE YOU'RE SOME ALTERNATE UNIVERSE BLACK WIDOW WHO LACKS SUBTLETY?
BUDDA BUDDA BUDDA BUDDA BUDDA BUDD
MAN, TARGET-LOCKING, SWIVEL-MOUNTED MACHINE GUNS, EH?
BET THEY DON'T WORK TOO WELL...
...IF THEY CAN'T SEE THEIR TARGET!
SLAM!
YOU KNOW, IF THIS DOESN'T END WITH YOU LEADING ME INTO A SURPRISE PARTY, I'M GONNA BE SO MAD.

COME ON! LET ME JUST WEB YOU UP AND THEN I CAN TAKE YOU TO A SPECIALIST!

SOMEONE WHO CAN TURN YOU BACK INTO A *NORMAL* ASSASSIN SLASH SPY SLASH SUPER HERO!

WIDOW!

THIS IS NUTS! LET'S JUST TALK AND--

--WHAT ARE--

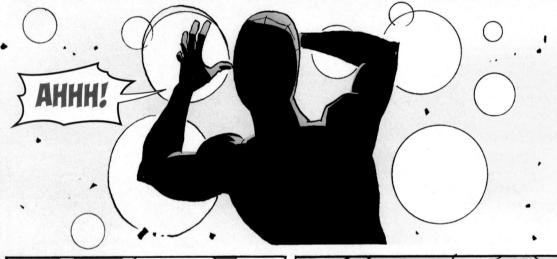

AHHH!

YOU--YOU *BLINDED* ME! THIS IS--THIS IS *WILDLY* UNFAIR!

WHOA! BUT BLIND OR NOT, I STILL GOT MY *SPIDER-SENSE,* LADY!

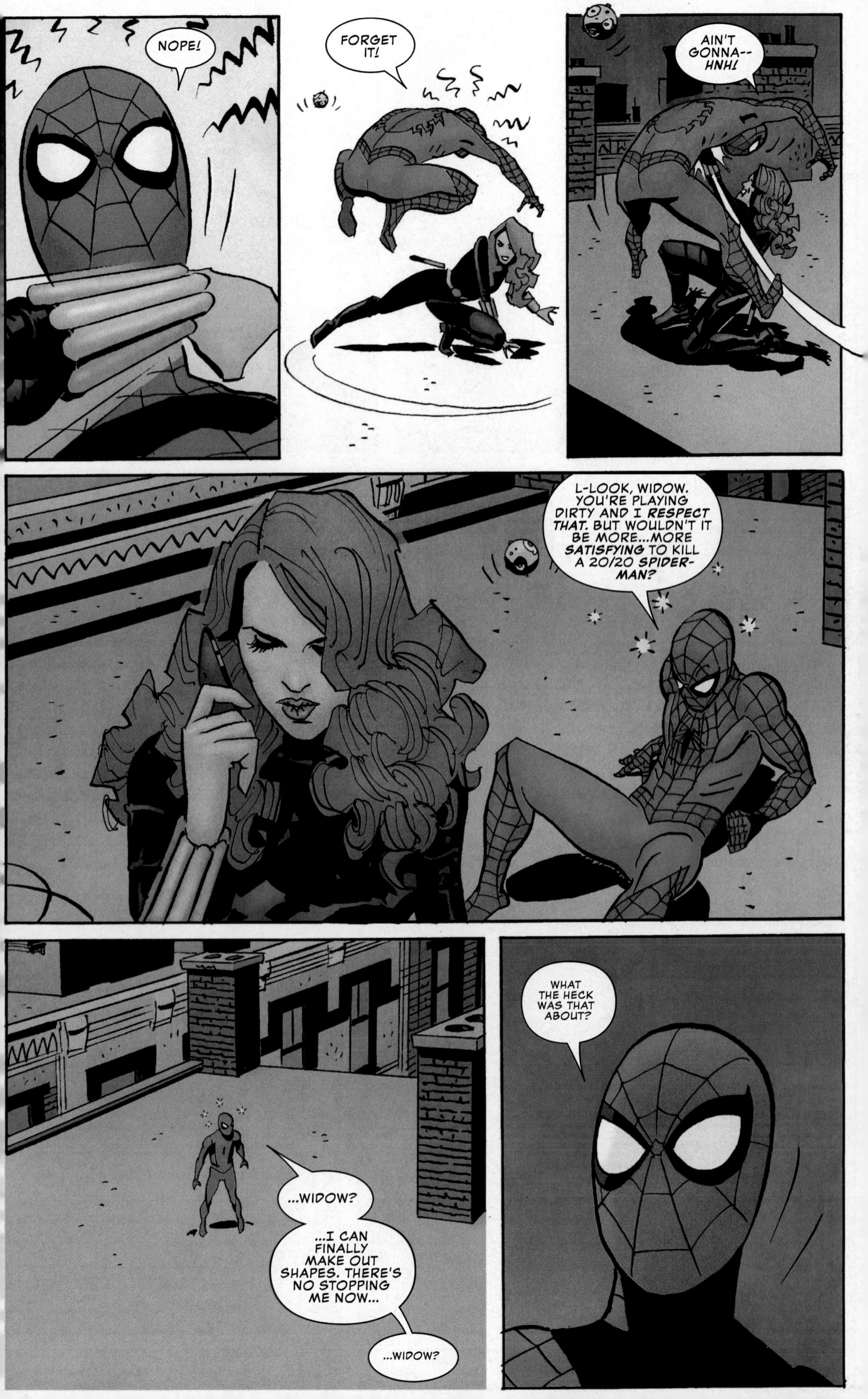
NOPE!
FORGET IT!
AIN'T GONNA-- HNH!
L-LOOK, WIDOW. YOU'RE PLAYING DIRTY AND I RESPECT THAT. BUT WOULDN'T IT BE MORE...MORE SATISFYING TO KILL A 20/20 SPIDER-MAN?
...WIDOW?
...I CAN FINALLY MAKE OUT SHAPES. THERE'S NO STOPPING ME NOW...
...WIDOW?
WHAT THE HECK WAS THAT ABOUT?

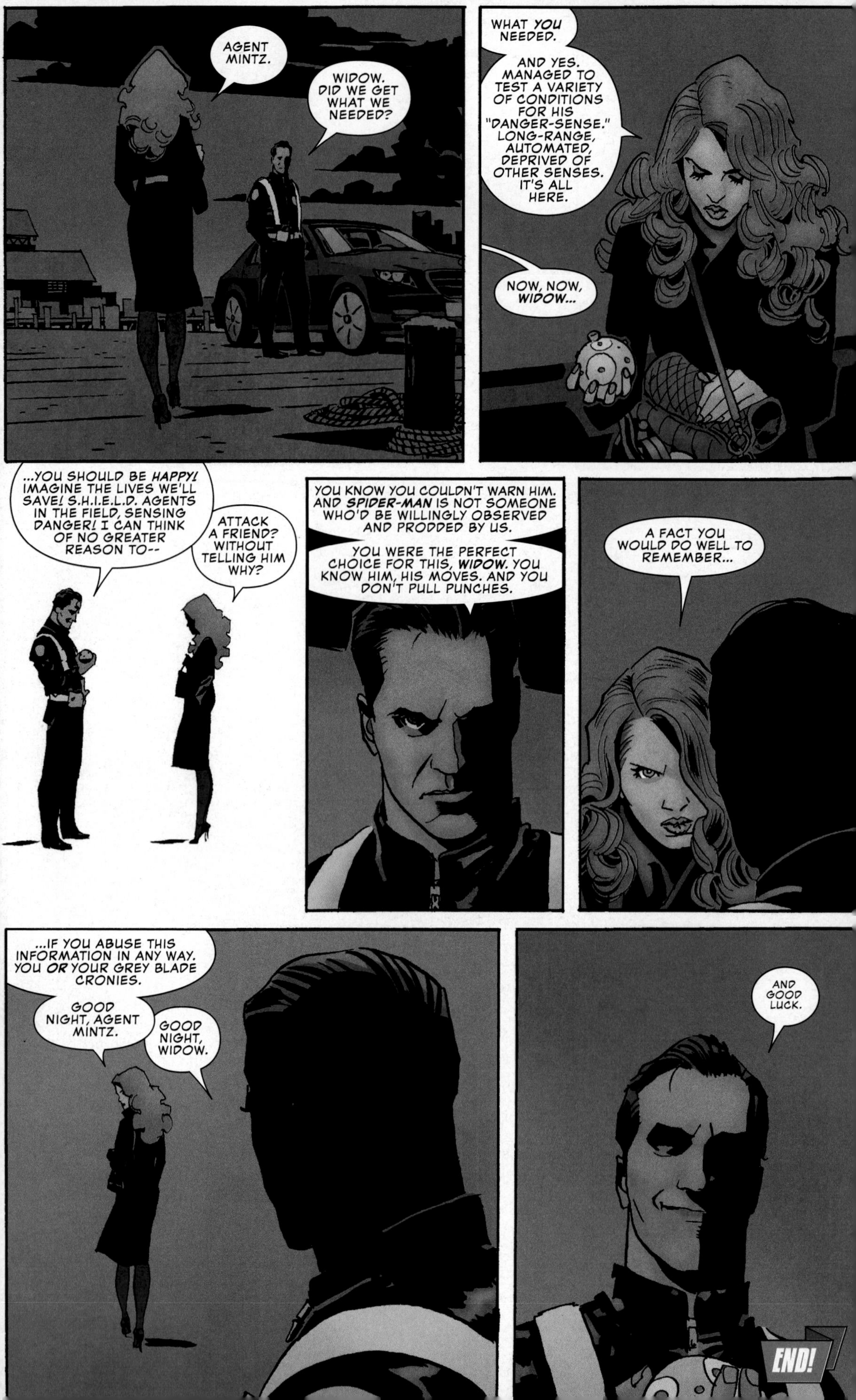
AGENT MINTZ.
WIDOW. DID WE GET WHAT WE NEEDED?
WHAT YOU NEEDED.
AND YES. MANAGED TO TEST A VARIETY OF CONDITIONS FOR HIS "DANGER-SENSE." LONG-RANGE, AUTOMATED, DEPRIVED OF OTHER SENSES. IT'S ALL HERE.
NOW, NOW, WIDOW...
...YOU SHOULD BE HAPPY! IMAGINE THE LIVES WE'LL SAVE! S.H.I.E.L.D. AGENTS IN THE FIELD, SENSING DANGER! I CAN THINK OF NO GREATER REASON TO--
ATTACK A FRIEND? WITHOUT TELLING HIM WHY?
YOU KNOW YOU COULDN'T WARN HIM. AND SPIDER-MAN IS NOT SOMEONE WHO'D BE WILLINGLY OBSERVED AND PRODDED BY US.
YOU WERE THE PERFECT CHOICE FOR THIS, WIDOW. YOU KNOW HIM, HIS MOVES. AND YOU DON'T PULL PUNCHES.
A FACT YOU WOULD DO WELL TO REMEMBER...
...IF YOU ABUSE THIS INFORMATION IN ANY WAY. YOU OR YOUR GREY BLADE CRONIES.
GOOD NIGHT, AGENT MINTZ.
GOOD NIGHT, WIDOW.
AND GOOD LUCK.
END!

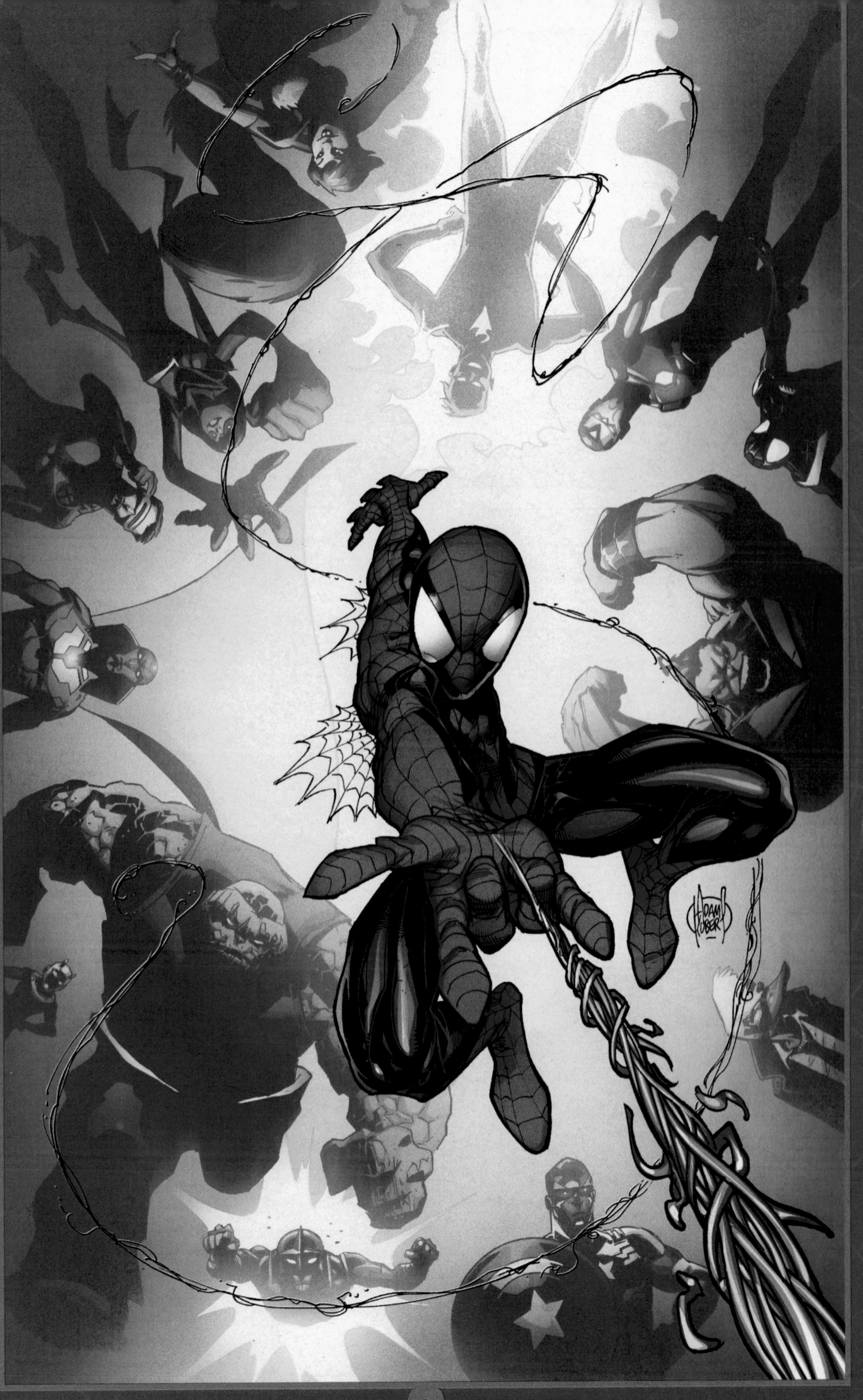
ADAM KUBERT

2

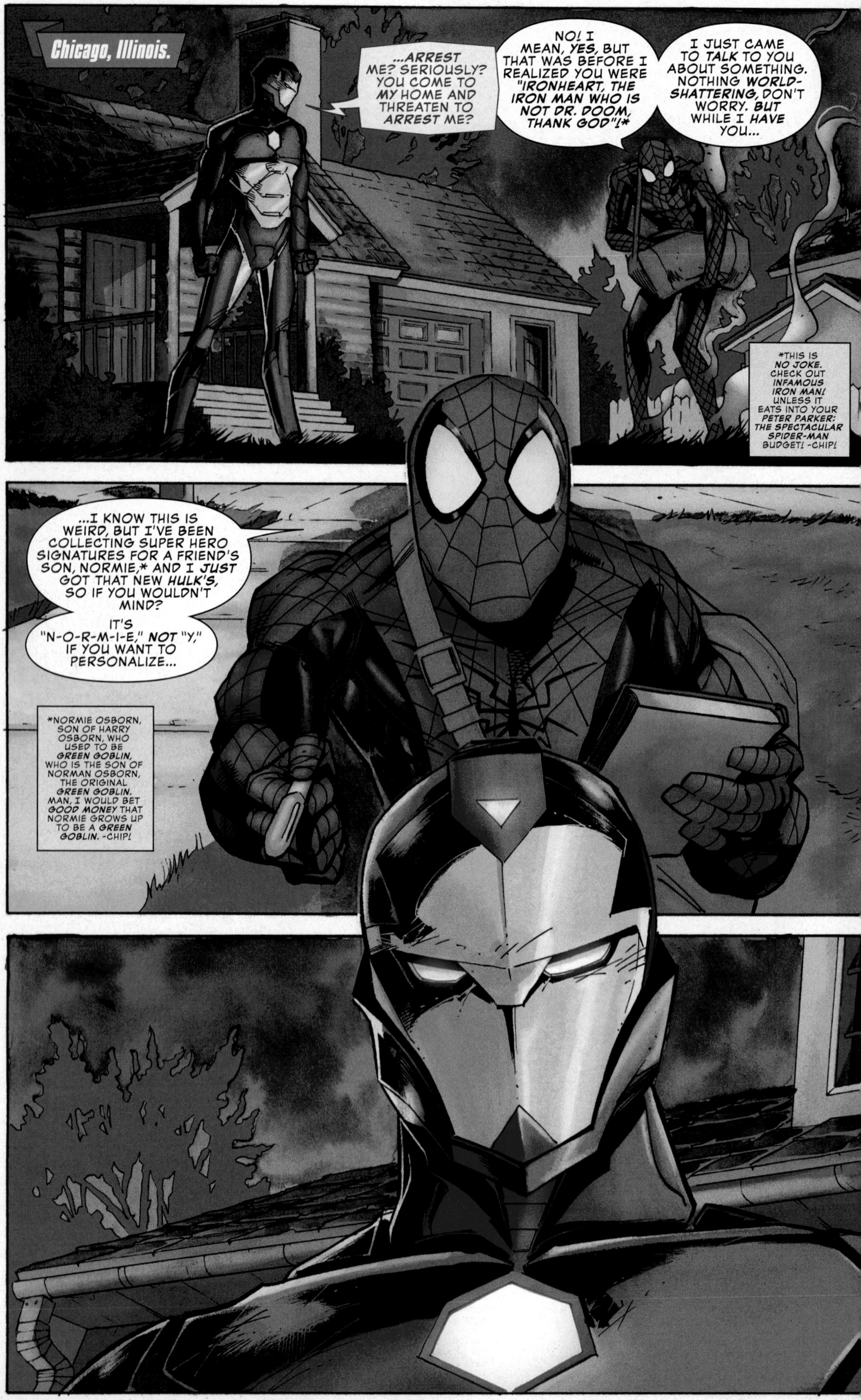
Chicago, Illinois.
...ARREST ME? SERIOUSLY? YOU COME TO MY HOME AND THREATEN TO ARREST ME?
NO! I MEAN, YES, BUT THAT WAS BEFORE I REALIZED YOU WERE "IRONHEART, THE IRON MAN WHO IS NOT DR. DOOM, THANK GOD"!*
I JUST CAME TO TALK TO YOU ABOUT SOMETHING. NOTHING WORLD-SHATTERING, DON'T WORRY. BUT WHILE I HAVE YOU...
*THIS IS NO JOKE. CHECK OUT INFAMOUS IRON MAN! UNLESS IT EATS INTO YOUR PETER PARKER: THE SPECTACULAR SPIDER-MAN BUDGET! -CHIP!
...I KNOW THIS IS WEIRD, BUT I'VE BEEN COLLECTING SUPER HERO SIGNATURES FOR A FRIEND'S SON, NORMIE,* AND I JUST GOT THAT NEW HULK'S, SO IF YOU WOULDN'T MIND?
IT'S "N-O-R-M-I-E," NOT "Y," IF YOU WANT TO PERSONALIZE...
*NORMIE OSBORN, SON OF HARRY OSBORN, WHO USED TO BE GREEN GOBLIN, WHO IS THE SON OF NORMAN OSBORN, THE ORIGINAL GREEN GOBLIN. MAN, I WOULD BET GOOD MONEY THAT NORMIE GROWS UP TO BE A GREEN GOBLIN. -CHIP!

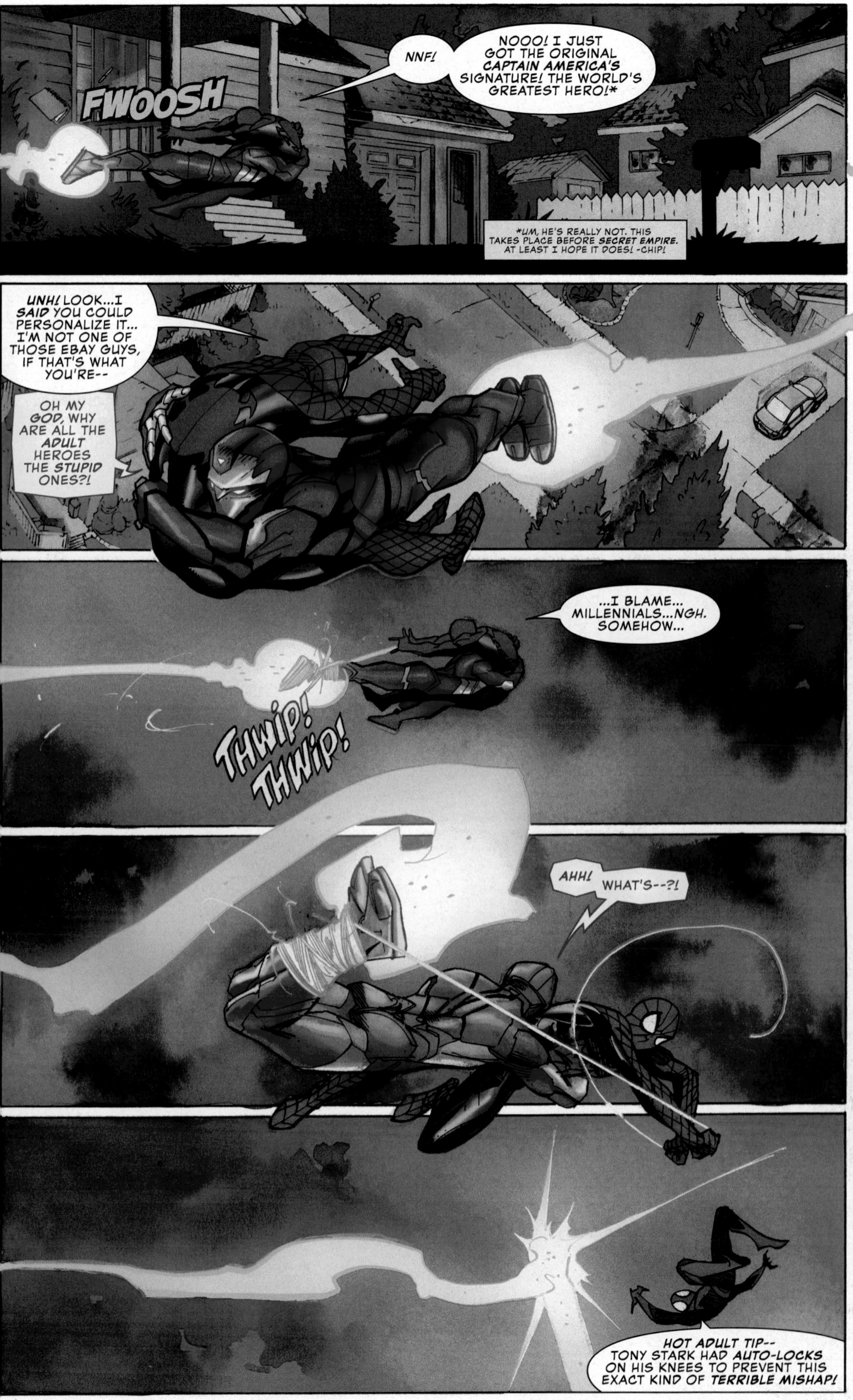
FWOOSH
NNF!
NOOO! I JUST GOT THE ORIGINAL CAPTAIN AMERICA'S SIGNATURE! THE WORLD'S GREATEST HERO!*
*UM, HE'S REALLY NOT. THIS TAKES PLACE BEFORE SECRET EMPIRE. AT LEAST I HOPE IT DOES! -CHIP!
UNH! LOOK...I SAID YOU COULD PERSONALIZE IT... I'M NOT ONE OF THOSE EBAY GUYS, IF THAT'S WHAT YOU'RE--
OH MY GOD, WHY ARE ALL THE ADULT HEROES THE STUPID ONES?!
...I BLAME... MILLENNIALS...NGH. SOMEHOW...
THWIP! THWIP!
AHH!
WHAT'S--?!
HOT ADULT TIP-- TONY STARK HAD AUTO-LOCKS ON HIS KNEES TO PREVENT THIS EXACT KIND OF TERRIBLE MISHAP!

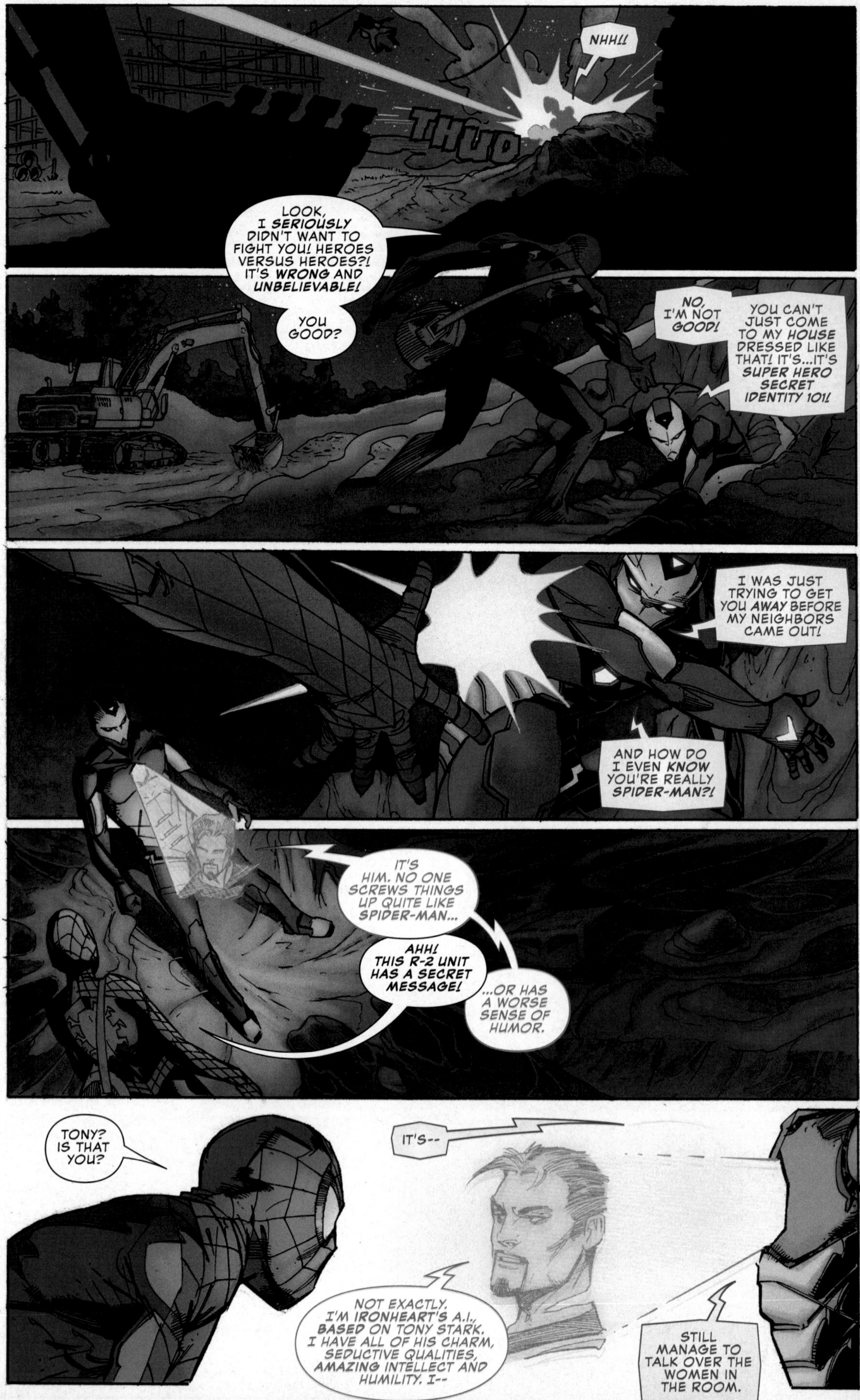
NHH!!
THUD
LOOK, I SERIOUSLY DIDN'T WANT TO FIGHT YOU! HEROES VERSUS HEROES?! IT'S WRONG AND UNBELIEVABLE!
YOU GOOD?
NO, I'M NOT GOOD!
YOU CAN'T JUST COME TO MY HOUSE DRESSED LIKE THAT! IT'S...IT'S SUPER HERO SECRET IDENTITY 101!
I WAS JUST TRYING TO GET YOU AWAY BEFORE MY NEIGHBORS CAME OUT!
AND HOW DO I EVEN KNOW YOU'RE REALLY SPIDER-MAN?!
IT'S HIM. NO ONE SCREWS THINGS UP QUITE LIKE SPIDER-MAN...
AHH! THIS R-2 UNIT HAS A SECRET MESSAGE!
...OR HAS A WORSE SENSE OF HUMOR.
TONY? IS THAT YOU?
IT'S--
NOT EXACTLY. I'M IRONHEART'S A.I., BASED ON TONY STARK. I HAVE ALL OF HIS CHARM, SEDUCTIVE QUALITIES, AMAZING INTELLECT AND HUMILITY. I--
STILL MANAGE TO TALK OVER THE WOMEN IN THE ROOM.

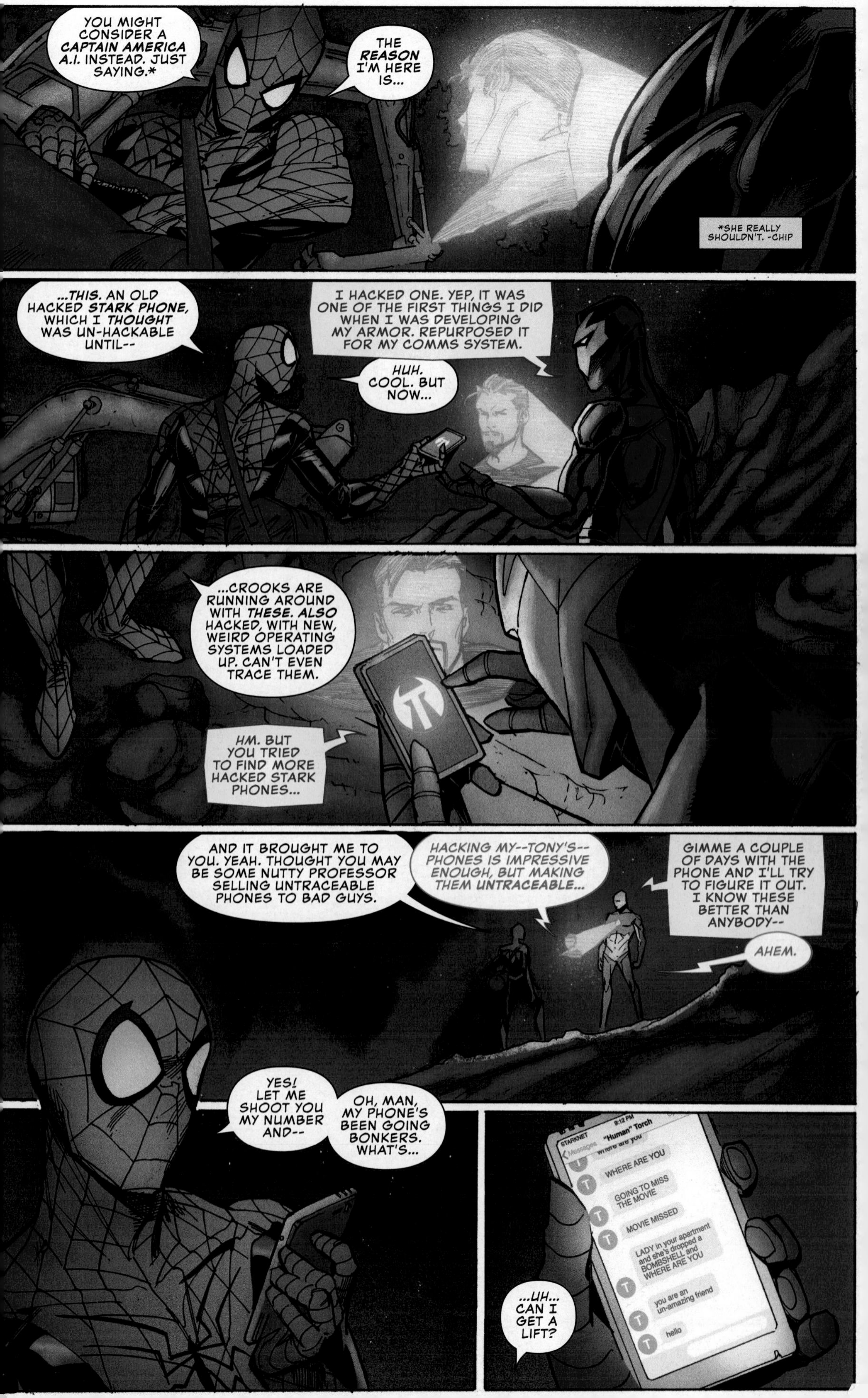

YOU MIGHT CONSIDER A CAPTAIN AMERICA A.I. INSTEAD. JUST SAYING.*
THE REASON I'M HERE IS...
*SHE REALLY SHOULDN'T. -CHIP
...THIS. AN OLD HACKED STARK PHONE, WHICH I THOUGHT WAS UN-HACKABLE UNTIL--
I HACKED ONE. YEP, IT WAS ONE OF THE FIRST THINGS I DID WHEN I WAS DEVELOPING MY ARMOR. REPURPOSED IT FOR MY COMMS SYSTEM.
HUH. COOL. BUT NOW...
...CROOKS ARE RUNNING AROUND WITH THESE. ALSO HACKED, WITH NEW, WEIRD OPERATING SYSTEMS LOADED UP. CAN'T EVEN TRACE THEM.
HM. BUT YOU TRIED TO FIND MORE HACKED STARK PHONES...
AND IT BROUGHT ME TO YOU. YEAH. THOUGHT YOU MAY BE SOME NUTTY PROFESSOR SELLING UNTRACEABLE PHONES TO BAD GUYS.
HACKING MY--TONY'S--PHONES IS IMPRESSIVE ENOUGH, BUT MAKING THEM UNTRACEABLE...
GIMME A COUPLE OF DAYS WITH THE PHONE AND I'LL TRY TO FIGURE IT OUT. I KNOW THESE BETTER THAN ANYBODY--
AHEM.
YES! LET ME SHOOT YOU MY NUMBER AND--
OH, MAN, MY PHONE'S BEEN GOING BONKERS. WHAT'S...
STARKNET
9:12 PM
Messages
"Human" Torch
WHERE ARE YOU
GOING TO MISS THE MOVIE
MOVIE MISSED
LADY in your apartment and she's dropped a BOMBSHELL and WHERE ARE YOU
you are an un-amazing friend
hello
...UH... CAN I GET A LIFT?

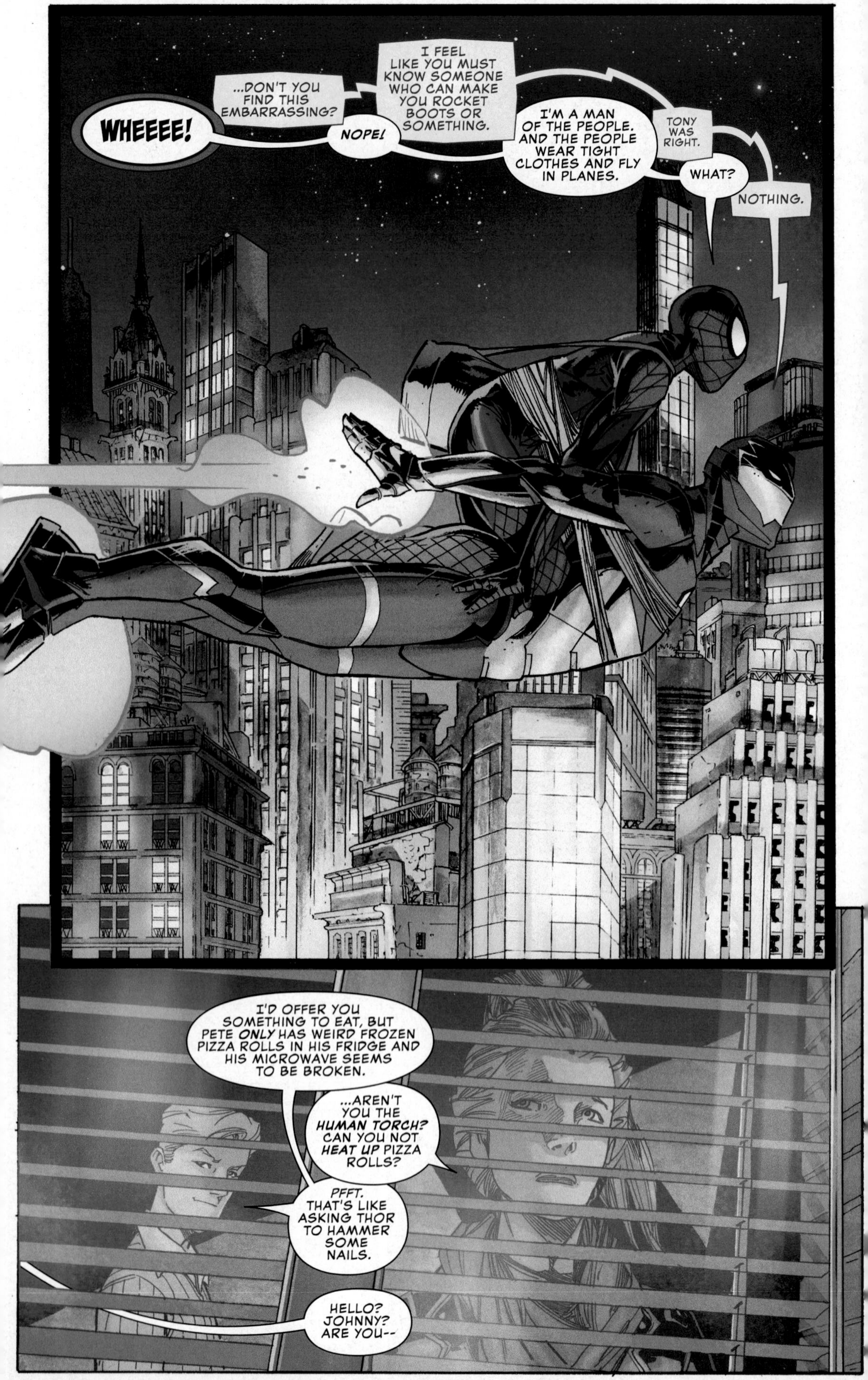
WHEEEE!
...DON'T YOU FIND THIS EMBARRASSING?
NOPE!
I FEEL LIKE YOU MUST KNOW SOMEONE WHO CAN MAKE YOU ROCKET BOOTS OR SOMETHING.
I'M A MAN OF THE PEOPLE. AND THE PEOPLE WEAR TIGHT CLOTHES AND FLY IN PLANES.
TONY WAS RIGHT.
WHAT?
NOTHING.
I'D OFFER YOU SOMETHING TO EAT, BUT PETE ONLY HAS WEIRD FROZEN PIZZA ROLLS IN HIS FRIDGE AND HIS MICROWAVE SEEMS TO BE BROKEN.
...AREN'T YOU THE HUMAN TORCH? CAN YOU NOT HEAT UP PIZZA ROLLS?
PFFT. THAT'S LIKE ASKING THOR TO HAMMER SOME NAILS.
HELLO? JOHNNY? ARE YOU--

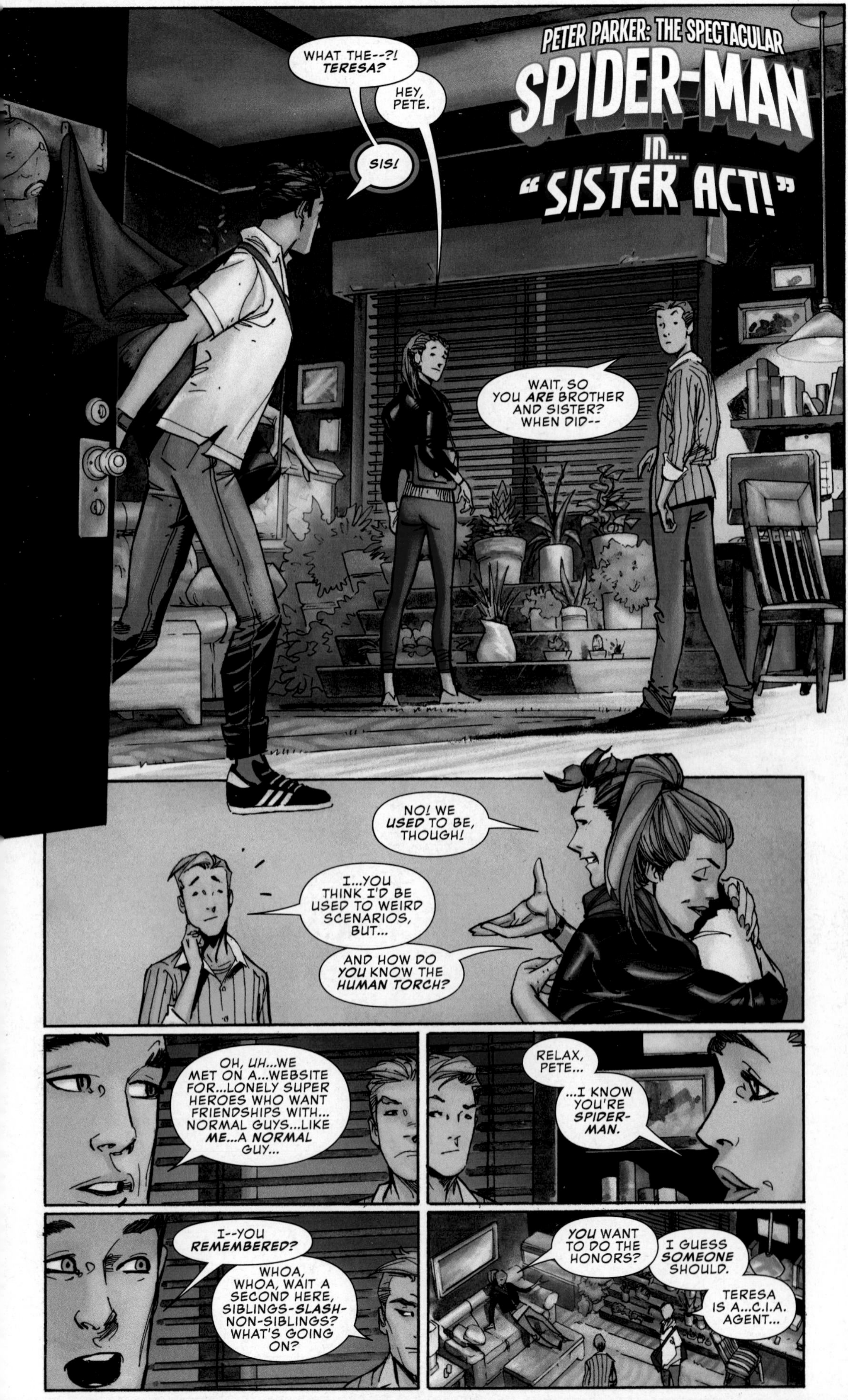
PETER PARKER: THE SPECTACULAR SPIDER-MAN IN... "SISTER ACT!"
WHAT THE--?! TERESA?
HEY, PETE.
SIS!
WAIT, SO YOU ARE BROTHER AND SISTER? WHEN DID--
NO! WE USED TO BE, THOUGH!
I...YOU THINK I'D BE USED TO WEIRD SCENARIOS, BUT...
AND HOW DO YOU KNOW THE HUMAN TORCH?
OH, UH...WE MET ON A...WEBSITE FOR...LONELY SUPER HEROES WHO WANT FRIENDSHIPS WITH... NORMAL GUYS...LIKE ME...A NORMAL GUY...
RELAX, PETE...
...I KNOW YOU'RE SPIDER-MAN.
I--YOU REMEMBERED?
WHOA, WHOA, WAIT A SECOND HERE, SIBLINGS-SLASH-NON-SIBLINGS? WHAT'S GOING ON?
YOU WANT TO DO THE HONORS?
I GUESS SOMEONE SHOULD.
TERESA IS A...C.I.A. AGENT...

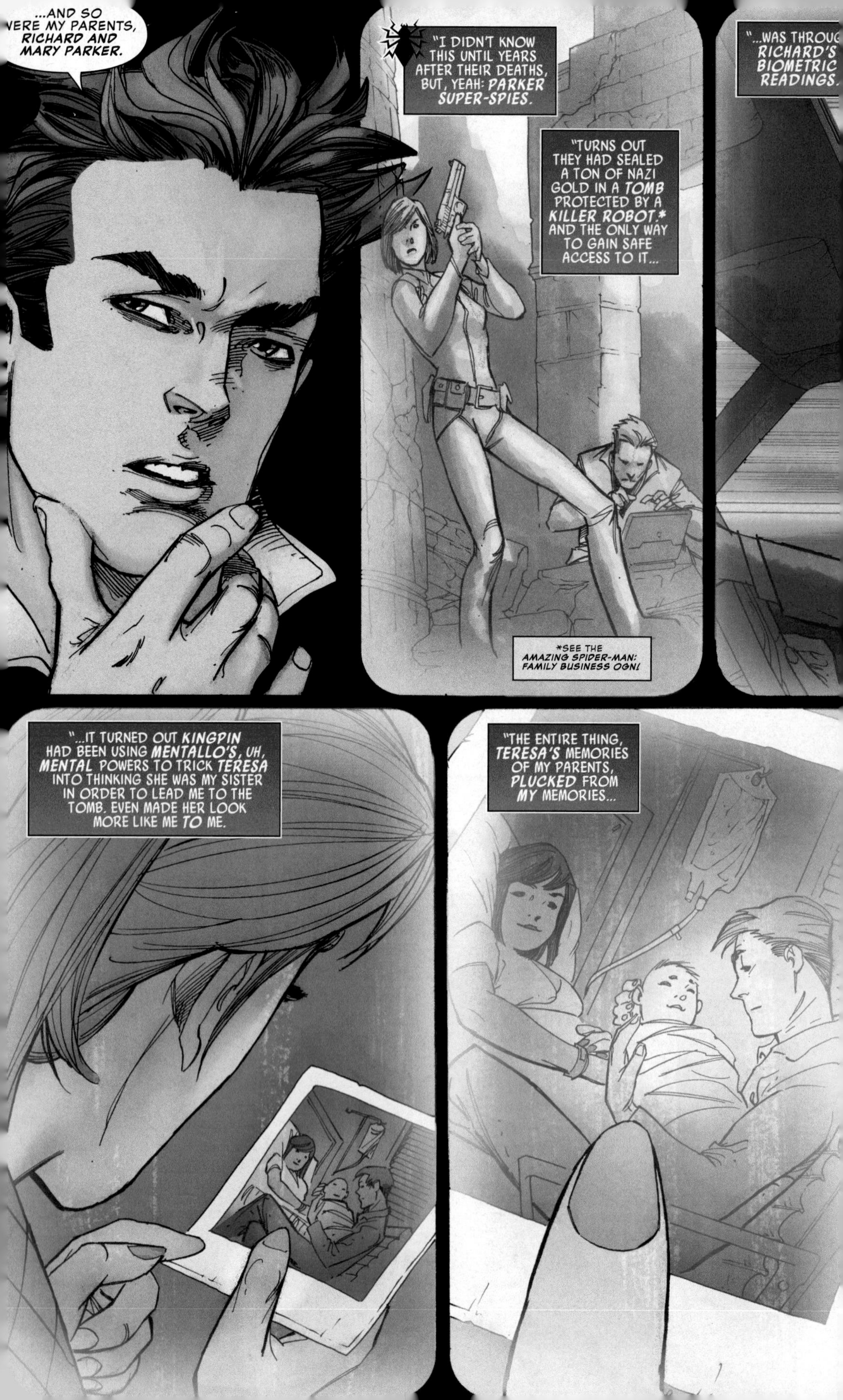
...AND SO WERE MY PARENTS, RICHARD AND MARY PARKER.
"I DIDN'T KNOW THIS UNTIL YEARS AFTER THEIR DEATHS, BUT, YEAH: PARKER SUPER-SPIES.
"TURNS OUT THEY HAD SEALED A TON OF NAZI GOLD IN A TOMB PROTECTED BY A KILLER ROBOT.* AND THE ONLY WAY TO GAIN SAFE ACCESS TO IT...
*SEE THE AMAZING SPIDER-MAN: FAMILY BUSINESS OGN!
"...WAS THROUG RICHARD'S BIOMETRIC READINGS.
"...IT TURNED OUT KINGPIN HAD BEEN USING MENTALLO'S, UH, MENTAL POWERS TO TRICK TERESA INTO THINKING SHE WAS MY SISTER IN ORDER TO LEAD ME TO THE TOMB. EVEN MADE HER LOOK MORE LIKE ME TO ME.
"THE ENTIRE THING, TERESA'S MEMORIES OF MY PARENTS, PLUCKED FROM MY MEMORIES...

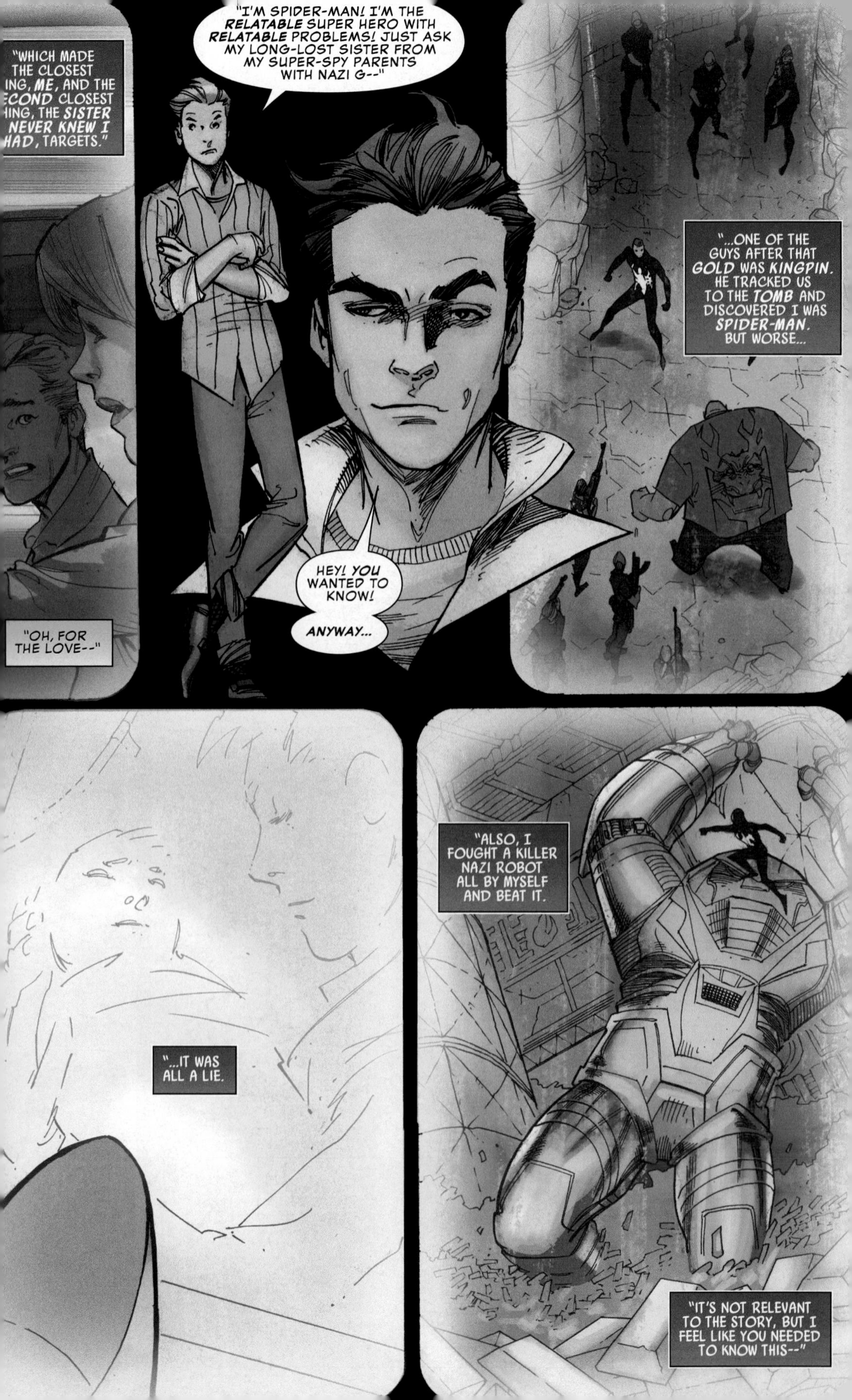
"WHICH MADE THE CLOSEST
ING, ME, AND THE
ECOND CLOSEST
HING, THE SISTER
NEVER KNEW I
HAD, TARGETS."
"OH, FOR THE LOVE--"
"I'M SPIDER-MAN! I'M THE RELATABLE SUPER HERO WITH RELATABLE PROBLEMS! JUST ASK MY LONG-LOST SISTER FROM MY SUPER-SPY PARENTS WITH NAZI G--"
HEY! YOU WANTED TO KNOW!
ANYWAY...
"...ONE OF THE GUYS AFTER THAT GOLD WAS KINGPIN. HE TRACKED US TO THE TOMB AND DISCOVERED I WAS SPIDER-MAN. BUT WORSE...
"...IT WAS ALL A LIE.
"ALSO, I FOUGHT A KILLER NAZI ROBOT ALL BY MYSELF AND BEAT IT.
"IT'S NOT RELEVANT TO THE STORY, BUT I FEEL LIKE YOU NEEDED TO KNOW THIS--"

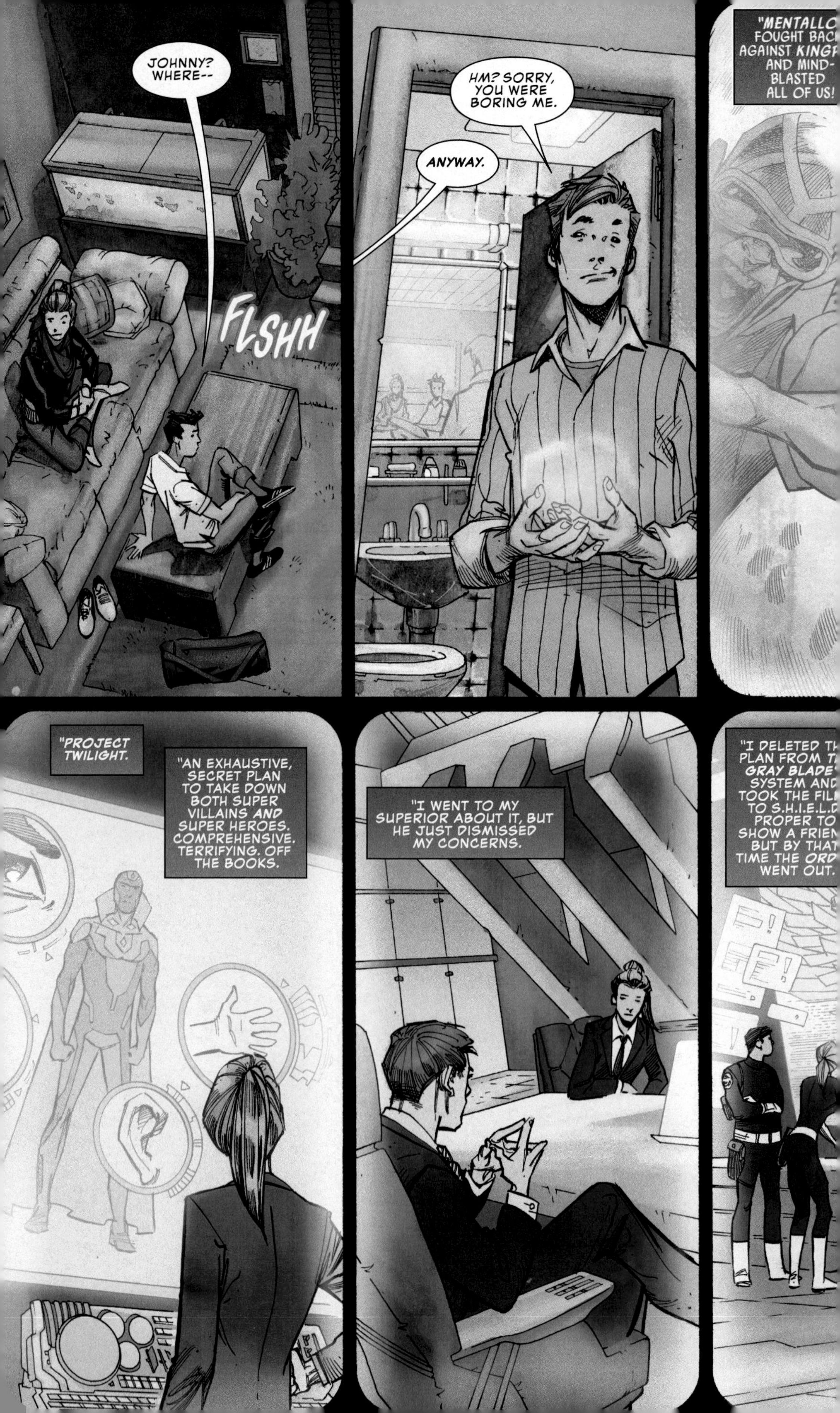
JOHNNY? WHERE--
FLSHH
HM? SORRY, YOU WERE BORING ME.
ANYWAY.
"MENTALLO FOUGHT BACK AGAINST KINGP AND MIND-BLASTED ALL OF US!
"PROJECT TWILIGHT.
"AN EXHAUSTIVE, SECRET PLAN TO TAKE DOWN BOTH SUPER VILLAINS AND SUPER HEROES. COMPREHENSIVE. TERRIFYING. OFF THE BOOKS.
"I WENT TO MY SUPERIOR ABOUT IT, BUT HE JUST DISMISSED MY CONCERNS.
"I DELETED TH PLAN FROM T GRAY BLADE SYSTEM AND TOOK THE FIL TO S.H.I.E.L.D PROPER TO SHOW A FRIEN BUT BY THAT TIME THE ORD WENT OUT.

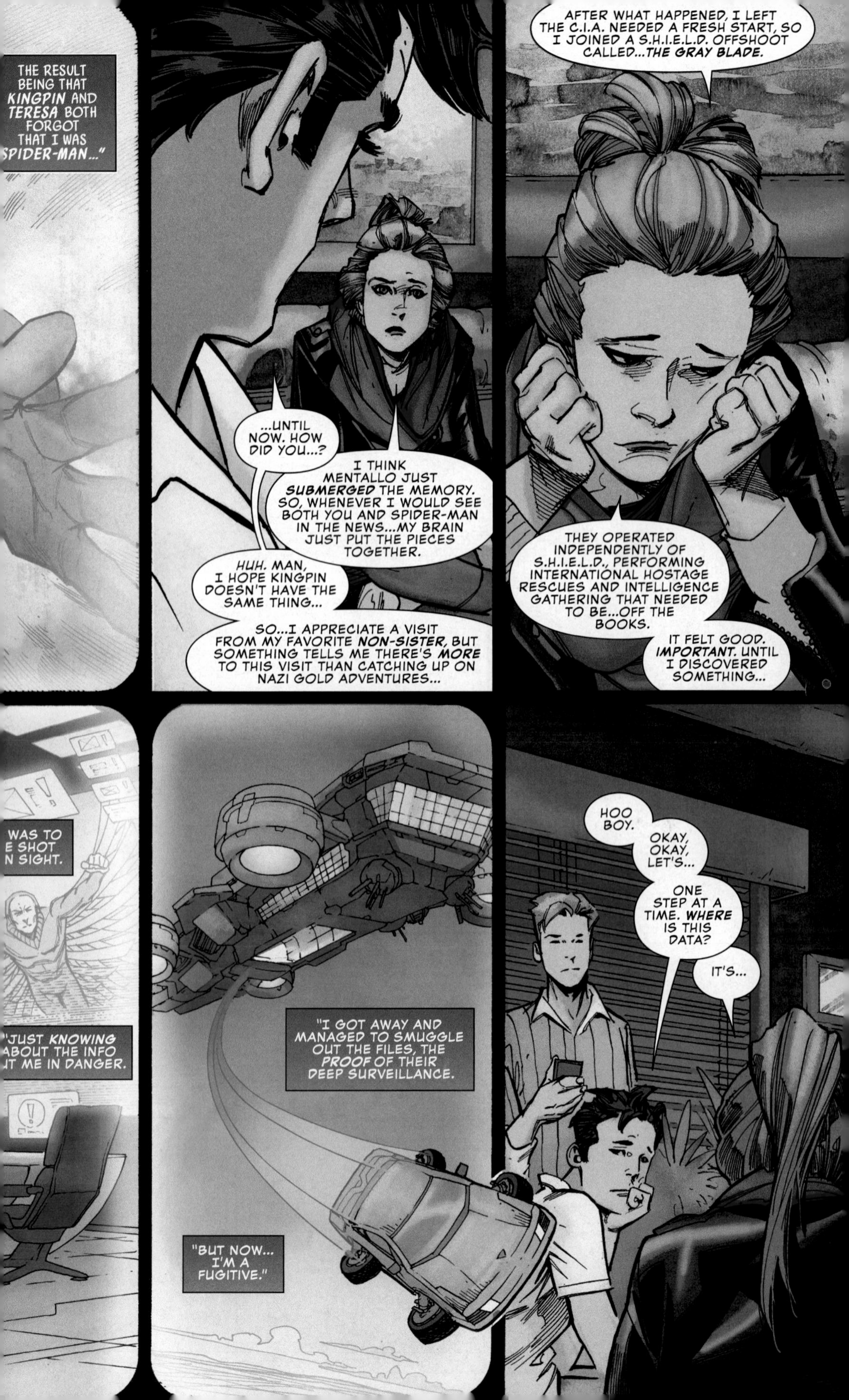
"THE RESULT BEING THAT KINGPIN AND TERESA BOTH FORGOT THAT I WAS SPIDER-MAN..."
...UNTIL NOW. HOW DID YOU...?
I THINK MENTALLO JUST SUBMERGED THE MEMORY. SO, WHENEVER I WOULD SEE BOTH YOU AND SPIDER-MAN IN THE NEWS...MY BRAIN JUST PUT THE PIECES TOGETHER.
HUH. MAN, I HOPE KINGPIN DOESN'T HAVE THE SAME THING...
SO...I APPRECIATE A VISIT FROM MY FAVORITE NON-SISTER, BUT SOMETHING TELLS ME THERE'S MORE TO THIS VISIT THAN CATCHING UP ON NAZI GOLD ADVENTURES...
AFTER WHAT HAPPENED, I LEFT THE C.I.A. NEEDED A FRESH START, SO I JOINED A S.H.I.E.L.D. OFFSHOOT CALLED...THE GRAY BLADE.
THEY OPERATED INDEPENDENTLY OF S.H.I.E.L.D., PERFORMING INTERNATIONAL HOSTAGE RESCUES AND INTELLIGENCE GATHERING THAT NEEDED TO BE...OFF THE BOOKS.
IT FELT GOOD. IMPORTANT. UNTIL I DISCOVERED SOMETHING...
WAS TO E SHOT N SIGHT.
"JUST KNOWING ABOUT THE INFO UT ME IN DANGER.
"I GOT AWAY AND MANAGED TO SMUGGLE OUT THE FILES, THE PROOF OF THEIR DEEP SURVEILLANCE.
"BUT NOW... I'M A FUGITIVE."
HOO BOY.
OKAY, OKAY, LET'S...
ONE STEP AT A TIME. WHERE IS THIS DATA?
IT'S...

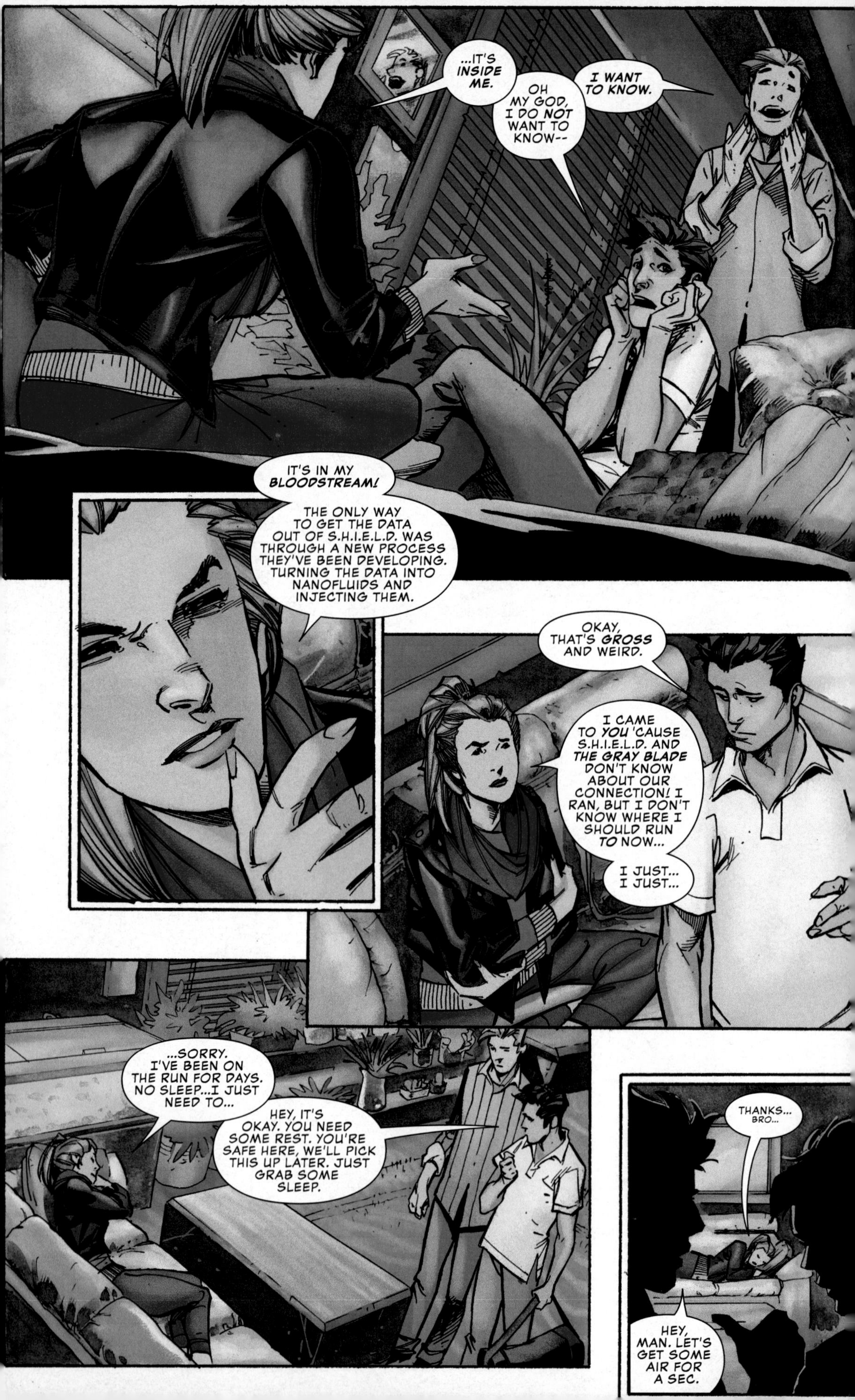
...IT'S INSIDE ME.
OH MY GOD, I DO NOT WANT TO KNOW--
I WANT TO KNOW.
IT'S IN MY BLOODSTREAM!
THE ONLY WAY TO GET THE DATA OUT OF S.H.I.E.L.D. WAS THROUGH A NEW PROCESS THEY'VE BEEN DEVELOPING. TURNING THE DATA INTO NANOFLUIDS AND INJECTING THEM.
OKAY, THAT'S GROSS AND WEIRD.
I CAME TO YOU 'CAUSE S.H.I.E.L.D. AND THE GRAY BLADE DON'T KNOW ABOUT OUR CONNECTION! I RAN, BUT I DON'T KNOW WHERE I SHOULD RUN TO NOW...
I JUST... I JUST...
...SORRY. I'VE BEEN ON THE RUN FOR DAYS. NO SLEEP...I JUST NEED TO...
HEY, IT'S OKAY. YOU NEED SOME REST. YOU'RE SAFE HERE, WE'LL PICK THIS UP LATER. JUST GRAB SOME SLEEP.
THANKS... BRO...
HEY, MAN. LET'S GET SOME AIR FOR A SEC.

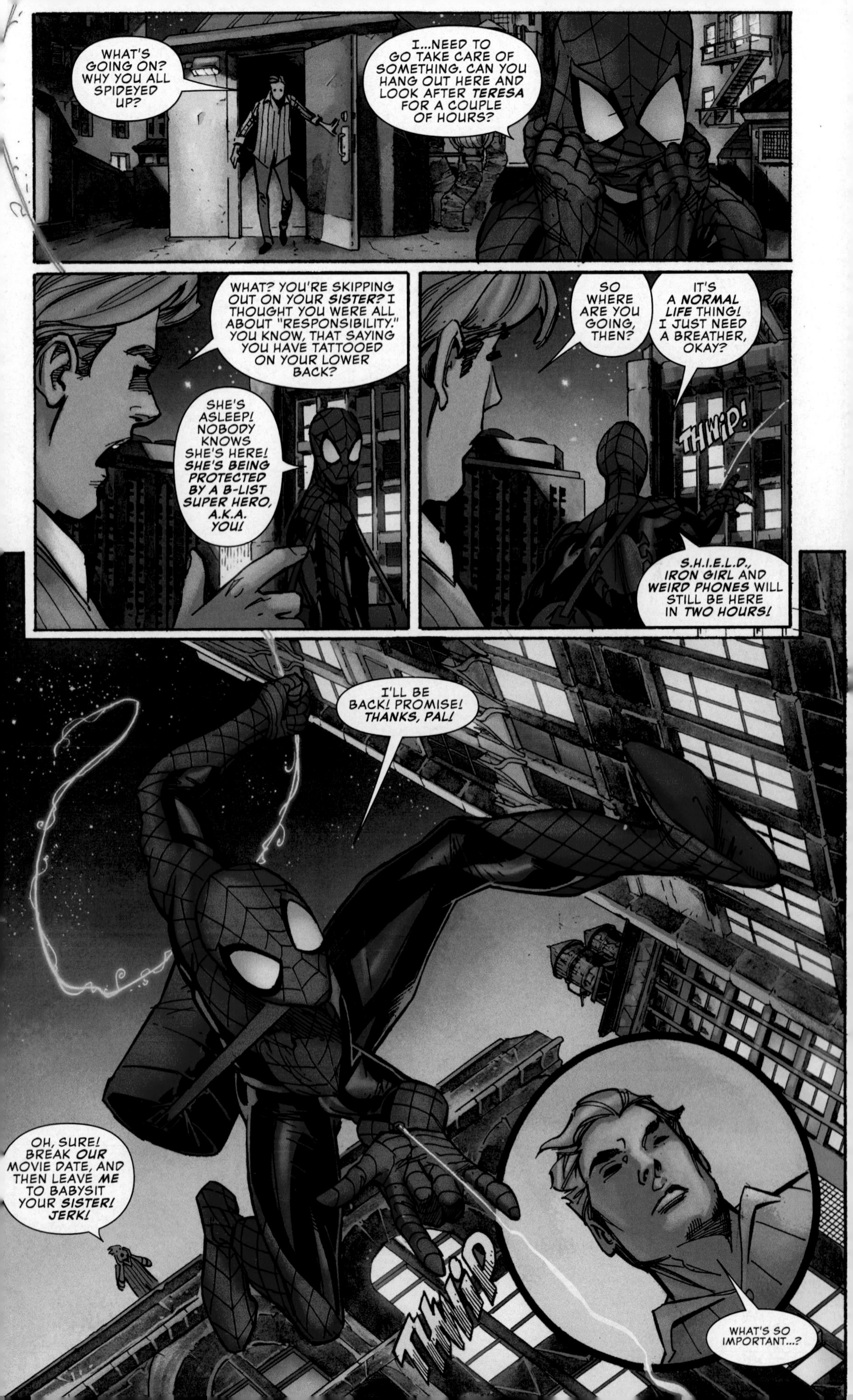
WHAT'S GOING ON? WHY YOU ALL SPIDEYED UP?
I...NEED TO GO TAKE CARE OF SOMETHING. CAN YOU HANG OUT HERE AND LOOK AFTER TERESA FOR A COUPLE OF HOURS?
WHAT? YOU'RE SKIPPING OUT ON YOUR SISTER? I THOUGHT YOU WERE ALL ABOUT "RESPONSIBILITY." YOU KNOW, THAT SAYING YOU HAVE TATTOOED ON YOUR LOWER BACK?
SHE'S ASLEEP! NOBODY KNOWS SHE'S HERE! SHE'S BEING PROTECTED BY A B-LIST SUPER HERO, A.K.A. YOU!
SO WHERE ARE YOU GOING, THEN?
IT'S A NORMAL LIFE THING! I JUST NEED A BREATHER, OKAY?
THWIP!
S.H.I.E.L.D., IRON GIRL AND WEIRD PHONES WILL STILL BE HERE IN TWO HOURS!
I'LL BE BACK! PROMISE! THANKS, PAL!
OH, SURE! BREAK OUR MOVIE DATE, AND THEN LEAVE ME TO BABYSIT YOUR SISTER! JERK!
THWIP
WHAT'S SO IMPORTANT...?

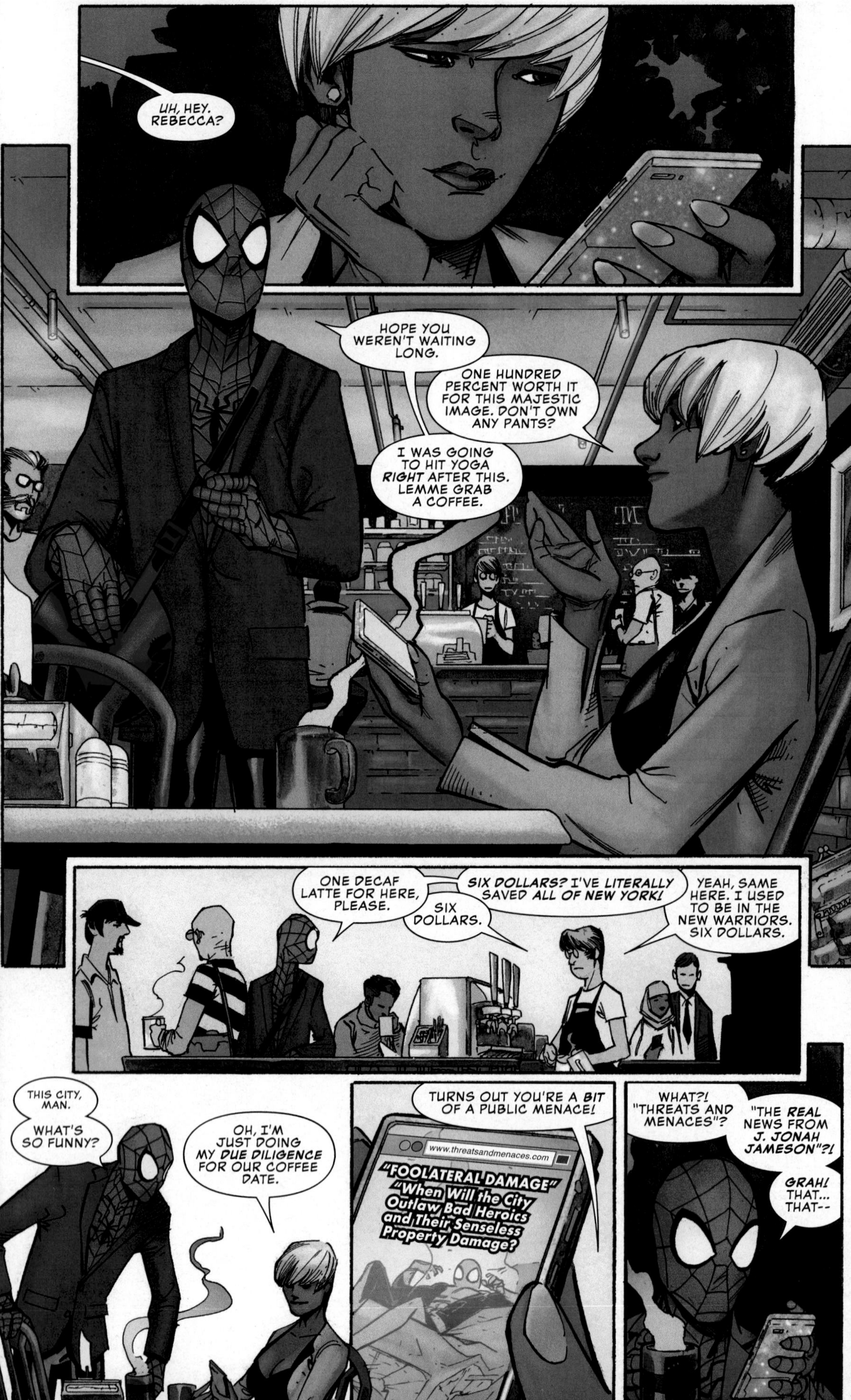
UH, HEY. REBECCA?
HOPE YOU WEREN'T WAITING LONG.
ONE HUNDRED PERCENT WORTH IT FOR THIS MAJESTIC IMAGE. DON'T OWN ANY PANTS?
I WAS GOING TO HIT YOGA *RIGHT* AFTER THIS. LEMME GRAB A COFFEE.
ONE DECAF LATTE FOR HERE, PLEASE.
SIX DOLLARS.
SIX DOLLARS? I'VE *LITERALLY* SAVED *ALL OF NEW YORK!*
YEAH, SAME HERE. I USED TO BE IN THE NEW WARRIORS. SIX DOLLARS.
THIS CITY, MAN.
WHAT'S SO FUNNY?
OH, I'M JUST DOING MY *DUE DILIGENCE* FOR OUR COFFEE DATE.
TURNS OUT YOU'RE A *BIT* OF A PUBLIC MENACE!
www.threatsandmenaces.com
"FOOLATERAL DAMAGE"
"When Will the City Outlaw Bad Heroics and Their Senseless Property Damage?
WHAT?! "THREATS AND MENACES"?
"THE *REAL* NEWS FROM J. JONAH JAMESON"?!
GRAH! THAT... THAT--

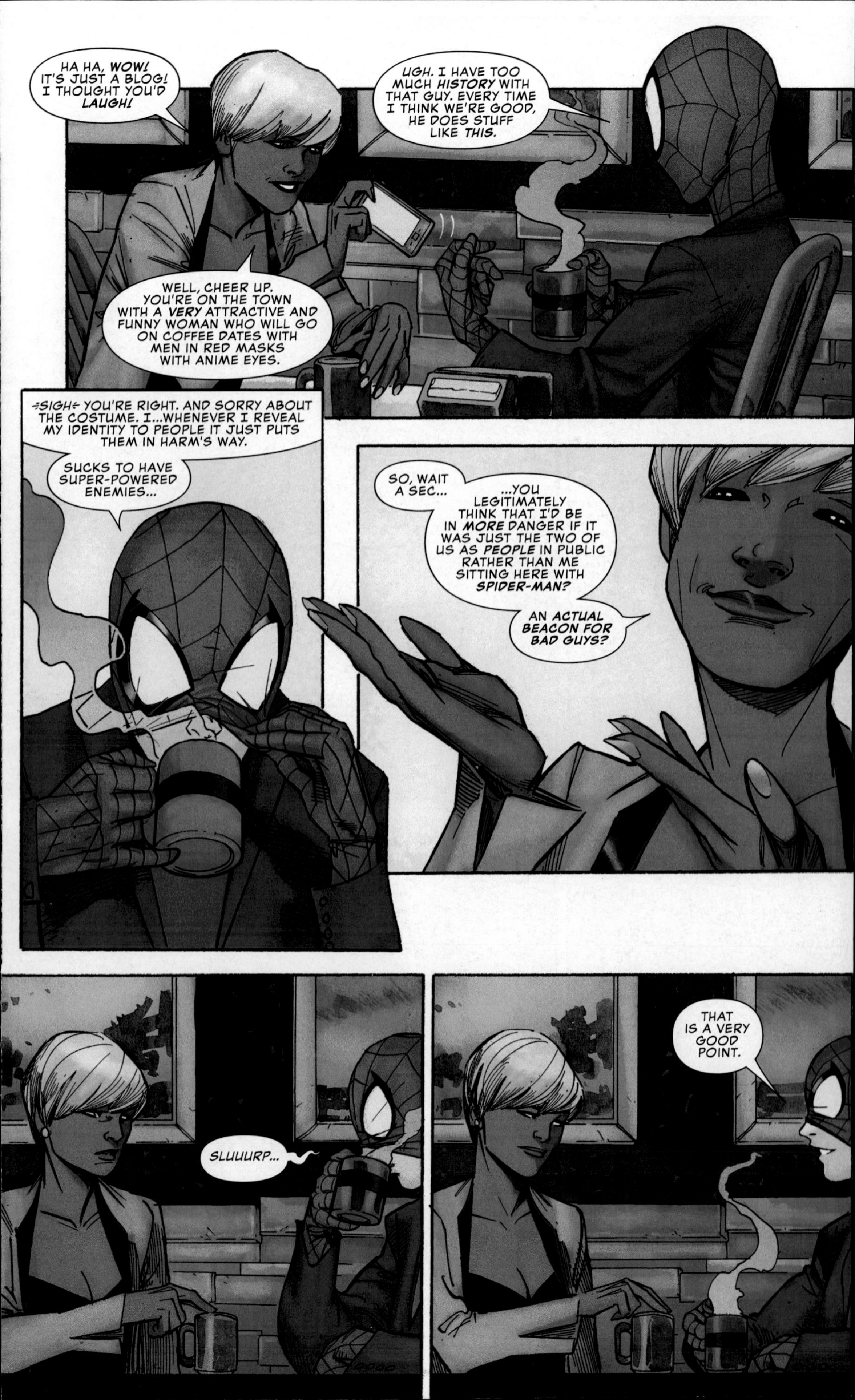
HA HA, WOW! IT'S JUST A BLOG! I THOUGHT YOU'D LAUGH!
UGH. I HAVE TOO MUCH HISTORY WITH THAT GUY. EVERY TIME I THINK WE'RE GOOD, HE DOES STUFF LIKE THIS.
WELL, CHEER UP. YOU'RE ON THE TOWN WITH A VERY ATTRACTIVE AND FUNNY WOMAN WHO WILL GO ON COFFEE DATES WITH MEN IN RED MASKS WITH ANIME EYES.
=SIGH= YOU'RE RIGHT. AND SORRY ABOUT THE COSTUME. I...WHENEVER I REVEAL MY IDENTITY TO PEOPLE IT JUST PUTS THEM IN HARM'S WAY.
SUCKS TO HAVE SUPER-POWERED ENEMIES...
SO, WAIT A SEC...
...YOU LEGITIMATELY THINK THAT I'D BE IN MORE DANGER IF IT WAS JUST THE TWO OF US AS PEOPLE IN PUBLIC RATHER THAN ME SITTING HERE WITH SPIDER-MAN?
AN ACTUAL BEACON FOR BAD GUYS?
SLUUURP...
THAT IS A VERY GOOD POINT.

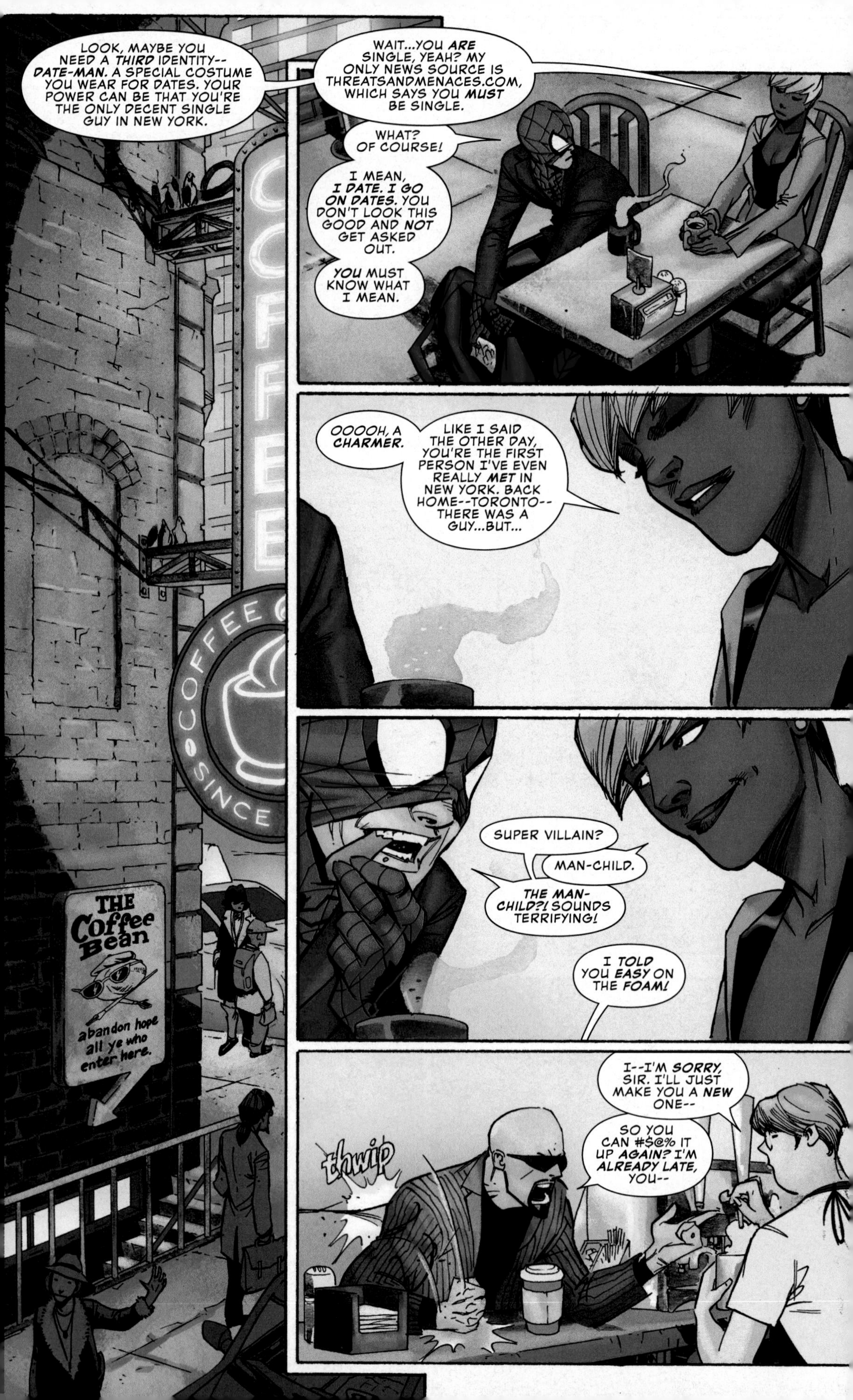
LOOK, MAYBE YOU NEED A THIRD IDENTITY-- DATE-MAN. A SPECIAL COSTUME YOU WEAR FOR DATES. YOUR POWER CAN BE THAT YOU'RE THE ONLY DECENT SINGLE GUY IN NEW YORK.
WAIT...YOU ARE SINGLE, YEAH? MY ONLY NEWS SOURCE IS THREATSANDMENACES.COM, WHICH SAYS YOU MUST BE SINGLE.
WHAT? OF COURSE!
I MEAN, I DATE. I GO ON DATES. YOU DON'T LOOK THIS GOOD AND NOT GET ASKED OUT.
YOU MUST KNOW WHAT I MEAN.
COFFEE
OOOOH, A CHARMER.
LIKE I SAID THE OTHER DAY, YOU'RE THE FIRST PERSON I'VE EVEN REALLY MET IN NEW YORK. BACK HOME--TORONTO-- THERE WAS A GUY...BUT...
COFFEE
SINCE
SUPER VILLAIN?
MAN-CHILD.
THE MAN-CHILD?! SOUNDS TERRIFYING!
I TOLD YOU EASY ON THE FOAM!
THE Coffee Bean
abandon hope all ye who enter here.
I--I'M SORRY, SIR. I'LL JUST MAKE YOU A NEW ONE--
SO YOU CAN #$@% IT UP AGAIN? I'M ALREADY LATE, YOU--
thwip

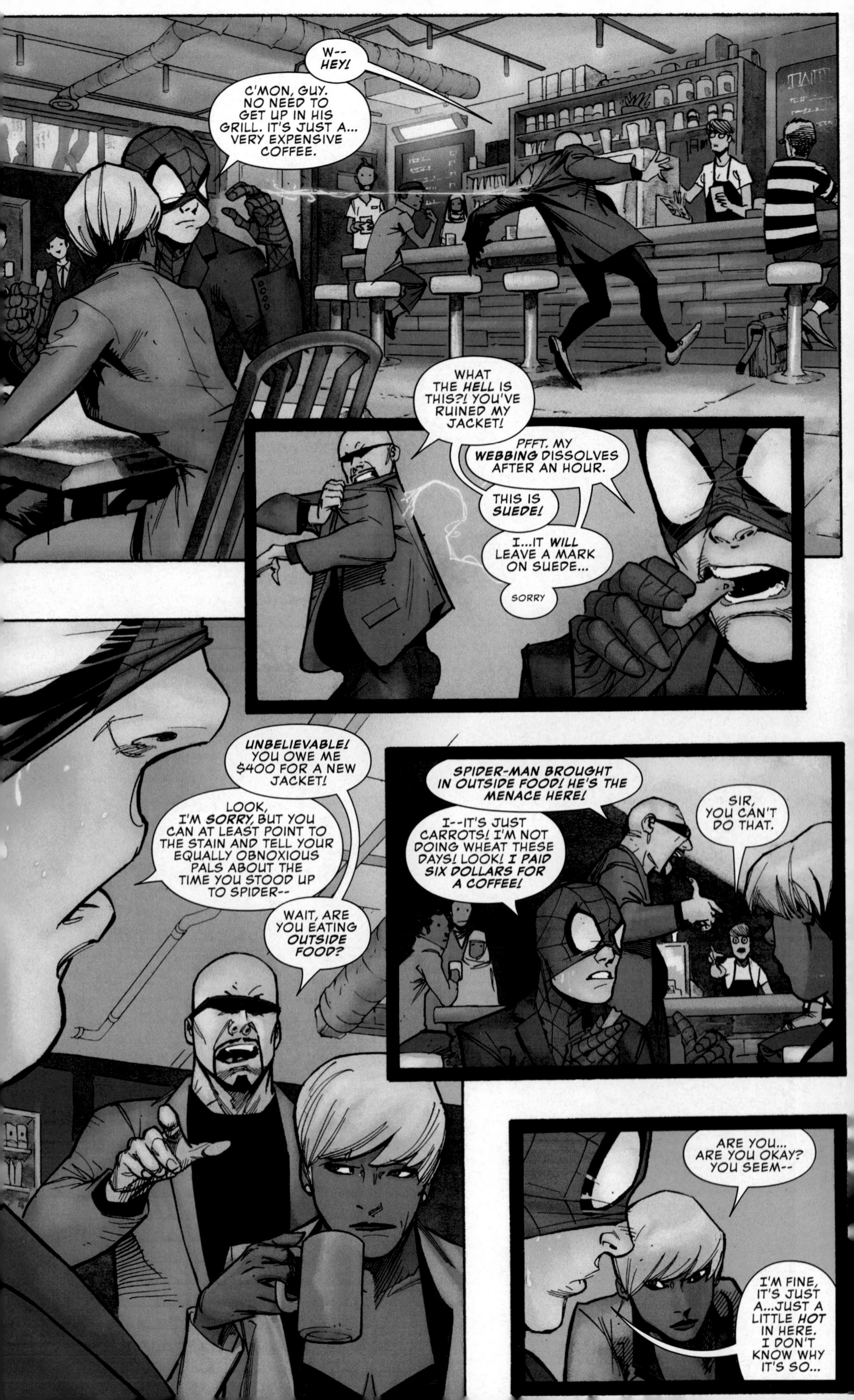
W-- HEY!
C'MON, GUY. NO NEED TO GET UP IN HIS GRILL. IT'S JUST A... VERY EXPENSIVE COFFEE.
WHAT THE HELL IS THIS?! YOU'VE RUINED MY JACKET!
PFFT. MY WEBBING DISSOLVES AFTER AN HOUR.
THIS IS SUEDE!
I...IT WILL LEAVE A MARK ON SUEDE...
SORRY
UNBELIEVABLE! YOU OWE ME $400 FOR A NEW JACKET!
LOOK, I'M SORRY, BUT YOU CAN AT LEAST POINT TO THE STAIN AND TELL YOUR EQUALLY OBNOXIOUS PALS ABOUT THE TIME YOU STOOD UP TO SPIDER--
WAIT, ARE YOU EATING OUTSIDE FOOD?
SPIDER-MAN BROUGHT IN OUTSIDE FOOD! HE'S THE MENACE HERE!
I--IT'S JUST CARROTS! I'M NOT DOING WHEAT THESE DAYS! LOOK! I PAID SIX DOLLARS FOR A COFFEE!
SIR, YOU CAN'T DO THAT.
ARE YOU... ARE YOU OKAY? YOU SEEM--
I'M FINE, IT'S JUST A...JUST A LITTLE HOT IN HERE. I DON'T KNOW WHY IT'S SO...

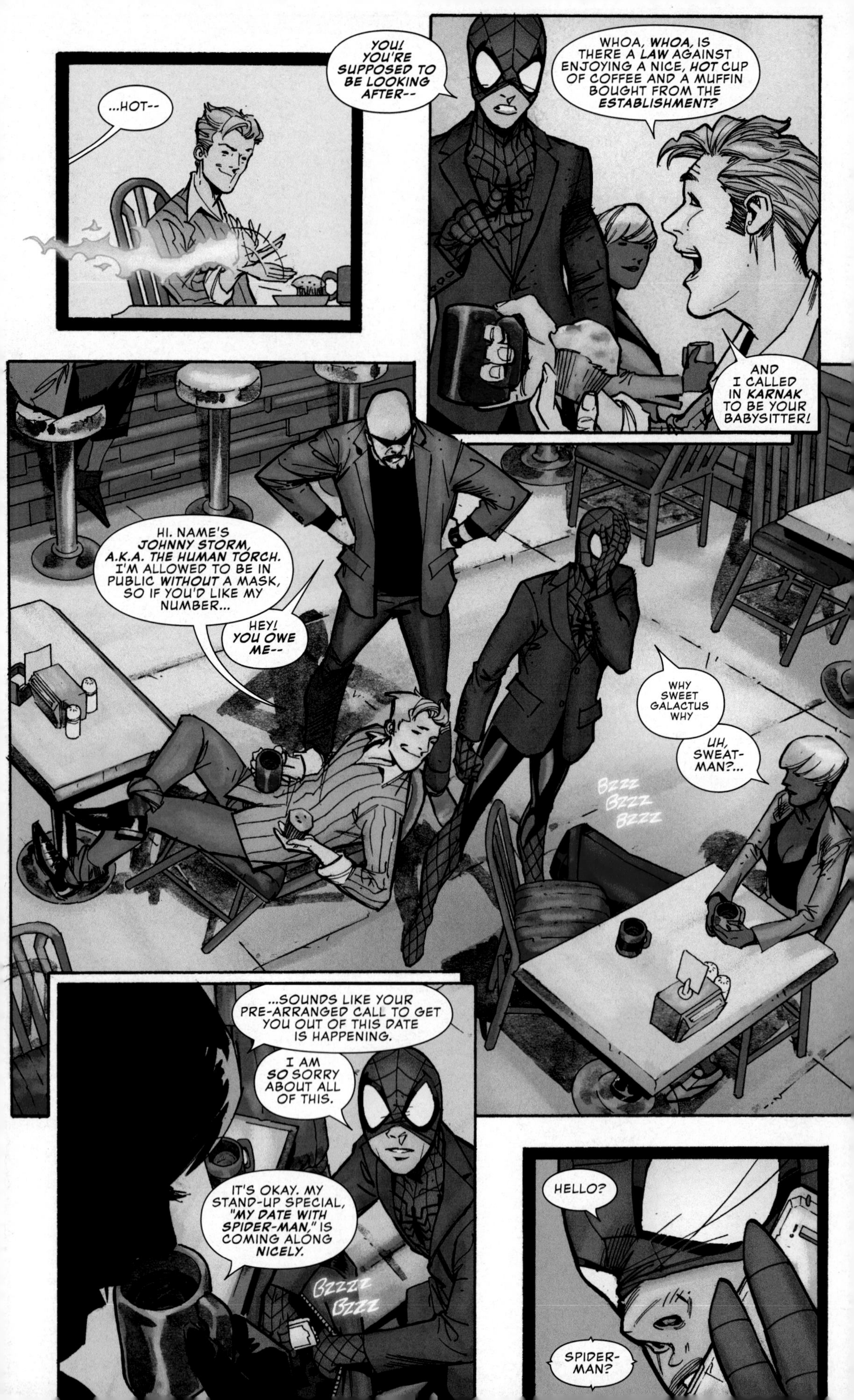
...HOT--
YOU! YOU'RE SUPPOSED TO BE LOOKING AFTER--
WHOA, WHOA, IS THERE A LAW AGAINST ENJOYING A NICE, HOT CUP OF COFFEE AND A MUFFIN BOUGHT FROM THE ESTABLISHMENT?
AND I CALLED IN KARNAK TO BE YOUR BABYSITTER!
HI. NAME'S JOHNNY STORM, A.K.A. THE HUMAN TORCH. I'M ALLOWED TO BE IN PUBLIC WITHOUT A MASK, SO IF YOU'D LIKE MY NUMBER...
HEY! YOU OWE ME--
WHY SWEET GALACTUS WHY
UH, SWEAT-MAN?...
BZZZ BZZZ BZZZ
...SOUNDS LIKE YOUR PRE-ARRANGED CALL TO GET YOU OUT OF THIS DATE IS HAPPENING.
I AM SO SORRY ABOUT ALL OF THIS.
IT'S OKAY. MY STAND-UP SPECIAL, "MY DATE WITH SPIDER-MAN," IS COMING ALONG NICELY.
BZZZZ BZZZ
HELLO?
SPIDER-MAN?

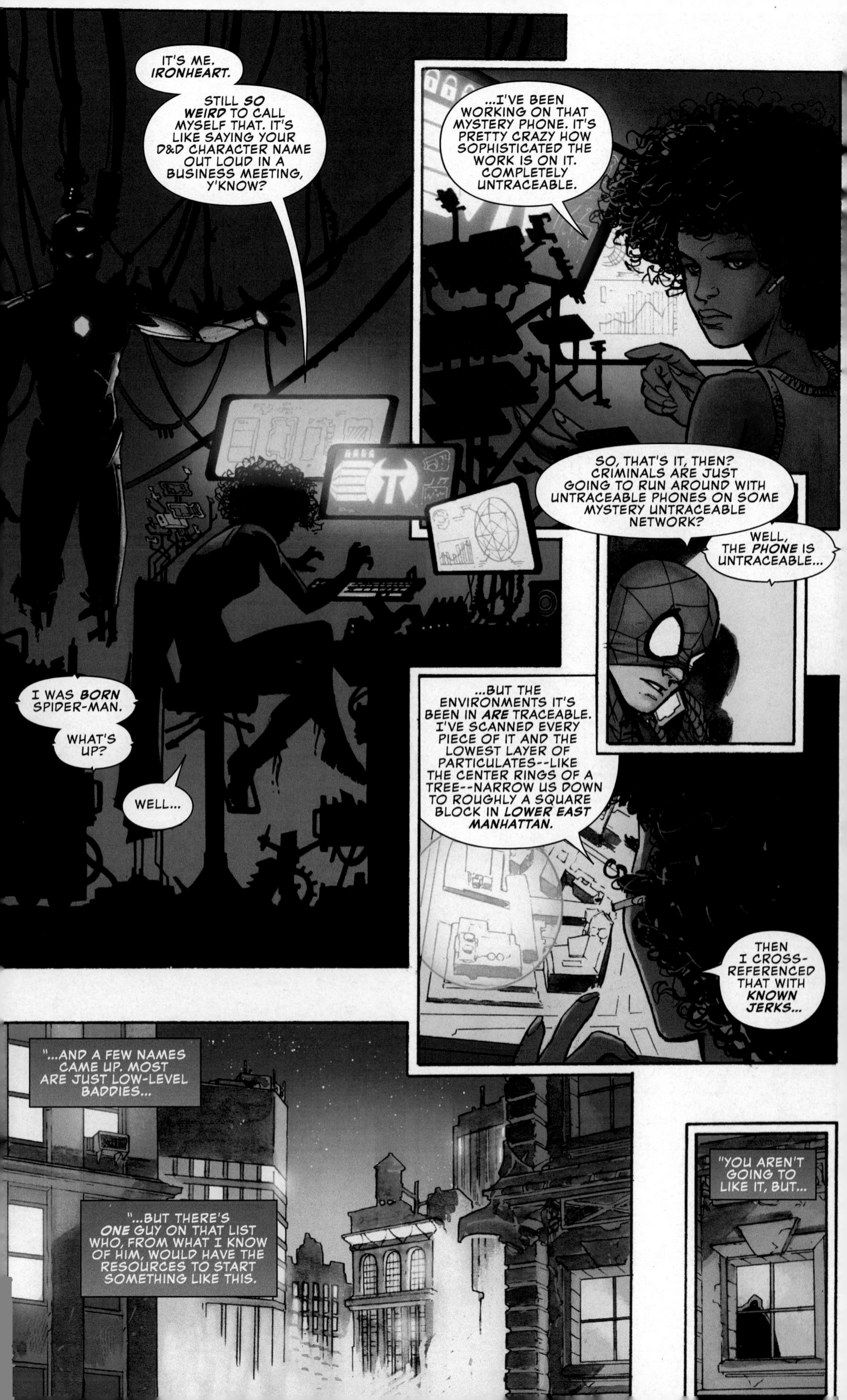
IT'S ME. IRONHEART.
STILL SO WEIRD TO CALL MYSELF THAT. IT'S LIKE SAYING YOUR D&D CHARACTER NAME OUT LOUD IN A BUSINESS MEETING, Y'KNOW?
I WAS BORN SPIDER-MAN.
WHAT'S UP?
WELL...
...I'VE BEEN WORKING ON THAT MYSTERY PHONE. IT'S PRETTY CRAZY HOW SOPHISTICATED THE WORK IS ON IT. COMPLETELY UNTRACEABLE.
SO, THAT'S IT, THEN? CRIMINALS ARE JUST GOING TO RUN AROUND WITH UNTRACEABLE PHONES ON SOME MYSTERY UNTRACEABLE NETWORK?
WELL, THE PHONE IS UNTRACEABLE...
...BUT THE ENVIRONMENTS IT'S BEEN IN ARE TRACEABLE. I'VE SCANNED EVERY PIECE OF IT AND THE LOWEST LAYER OF PARTICULATES--LIKE THE CENTER RINGS OF A TREE--NARROW US DOWN TO ROUGHLY A SQUARE BLOCK IN LOWER EAST MANHATTAN.
THEN I CROSS-REFERENCED THAT WITH KNOWN JERKS...
"...AND A FEW NAMES CAME UP. MOST ARE JUST LOW-LEVEL BADDIES...
"...BUT THERE'S ONE GUY ON THAT LIST WHO, FROM WHAT I KNOW OF HIM, WOULD HAVE THE RESOURCES TO START SOMETHING LIKE THIS.
"YOU AREN'T GOING TO LIKE IT, BUT...

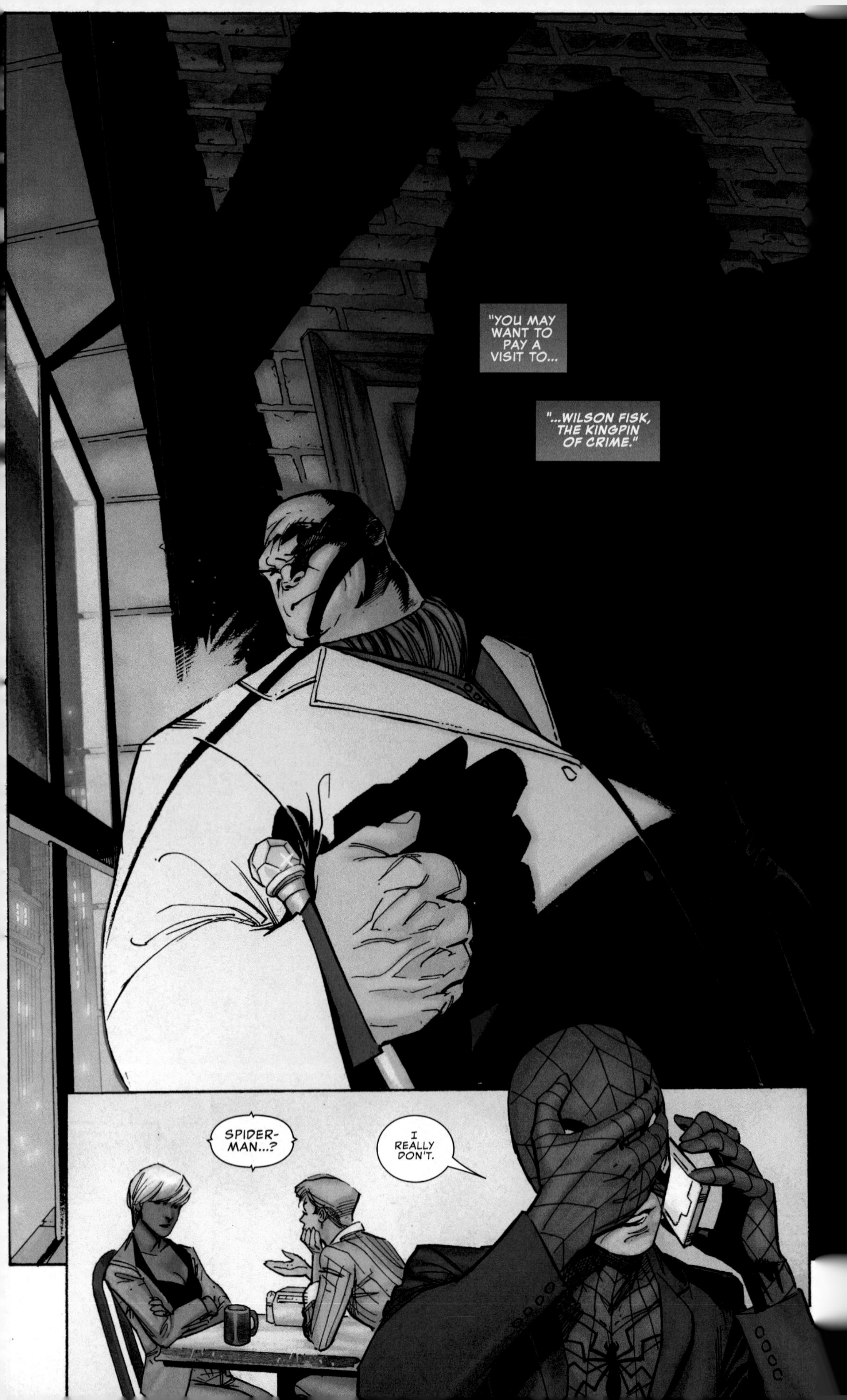
"YOU MAY WANT TO PAY A VISIT TO...
"...WILSON FISK, THE KINGPIN OF CRIME."
SPIDER-MAN...?
I REALLY DON'T.

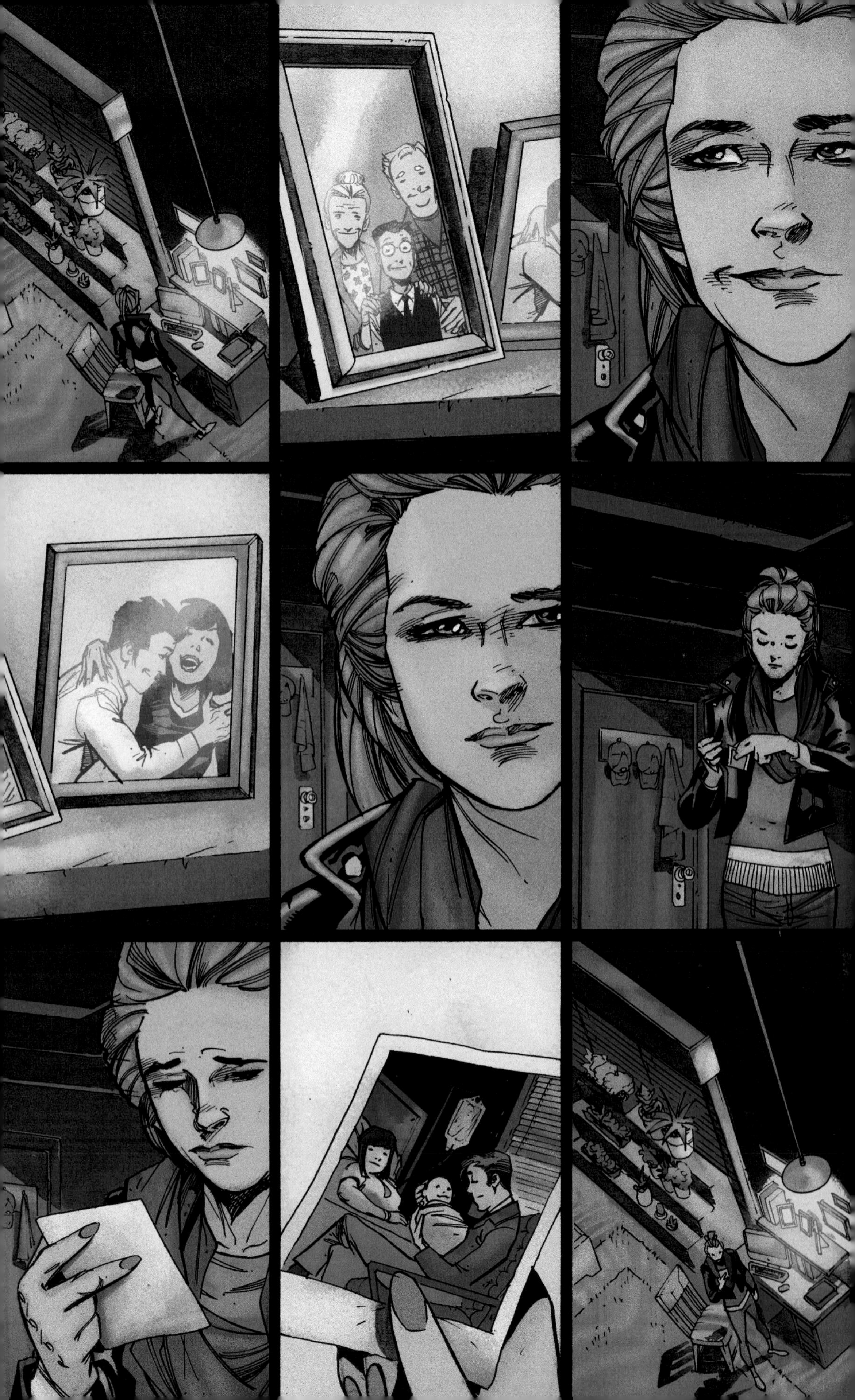

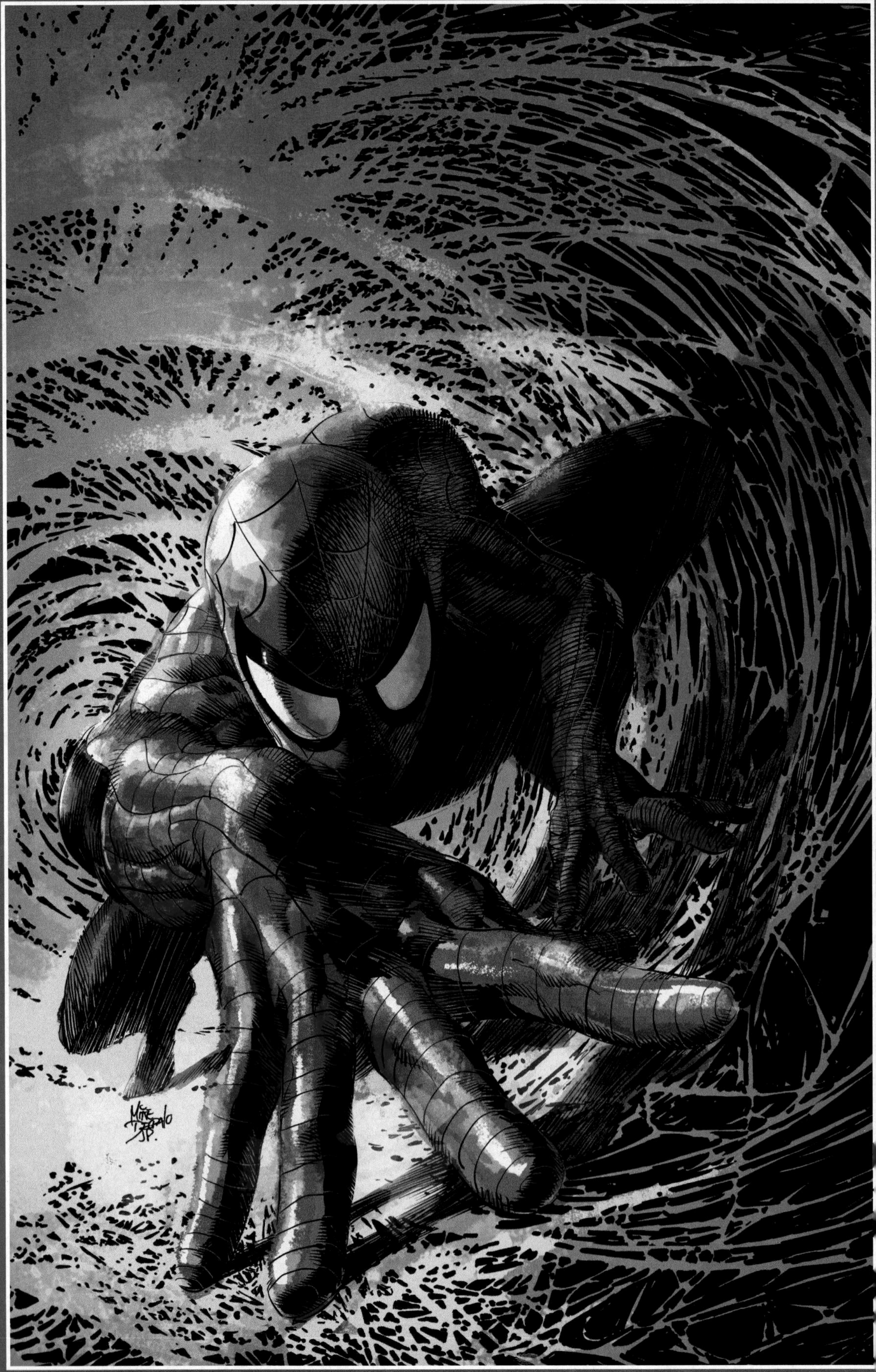

#1 VARIANT BY **MIKE DEODATO JR.** & **RAIN BEREDO**

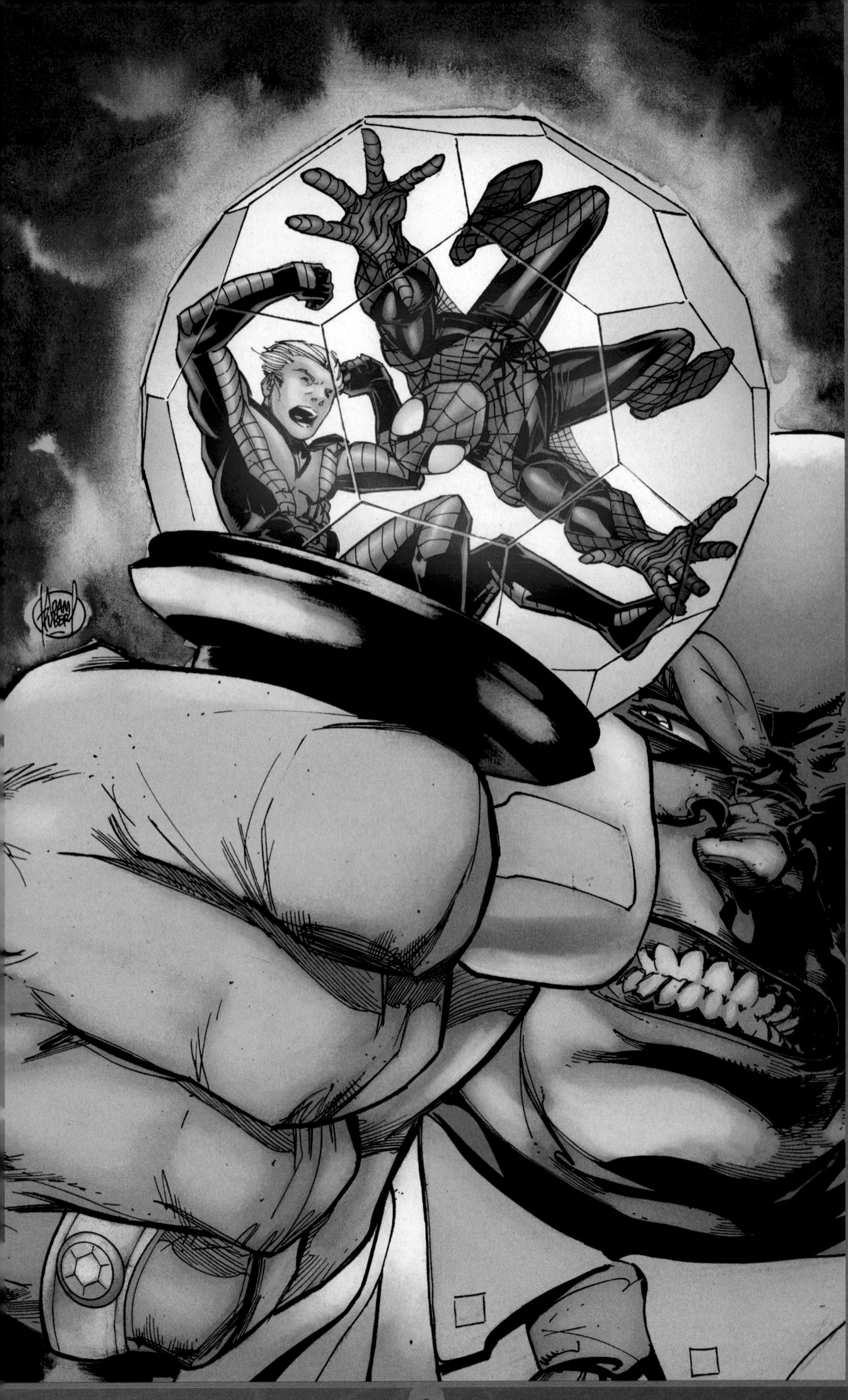

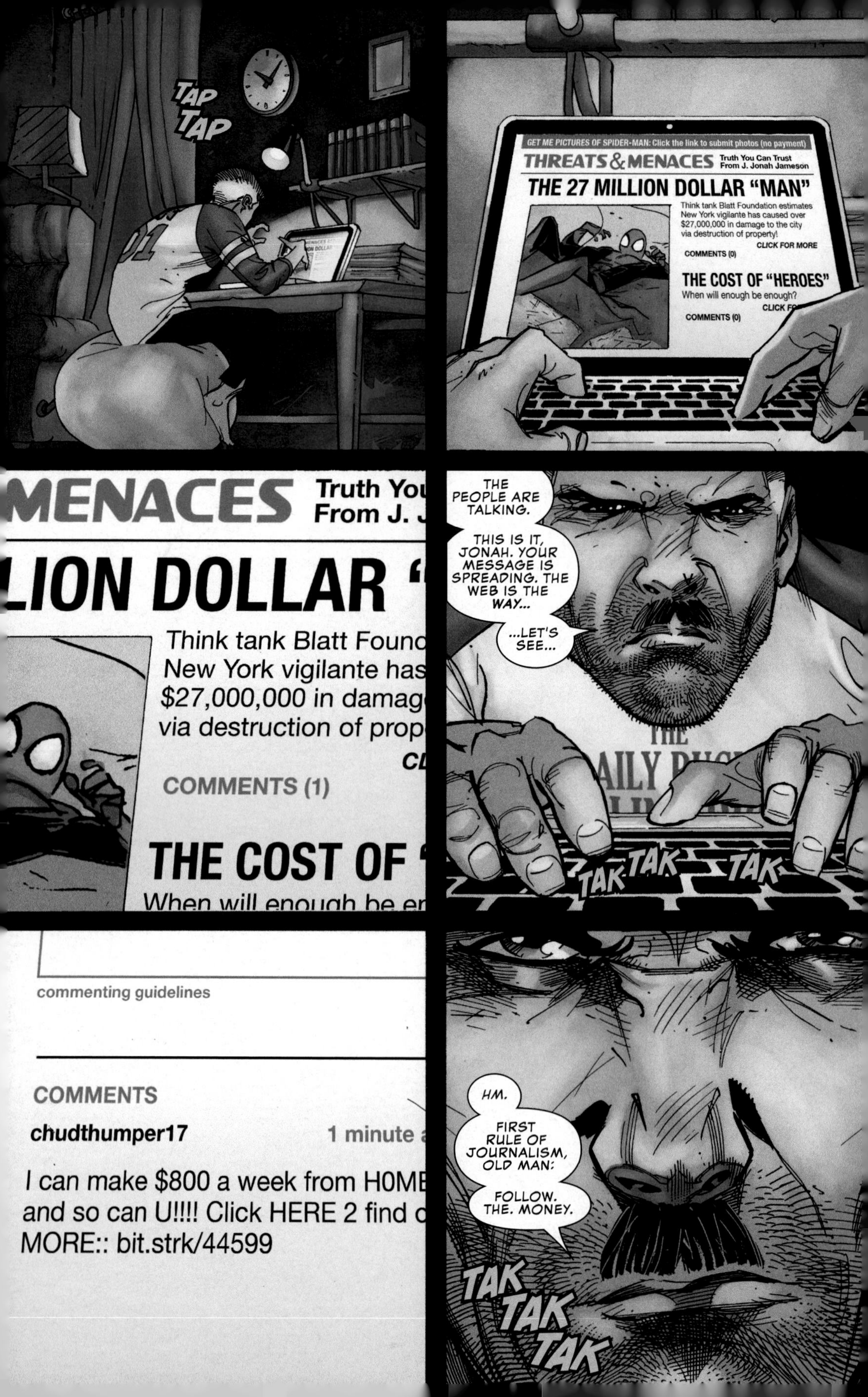
TAP TAP
GET ME PICTURES OF SPIDER-MAN: Click the link to submit photos (no payment)
THREATS & MENACES
Truth You Can Trust From J. Jonah Jameson
THE 27 MILLION DOLLAR "MAN"
Think tank Blatt Foundation estimates New York vigilante has caused over $27,000,000 in damage to the city via destruction of property!
CLICK FOR MORE
COMMENTS (0)
THE COST OF "HEROES"
When will enough be enough?
COMMENTS (0)
MENACES
LION DOLLAR
COMMENTS (1)
THE COST OF
THE PEOPLE ARE TALKING.
THIS IS IT, JONAH. YOUR MESSAGE IS SPREADING. THE WEB IS THE WAY...
...LET'S SEE...
TAK TAK TAK
commenting guidelines
COMMENTS
chudthumper17
I can make $800 a week from H0ME
and so can U!!!! Click HERE 2 find
MORE:: bit.strk/44599
HM.
FIRST RULE OF JOURNALISM, OLD MAN:
FOLLOW. THE. MONEY.
TAK TAK TAK

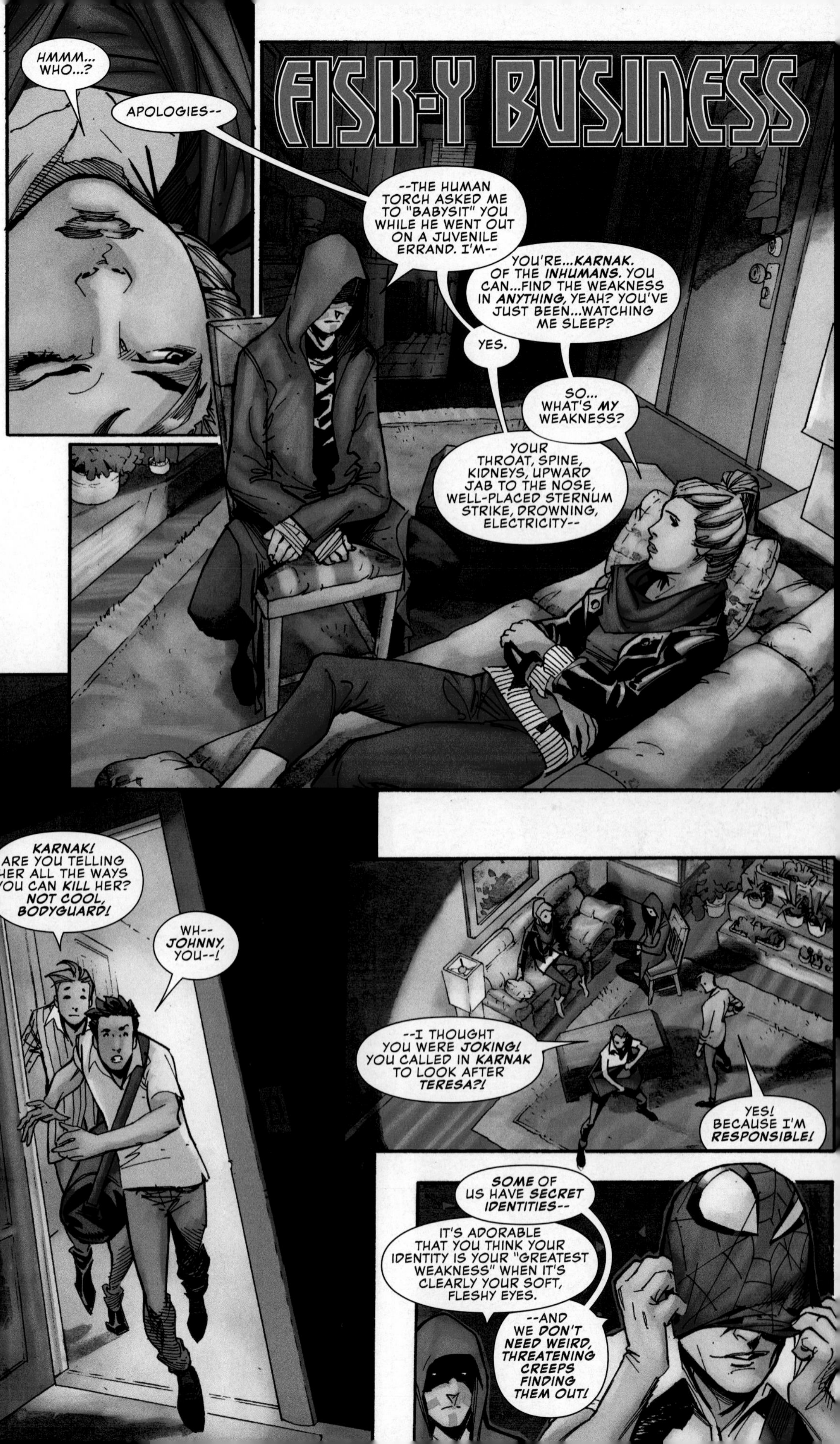

FISK-Y BUSINESS
HMMM... WHO...?
APOLOGIES--
--THE HUMAN TORCH ASKED ME TO "BABYSIT" YOU WHILE HE WENT OUT ON A JUVENILE ERRAND. I'M--
YOU'RE...KARNAK. OF THE INHUMANS. YOU CAN...FIND THE WEAKNESS IN ANYTHING, YEAH? YOU'VE JUST BEEN...WATCHING ME SLEEP?
YES.
SO... WHAT'S MY WEAKNESS?
YOUR THROAT, SPINE, KIDNEYS, UPWARD JAB TO THE NOSE, WELL-PLACED STERNUM STRIKE, DROWNING, ELECTRICITY--
KARNAK! ARE YOU TELLING HER ALL THE WAYS YOU CAN KILL HER? NOT COOL, BODYGUARD!
WH-- JOHNNY, YOU--!
--I THOUGHT YOU WERE JOKING! YOU CALLED IN KARNAK TO LOOK AFTER TERESA?!
YES! BECAUSE I'M RESPONSIBLE!
SOME OF US HAVE SECRET IDENTITIES--
IT'S ADORABLE THAT YOU THINK YOUR IDENTITY IS YOUR "GREATEST WEAKNESS" WHEN IT'S CLEARLY YOUR SOFT, FLESHY EYES.
--AND WE DON'T NEED WEIRD, THREATENING CREEPS FINDING THEM OUT!

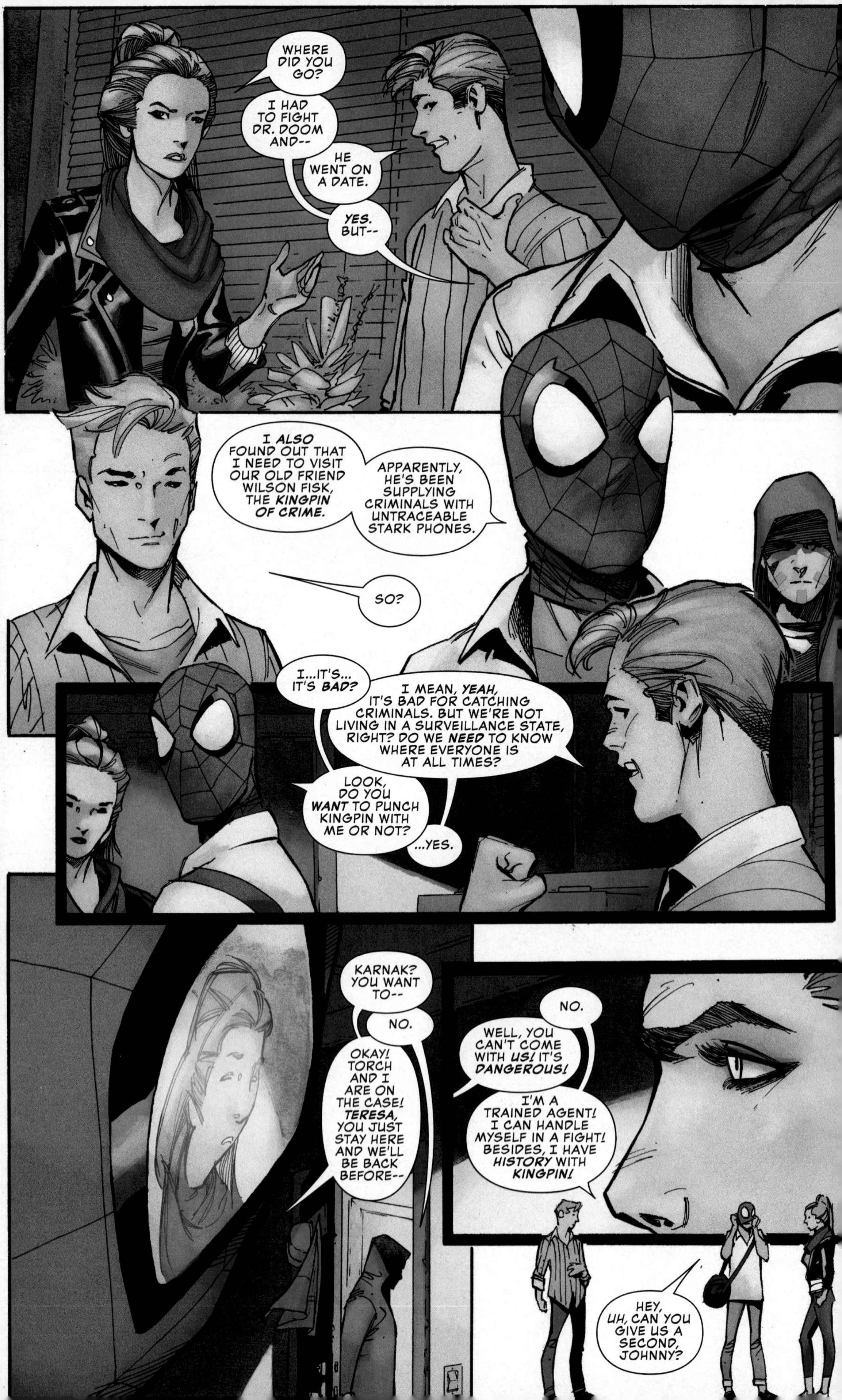
WHERE DID YOU GO?
I HAD TO FIGHT DR. DOOM AND--
HE WENT ON A DATE.
YES. BUT--
I ALSO FOUND OUT THAT I NEED TO VISIT OUR OLD FRIEND WILSON FISK, THE KINGPIN OF CRIME.
APPARENTLY, HE'S BEEN SUPPLYING CRIMINALS WITH UNTRACEABLE STARK PHONES.
SO?
I...IT'S... IT'S BAD?
I MEAN, YEAH, IT'S BAD FOR CATCHING CRIMINALS. BUT WE'RE NOT LIVING IN A SURVEILLANCE STATE, RIGHT? DO WE NEED TO KNOW WHERE EVERYONE IS AT ALL TIMES?
LOOK, DO YOU WANT TO PUNCH KINGPIN WITH ME OR NOT?
...YES.
KARNAK? YOU WANT TO--
NO.
OKAY! TORCH AND I ARE ON THE CASE! TERESA, YOU JUST STAY HERE AND WE'LL BE BACK BEFORE--
NO.
WELL, YOU CAN'T COME WITH US! IT'S DANGEROUS!
I'M A TRAINED AGENT! I CAN HANDLE MYSELF IN A FIGHT! BESIDES, I HAVE HISTORY WITH KINGPIN!
HEY, UH, CAN YOU GIVE US A SECOND, JOHNNY?

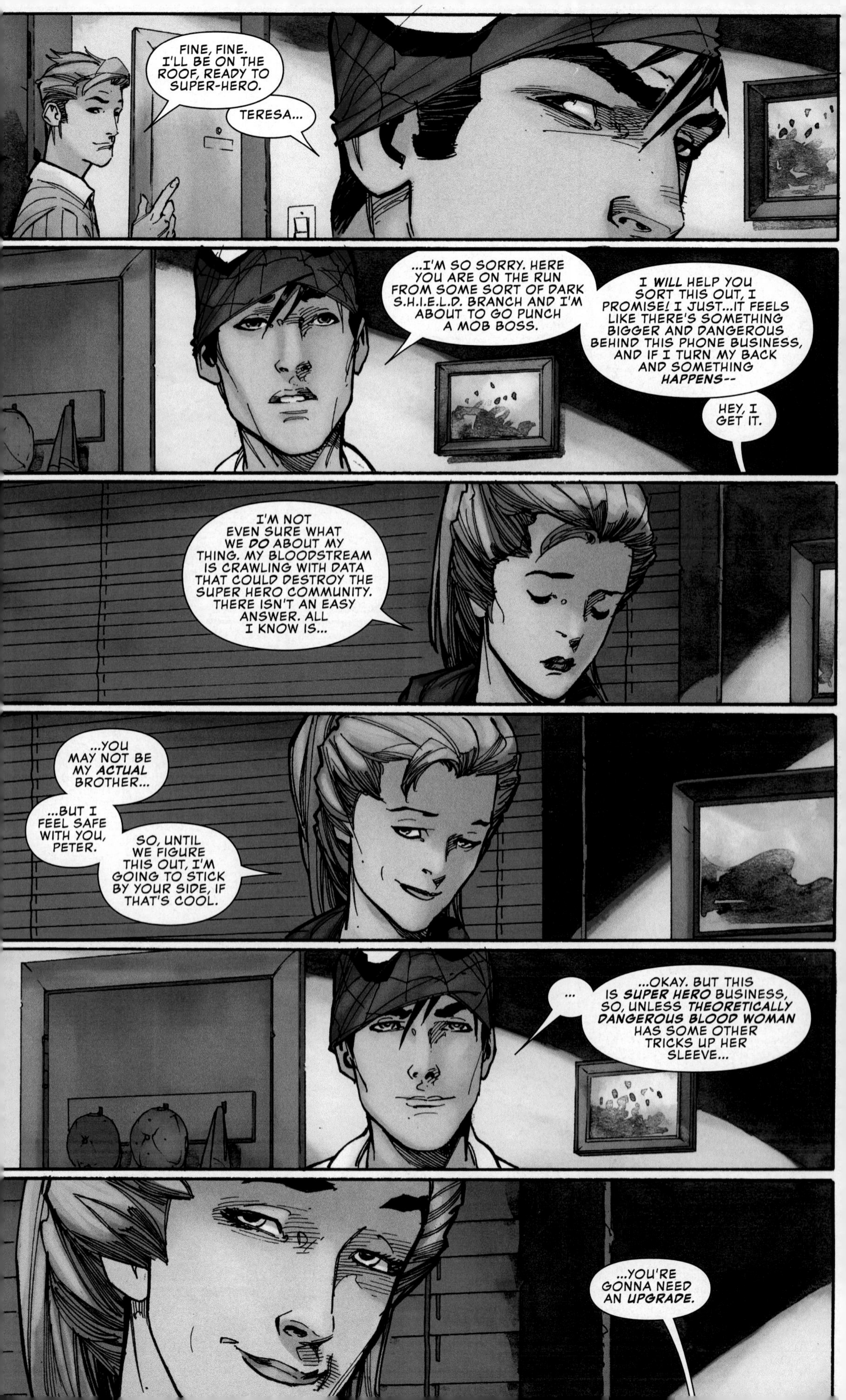
FINE, FINE. I'LL BE ON THE ROOF, READY TO SUPER-HERO.
TERESA...
...I'M SO SORRY. HERE YOU ARE ON THE RUN FROM SOME SORT OF DARK S.H.I.E.L.D. BRANCH AND I'M ABOUT TO GO PUNCH A MOB BOSS.
I *WILL* HELP YOU SORT THIS OUT, I PROMISE! I JUST...IT FEELS LIKE THERE'S SOMETHING BIGGER AND DANGEROUS BEHIND THIS PHONE BUSINESS, AND IF I TURN MY BACK AND SOMETHING *HAPPENS*--
HEY, I GET IT.
I'M NOT EVEN SURE WHAT WE *DO* ABOUT MY THING. MY BLOODSTREAM IS CRAWLING WITH DATA THAT COULD DESTROY THE SUPER HERO COMMUNITY. THERE ISN'T AN EASY ANSWER. ALL I KNOW IS...
...YOU MAY NOT BE MY *ACTUAL* BROTHER...
...BUT I FEEL SAFE WITH YOU, PETER.
SO, UNTIL WE FIGURE THIS OUT, I'M GOING TO STICK BY YOUR SIDE, IF THAT'S COOL.
...
...OKAY. BUT THIS IS *SUPER HERO* BUSINESS, SO, UNLESS *THEORETICALLY DANGEROUS BLOOD WOMAN* HAS SOME OTHER TRICKS UP HER SLEEVE...
...YOU'RE GONNA NEED AN *UPGRADE.*

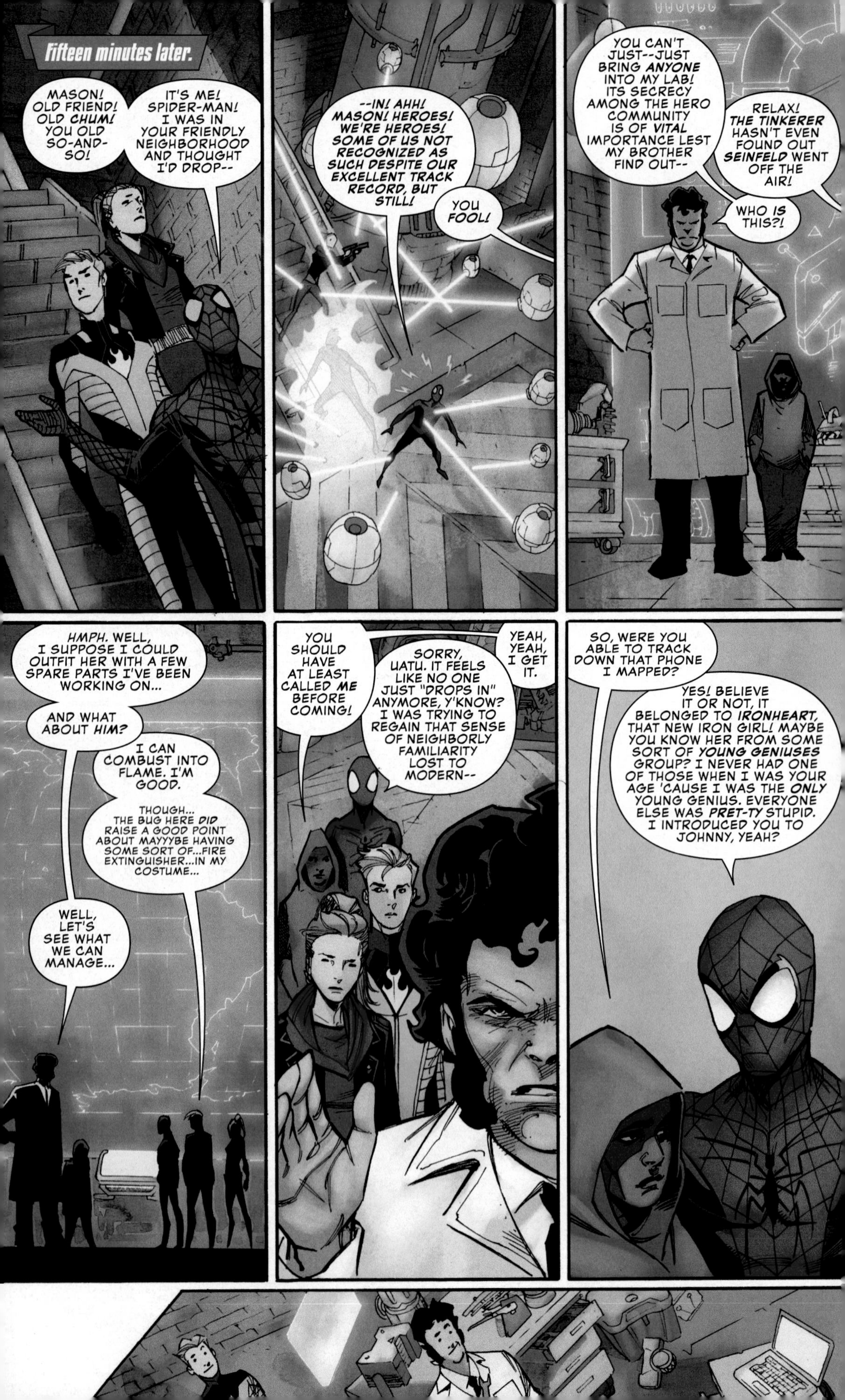
Fifteen minutes later.
MASON! OLD FRIEND! OLD CHUM! YOU OLD SO-AND-SO!
IT'S ME! SPIDER-MAN! I WAS IN YOUR FRIENDLY NEIGHBORHOOD AND THOUGHT I'D DROP--
--IN! AHH! MASON! HEROES! WE'RE HEROES! SOME OF US NOT RECOGNIZED AS SUCH DESPITE OUR EXCELLENT TRACK RECORD, BUT STILL!
YOU FOOL!
YOU CAN'T JUST--JUST BRING ANYONE INTO MY LAB! ITS SECRECY AMONG THE HERO COMMUNITY IS OF VITAL IMPORTANCE LEST MY BROTHER FIND OUT--
RELAX! THE TINKERER HASN'T EVEN FOUND OUT SEINFELD WENT OFF THE AIR!
WHO IS THIS?!
HMPH. WELL, I SUPPOSE I COULD OUTFIT HER WITH A FEW SPARE PARTS I'VE BEEN WORKING ON...
AND WHAT ABOUT HIM?
I CAN COMBUST INTO FLAME. I'M GOOD.
THOUGH... THE BUG HERE DID RAISE A GOOD POINT ABOUT MAYYYBE HAVING SOME SORT OF...FIRE EXTINGUISHER...IN MY COSTUME...
WELL, LET'S SEE WHAT WE CAN MANAGE...
YOU SHOULD HAVE AT LEAST CALLED ME BEFORE COMING!
SORRY, UATU. IT FEELS LIKE NO ONE JUST "DROPS IN" ANYMORE, Y'KNOW? I WAS TRYING TO REGAIN THAT SENSE OF NEIGHBORLY FAMILIARITY LOST TO MODERN--
YEAH, YEAH, I GET IT.
SO, WERE YOU ABLE TO TRACK DOWN THAT PHONE I MAPPED?
YES! BELIEVE IT OR NOT, IT BELONGED TO IRONHEART, THAT NEW IRON GIRL! MAYBE YOU KNOW HER FROM SOME SORT OF YOUNG GENIUSES GROUP? I NEVER HAD ONE OF THOSE WHEN I WAS YOUR AGE 'CAUSE I WAS THE ONLY YOUNG GENIUS. EVERYONE ELSE WAS PRET-TY STUPID. I INTRODUCED YOU TO JOHNNY, YEAH?

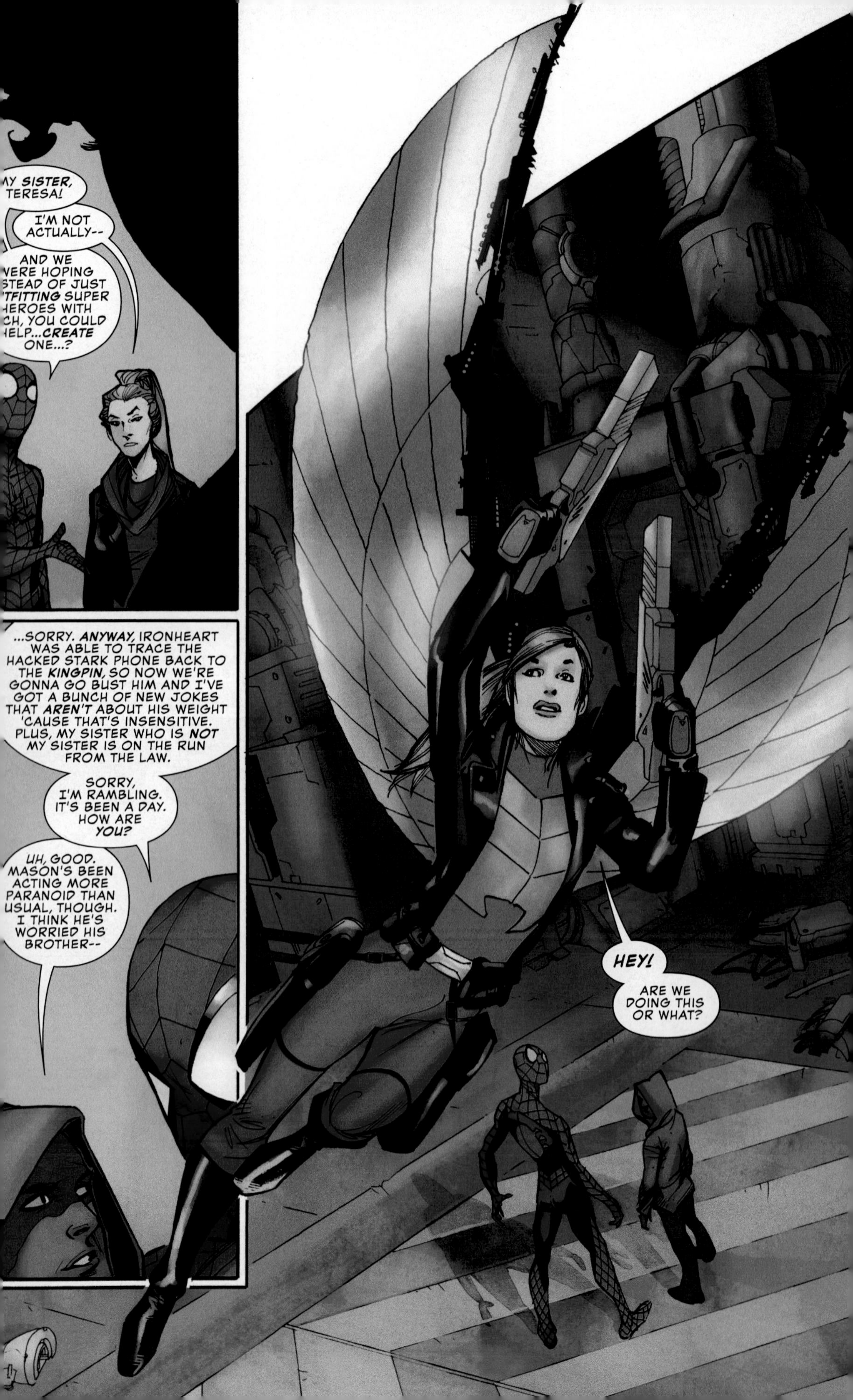
MY SISTER, TERESA!
I'M NOT ACTUALLY--
AND WE WERE HOPING INSTEAD OF JUST OUTFITTING SUPER HEROES WITH TECH, YOU COULD HELP...CREATE ONE...?
...SORRY. ANYWAY, IRONHEART WAS ABLE TO TRACE THE HACKED STARK PHONE BACK TO THE KINGPIN, SO NOW WE'RE GONNA GO BUST HIM AND I'VE GOT A BUNCH OF NEW JOKES THAT AREN'T ABOUT HIS WEIGHT 'CAUSE THAT'S INSENSITIVE. PLUS, MY SISTER WHO IS NOT MY SISTER IS ON THE RUN FROM THE LAW.
SORRY, I'M RAMBLING. IT'S BEEN A DAY. HOW ARE YOU?
UH, GOOD. MASON'S BEEN ACTING MORE PARANOID THAN USUAL, THOUGH. I THINK HE'S WORRIED HIS BROTHER--
HEY!
ARE WE DOING THIS OR WHAT?

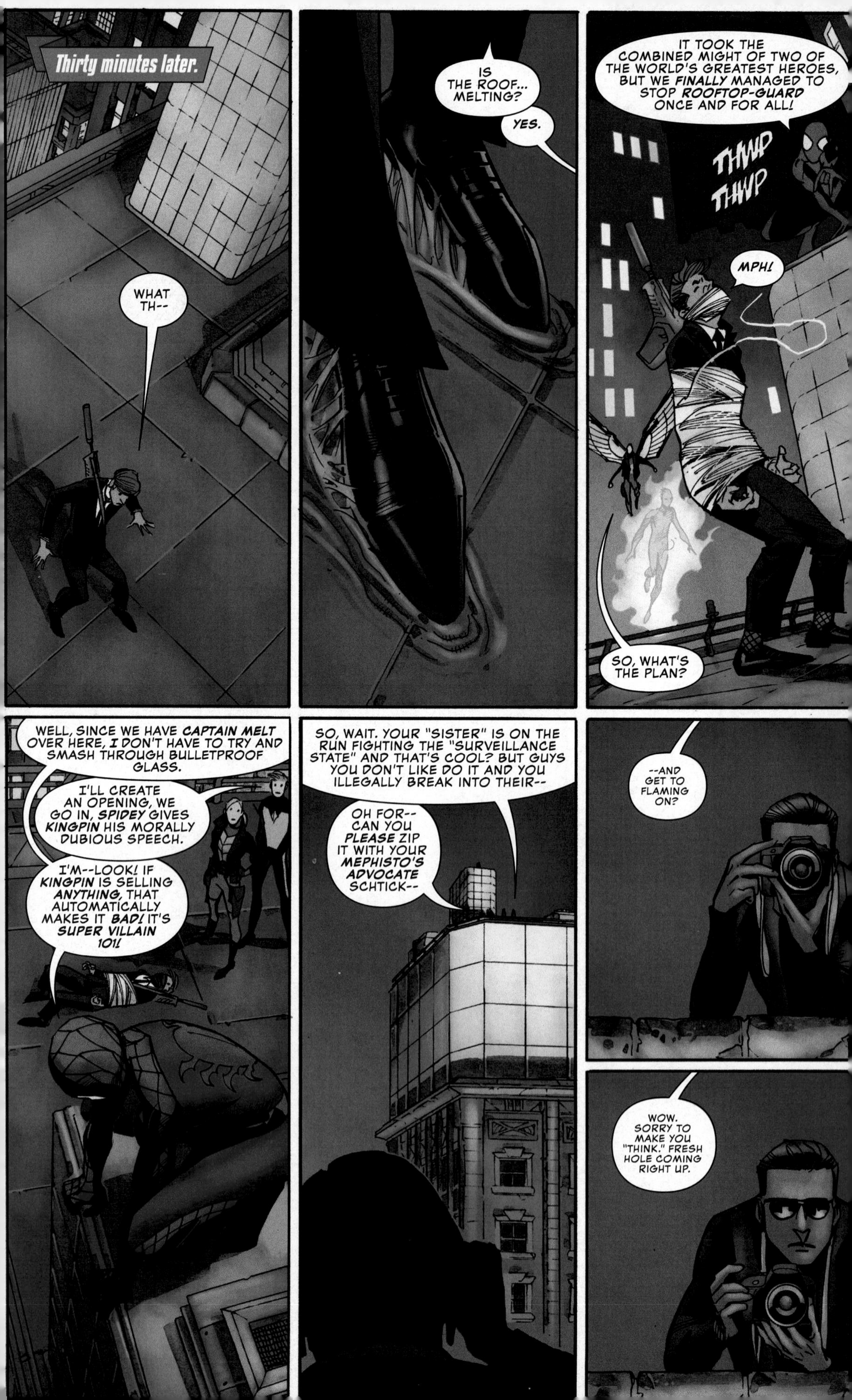
Thirty minutes later.
WHAT TH--
IS THE ROOF... MELTING?
YES.
IT TOOK THE COMBINED MIGHT OF TWO OF THE WORLD'S GREATEST HEROES, BUT WE FINALLY MANAGED TO STOP ROOFTOP-GUARD ONCE AND FOR ALL!
THWP THWP
MPH!
SO, WHAT'S THE PLAN?
WELL, SINCE WE HAVE CAPTAIN MELT OVER HERE, I DON'T HAVE TO TRY AND SMASH THROUGH BULLETPROOF GLASS.
I'LL CREATE AN OPENING, WE GO IN, SPIDEY GIVES KINGPIN HIS MORALLY DUBIOUS SPEECH.
I'M--LOOK! IF KINGPIN IS SELLING ANYTHING, THAT AUTOMATICALLY MAKES IT BAD! IT'S SUPER VILLAIN 101!
SO, WAIT. YOUR "SISTER" IS ON THE RUN FIGHTING THE "SURVEILLANCE STATE" AND THAT'S COOL? BUT GUYS YOU DON'T LIKE DO IT AND YOU ILLEGALLY BREAK INTO THEIR--
OH FOR-- CAN YOU PLEASE ZIP IT WITH YOUR MEPHISTO'S ADVOCATE SCHTICK--
--AND GET TO FLAMING ON?
WOW. SORRY TO MAKE YOU "THINK." FRESH HOLE COMING RIGHT UP.

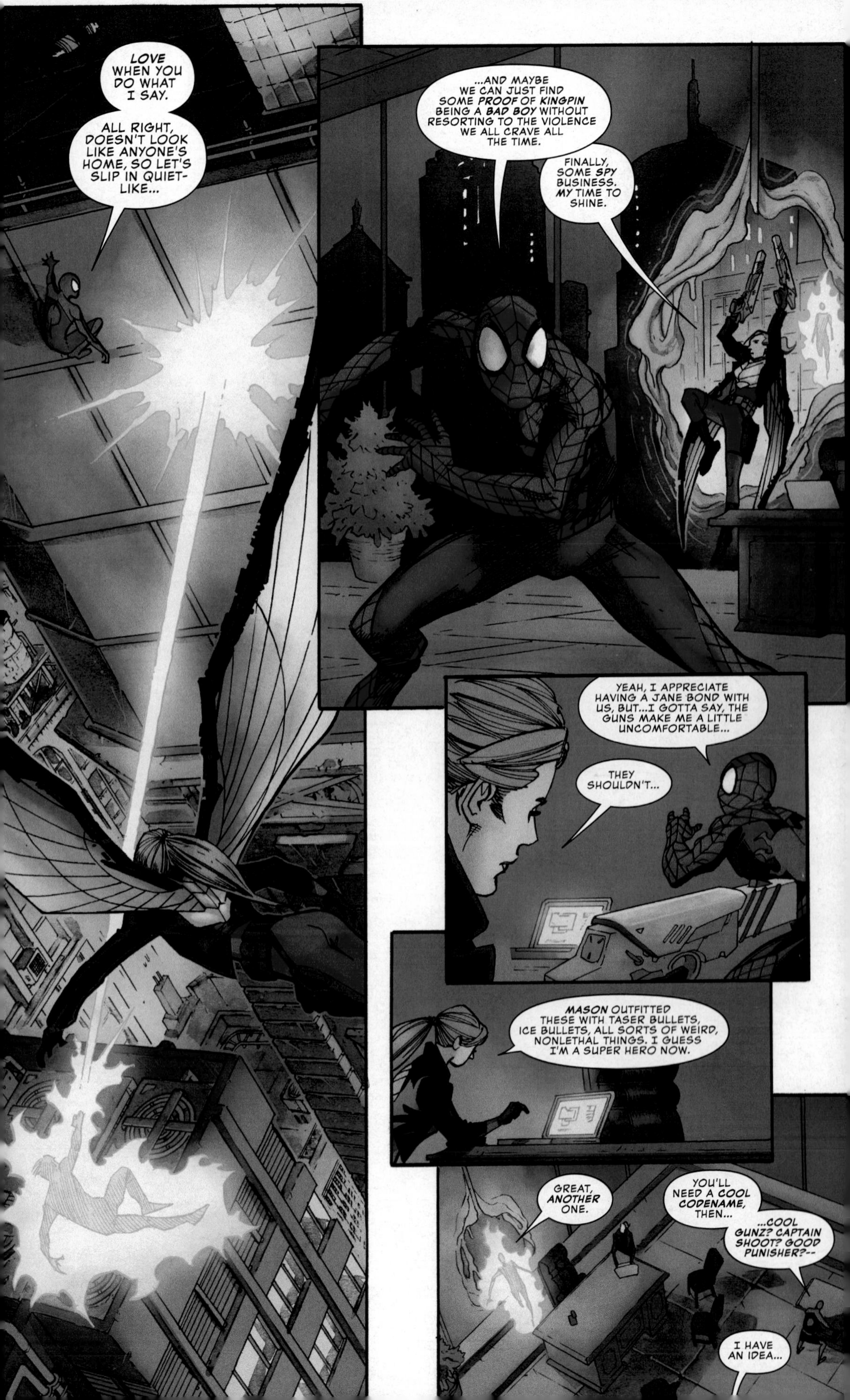

LOVE WHEN YOU DO WHAT I SAY.
ALL RIGHT, DOESN'T LOOK LIKE ANYONE'S HOME, SO LET'S SLIP IN QUIET-LIKE...
...AND MAYBE WE CAN JUST FIND SOME PROOF OF KINGPIN BEING A BAD BOY WITHOUT RESORTING TO THE VIOLENCE WE ALL CRAVE ALL THE TIME.
FINALLY, SOME SPY BUSINESS. MY TIME TO SHINE.
YEAH, I APPRECIATE HAVING A JANE BOND WITH US, BUT...I GOTTA SAY, THE GUNS MAKE ME A LITTLE UNCOMFORTABLE...
THEY SHOULDN'T...
MASON OUTFITTED THESE WITH TASER BULLETS, ICE BULLETS, ALL SORTS OF WEIRD, NONLETHAL THINGS. I GUESS I'M A SUPER HERO NOW.
GREAT, ANOTHER ONE.
YOU'LL NEED A COOL CODENAME, THEN...
...COOL GUNZ? CAPTAIN SHOOT? GOOD PUNISHER?--
I HAVE AN IDEA...

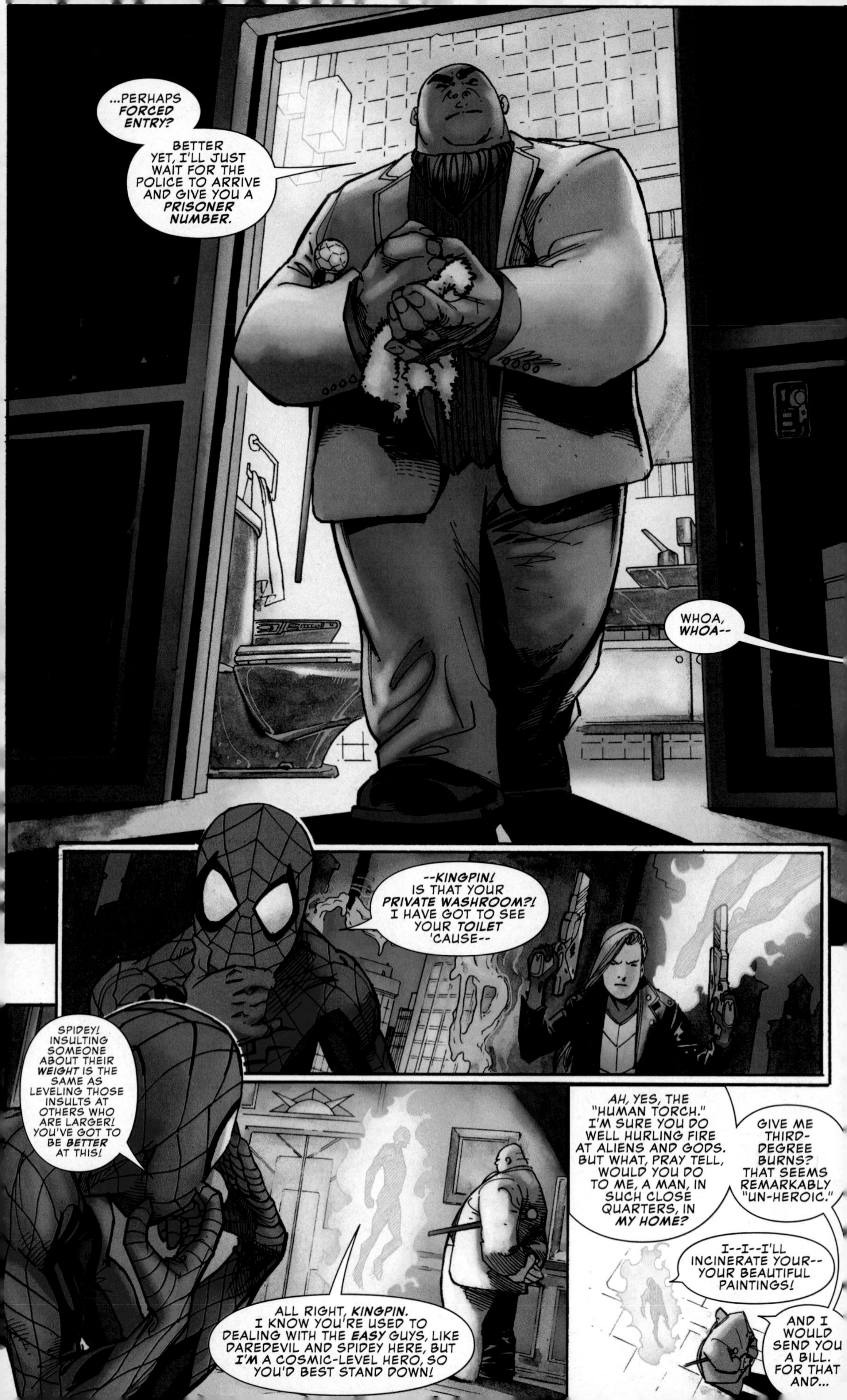
...PERHAPS FORCED ENTRY?
BETTER YET, I'LL JUST WAIT FOR THE POLICE TO ARRIVE AND GIVE YOU A PRISONER NUMBER.
WHOA, WHOA--
--KINGPIN! IS THAT YOUR PRIVATE WASHROOM?! I HAVE GOT TO SEE YOUR TOILET 'CAUSE--
SPIDEY! INSULTING SOMEONE ABOUT THEIR WEIGHT IS THE SAME AS LEVELING THOSE INSULTS AT OTHERS WHO ARE LARGER! YOU'VE GOT TO BE BETTER AT THIS!
ALL RIGHT, KINGPIN. I KNOW YOU'RE USED TO DEALING WITH THE EASY GUYS, LIKE DAREDEVIL AND SPIDEY HERE, BUT I'M A COSMIC-LEVEL HERO, SO YOU'D BEST STAND DOWN!
AH, YES, THE "HUMAN TORCH." I'M SURE YOU DO WELL HURLING FIRE AT ALIENS AND GODS. BUT WHAT, PRAY TELL, WOULD YOU DO TO ME, A MAN, IN SUCH CLOSE QUARTERS, IN MY HOME?
GIVE ME THIRD-DEGREE BURNS? THAT SEEMS REMARKABLY "UN-HEROIC."
I--I--I'LL INCINERATE YOUR-- YOUR BEAUTIFUL PAINTINGS!
AND I WOULD SEND YOU A BILL. FOR THAT AND...

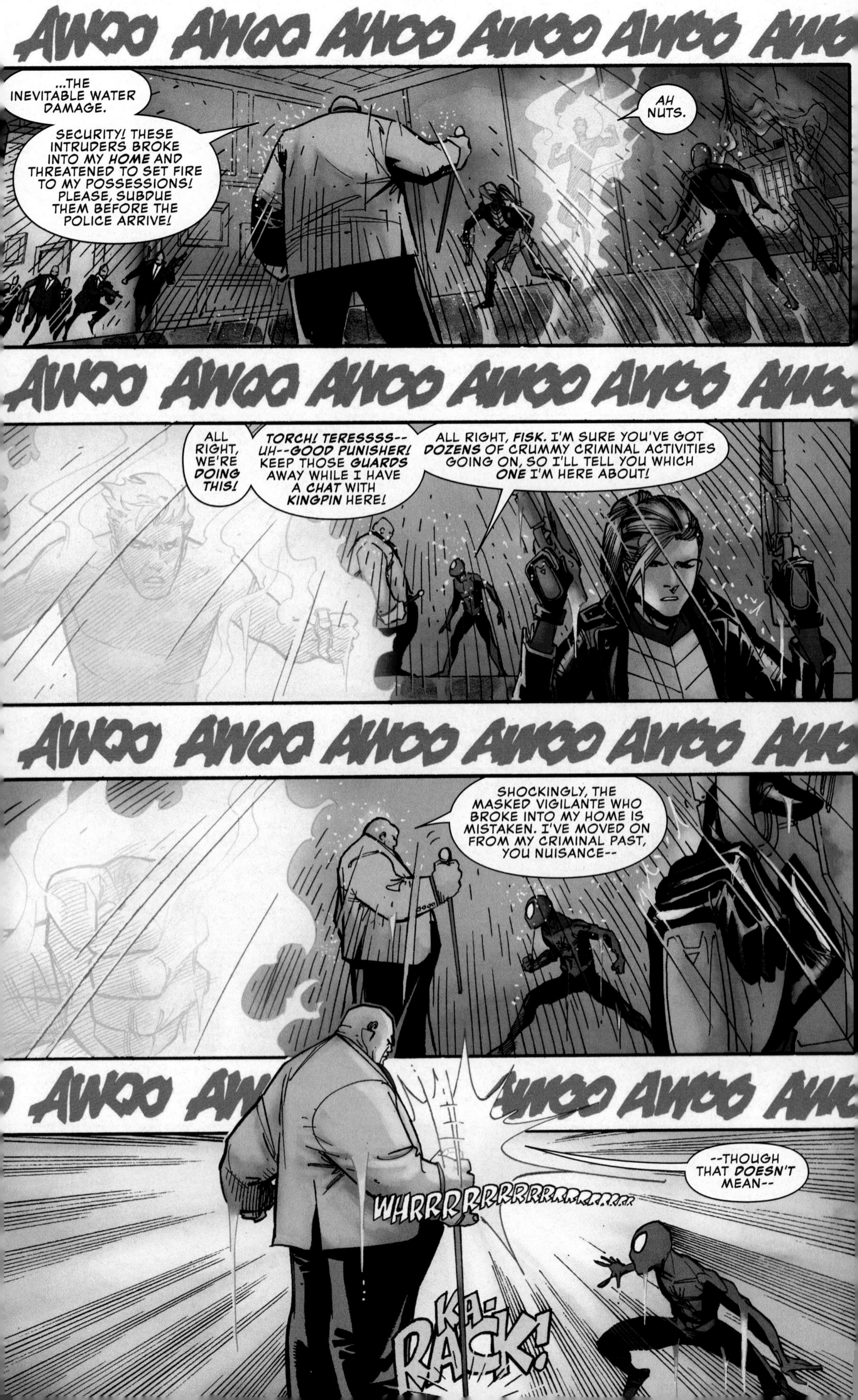

AWOO AWOO AWOO AWOO AWOO AWOO
...THE INEVITABLE WATER DAMAGE.
SECURITY! THESE INTRUDERS BROKE INTO MY HOME AND THREATENED TO SET FIRE TO MY POSSESSIONS! PLEASE, SUBDUE THEM BEFORE THE POLICE ARRIVE!
AH NUTS.
AWOO AWOO AWOO AWOO AWOO AWOO
ALL RIGHT, WE'RE DOING THIS!
TORCH! TERESSSS--UH--GOOD PUNISHER! KEEP THOSE GUARDS AWAY WHILE I HAVE A CHAT WITH KINGPIN HERE!
ALL RIGHT, FISK. I'M SURE YOU'VE GOT DOZENS OF CRUMMY CRIMINAL ACTIVITIES GOING ON, SO I'LL TELL YOU WHICH ONE I'M HERE ABOUT!
AWOO AWOO AWOO AWOO AWOO AWOO
SHOCKINGLY, THE MASKED VIGILANTE WHO BROKE INTO MY HOME IS MISTAKEN. I'VE MOVED ON FROM MY CRIMINAL PAST, YOU NUISANCE--
AWOO AWOO AWOO AWOO
--THOUGH THAT DOESN'T MEAN--
WHRRRRRRRRRRRRRRRR
KA-RACK!

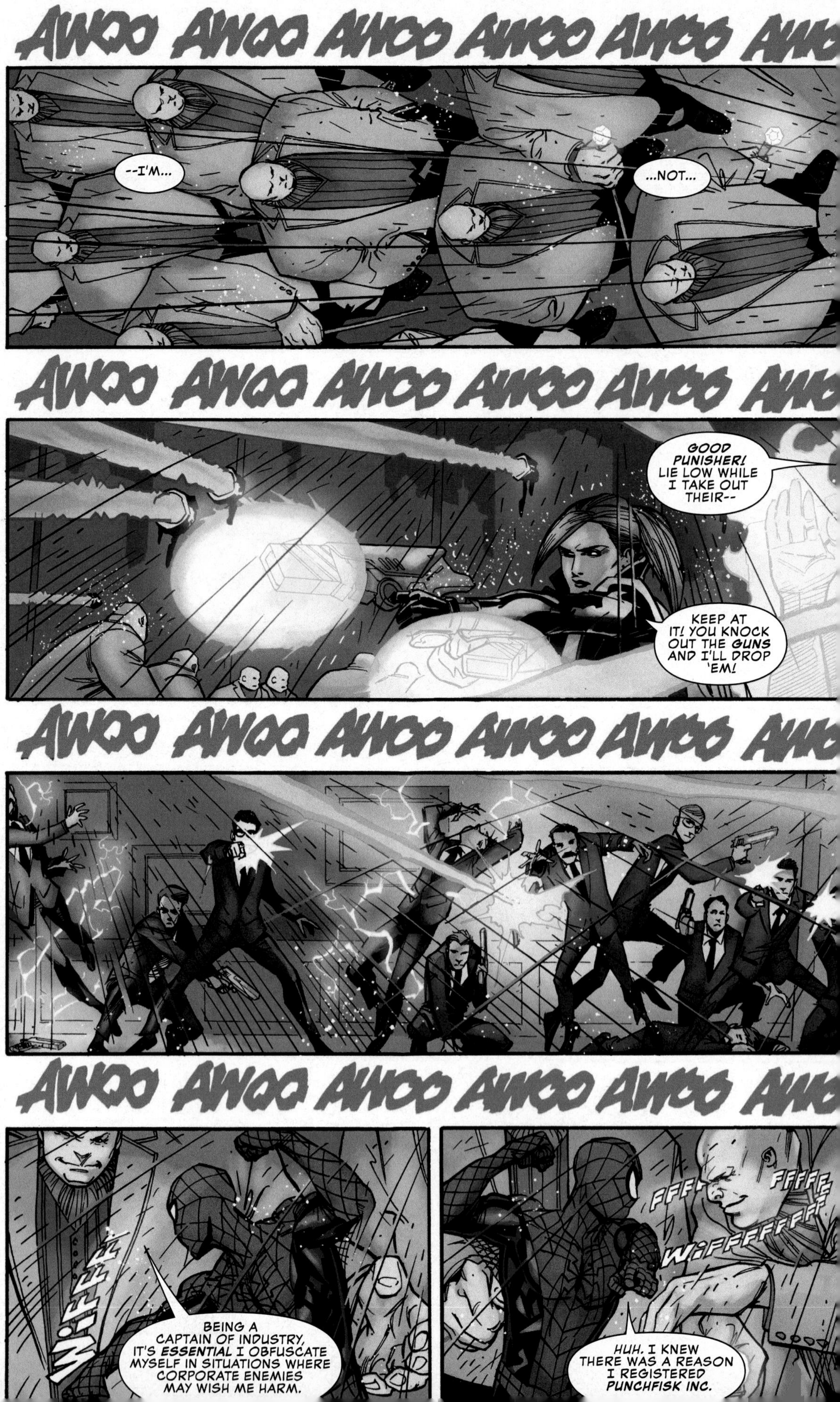
AWOO AWOO AWOO AWOO AWOO
--I'M...
...NOT...
AWOO AWOO AWOO AWOO AWOO
GOOD PUNISHER! LIE LOW WHILE I TAKE OUT THEIR--
KEEP AT IT! YOU KNOCK OUT THE GUNS AND I'LL DROP 'EM!
AWOO AWOO AWOO AWOO AWOO
AWOO AWOO AWOO AWOO AWOO
WiFFFF
BEING A CAPTAIN OF INDUSTRY, IT'S ESSENTIAL I OBFUSCATE MYSELF IN SITUATIONS WHERE CORPORATE ENEMIES MAY WISH ME HARM.
FFFF
FFFFF
WiFFFFFFFFF
HUH. I KNEW THERE WAS A REASON I REGISTERED PUNCHFISK INC.

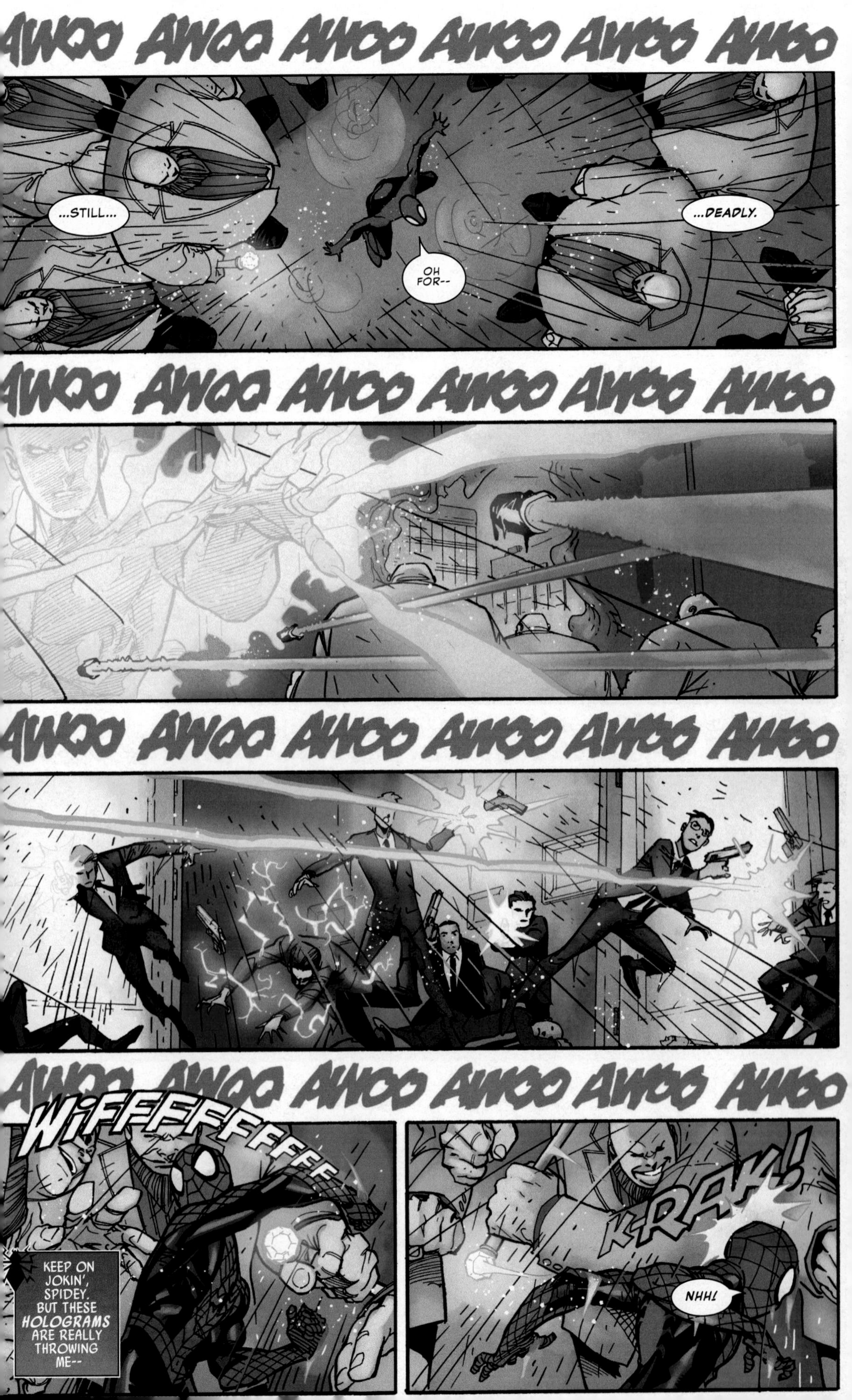
AWOO AWOO AWOO AWOO AWOO AWOO
...STILL...
OH FOR--
...DEADLY.
AWOO AWOO AWOO AWOO AWOO AWOO
AWOO AWOO AWOO AWOO AWOO AWOO
AWOO AWOO AWOO AWOO AWOO AWOO
WIFFFFFFFFF
KEEP ON JOKIN', SPIDEY, BUT THESE HOLOGRAMS ARE REALLY THROWING ME--
K-RAK!
NHH!

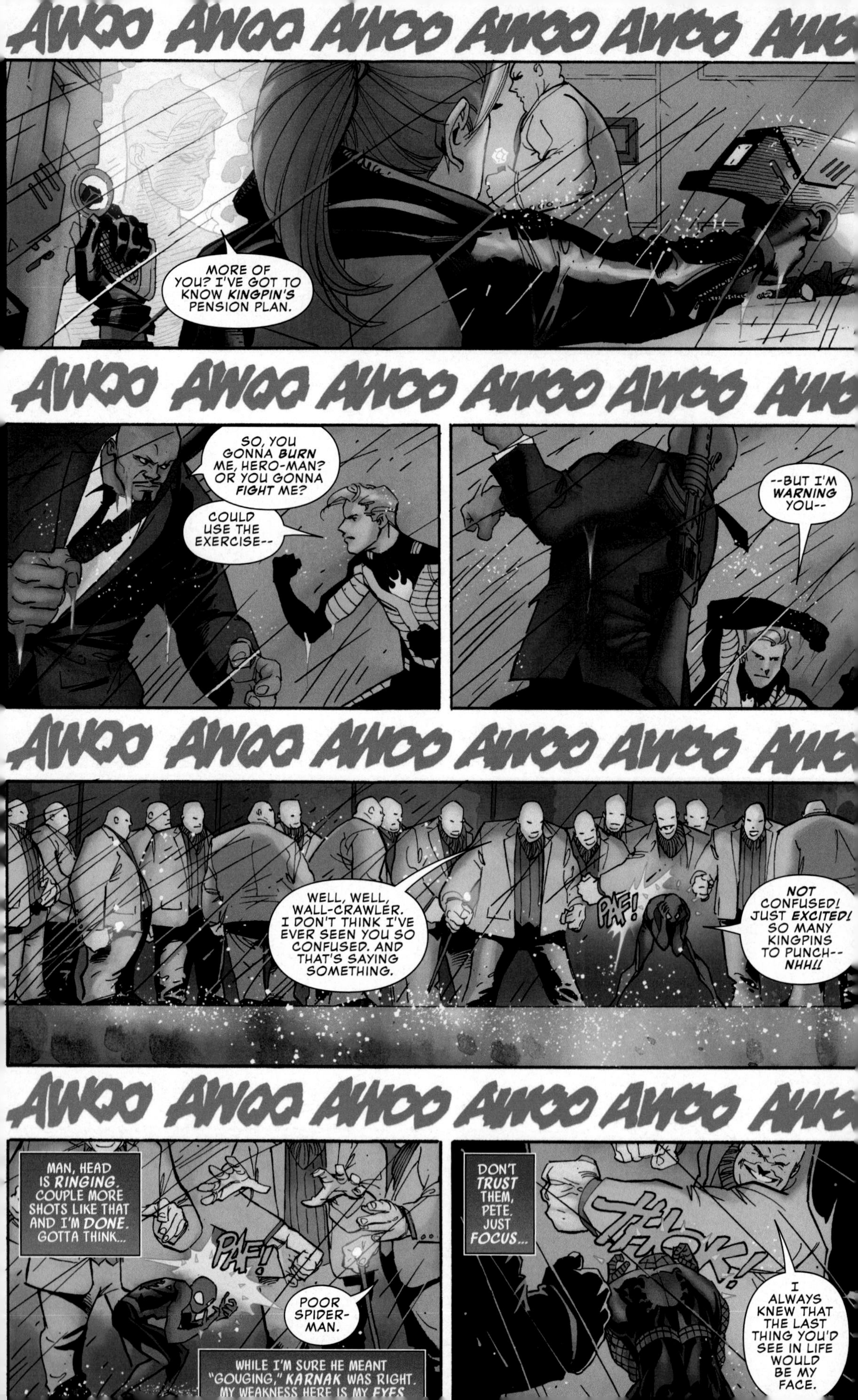
AWOO AWOO AWOO AWOO AWOO
MORE OF YOU? I'VE GOT TO KNOW KINGPIN'S PENSION PLAN.
AWOO AWOO AWOO AWOO AWOO
SO, YOU GONNA BURN ME, HERO-MAN? OR YOU GONNA FIGHT ME?
COULD USE THE EXERCISE--
--BUT I'M WARNING YOU--
AWOO AWOO AWOO AWOO AWOO
WELL, WELL, WALL-CRAWLER. I DON'T THINK I'VE EVER SEEN YOU SO CONFUSED. AND THAT'S SAYING SOMETHING.
PAF!
NOT CONFUSED! JUST EXCITED! SO MANY KINGPINS TO PUNCH-- NHH!!
AWOO AWOO AWOO AWOO AWOO
MAN, HEAD IS RINGING. COUPLE MORE SHOTS LIKE THAT AND I'M DONE. GOTTA THINK...
PAF!
POOR SPIDER-MAN.
WHILE I'M SURE HE MEANT "GOUGING," KARNAK WAS RIGHT. MY WEAKNESS HERE IS MY EYES
DON'T TRUST THEM, PETE. JUST FOCUS...
THOK!
I ALWAYS KNEW THAT THE LAST THING YOU'D SEE IN LIFE WOULD BE MY FACE.

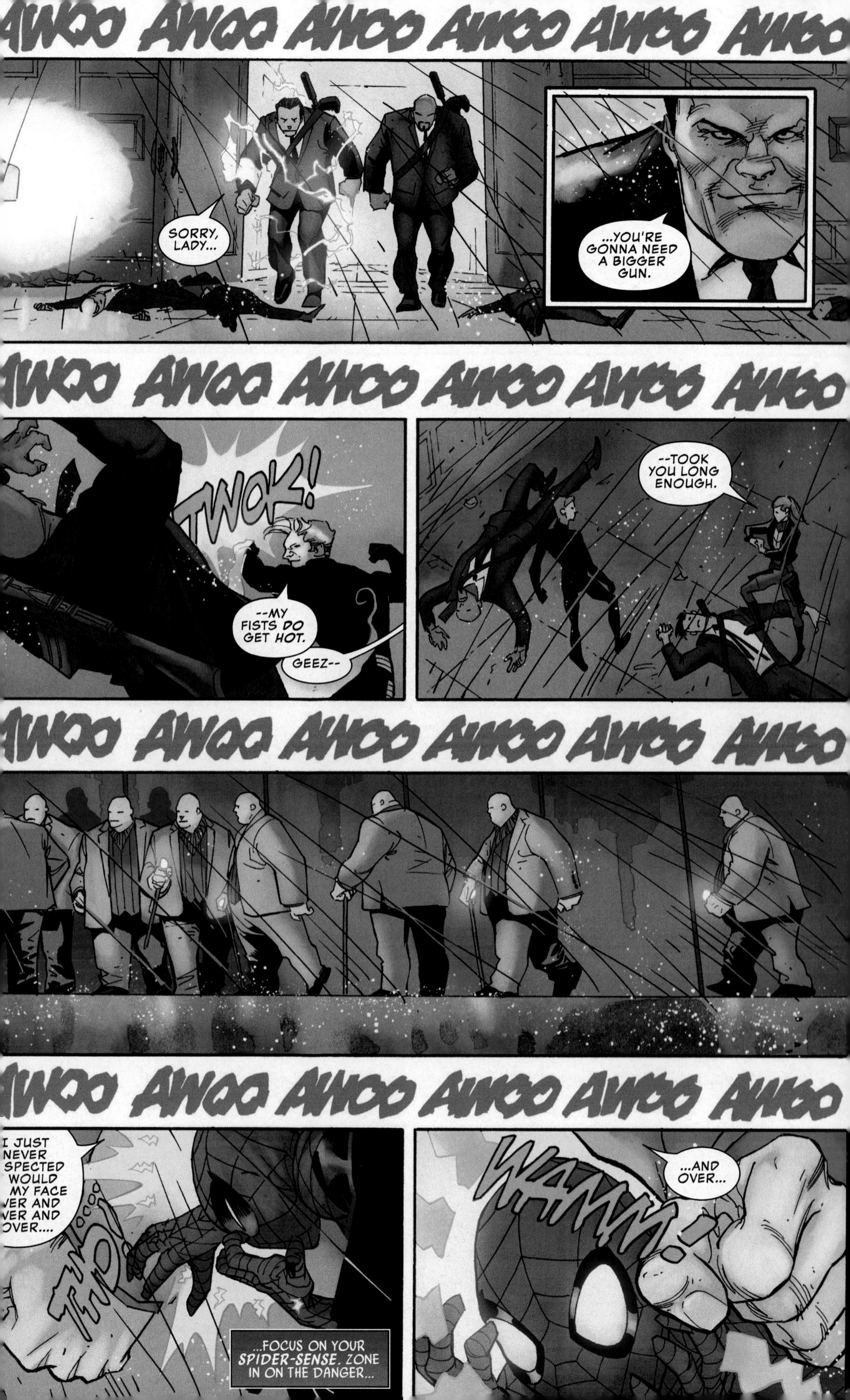
AWOO AWOO AWOO AWOO AWOO AWOO
SORRY, LADY...
...YOU'RE GONNA NEED A BIGGER GUN.
AWOO AWOO AWOO AWOO AWOO AWOO
TWOK!
GEEZ--
--MY FISTS DO GET HOT.
--TOOK YOU LONG ENOUGH.
AWOO AWOO AWOO AWOO AWOO AWOO
AWOO AWOO AWOO AWOO AWOO AWOO
I JUST NEVER SPECTED WOULD MY FACE VER AND VER AND OVER....
THOCOOO
...FOCUS ON YOUR SPIDER-SENSE. ZONE IN ON THE DANGER...
WAMM
...AND OVER...

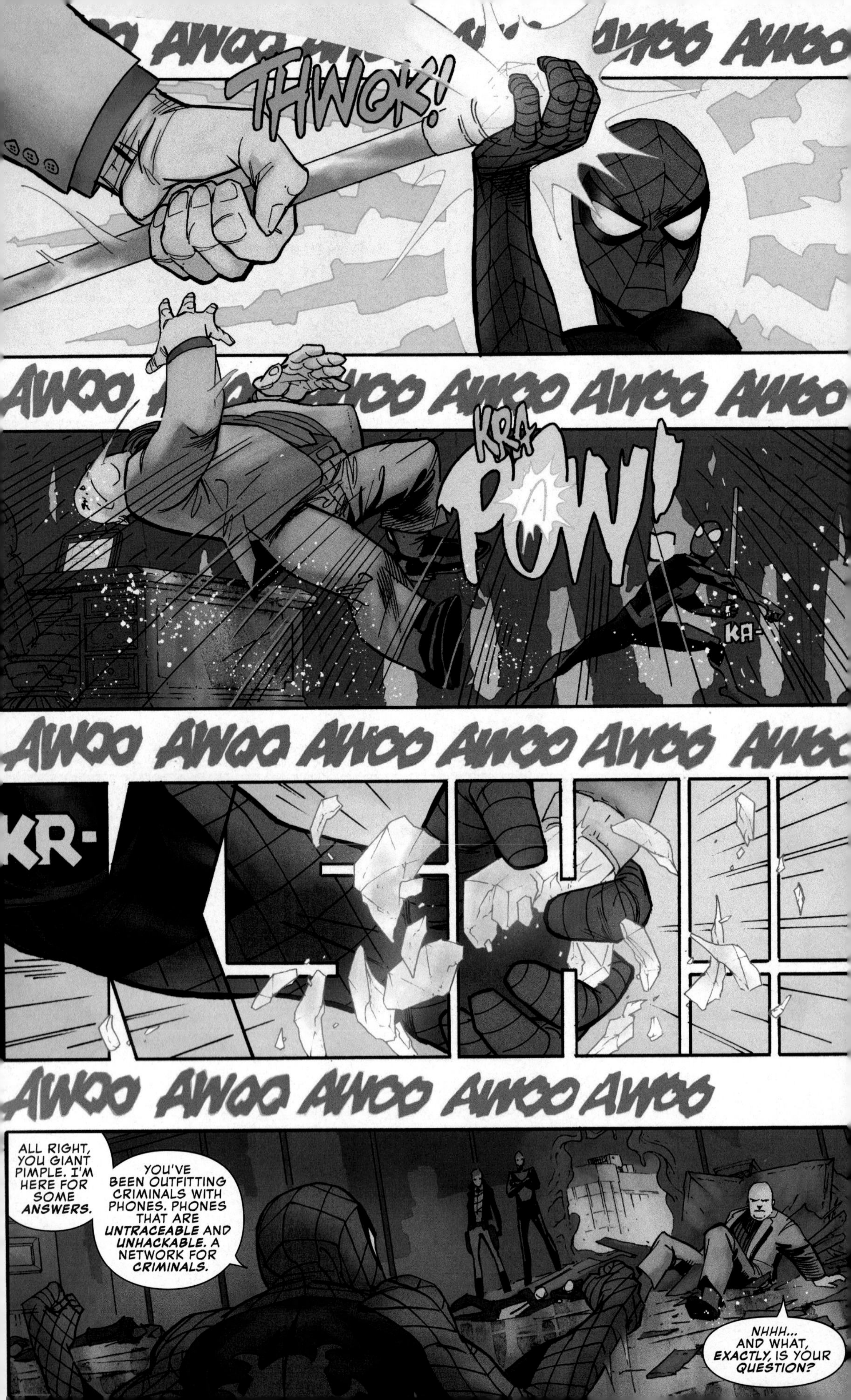
AWOO AWOO AWOO AWOO
THWOK!
AWOO AWOO AWOO AWOO AWOO AWOO
KRA-POW!
KA-
AWOO AWOO AWOO AWOO AWOO AWOO
KR-
AWOO AWOO AWOO AWOO AWOO
ALL RIGHT, YOU GIANT PIMPLE. I'M HERE FOR SOME ANSWERS.
YOU'VE BEEN OUTFITTING CRIMINALS WITH PHONES. PHONES THAT ARE UNTRACEABLE AND UNHACKABLE. A NETWORK FOR CRIMINALS.
NHHH... AND WHAT, EXACTLY, IS YOUR QUESTION?

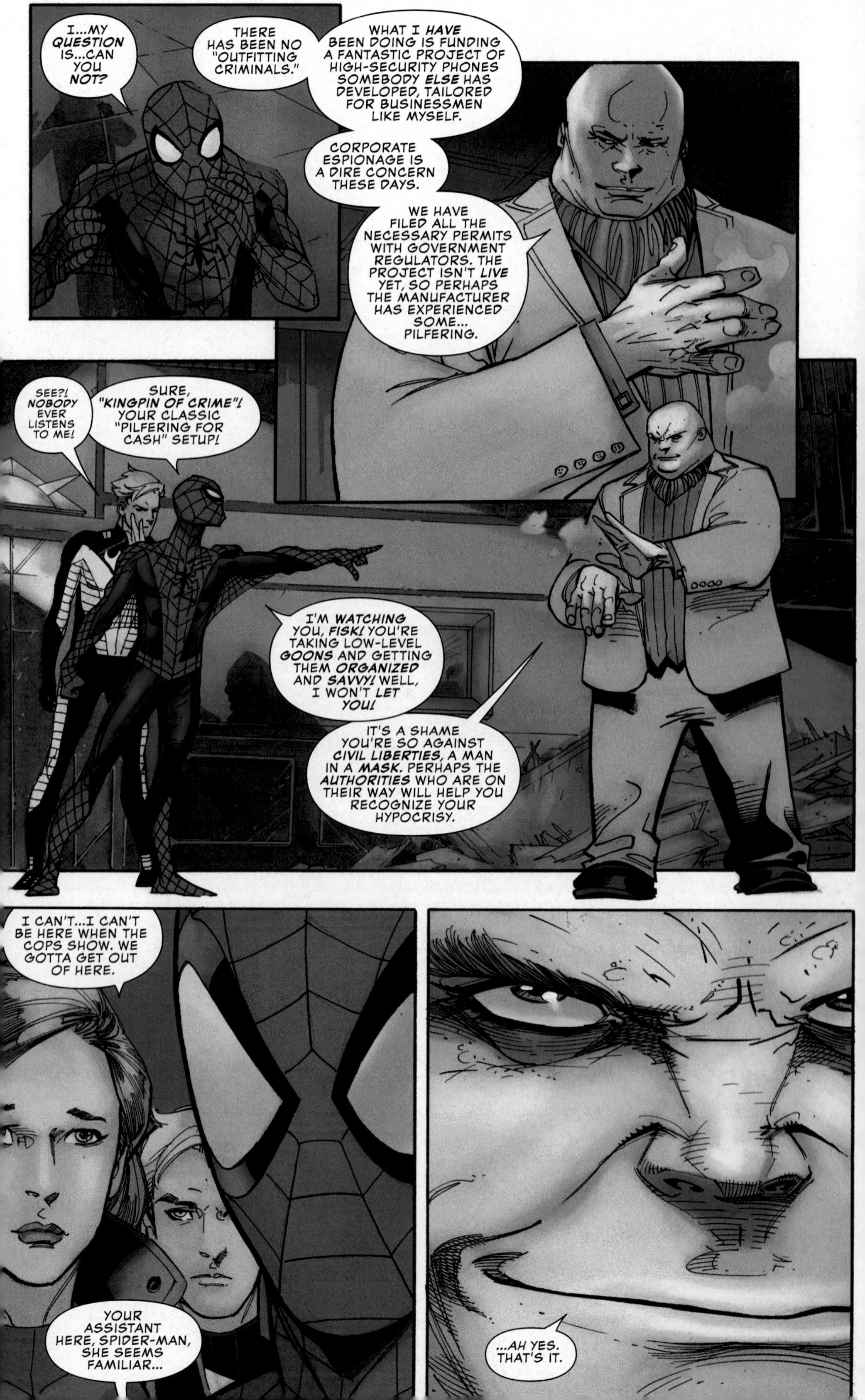
I...MY QUESTION IS...CAN YOU NOT?
THERE HAS BEEN NO "OUTFITTING CRIMINALS."
WHAT I HAVE BEEN DOING IS FUNDING A FANTASTIC PROJECT OF HIGH-SECURITY PHONES SOMEBODY ELSE HAS DEVELOPED, TAILORED FOR BUSINESSMEN LIKE MYSELF.
CORPORATE ESPIONAGE IS A DIRE CONCERN THESE DAYS.
WE HAVE FILED ALL THE NECESSARY PERMITS WITH GOVERNMENT REGULATORS. THE PROJECT ISN'T LIVE YET, SO PERHAPS THE MANUFACTURER HAS EXPERIENCED SOME... PILFERING.
SEE?! NOBODY EVER LISTENS TO ME!
SURE, "KINGPIN OF CRIME"! YOUR CLASSIC "PILFERING FOR CASH" SETUP!
I'M WATCHING YOU, FISK! YOU'RE TAKING LOW-LEVEL GOONS AND GETTING THEM ORGANIZED AND SAVVY! WELL, I WON'T LET YOU!
IT'S A SHAME YOU'RE SO AGAINST CIVIL LIBERTIES, A MAN IN A MASK. PERHAPS THE AUTHORITIES WHO ARE ON THEIR WAY WILL HELP YOU RECOGNIZE YOUR HYPOCRISY.
I CAN'T...I CAN'T BE HERE WHEN THE COPS SHOW. WE GOTTA GET OUT OF HERE.
YOUR ASSISTANT HERE, SPIDER-MAN, SHE SEEMS FAMILIAR...
...AH YES. THAT'S IT.

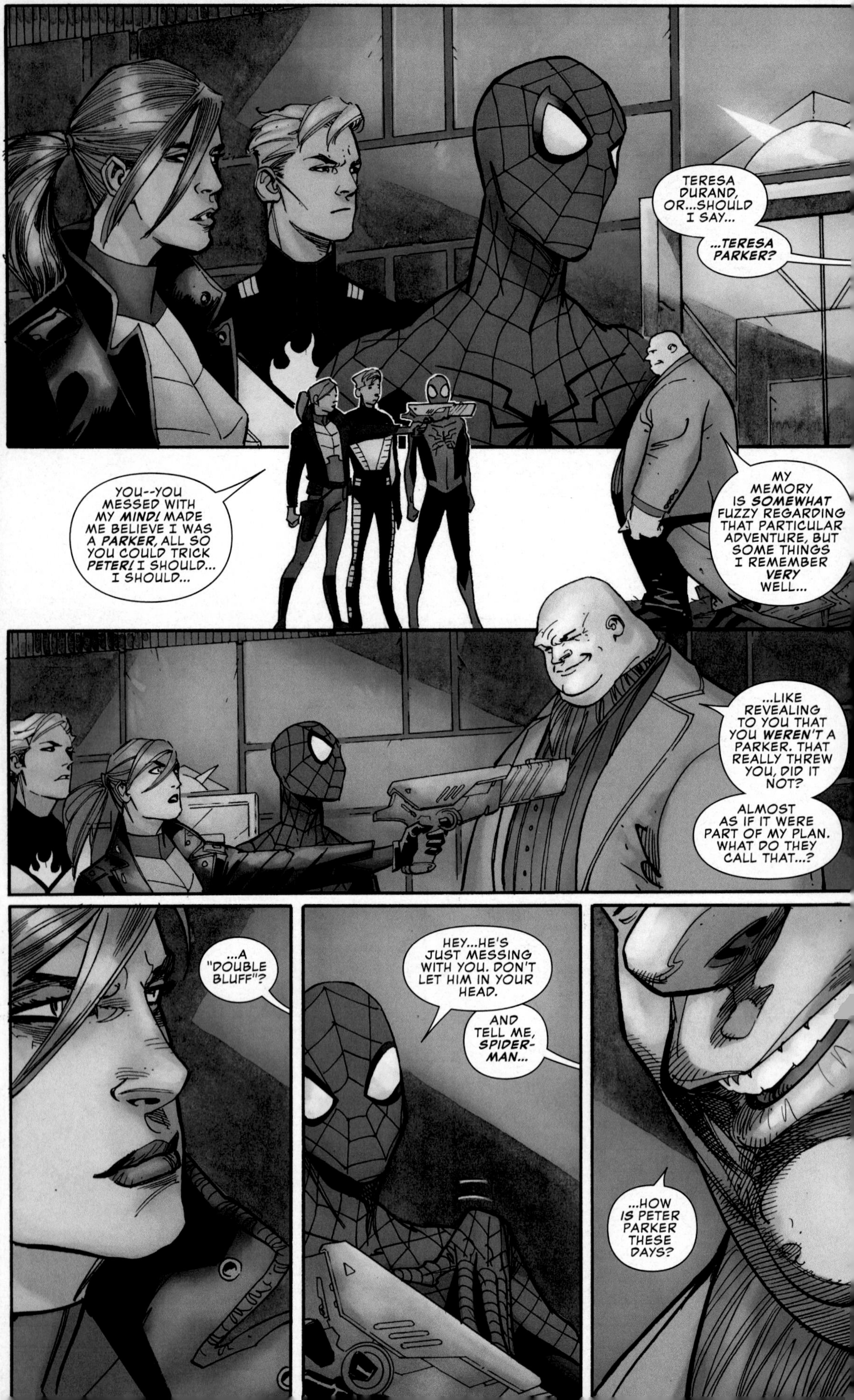
TERESA DURAND, OR...SHOULD I SAY...
...TERESA PARKER?
YOU--YOU MESSED WITH MY MIND! MADE ME BELIEVE I WAS A PARKER, ALL SO YOU COULD TRICK PETER! I SHOULD... I SHOULD...
MY MEMORY IS SOMEWHAT FUZZY REGARDING THAT PARTICULAR ADVENTURE, BUT SOME THINGS I REMEMBER VERY WELL...
...LIKE REVEALING TO YOU THAT YOU WEREN'T A PARKER. THAT REALLY THREW YOU, DID IT NOT?
ALMOST AS IF IT WERE PART OF MY PLAN. WHAT DO THEY CALL THAT...?
...A "DOUBLE BLUFF"?
HEY...HE'S JUST MESSING WITH YOU. DON'T LET HIM IN YOUR HEAD.
AND TELL ME, SPIDER-MAN...
...HOW IS PETER PARKER THESE DAYS?

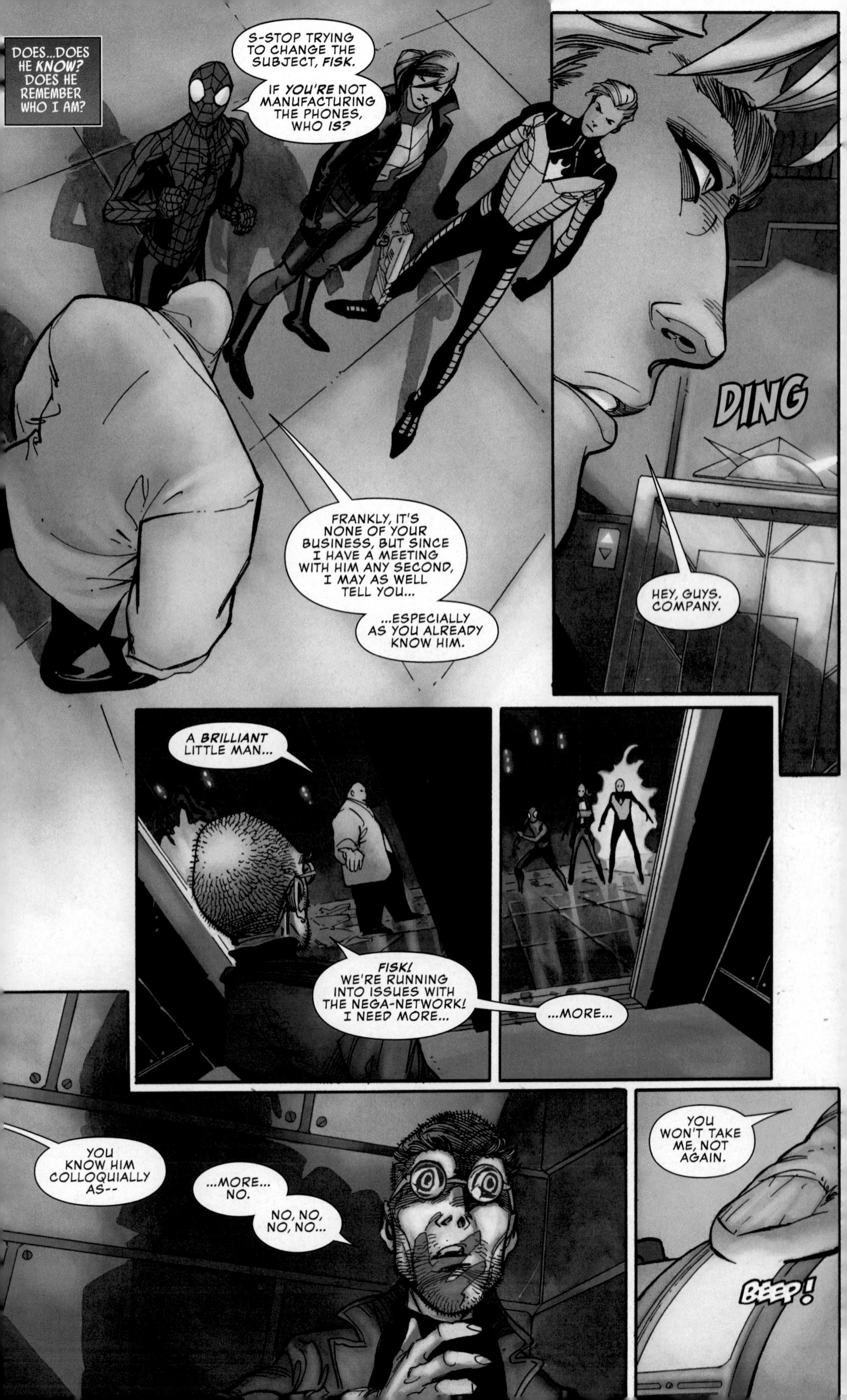
DOES...DOES HE *KNOW?* DOES HE REMEMBER WHO I AM?
S-STOP TRYING TO CHANGE THE SUBJECT, *FISK.*
IF *YOU'RE* NOT MANUFACTURING THE PHONES, WHO *IS?*
FRANKLY, IT'S NONE OF YOUR BUSINESS, BUT SINCE I HAVE A MEETING WITH HIM ANY SECOND, I MAY AS WELL TELL YOU...
...ESPECIALLY AS YOU ALREADY KNOW HIM.
DING
HEY, GUYS. COMPANY.
A *BRILLIANT* LITTLE MAN...
FISK! WE'RE RUNNING INTO ISSUES WITH THE NEGA-NETWORK! I NEED MORE...
...MORE...
YOU KNOW HIM COLLOQUIALLY AS--
...MORE... NO.
NO, NO, NO, NO...
YOU WON'T TAKE ME, NOT AGAIN.
BEEP!

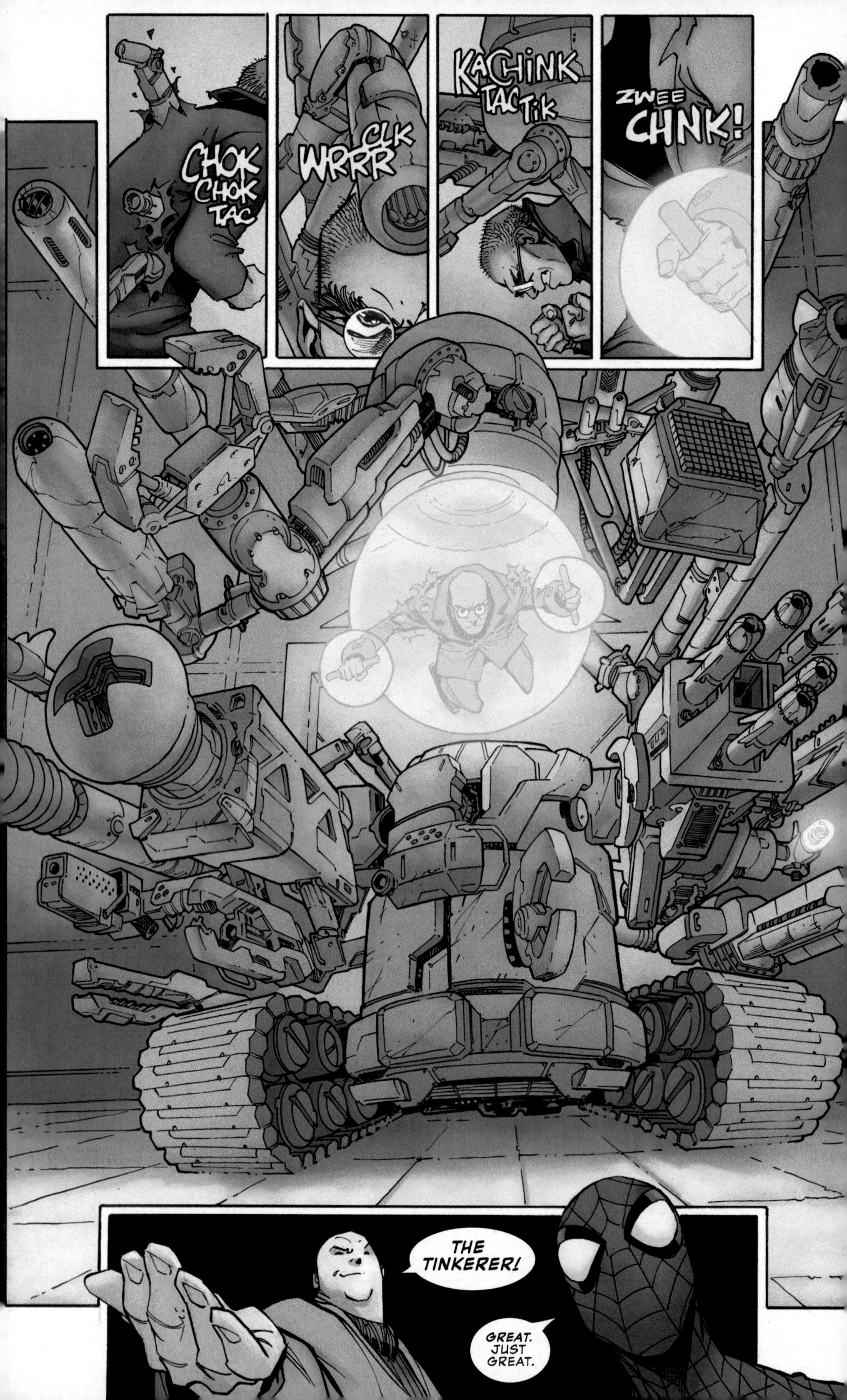
CHOK
CHOK
TAC
WRRR
CLK
KACHINK
TAC TIK
ZWEE
CHNK!
THE TINKERER!
GREAT. JUST GREAT.

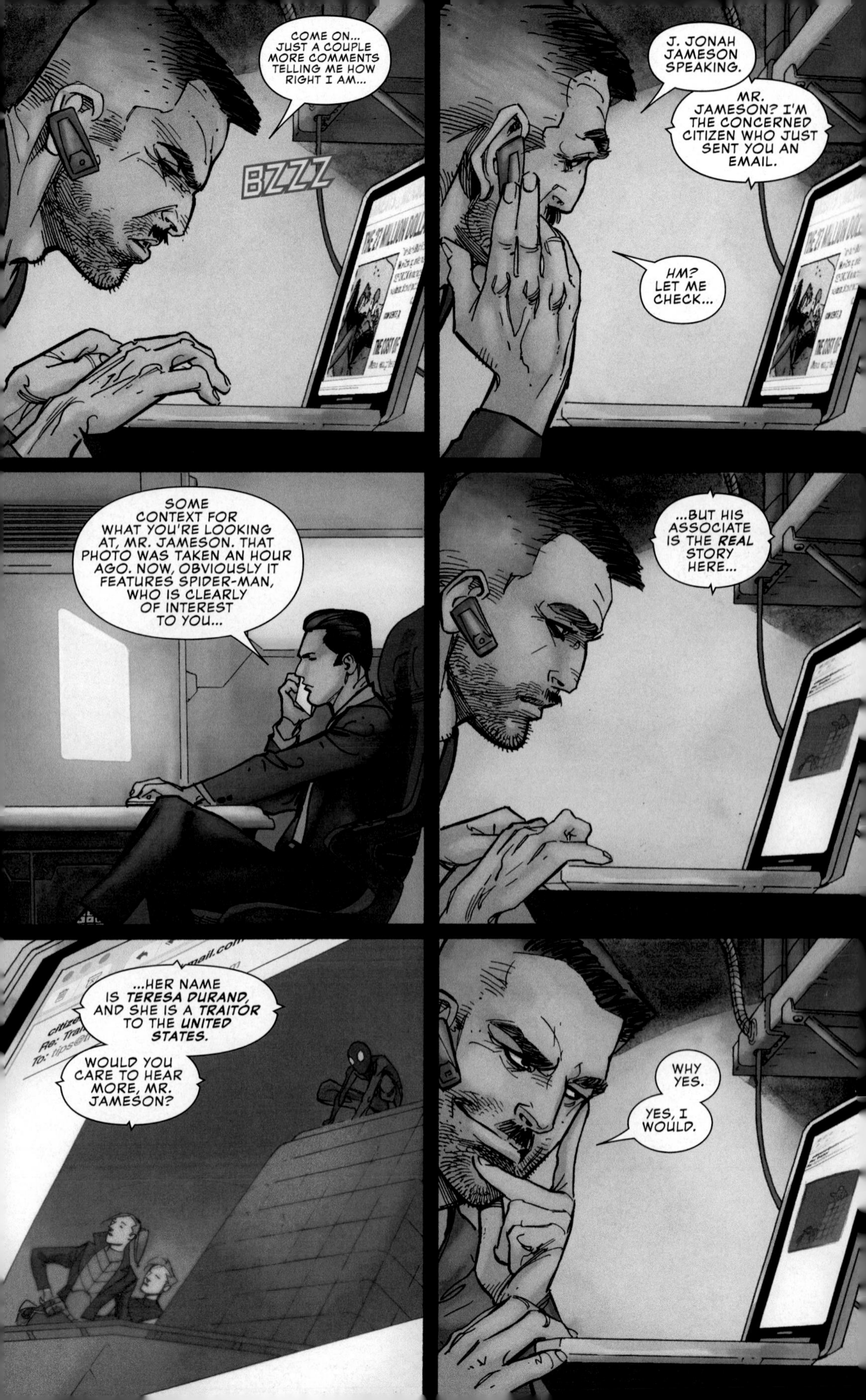
COME ON... JUST A COUPLE MORE COMMENTS TELLING ME HOW RIGHT I AM...
BZZZ
J. JONAH JAMESON SPEAKING.
MR. JAMESON? I'M THE CONCERNED CITIZEN WHO JUST SENT YOU AN EMAIL.
HM? LET ME CHECK...
SOME CONTEXT FOR WHAT YOU'RE LOOKING AT, MR. JAMESON. THAT PHOTO WAS TAKEN AN HOUR AGO. NOW, OBVIOUSLY IT FEATURES SPIDER-MAN, WHO IS CLEARLY OF INTEREST TO YOU...
...BUT HIS ASSOCIATE IS THE *REAL* STORY HERE...
...HER NAME IS *TERESA DURAND*, AND SHE IS A *TRAITOR* TO THE *UNITED STATES*.
WOULD YOU CARE TO HEAR MORE, MR. JAMESON?
WHY YES.
YES, I WOULD.

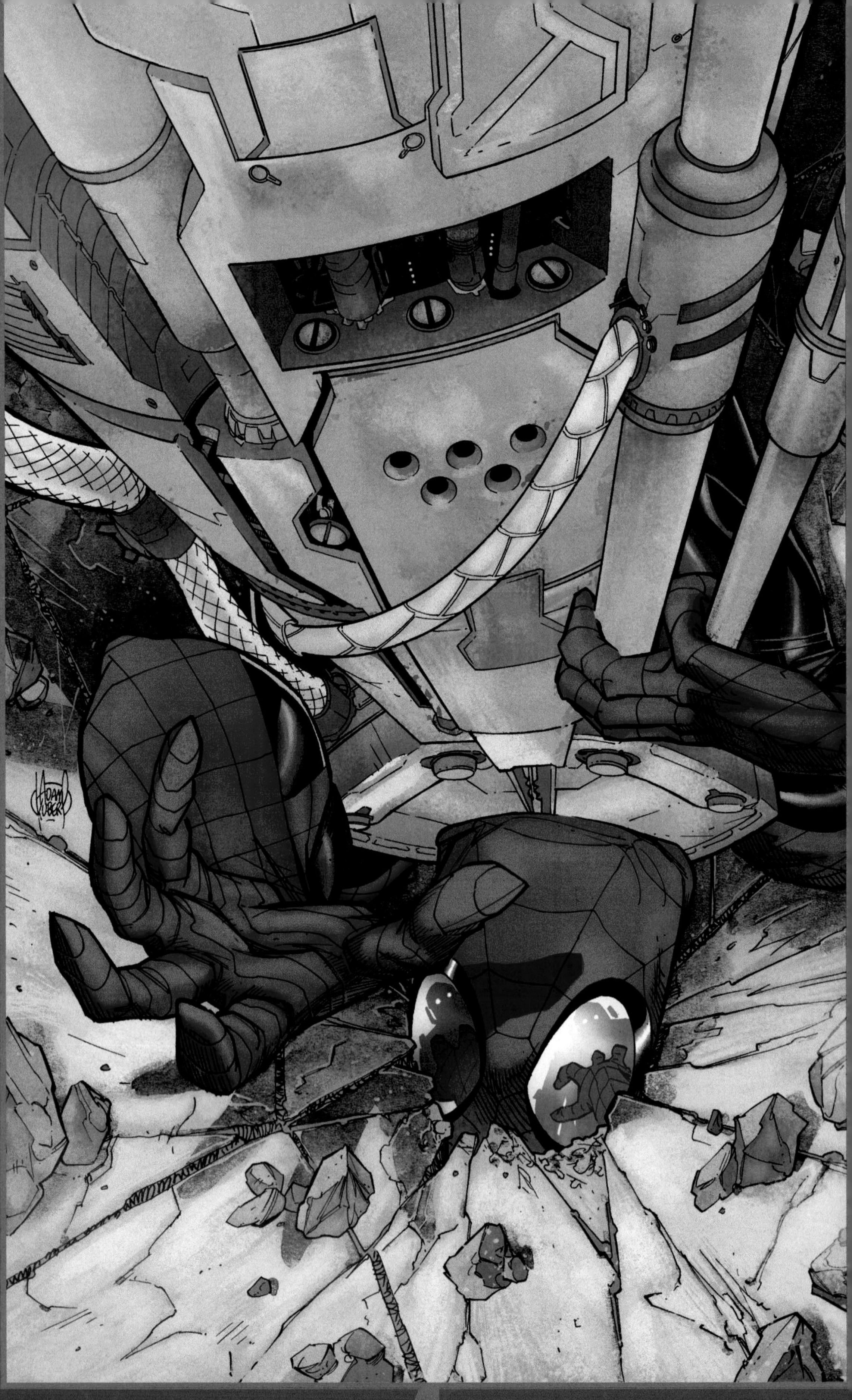

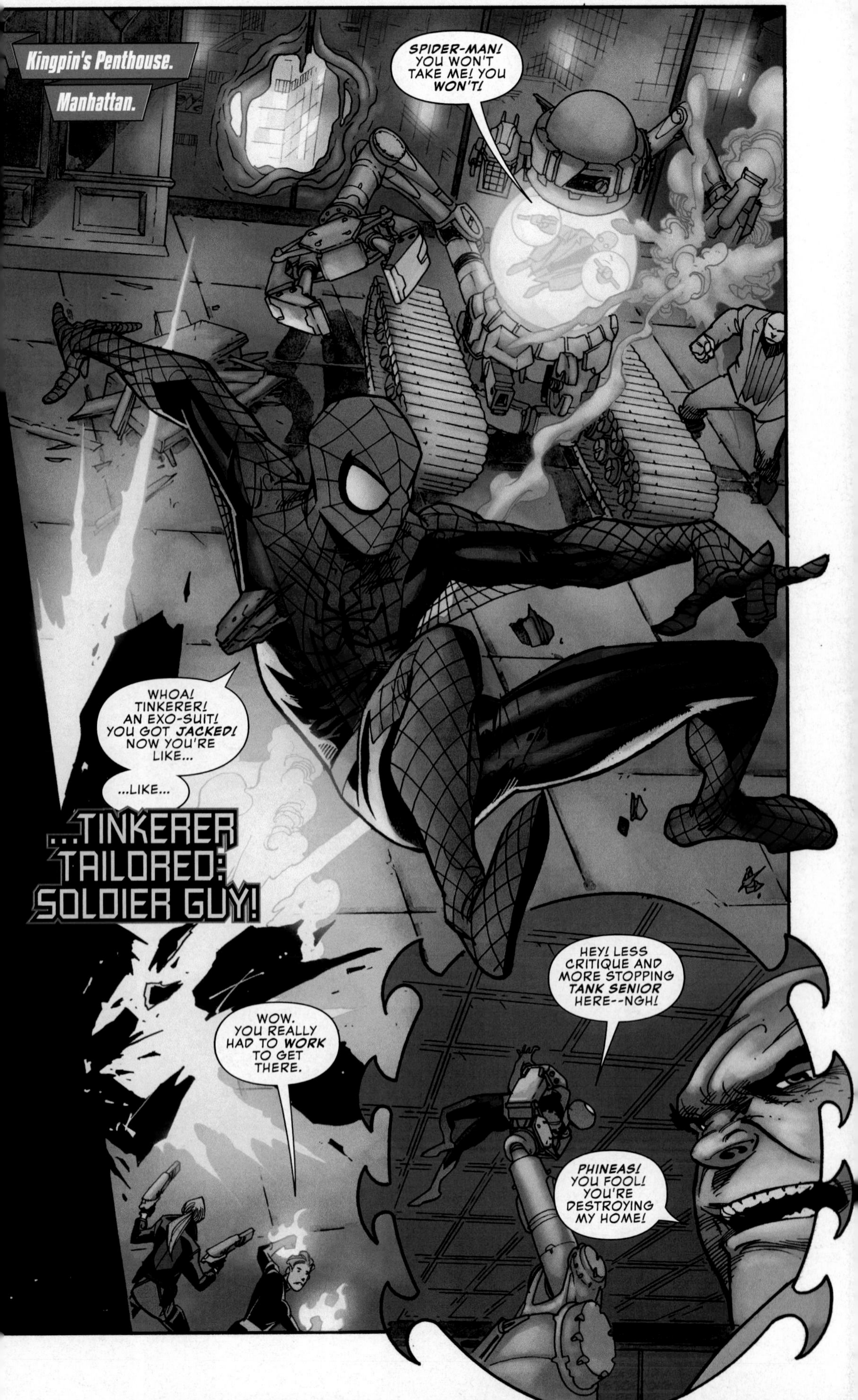
Kingpin's Penthouse.
Manhattan.
SPIDER-MAN! YOU WON'T TAKE ME! YOU WON'T!
WHOA! TINKERER! AN EXO-SUIT! YOU GOT JACKED! NOW YOU'RE LIKE...
...LIKE...
...TINKERER TAILORED: SOLDIER GUY!
WOW. YOU REALLY HAD TO WORK TO GET THERE.
HEY! LESS CRITIQUE AND MORE STOPPING TANK SENIOR HERE--NGH!
PHINEAS! YOU FOOL! YOU'RE DESTROYING MY HOME!

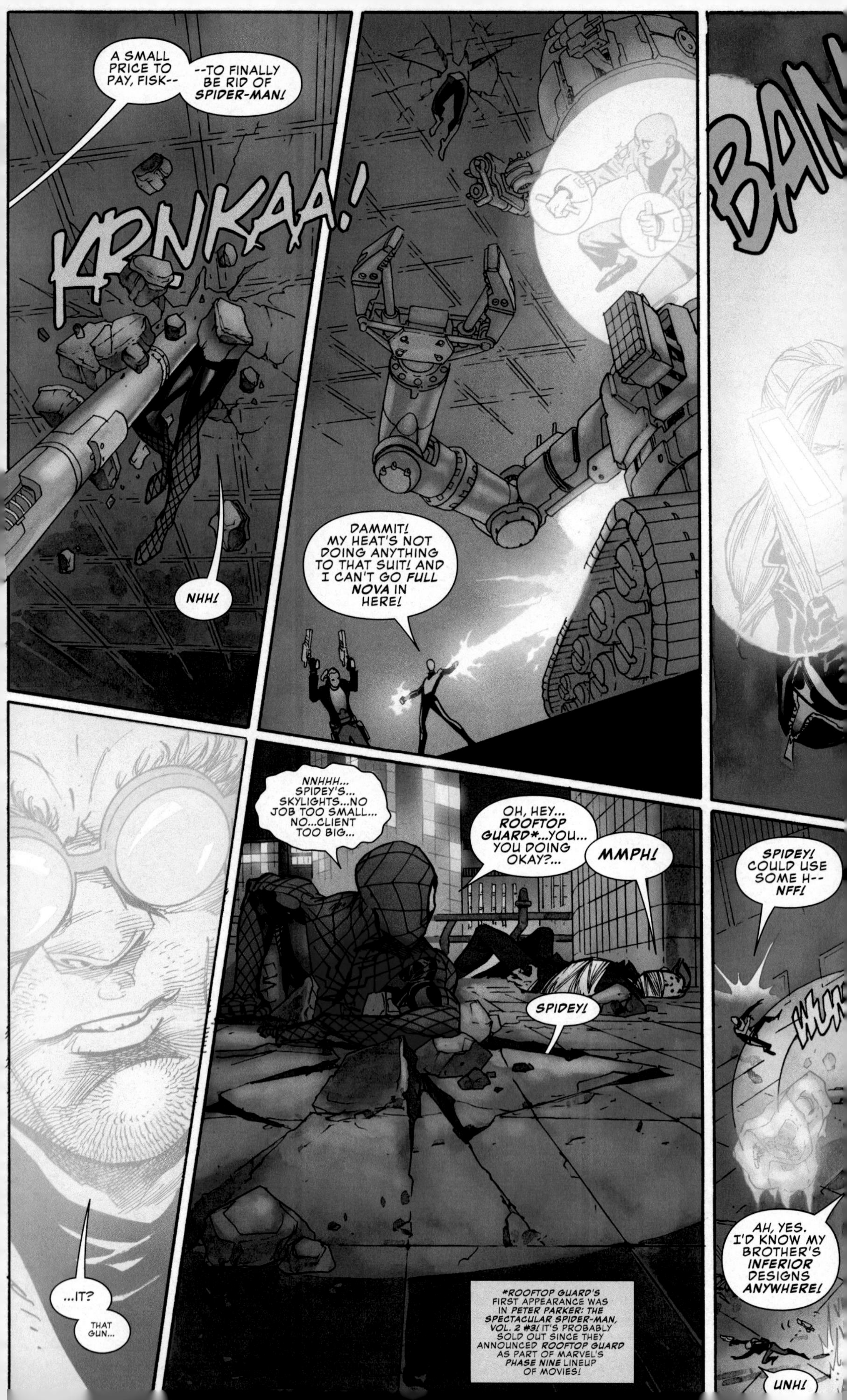

A SMALL PRICE TO PAY, FISK--
--TO FINALLY BE RID OF SPIDER-MAN!
KRNKAA!
NHH!
DAMMIT! MY HEAT'S NOT DOING ANYTHING TO THAT SUIT! AND I CAN'T GO FULL NOVA IN HERE!
...IT?
THAT GUN...
NNHHH... SPIDEY'S... SKYLIGHTS...NO JOB TOO SMALL... NO...CLIENT TOO BIG...
OH, HEY... ROOFTOP GUARD*...YOU... YOU DOING OKAY?...
MMPH!
SPIDEY!
*ROOFTOP GUARD'S FIRST APPEARANCE WAS IN PETER PARKER: THE SPECTACULAR SPIDER-MAN, VOL. 2 #3! IT'S PROBABLY SOLD OUT SINCE THEY ANNOUNCED ROOFTOP GUARD AS PART OF MARVEL'S PHASE NINE LINEUP OF MOVIES!
SPIDEY! COULD USE SOME H-- NFF!
AH, YES. I'D KNOW MY BROTHER'S INFERIOR DESIGNS ANYWHERE!
UNH!

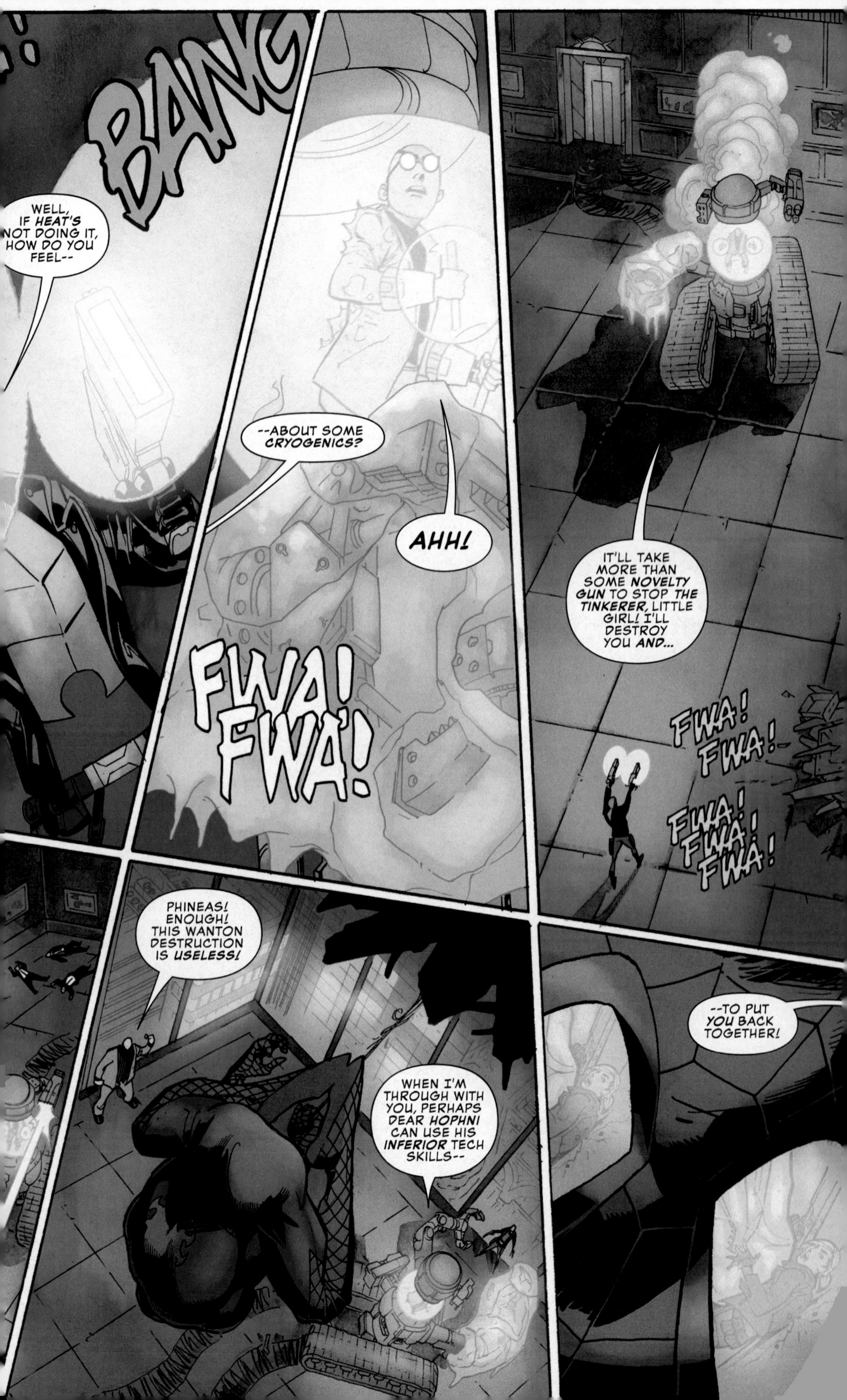
BANG
WELL, IF HEAT'S NOT DOING IT, HOW DO YOU FEEL--
--ABOUT SOME CRYOGENICS?
AHH!
FWA! FWA!
IT'LL TAKE MORE THAN SOME NOVELTY GUN TO STOP THE TINKERER, LITTLE GIRL! I'LL DESTROY YOU AND...
FWA! FWA!
FWA! FWA! FWA!
PHINEAS! ENOUGH! THIS WANTON DESTRUCTION IS USELESS!
WHEN I'M THROUGH WITH YOU, PERHAPS DEAR HOPHNI CAN USE HIS INFERIOR TECH SKILLS--
--TO PUT YOU BACK TOGETHER!

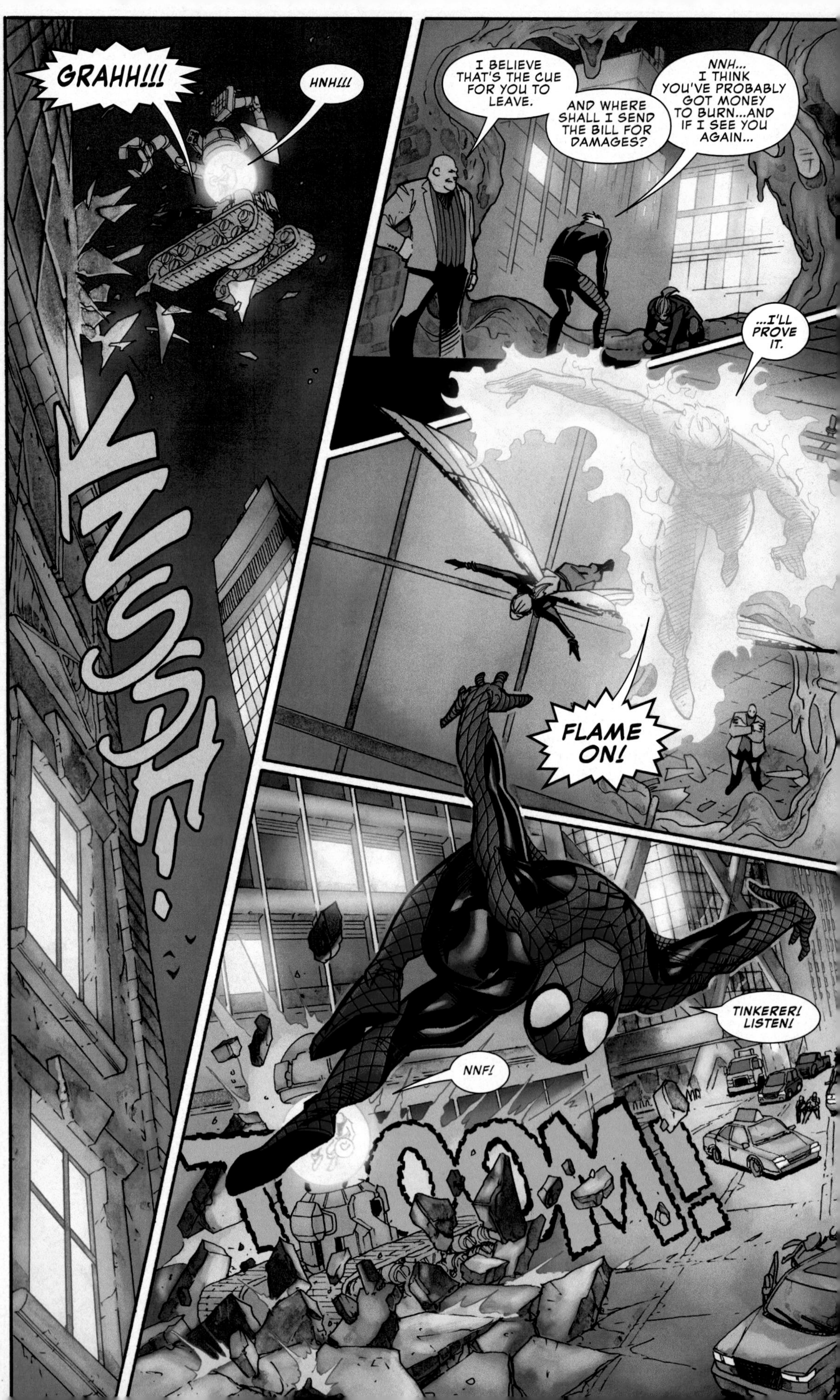
GRAHH!!!
HNH!!!
YANK!
I BELIEVE THAT'S THE CUE FOR YOU TO LEAVE.
AND WHERE SHALL I SEND THE BILL FOR DAMAGES?
NNH... I THINK YOU'VE PROBABLY GOT MONEY TO BURN...AND IF I SEE YOU AGAIN...
...I'LL PROVE IT.
FLAME ON!
TINKERER! LISTEN!
NNF!
BOOM!

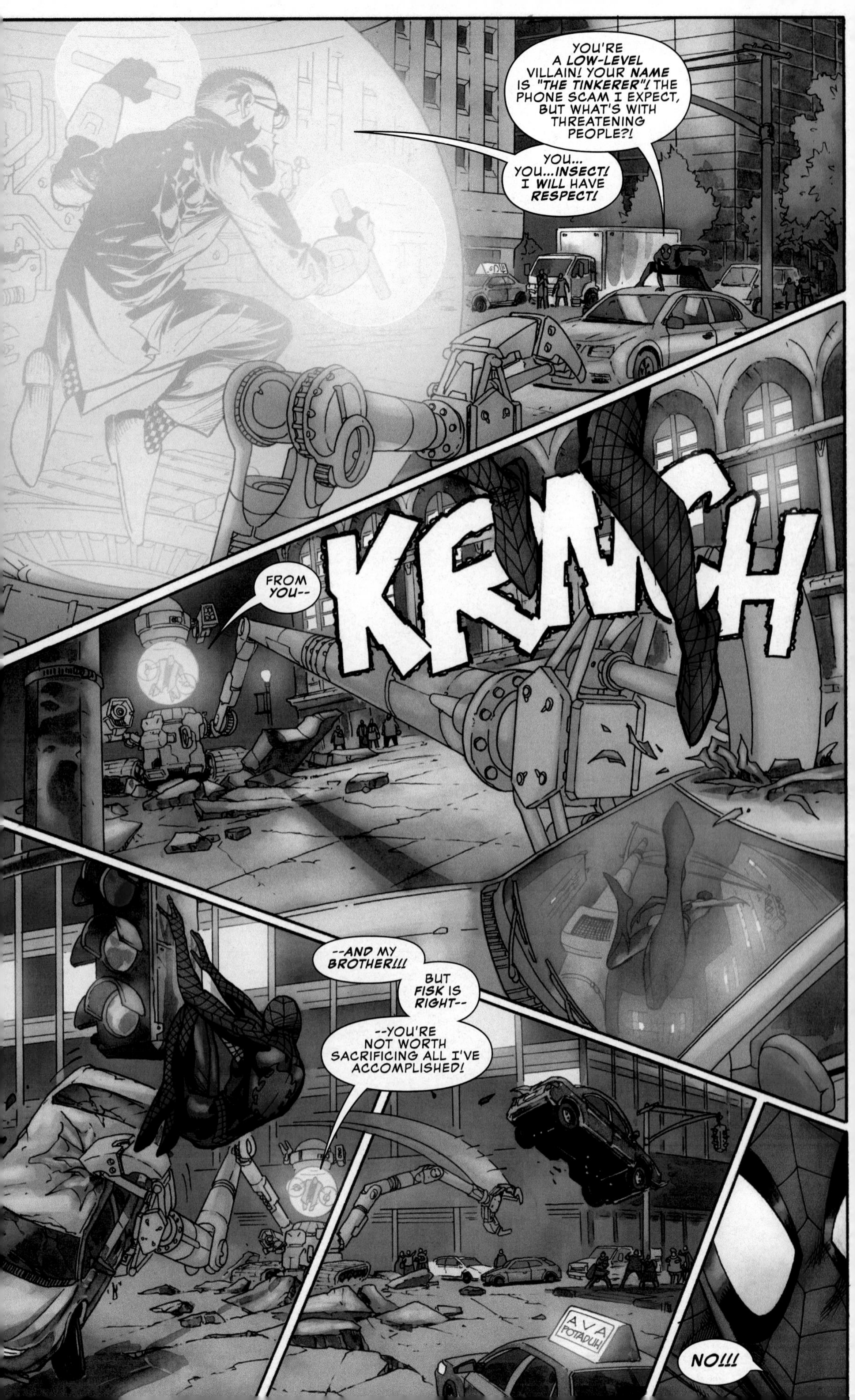
YOU'RE A LOW-LEVEL VILLAIN! YOUR NAME IS "THE TINKERER"! THE PHONE SCAM I EXPECT, BUT WHAT'S WITH THREATENING PEOPLE?!
YOU... YOU...INSECT! I WILL HAVE RESPECT!
FROM YOU--
KRNCH
--AND MY BROTHER!!!
BUT FISK IS RIGHT--
--YOU'RE NOT WORTH SACRIFICING ALL I'VE ACCOMPLISHED!
AVA POTADUH
NO!!!

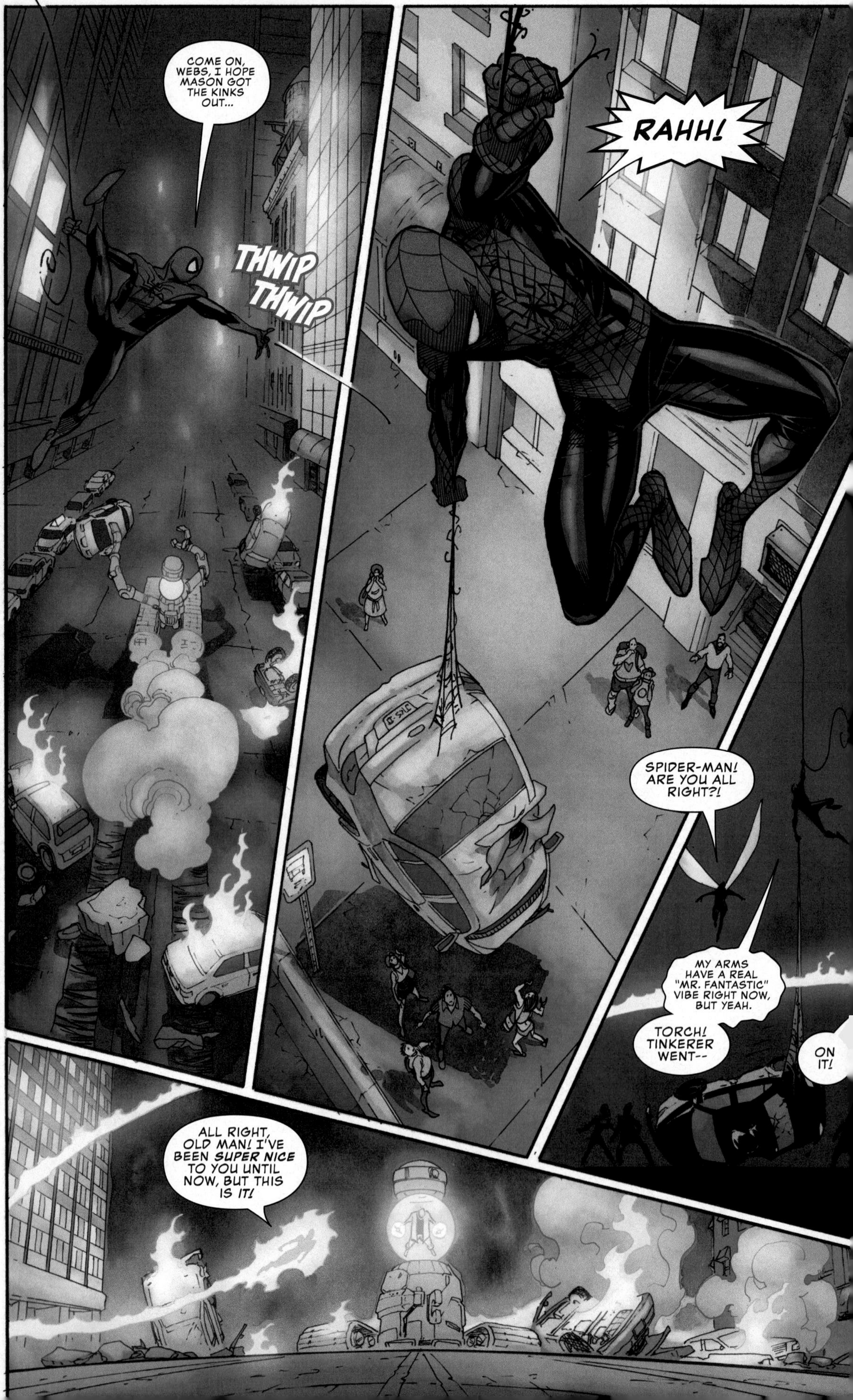
COME ON, WEBS, I HOPE MASON GOT THE KINKS OUT...
THWIP THWIP
RAHH!
SPIDER-MAN! ARE YOU ALL RIGHT?!
MY ARMS HAVE A REAL "MR. FANTASTIC" VIBE RIGHT NOW, BUT YEAH.
TORCH! TINKERER WENT--
ON IT!
ALL RIGHT, OLD MAN! I'VE BEEN SUPER NICE TO YOU UNTIL NOW, BUT THIS IS IT!

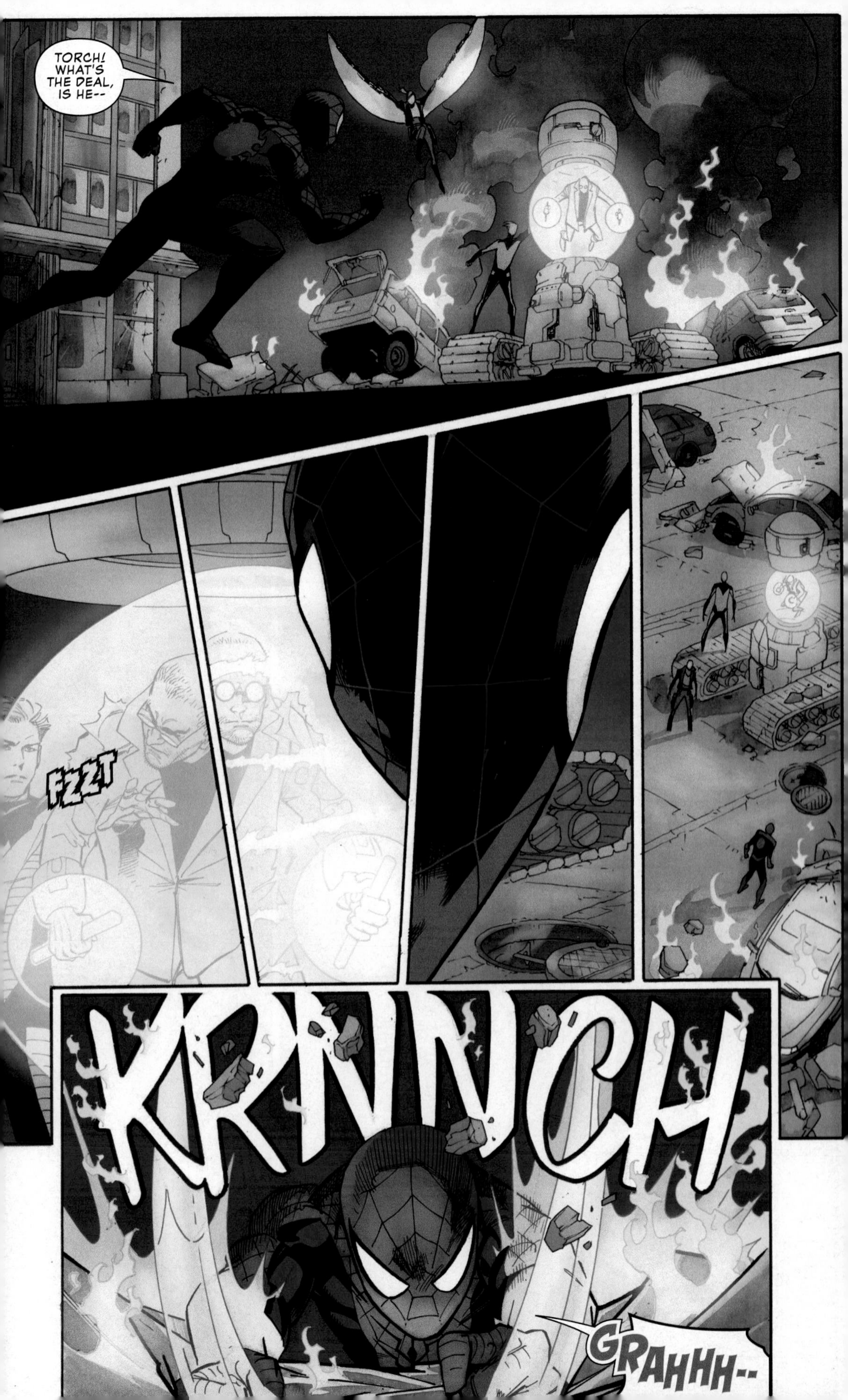
TORCH! WHAT'S THE DEAL, IS HE--
FZZT
KRNNCH
GRAHHH--

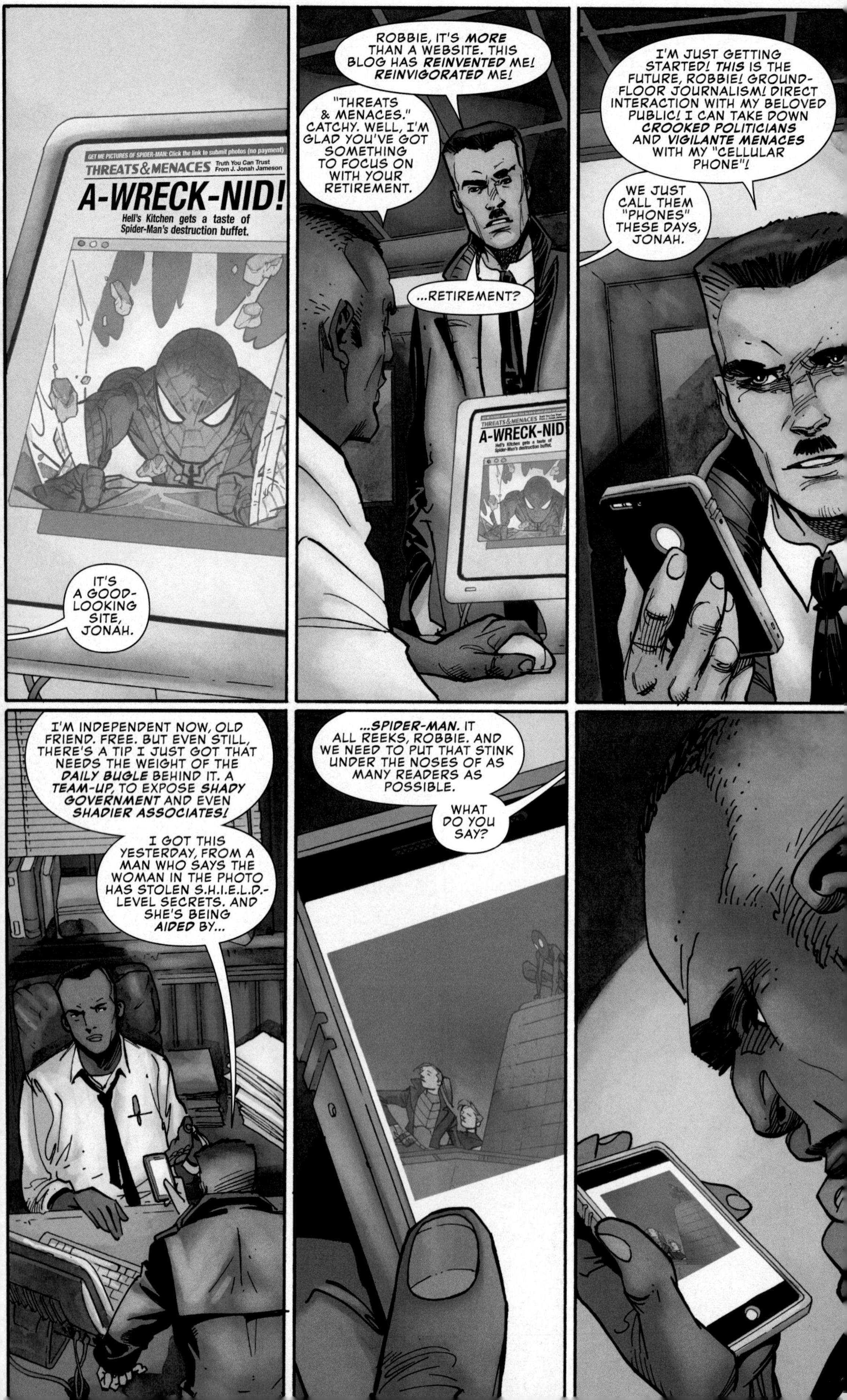
GET ME PICTURES OF SPIDER-MAN: Click the link to submit photos (no payment)
THREATS & MENACES Truth You Can Trust From J. Jonah Jameson
A-WRECK-NID!
Hell's Kitchen gets a taste of Spider-Man's destruction buffet.
IT'S A GOOD-LOOKING SITE, JONAH.
ROBBIE, IT'S MORE THAN A WEBSITE. THIS BLOG HAS REINVENTED ME! REINVIGORATED ME!
"THREATS & MENACES." CATCHY. WELL, I'M GLAD YOU'VE GOT SOMETHING TO FOCUS ON WITH YOUR RETIREMENT.
...RETIREMENT?
I'M JUST GETTING STARTED! THIS IS THE FUTURE, ROBBIE! GROUND-FLOOR JOURNALISM! DIRECT INTERACTION WITH MY BELOVED PUBLIC! I CAN TAKE DOWN CROOKED POLITICIANS AND VIGILANTE MENACES WITH MY "CELLULAR PHONE"!
WE JUST CALL THEM "PHONES" THESE DAYS, JONAH.
I'M INDEPENDENT NOW, OLD FRIEND. FREE. BUT EVEN STILL, THERE'S A TIP I JUST GOT THAT NEEDS THE WEIGHT OF THE DAILY BUGLE BEHIND IT. A TEAM-UP, TO EXPOSE SHADY GOVERNMENT AND EVEN SHADIER ASSOCIATES!
I GOT THIS YESTERDAY, FROM A MAN WHO SAYS THE WOMAN IN THE PHOTO HAS STOLEN S.H.I.E.L.D.-LEVEL SECRETS. AND SHE'S BEING AIDED BY...
...SPIDER-MAN. IT ALL REEKS, ROBBIE. AND WE NEED TO PUT THAT STINK UNDER THE NOSES OF AS MANY READERS AS POSSIBLE.
WHAT DO YOU SAY?

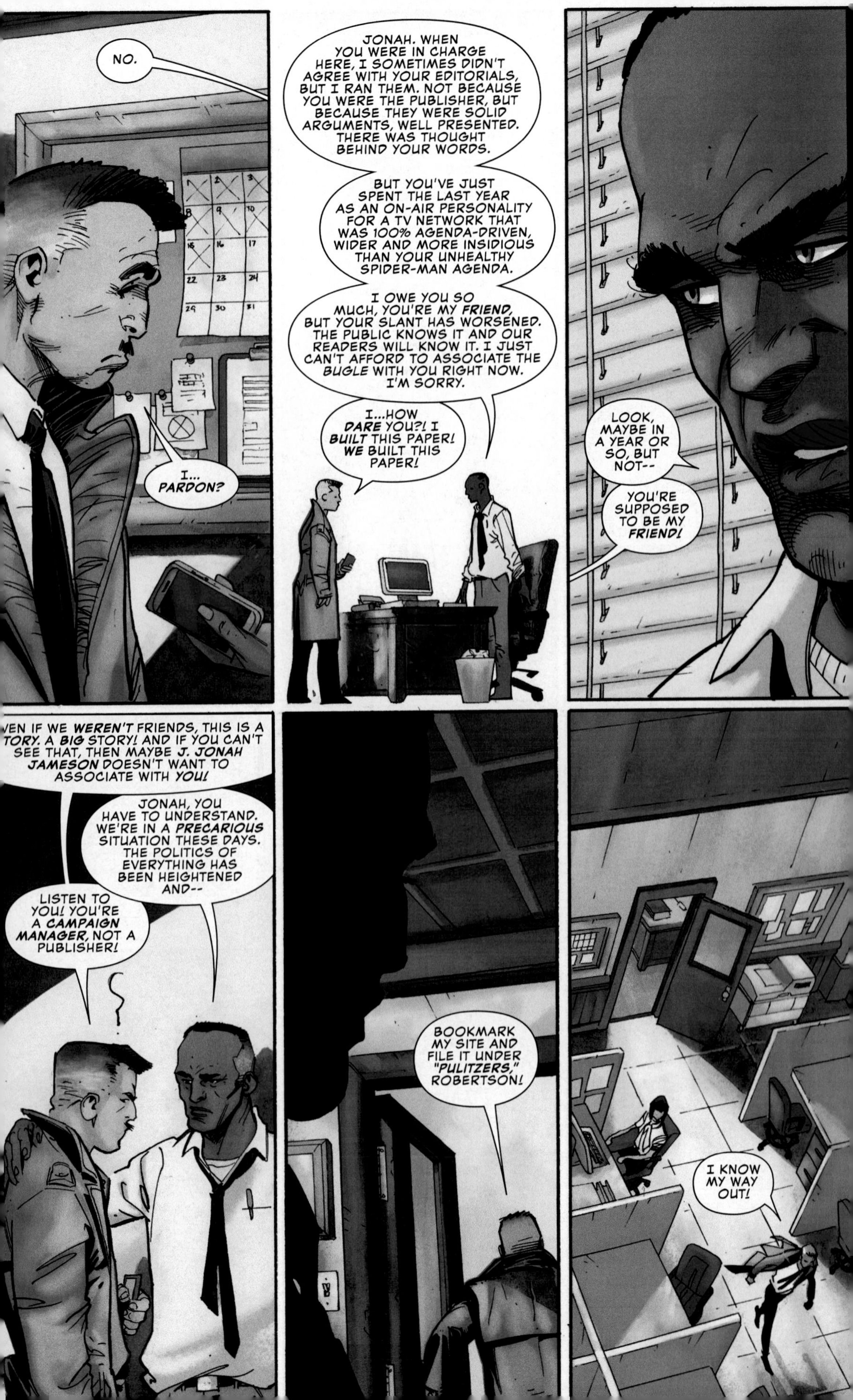
NO.
JONAH. WHEN YOU WERE IN CHARGE HERE, I SOMETIMES DIDN'T AGREE WITH YOUR EDITORIALS, BUT I RAN THEM. NOT BECAUSE YOU WERE THE PUBLISHER, BUT BECAUSE THEY WERE SOLID ARGUMENTS, WELL PRESENTED. THERE WAS THOUGHT BEHIND YOUR WORDS.
BUT YOU'VE JUST SPENT THE LAST YEAR AS AN ON-AIR PERSONALITY FOR A TV NETWORK THAT WAS 100% AGENDA-DRIVEN, WIDER AND MORE INSIDIOUS THAN YOUR UNHEALTHY SPIDER-MAN AGENDA.
I OWE YOU SO MUCH, YOU'RE MY FRIEND, BUT YOUR SLANT HAS WORSENED. THE PUBLIC KNOWS IT AND OUR READERS WILL KNOW IT. I JUST CAN'T AFFORD TO ASSOCIATE THE BUGLE WITH YOU RIGHT NOW. I'M SORRY.
I... PARDON?
I...HOW DARE YOU?! I BUILT THIS PAPER! WE BUILT THIS PAPER!
LOOK, MAYBE IN A YEAR OR SO, BUT NOT--
YOU'RE SUPPOSED TO BE MY FRIEND!
VEN IF WE WEREN'T FRIENDS, THIS IS A TORY. A BIG STORY! AND IF YOU CAN'T SEE THAT, THEN MAYBE J. JONAH JAMESON DOESN'T WANT TO ASSOCIATE WITH YOU!
JONAH, YOU HAVE TO UNDERSTAND. WE'RE IN A PRECARIOUS SITUATION THESE DAYS. THE POLITICS OF EVERYTHING HAS BEEN HEIGHTENED AND--
LISTEN TO YOU! YOU'RE A CAMPAIGN MANAGER, NOT A PUBLISHER!
BOOKMARK MY SITE AND FILE IT UNDER "PULITZERS," ROBERTSON!
I KNOW MY WAY OUT!

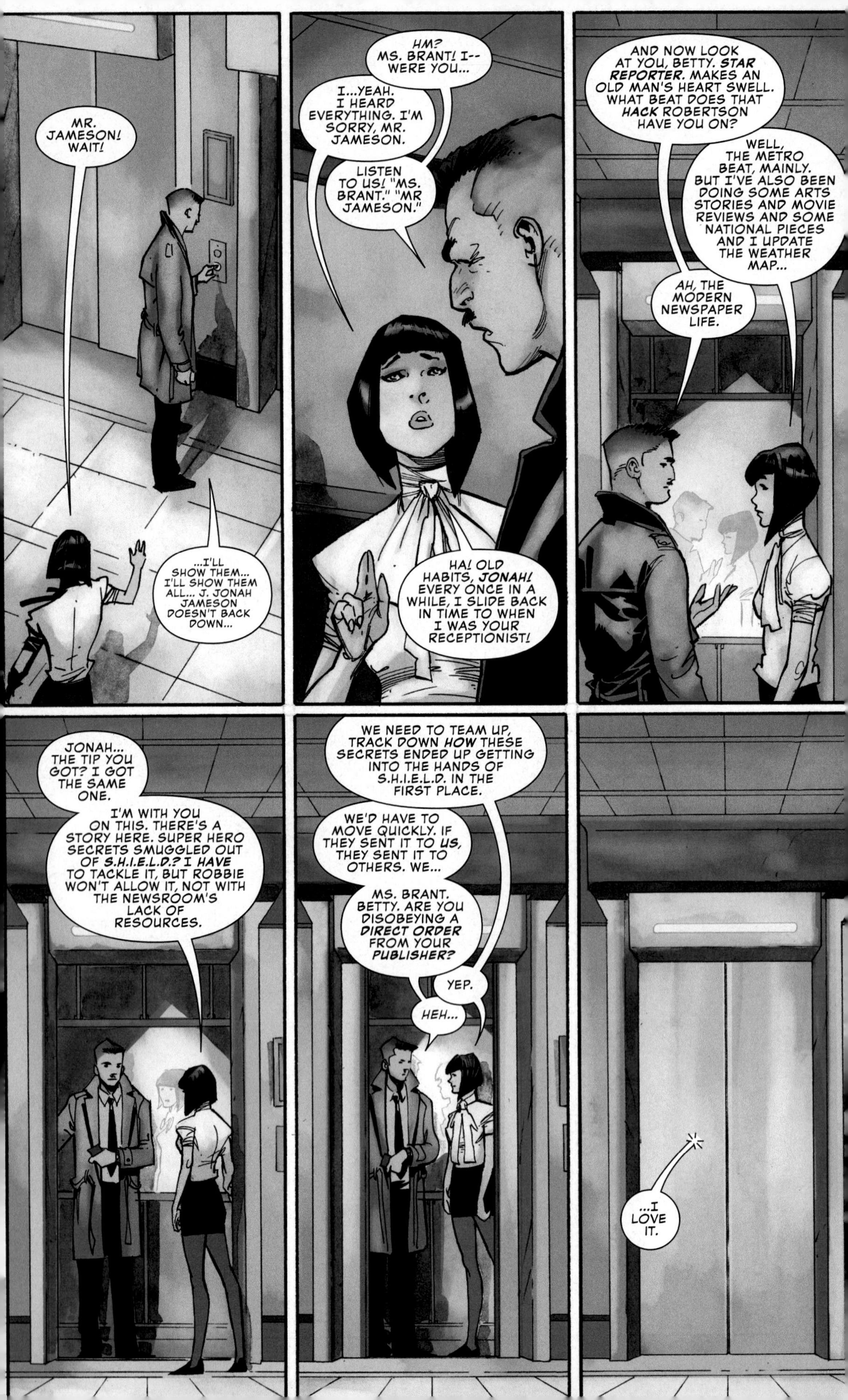

MR. JAMESON! WAIT!
...I'LL SHOW THEM... I'LL SHOW THEM ALL... J. JONAH JAMESON DOESN'T BACK DOWN...
HM? MS. BRANT! I--WERE YOU...
I...YEAH. I HEARD EVERYTHING. I'M SORRY, MR. JAMESON.
LISTEN TO US! "MS. BRANT." "MR JAMESON."
HA! OLD HABITS, JONAH! EVERY ONCE IN A WHILE, I SLIDE BACK IN TIME TO WHEN I WAS YOUR RECEPTIONIST!
AND NOW LOOK AT YOU, BETTY. STAR REPORTER. MAKES AN OLD MAN'S HEART SWELL. WHAT BEAT DOES THAT HACK ROBERTSON HAVE YOU ON?
WELL, THE METRO BEAT, MAINLY. BUT I'VE ALSO BEEN DOING SOME ARTS STORIES AND MOVIE REVIEWS AND SOME NATIONAL PIECES AND I UPDATE THE WEATHER MAP...
AH, THE MODERN NEWSPAPER LIFE.
JONAH... THE TIP YOU GOT? I GOT THE SAME ONE.
I'M WITH YOU ON THIS. THERE'S A STORY HERE. SUPER HERO SECRETS SMUGGLED OUT OF S.H.I.E.L.D.? I HAVE TO TACKLE IT, BUT ROBBIE WON'T ALLOW IT, NOT WITH THE NEWSROOM'S LACK OF RESOURCES.
WE NEED TO TEAM UP, TRACK DOWN HOW THESE SECRETS ENDED UP GETTING INTO THE HANDS OF S.H.I.E.L.D. IN THE FIRST PLACE.
WE'D HAVE TO MOVE QUICKLY. IF THEY SENT IT TO US, THEY SENT IT TO OTHERS. WE...
MS. BRANT. BETTY. ARE YOU DISOBEYING A DIRECT ORDER FROM YOUR PUBLISHER?
YEP.
HEH...
...I LOVE IT.

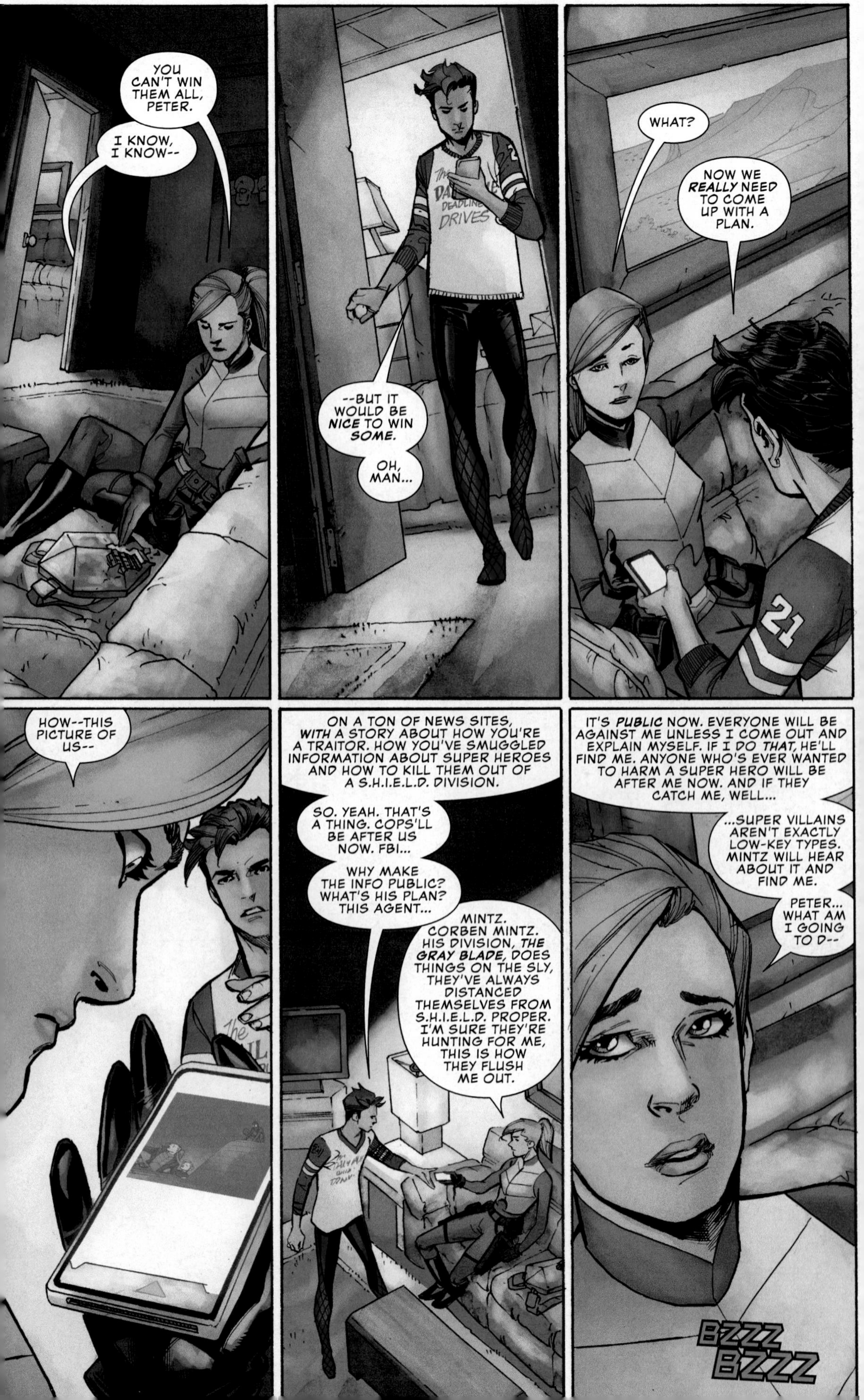
YOU CAN'T WIN THEM ALL, PETER.
I KNOW, I KNOW--
--BUT IT WOULD BE NICE TO WIN SOME.
OH, MAN...
WHAT?
NOW WE REALLY NEED TO COME UP WITH A PLAN.
HOW--THIS PICTURE OF US--
ON A TON OF NEWS SITES, WITH A STORY ABOUT HOW YOU'RE A TRAITOR. HOW YOU'VE SMUGGLED INFORMATION ABOUT SUPER HEROES AND HOW TO KILL THEM OUT OF A S.H.I.E.L.D. DIVISION.
SO. YEAH. THAT'S A THING. COPS'LL BE AFTER US NOW. FBI...
WHY MAKE THE INFO PUBLIC? WHAT'S HIS PLAN? THIS AGENT...
MINTZ. CORBEN MINTZ. HIS DIVISION, THE GRAY BLADE, DOES THINGS ON THE SLY, THEY'VE ALWAYS DISTANCED THEMSELVES FROM S.H.I.E.L.D. PROPER. I'M SURE THEY'RE HUNTING FOR ME, THIS IS HOW THEY FLUSH ME OUT.
IT'S PUBLIC NOW. EVERYONE WILL BE AGAINST ME UNLESS I COME OUT AND EXPLAIN MYSELF. IF I DO THAT, HE'LL FIND ME. ANYONE WHO'S EVER WANTED TO HARM A SUPER HERO WILL BE AFTER ME NOW. AND IF THEY CATCH ME, WELL...
...SUPER VILLAINS AREN'T EXACTLY LOW-KEY TYPES. MINTZ WILL HEAR ABOUT IT AND FIND ME.
PETER... WHAT AM I GOING TO D--
BZZZ BZZZ

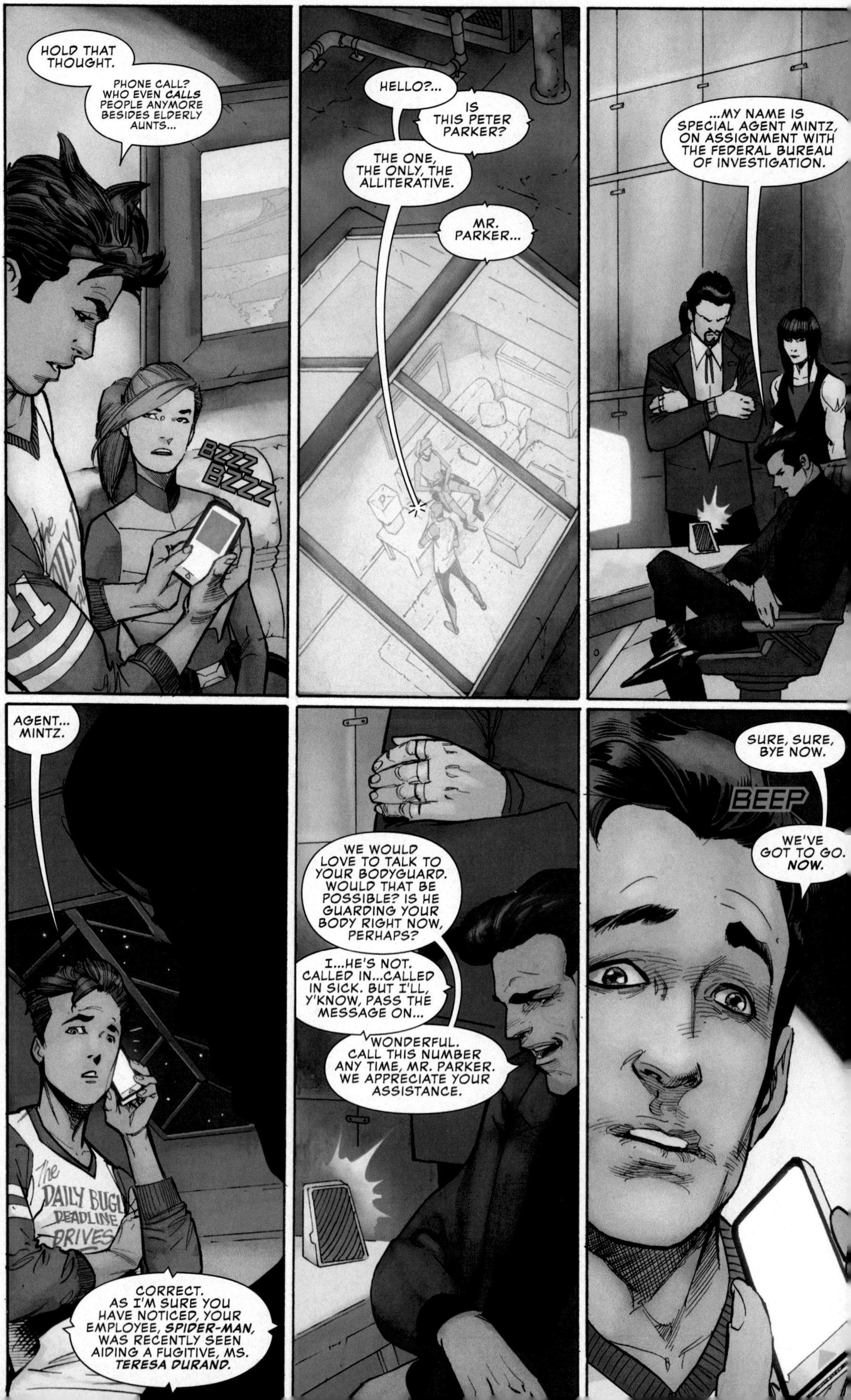
HOLD THAT THOUGHT.
PHONE CALL? WHO EVEN CALLS PEOPLE ANYMORE BESIDES ELDERLY AUNTS...
BZZZ BZZZ
HELLO?...
IS THIS PETER PARKER?
THE ONE, THE ONLY, THE ALLITERATIVE.
MR. PARKER...
...MY NAME IS SPECIAL AGENT MINTZ, ON ASSIGNMENT WITH THE FEDERAL BUREAU OF INVESTIGATION.
AGENT... MINTZ.
CORRECT. AS I'M SURE YOU HAVE NOTICED, YOUR EMPLOYEE, SPIDER-MAN, WAS RECENTLY SEEN AIDING A FUGITIVE, MS. TERESA DURAND.
WE WOULD LOVE TO TALK TO YOUR BODYGUARD. WOULD THAT BE POSSIBLE? IS HE GUARDING YOUR BODY RIGHT NOW, PERHAPS?
I...HE'S NOT. CALLED IN...CALLED IN SICK. BUT I'LL, Y'KNOW, PASS THE MESSAGE ON...
WONDERFUL. CALL THIS NUMBER ANY TIME, MR. PARKER. WE APPRECIATE YOUR ASSISTANCE.
SURE, SURE, BYE NOW.
BEEP
WE'VE GOT TO GO. NOW.

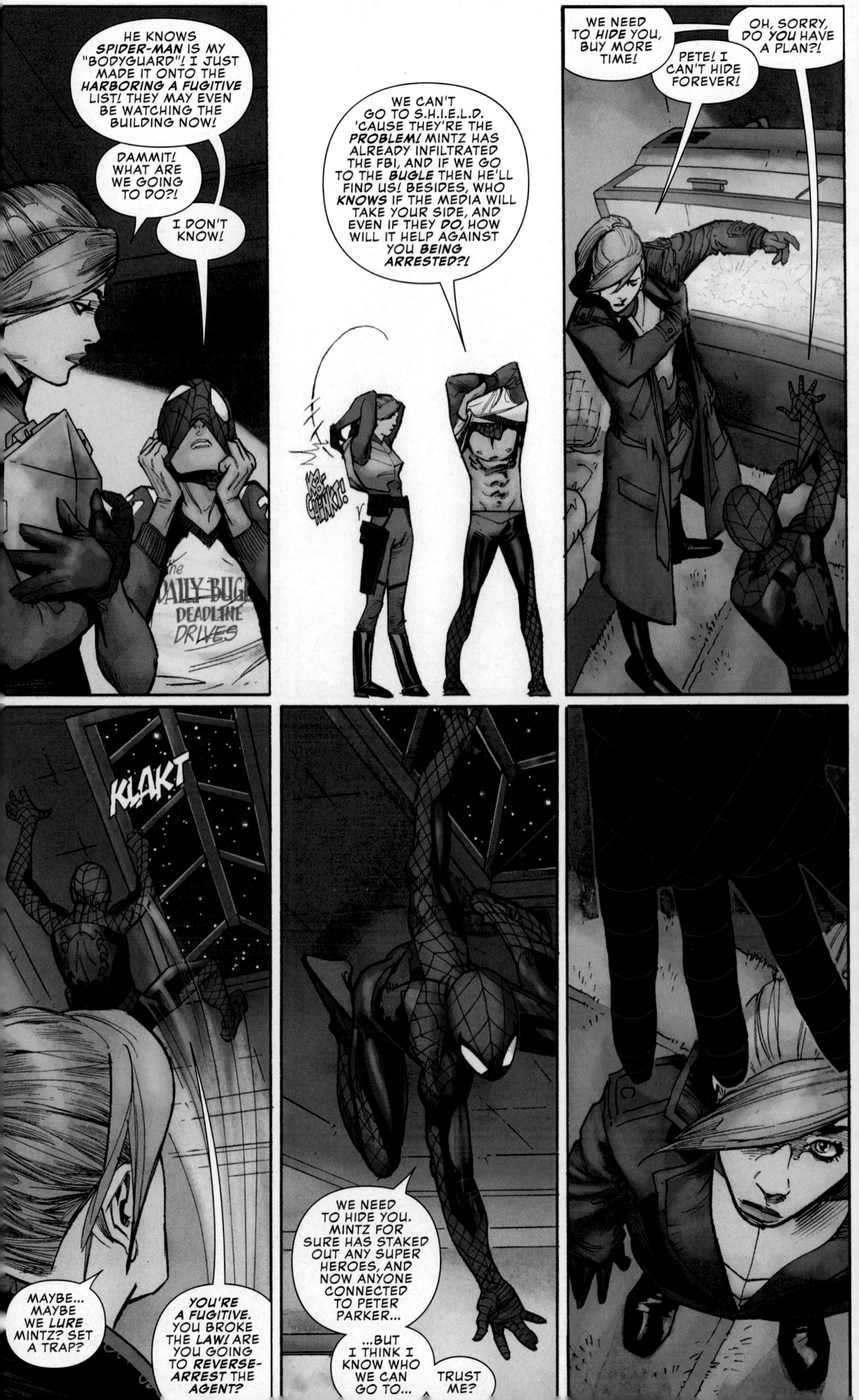
HE KNOWS SPIDER-MAN IS MY "BODYGUARD"! I JUST MADE IT ONTO THE HARBORING A FUGITIVE LIST! THEY MAY EVEN BE WATCHING THE BUILDING NOW!
DAMMIT! WHAT ARE WE GOING TO DO?!
I DON'T KNOW!
The DAILY BUGLE DEADLINE DRIVES
WE CAN'T GO TO S.H.I.E.L.D. 'CAUSE THEY'RE THE PROBLEM! MINTZ HAS ALREADY INFILTRATED THE FBI, AND IF WE GO TO THE BUGLE THEN HE'LL FIND US! BESIDES, WHO KNOWS IF THE MEDIA WILL TAKE YOUR SIDE, AND EVEN IF THEY DO, HOW WILL IT HELP AGAINST YOU BEING ARRESTED?!
KA-CHUNK!
WE NEED TO HIDE YOU, BUY MORE TIME!
PETE! I CAN'T HIDE FOREVER!
OH, SORRY, DO YOU HAVE A PLAN?!
KLAKT
MAYBE... MAYBE WE LURE MINTZ? SET A TRAP?
YOU'RE A FUGITIVE. YOU BROKE THE LAW! ARE YOU GOING TO REVERSE-ARREST THE AGENT?
WE NEED TO HIDE YOU. MINTZ FOR SURE HAS STAKED OUT ANY SUPER HEROES, AND NOW ANYONE CONNECTED TO PETER PARKER...
...BUT I THINK I KNOW WHO WE CAN GO TO...
TRUST ME?

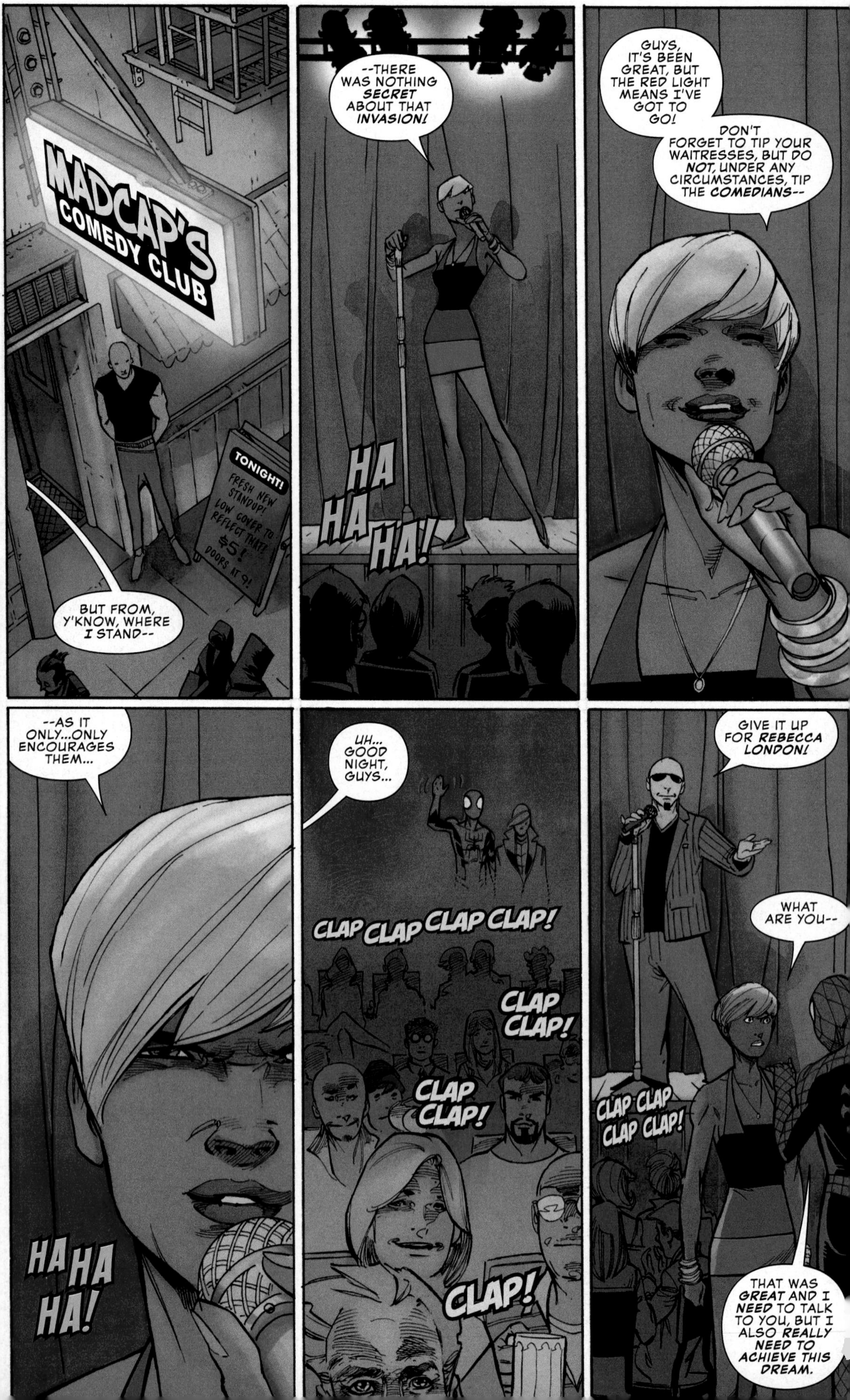
MADCAP'S COMEDY CLUB
TONIGHT!
FRESH NEW STANDUP! LOW COVER TO REFLECT THAT! $5! DOORS AT 9!
BUT FROM, Y'KNOW, WHERE I STAND--
--THERE WAS NOTHING SECRET ABOUT THAT INVASION!
HA HA HA!
GUYS, IT'S BEEN GREAT, BUT THE RED LIGHT MEANS I'VE GOT TO GO!
DON'T FORGET TO TIP YOUR WAITRESSES, BUT DO NOT, UNDER ANY CIRCUMSTANCES, TIP THE COMEDIANS--
--AS IT ONLY...ONLY ENCOURAGES THEM...
HA HA HA HA!
UH... GOOD NIGHT, GUYS...
CLAP CLAP CLAP CLAP!
CLAP CLAP!
CLAP CLAP!
CLAP!
GIVE IT UP FOR REBECCA LONDON!
WHAT ARE YOU--
CLAP CLAP CLAP CLAP!
THAT WAS GREAT AND I NEED TO TALK TO YOU, BUT I ALSO REALLY NEED TO ACHIEVE THIS DREAM.

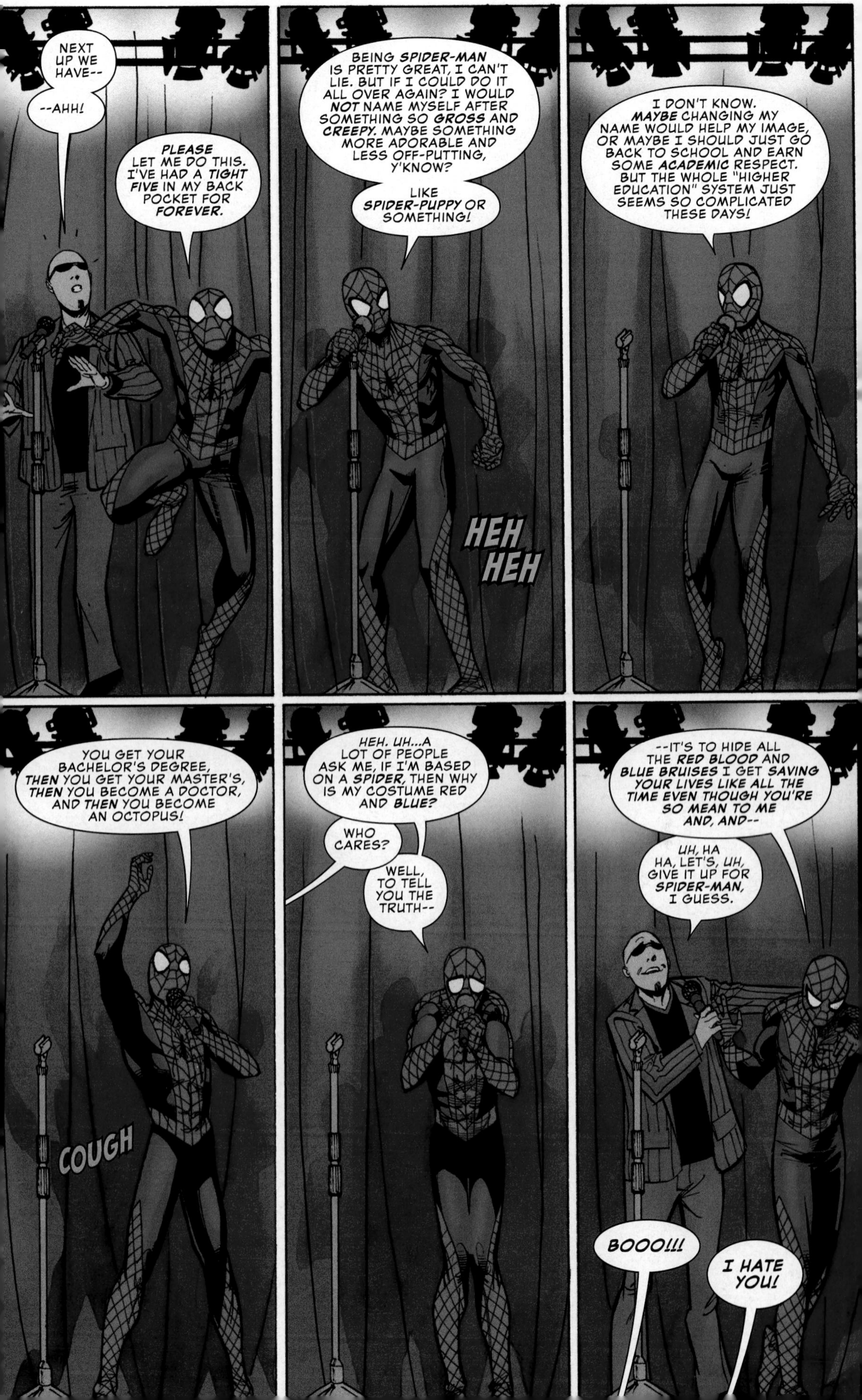
NEXT UP WE HAVE--
--AHH!
PLEASE LET ME DO THIS. I'VE HAD A TIGHT FIVE IN MY BACK POCKET FOR FOREVER.
BEING SPIDER-MAN IS PRETTY GREAT, I CAN'T LIE. BUT IF I COULD DO IT ALL OVER AGAIN? I WOULD NOT NAME MYSELF AFTER SOMETHING SO GROSS AND CREEPY. MAYBE SOMETHING MORE ADORABLE AND LESS OFF-PUTTING, Y'KNOW?
LIKE SPIDER-PUPPY OR SOMETHING!
HEH HEH
I DON'T KNOW. MAYBE CHANGING MY NAME WOULD HELP MY IMAGE, OR MAYBE I SHOULD JUST GO BACK TO SCHOOL AND EARN SOME ACADEMIC RESPECT. BUT THE WHOLE "HIGHER EDUCATION" SYSTEM JUST SEEMS SO COMPLICATED THESE DAYS!
YOU GET YOUR BACHELOR'S DEGREE, THEN YOU GET YOUR MASTER'S, THEN YOU BECOME A DOCTOR, AND THEN YOU BECOME AN OCTOPUS!
COUGH
HEH. UH...A LOT OF PEOPLE ASK ME, IF I'M BASED ON A SPIDER, THEN WHY IS MY COSTUME RED AND BLUE?
WHO CARES?
WELL, TO TELL YOU THE TRUTH--
--IT'S TO HIDE ALL THE RED BLOOD AND BLUE BRUISES I GET SAVING YOUR LIVES LIKE ALL THE TIME EVEN THOUGH YOU'RE SO MEAN TO ME AND, AND--
UH, HA HA, LET'S, UH, GIVE IT UP FOR SPIDER-MAN, I GUESS.
BOOO!!!
I HATE YOU!

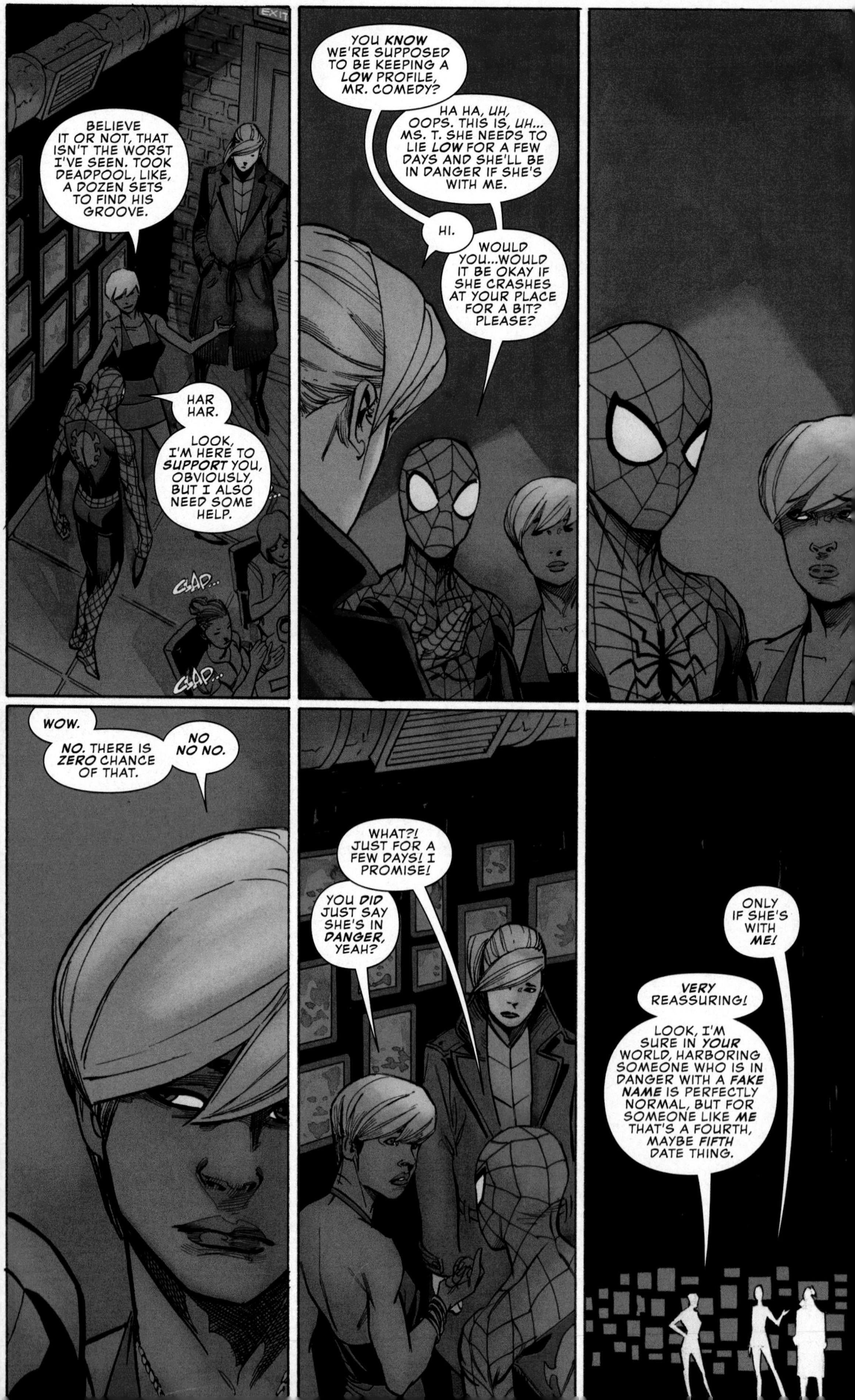
EXIT
BELIEVE IT OR NOT, THAT ISN'T THE WORST I'VE SEEN. TOOK DEADPOOL, LIKE, A DOZEN SETS TO FIND HIS GROOVE.
HAR HAR.
LOOK, I'M HERE TO SUPPORT YOU, OBVIOUSLY, BUT I ALSO NEED SOME HELP.
CLAP...
CLAP...
YOU KNOW WE'RE SUPPOSED TO BE KEEPING A LOW PROFILE, MR. COMEDY?
HA HA, UH, OOPS. THIS IS, UH... MS. T. SHE NEEDS TO LIE LOW FOR A FEW DAYS AND SHE'LL BE IN DANGER IF SHE'S WITH ME.
HI.
WOULD YOU...WOULD IT BE OKAY IF SHE CRASHES AT YOUR PLACE FOR A BIT? PLEASE?
WOW.
NO. THERE IS ZERO CHANCE OF THAT.
NO NO NO.
WHAT?! JUST FOR A FEW DAYS! I PROMISE!
YOU DID JUST SAY SHE'S IN DANGER, YEAH?
ONLY IF SHE'S WITH ME!
VERY REASSURING!
LOOK, I'M SURE IN YOUR WORLD, HARBORING SOMEONE WHO IS IN DANGER WITH A FAKE NAME IS PERFECTLY NORMAL, BUT FOR SOMEONE LIKE ME THAT'S A FOURTH, MAYBE FIFTH DATE THING.

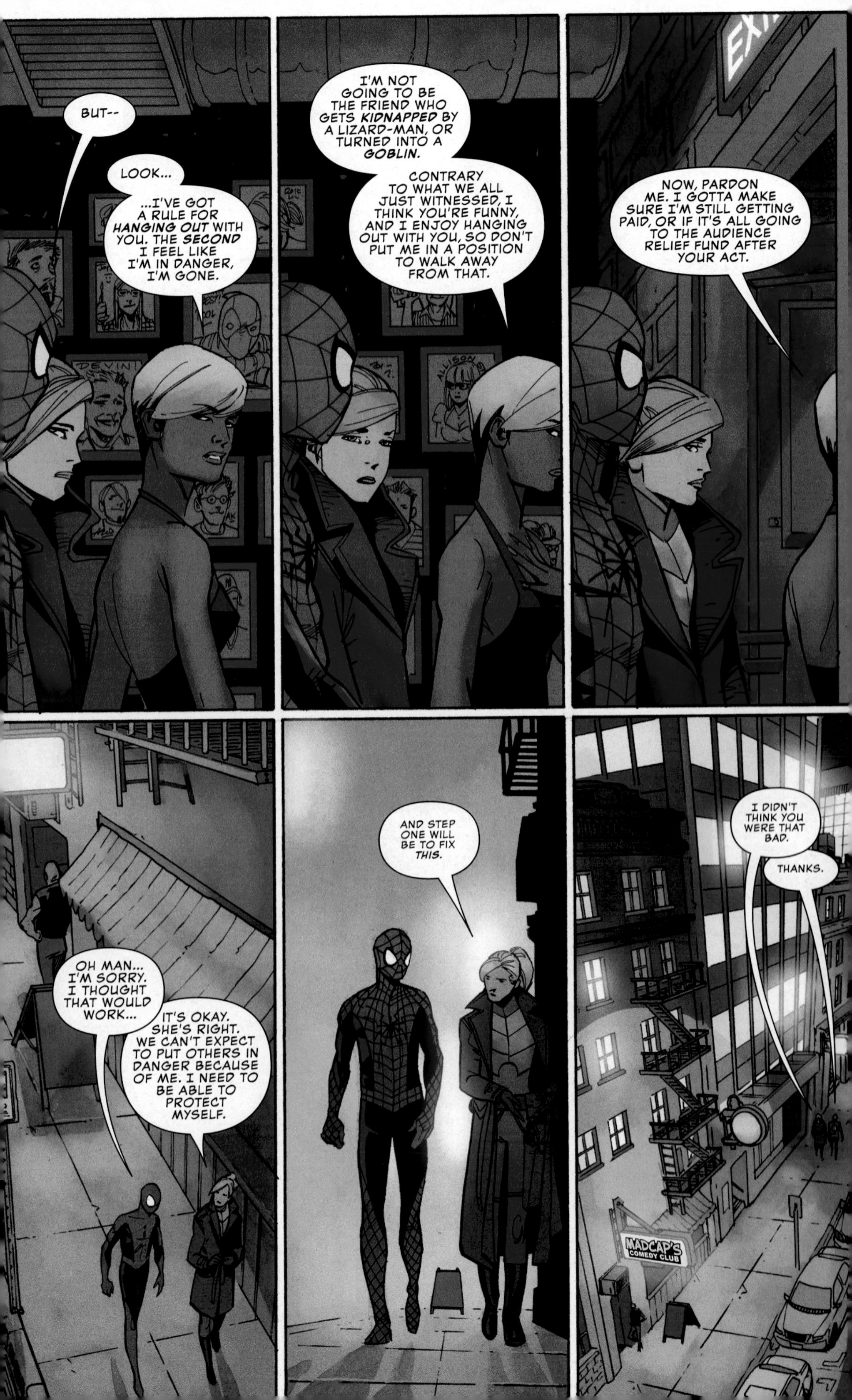
BUT--
LOOK...
...I'VE GOT A RULE FOR HANGING OUT WITH YOU. THE SECOND I FEEL LIKE I'M IN DANGER, I'M GONE.
I'M NOT GOING TO BE THE FRIEND WHO GETS KIDNAPPED BY A LIZARD-MAN, OR TURNED INTO A GOBLIN.
CONTRARY TO WHAT WE ALL JUST WITNESSED, I THINK YOU'RE FUNNY, AND I ENJOY HANGING OUT WITH YOU, SO DON'T PUT ME IN A POSITION TO WALK AWAY FROM THAT.
NOW, PARDON ME. I GOTTA MAKE SURE I'M STILL GETTING PAID, OR IF IT'S ALL GOING TO THE AUDIENCE RELIEF FUND AFTER YOUR ACT.
OH MAN... I'M SORRY. I THOUGHT THAT WOULD WORK...
IT'S OKAY. SHE'S RIGHT. WE CAN'T EXPECT TO PUT OTHERS IN DANGER BECAUSE OF ME. I NEED TO BE ABLE TO PROTECT MYSELF.
AND STEP ONE WILL BE TO FIX THIS.
I DIDN'T THINK YOU WERE THAT BAD.
THANKS.
MADCAP'S COMEDY CLUB

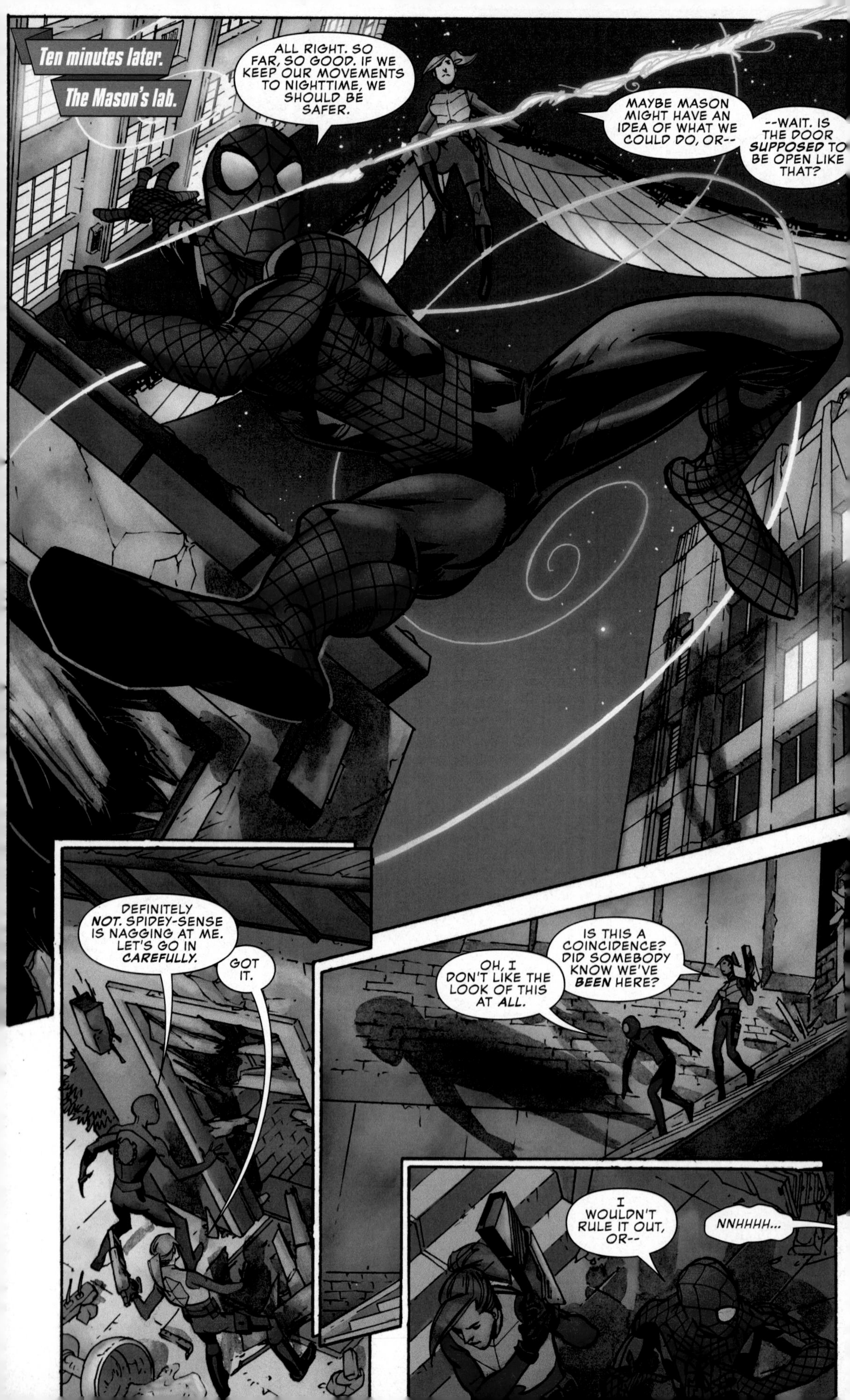
Ten minutes later.
The Mason's lab.
ALL RIGHT. SO FAR, SO GOOD. IF WE KEEP OUR MOVEMENTS TO NIGHTTIME, WE SHOULD BE SAFER.
MAYBE MASON MIGHT HAVE AN IDEA OF WHAT WE COULD DO, OR--
--WAIT. IS THE DOOR SUPPOSED TO BE OPEN LIKE THAT?
DEFINITELY NOT. SPIDEY-SENSE IS NAGGING AT ME. LET'S GO IN CAREFULLY.
GOT IT.
OH, I DON'T LIKE THE LOOK OF THIS AT ALL.
IS THIS A COINCIDENCE? DID SOMEBODY KNOW WE'VE BEEN HERE?
I WOULDN'T RULE IT OUT, OR--
NNHHHH...

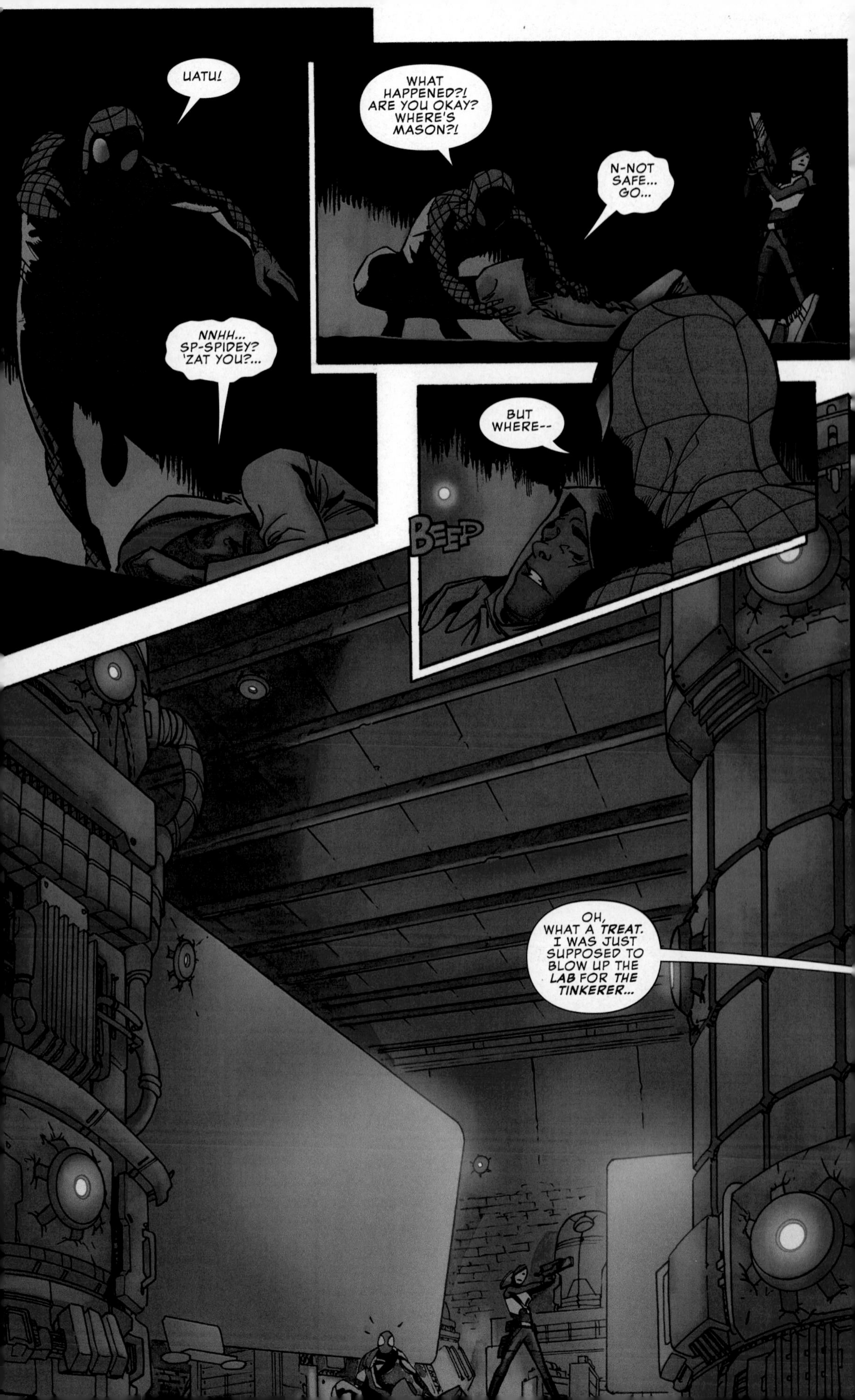
UATU!
WHAT HAPPENED?! ARE YOU OKAY? WHERE'S MASON?!
NNHH... SP-SPIDEY? 'ZAT YOU?...
N-NOT SAFE... GO...
BUT WHERE--
BEEP
OH, WHAT A TREAT. I WAS JUST SUPPOSED TO BLOW UP THE LAB FOR THE TINKERER...

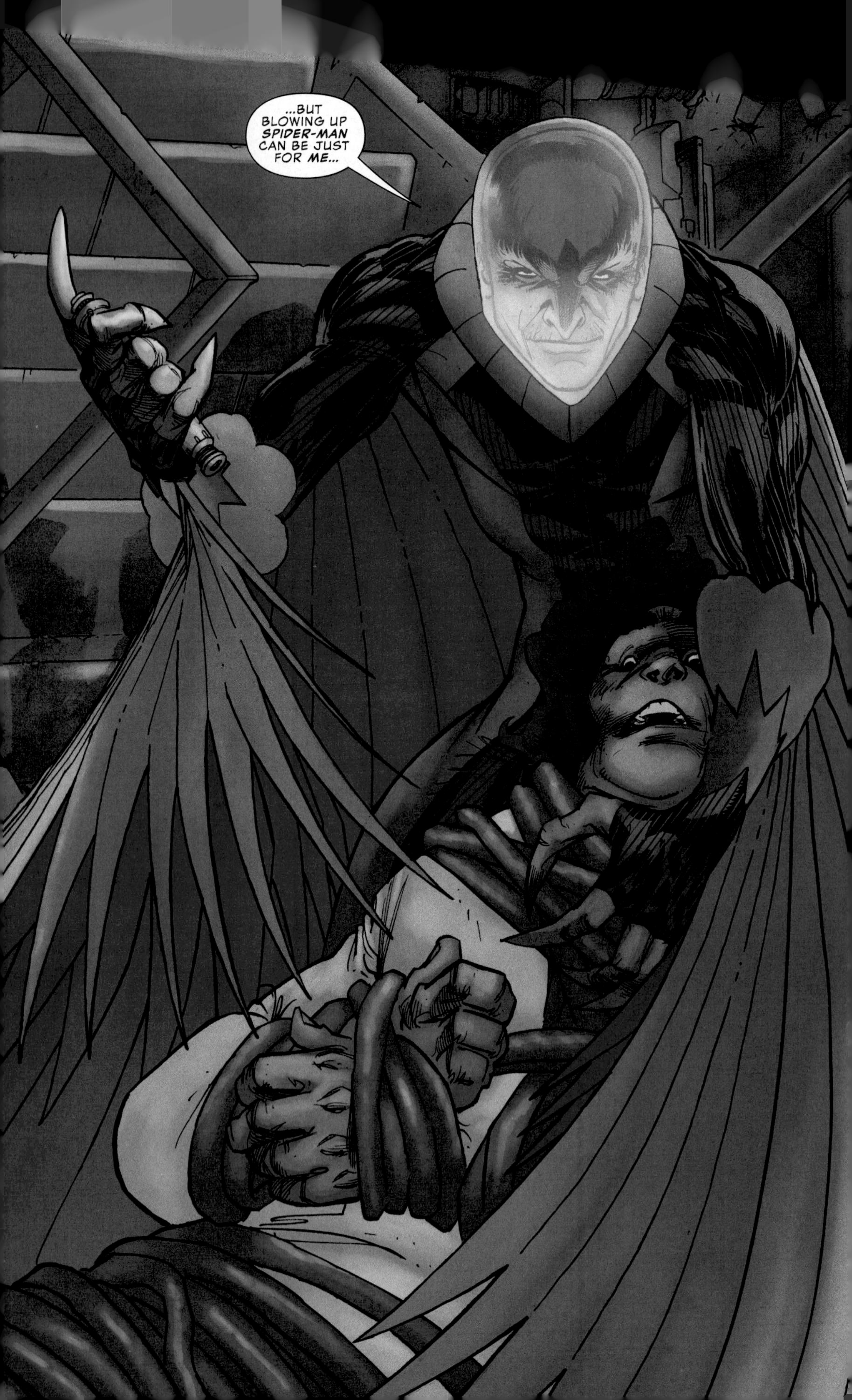
...BUT BLOWING UP *SPIDER-MAN* CAN BE JUST FOR *ME*...

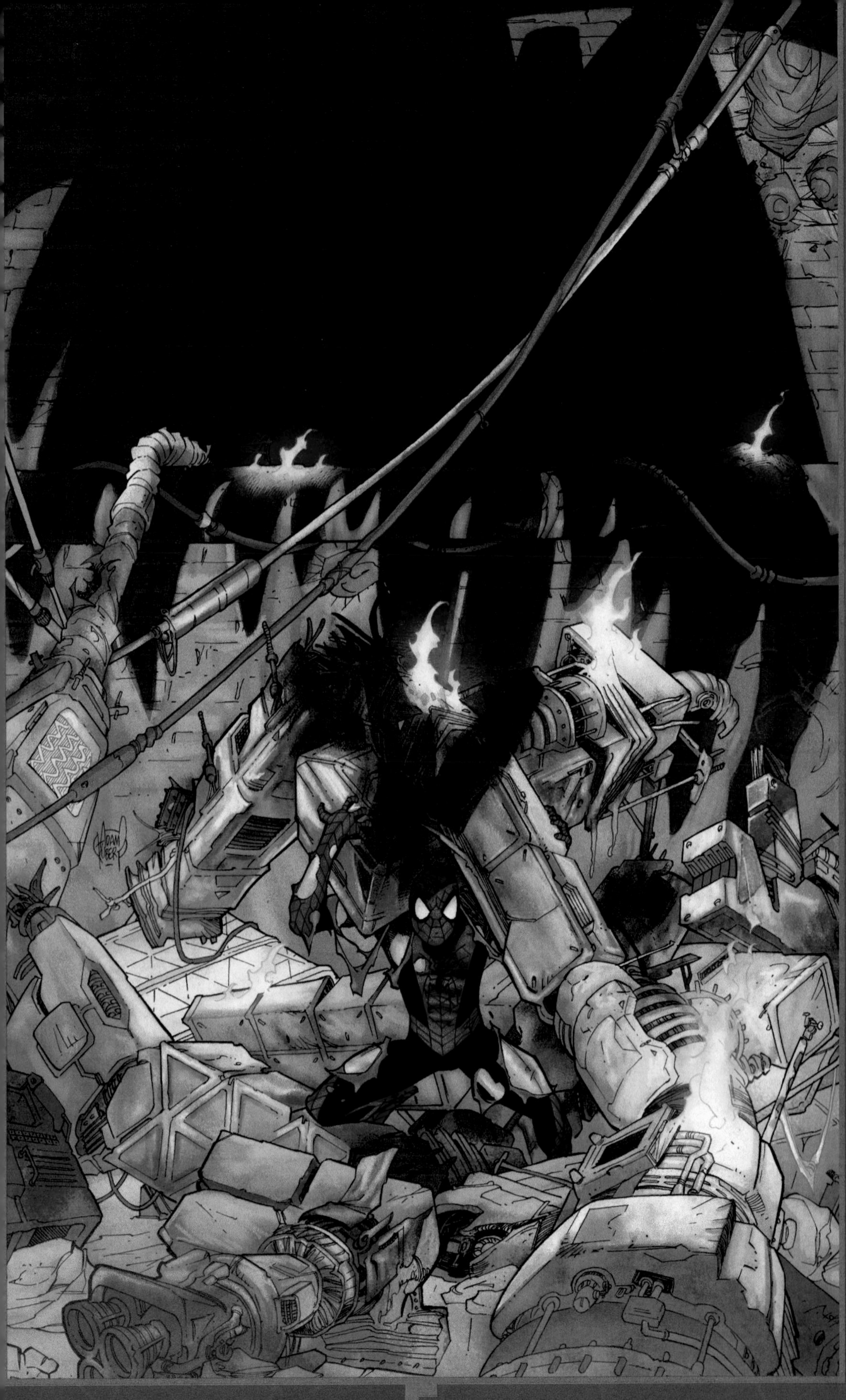

5

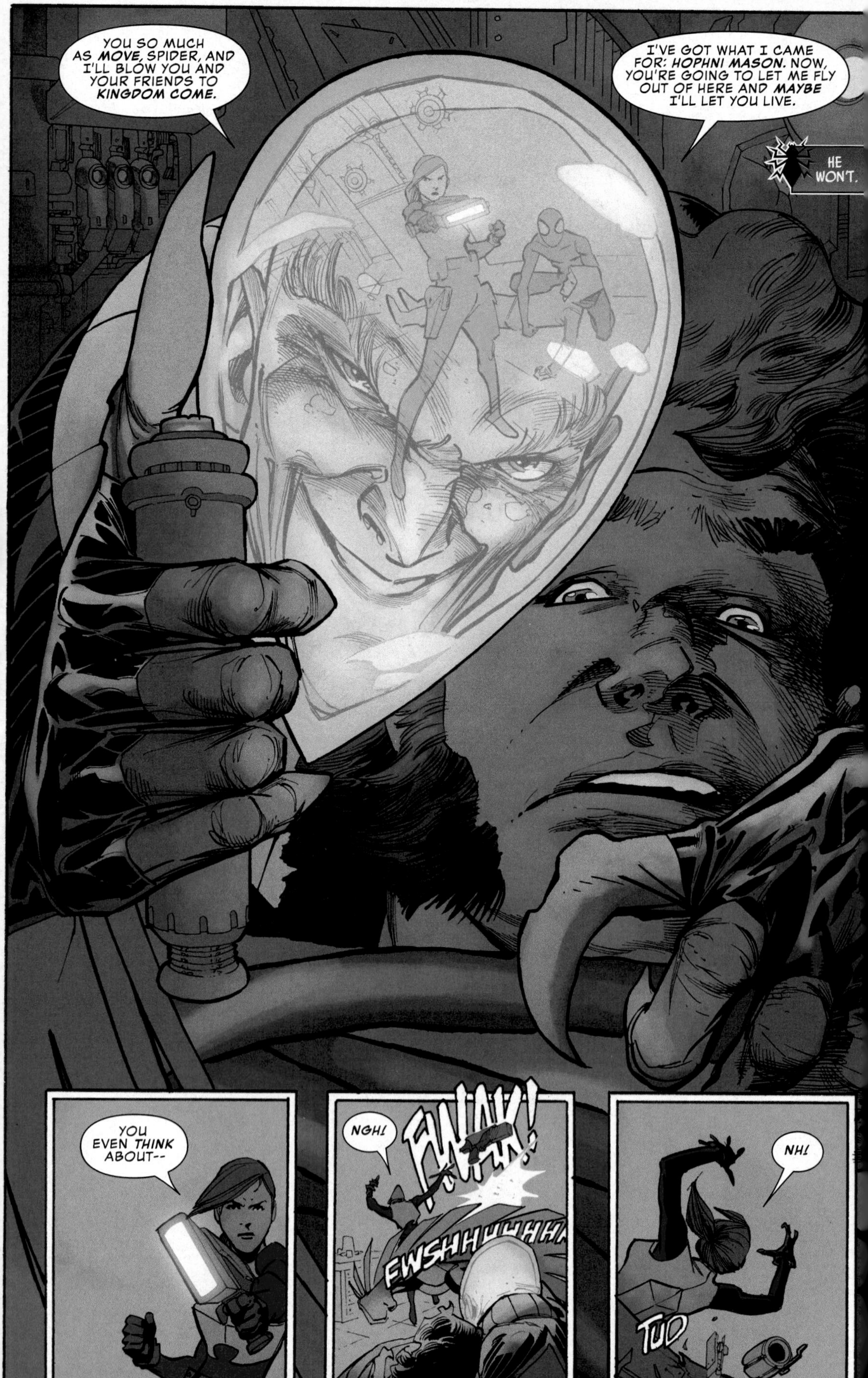

YOU SO MUCH AS MOVE, SPIDER, AND I'LL BLOW YOU AND YOUR FRIENDS TO KINGDOM COME.
I'VE GOT WHAT I CAME FOR: HOPHNI MASON. NOW, YOU'RE GOING TO LET ME FLY OUT OF HERE AND MAYBE I'LL LET YOU LIVE.
HE WON'T.
YOU EVEN THINK ABOUT--
NGH!
FWSHHHHHHH
NH!
TUD

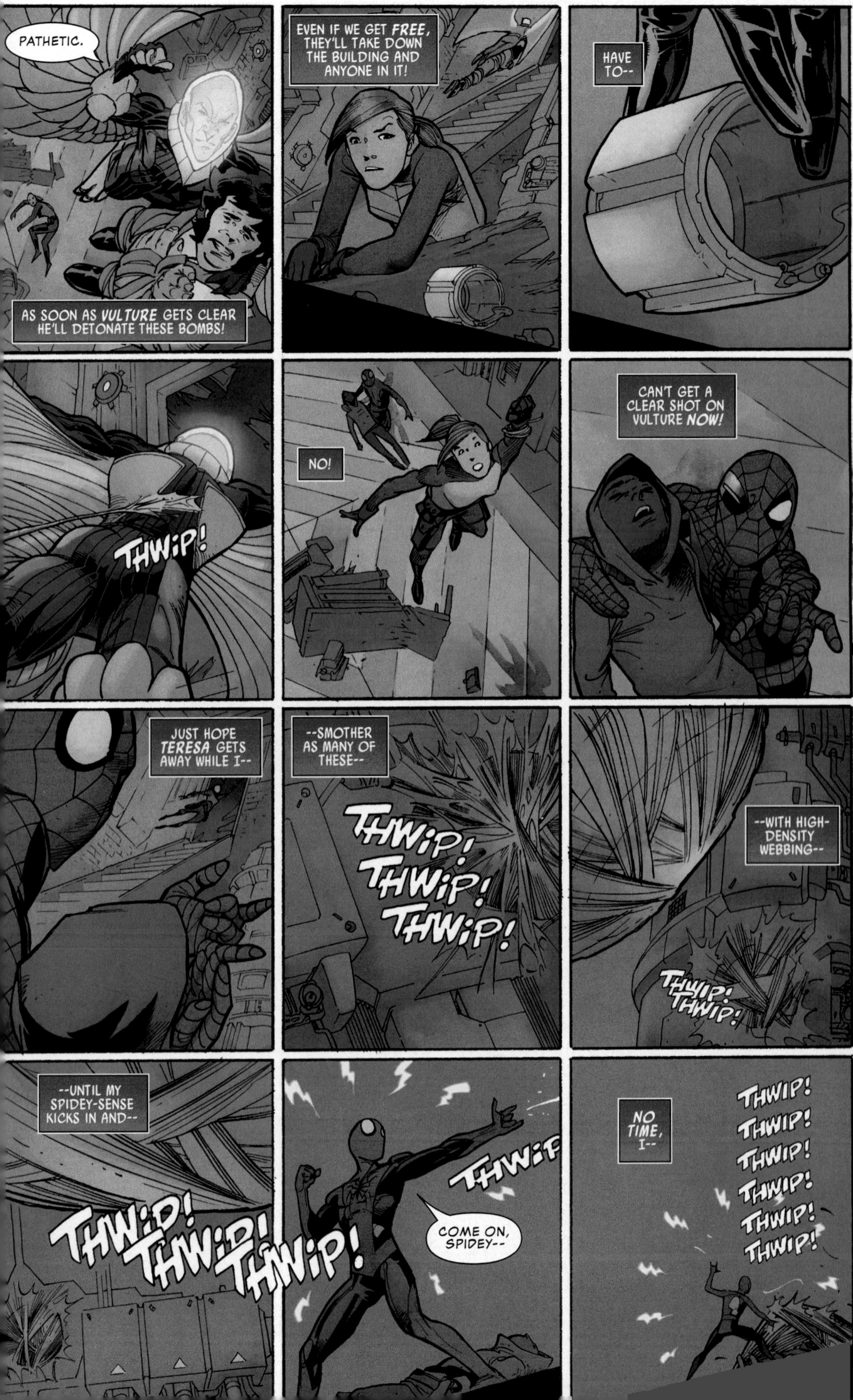
PATHETIC.
AS SOON AS VULTURE GETS CLEAR HE'LL DETONATE THESE BOMBS!
EVEN IF WE GET FREE, THEY'LL TAKE DOWN THE BUILDING AND ANYONE IN IT!
HAVE TO--
THWIP!
NO!
CAN'T GET A CLEAR SHOT ON VULTURE NOW!
JUST HOPE TERESA GETS AWAY WHILE I--
--SMOTHER AS MANY OF THESE--
THWIP! THWIP! THWIP!
--WITH HIGH-DENSITY WEBBING--
THWIP! THWIP!
--UNTIL MY SPIDEY-SENSE KICKS IN AND--
THWIP! THWIP! THWIP!
THWIP
COME ON, SPIDEY--
NO TIME, I--
THWIP! THWIP! THWIP! THWIP! THWIP! THWIP!

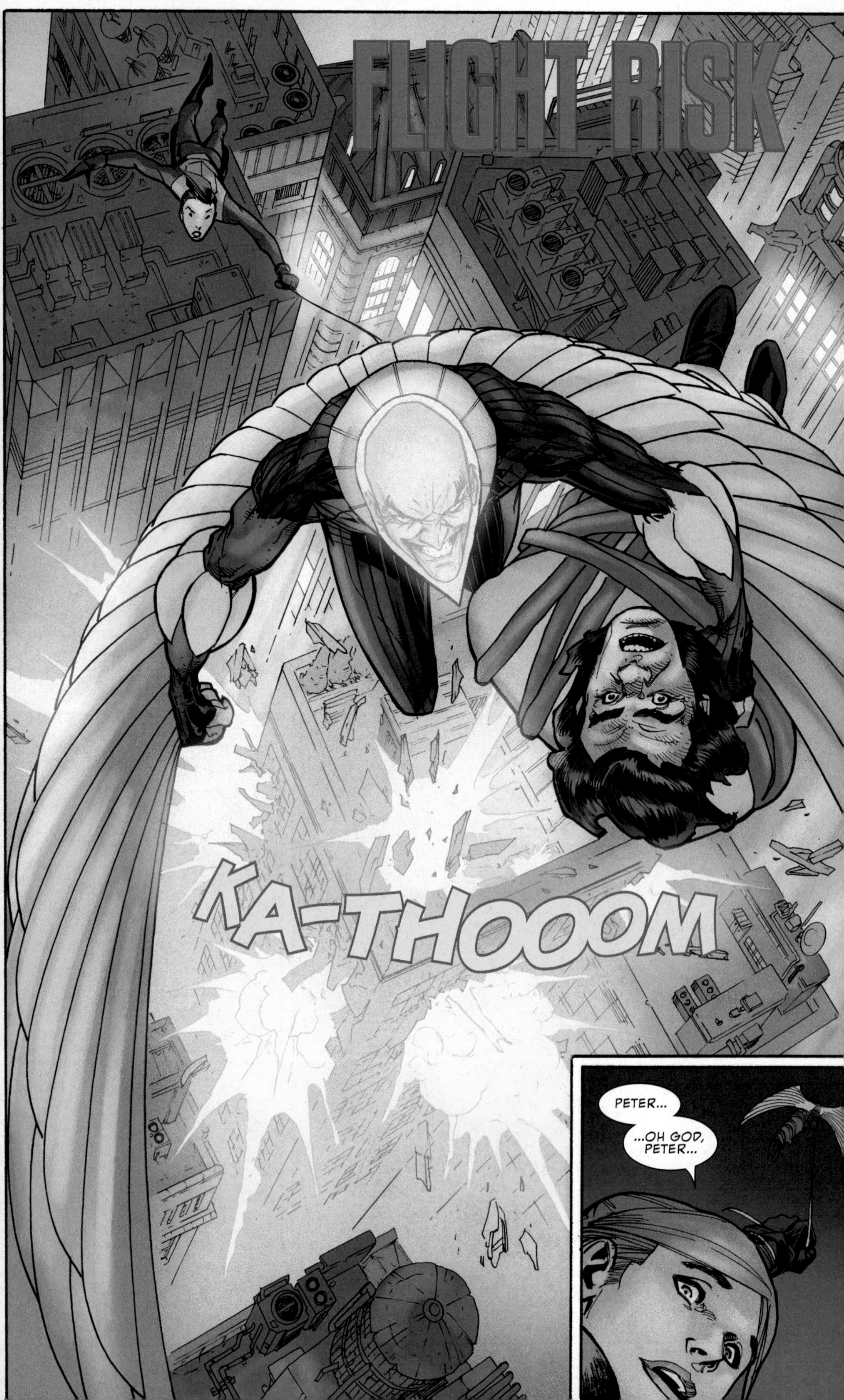
FLIGHT RISK
KA-THOOOM
PETER...
...OH GOD, PETER...

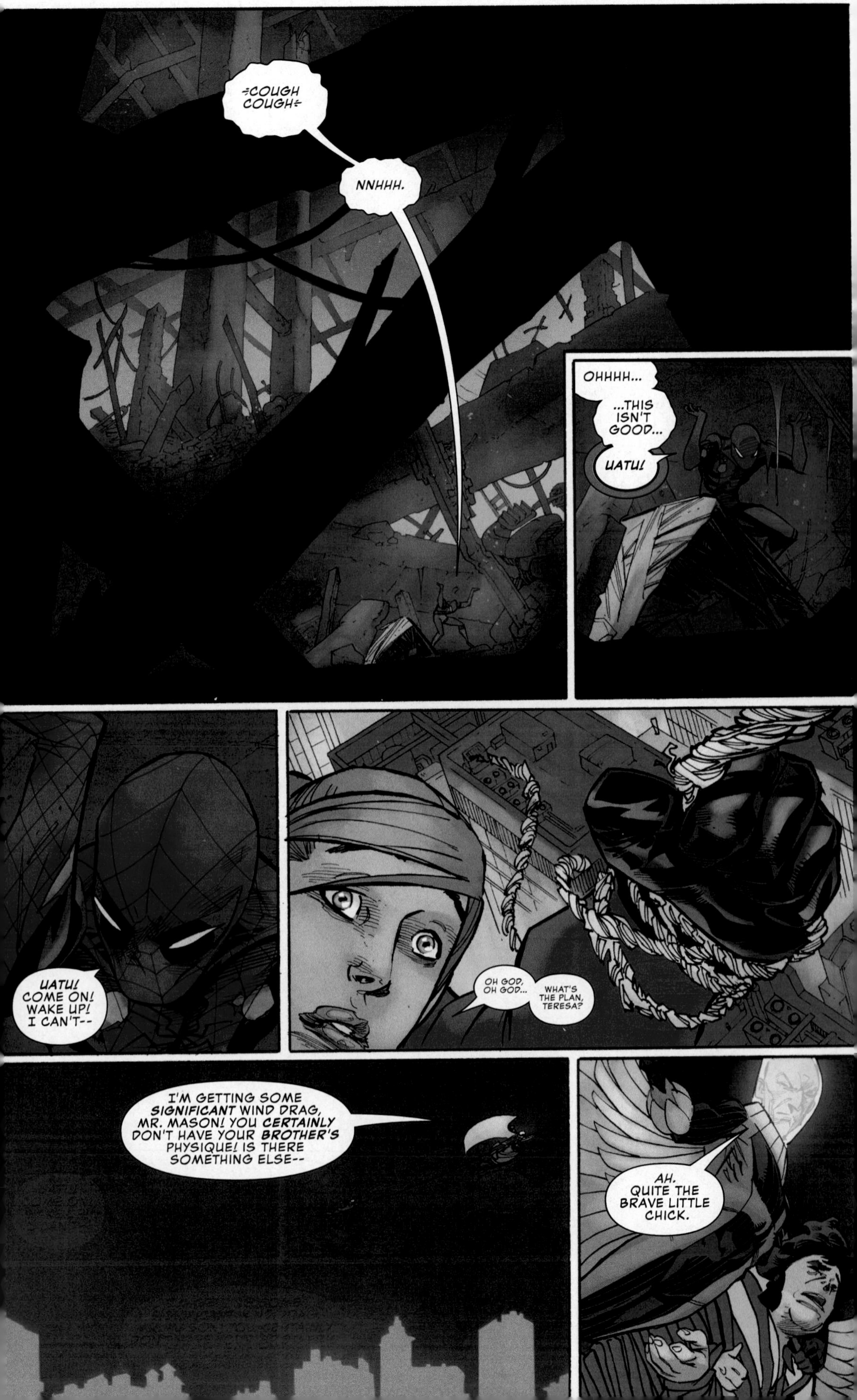

=COUGH COUGH=
NNHHH.
OHHHH...
...THIS ISN'T GOOD...
UATU!
UATU! COME ON! WAKE UP! I CAN'T--
OH GOD, OH GOD...
WHAT'S THE PLAN, TERESA?
I'M GETTING SOME SIGNIFICANT WIND DRAG, MR. MASON! YOU CERTAINLY DON'T HAVE YOUR BROTHER'S PHYSIQUE! IS THERE SOMETHING ELSE--
AH. QUITE THE BRAVE LITTLE CHICK.

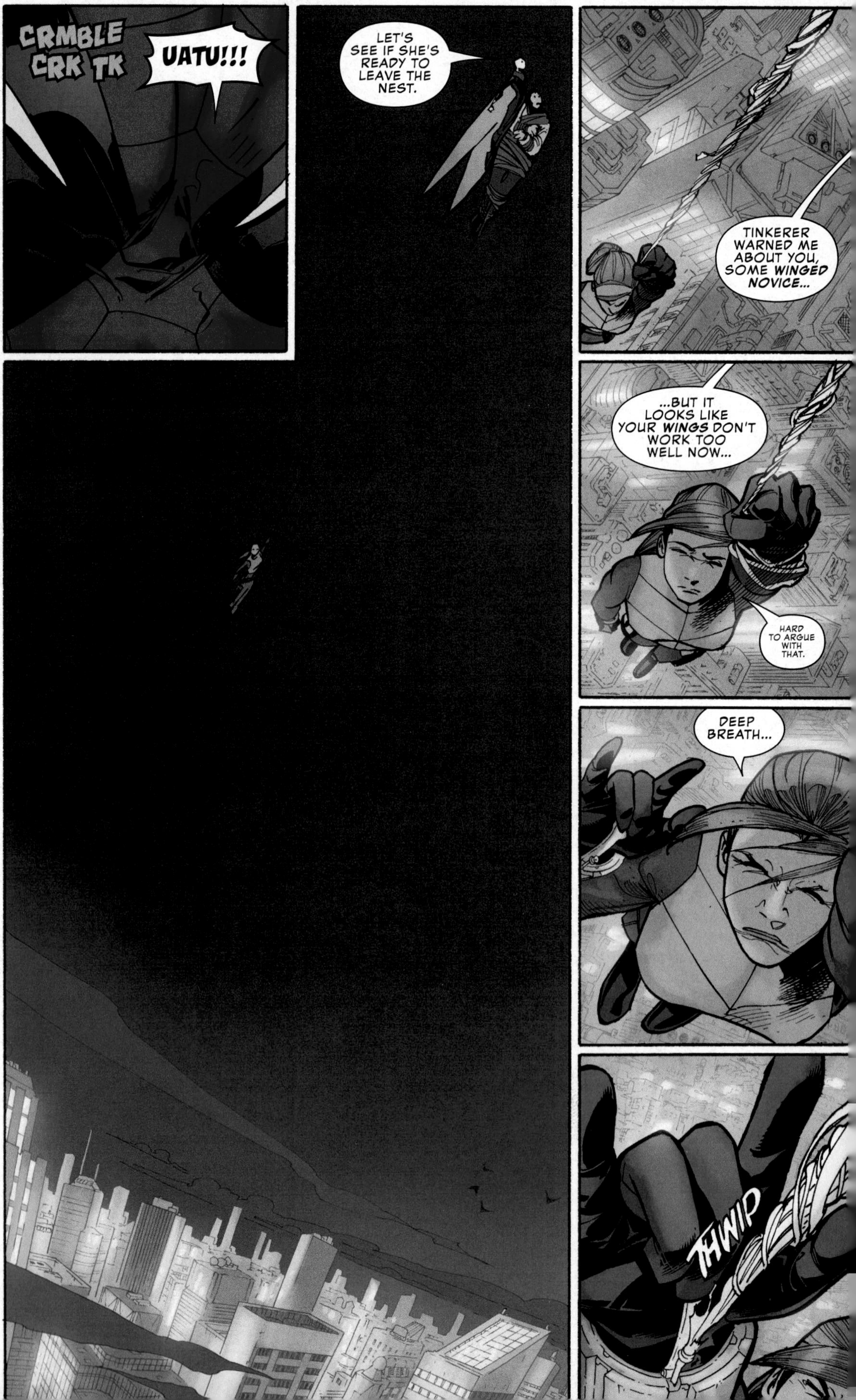
CRMBLE CRK TK
UATU!!!
LET'S SEE IF SHE'S READY TO LEAVE THE NEST.
TINKERER WARNED ME ABOUT YOU, SOME WINGED NOVICE...
...BUT IT LOOKS LIKE YOUR WINGS DON'T WORK TOO WELL NOW...
HARD TO ARGUE WITH THAT.
DEEP BREATH...
THWIP

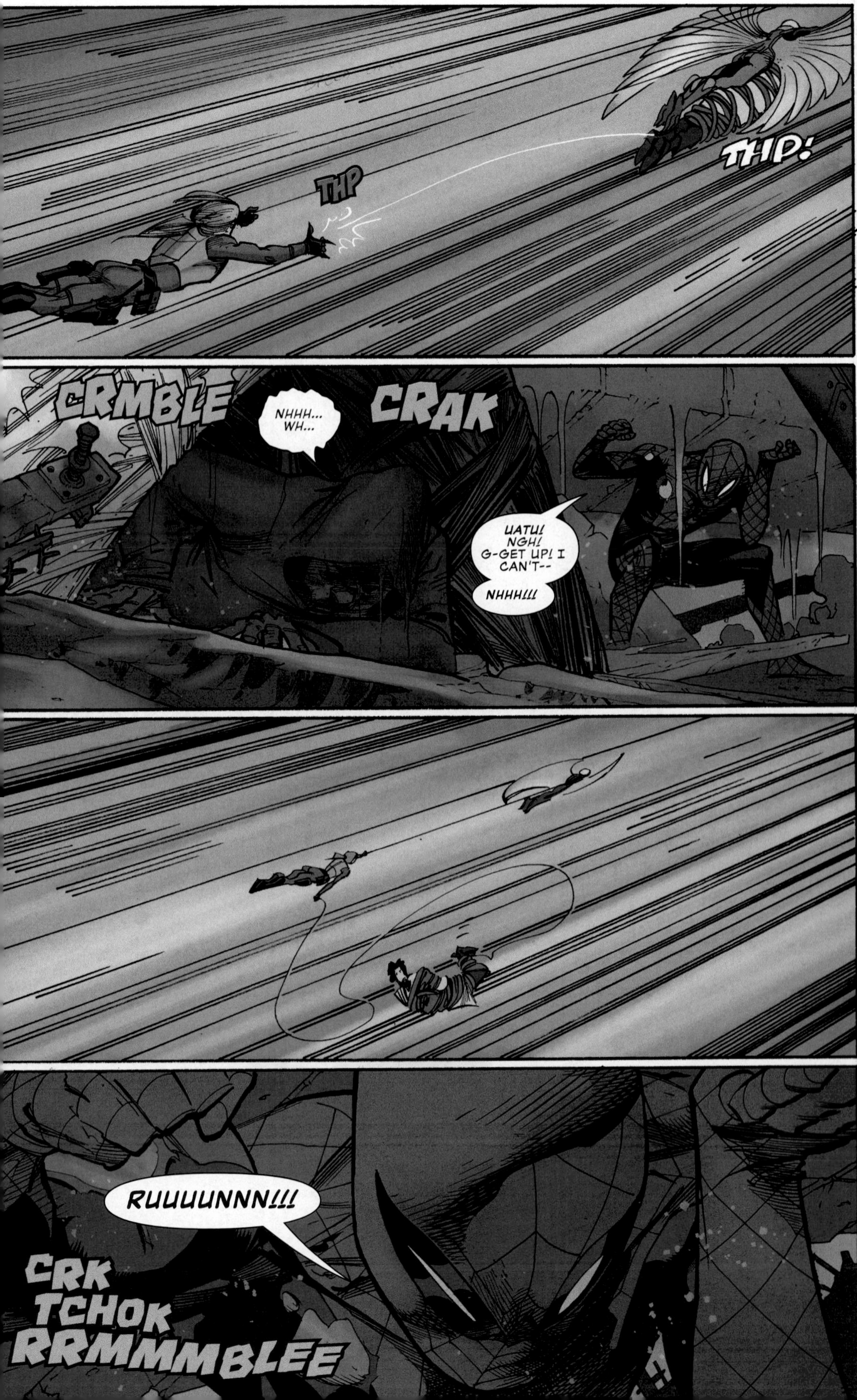
THP
THIP!
CRMBLE
NHHH... WH...
CRAK
UATU! NGH! G-GET UP! I CAN'T--
NHHH!!!
RUUUUNNN!!!
CRK TCHOK RRMMMBLEE

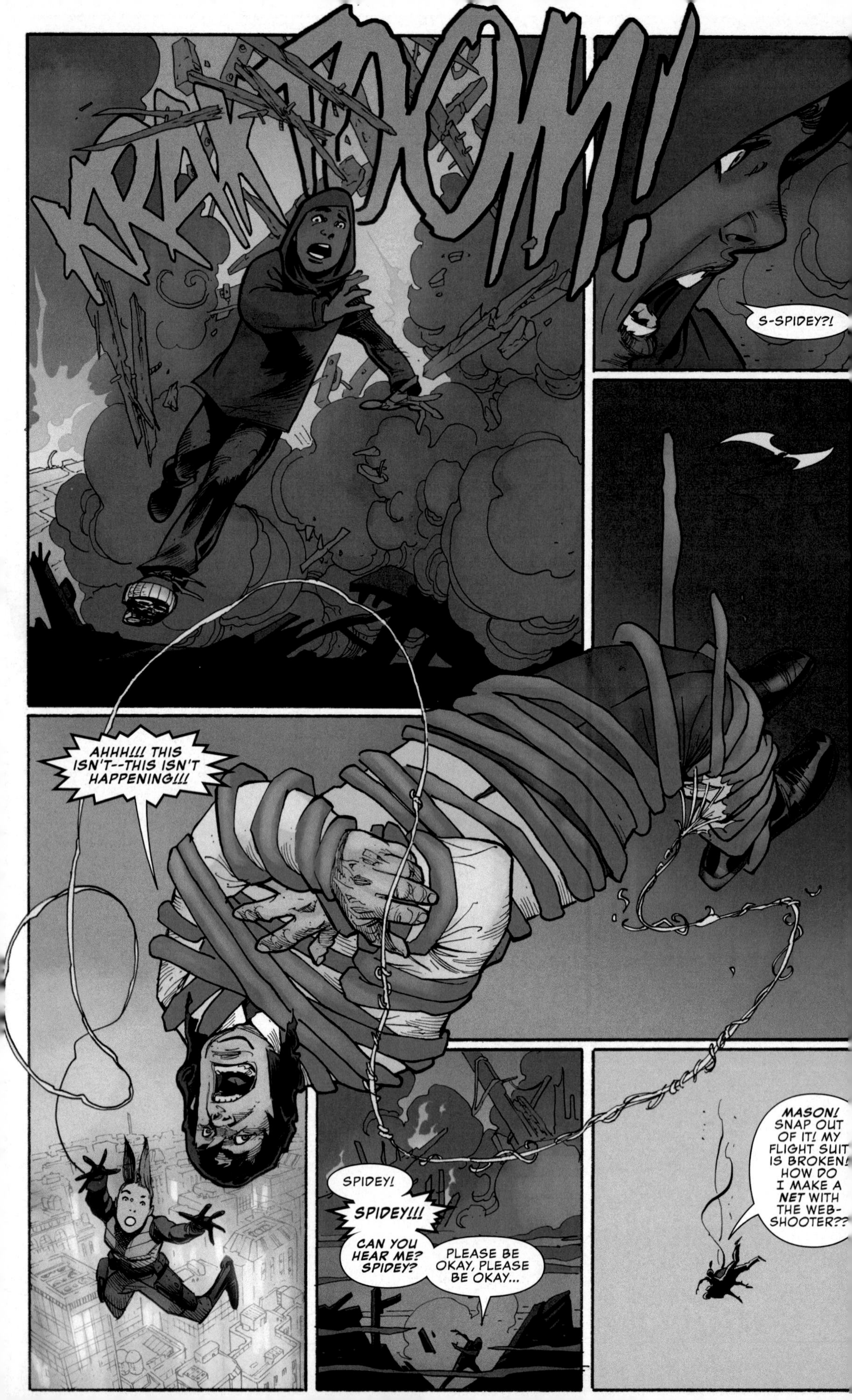
KRAKADOOM!
S-SPIDEY?!
AHHH!!! THIS ISN'T--THIS ISN'T HAPPENING!!!
SPIDEY!
SPIDEY!!!
CAN YOU HEAR ME? SPIDEY?
PLEASE BE OKAY, PLEASE BE OKAY...
MASON! SNAP OUT OF IT! MY FLIGHT SUIT IS BROKEN! HOW DO I MAKE A NET WITH THE WEB-SHOOTER??

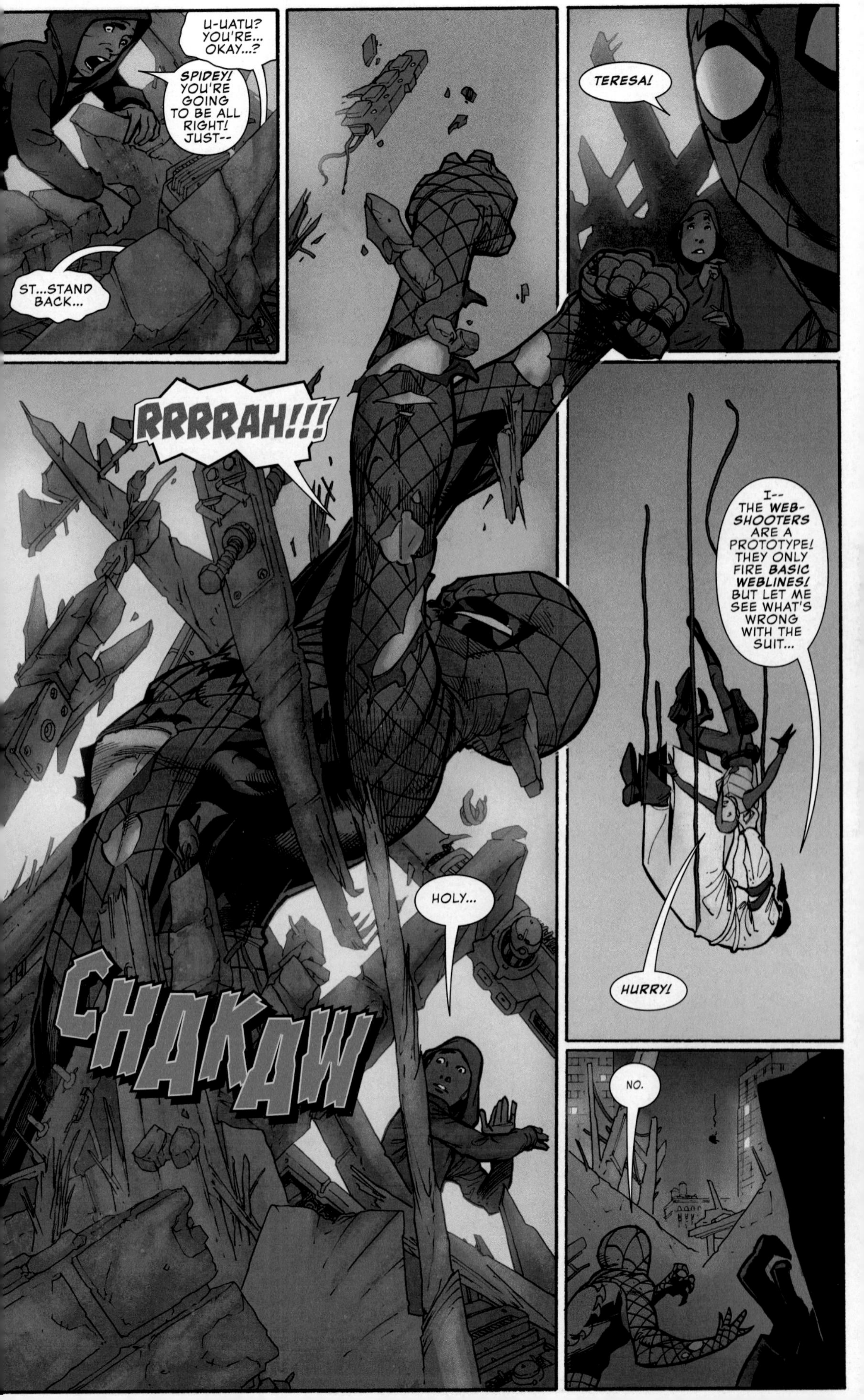
U-UATU? YOU'RE... OKAY...?
SPIDEY! YOU'RE GOING TO BE ALL RIGHT! JUST--
ST...STAND BACK...
TERESA!
RRRRAH!!!
HOLY...
CHAKAW
I-- THE WEB-SHOOTERS ARE A PROTOTYPE! THEY ONLY FIRE BASIC WEBLINES! BUT LET ME SEE WHAT'S WRONG WITH THE SUIT...
HURRY!
NO.

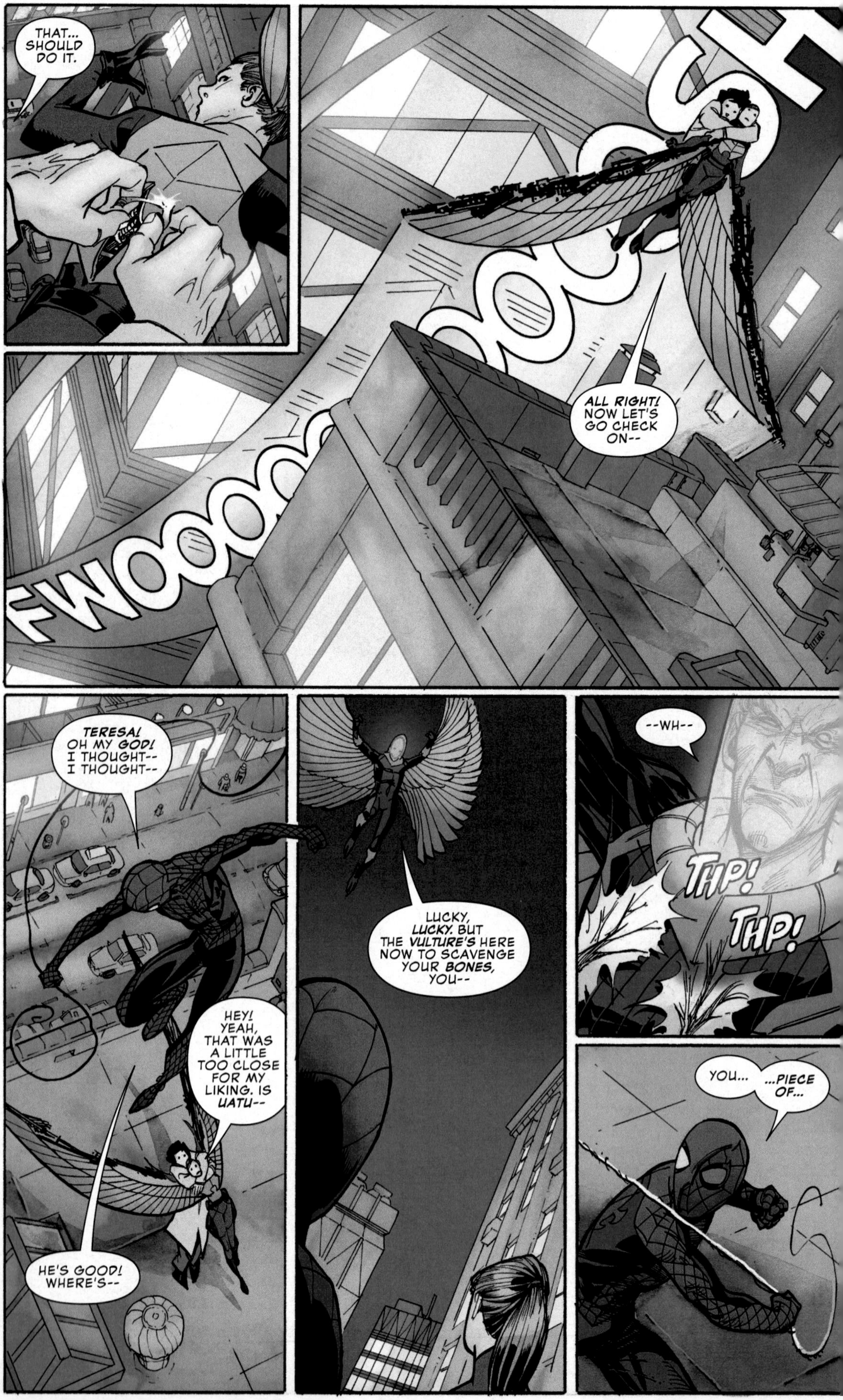
THAT... SHOULD DO IT.
FWOOOOOOOOSH
ALL RIGHT! NOW LET'S GO CHECK ON--
TERESA! OH MY GOD! I THOUGHT-- I THOUGHT--
HEY! YEAH, THAT WAS A LITTLE TOO CLOSE FOR MY LIKING. IS UATU--
HE'S GOOD! WHERE'S--
LUCKY, LUCKY. BUT THE VULTURE'S HERE NOW TO SCAVENGE YOUR BONES, YOU--
--WH--
THP!
THP!
YOU...
...PIECE OF...

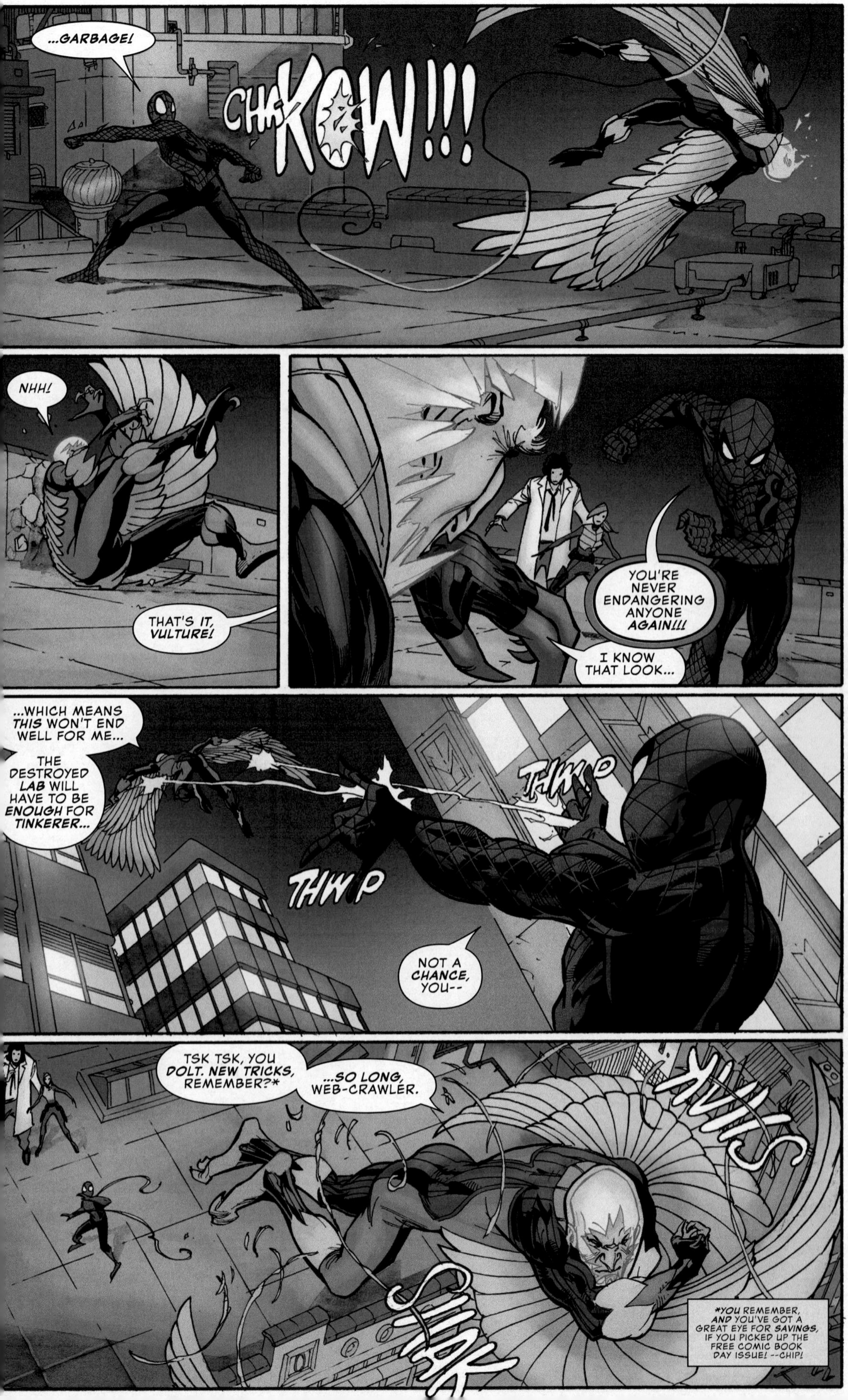
...GARBAGE!
CHAKOW!!!
NHH!
THAT'S IT, VULTURE!
YOU'RE NEVER ENDANGERING ANYONE AGAIN!!!
I KNOW THAT LOOK...
...WHICH MEANS THIS WON'T END WELL FOR ME...
THE DESTROYED LAB WILL HAVE TO BE ENOUGH FOR TINKERER...
THWIP
THWIP
NOT A CHANCE, YOU--
TSK TSK, YOU DOLT. NEW TRICKS, REMEMBER?*
...SO LONG, WEB-CRAWLER.
SHAK
SHAK
*YOU REMEMBER, AND YOU'VE GOT A GREAT EYE FOR SAVINGS, IF YOU PICKED UP THE FREE COMIC BOOK DAY ISSUE! --CHIP!

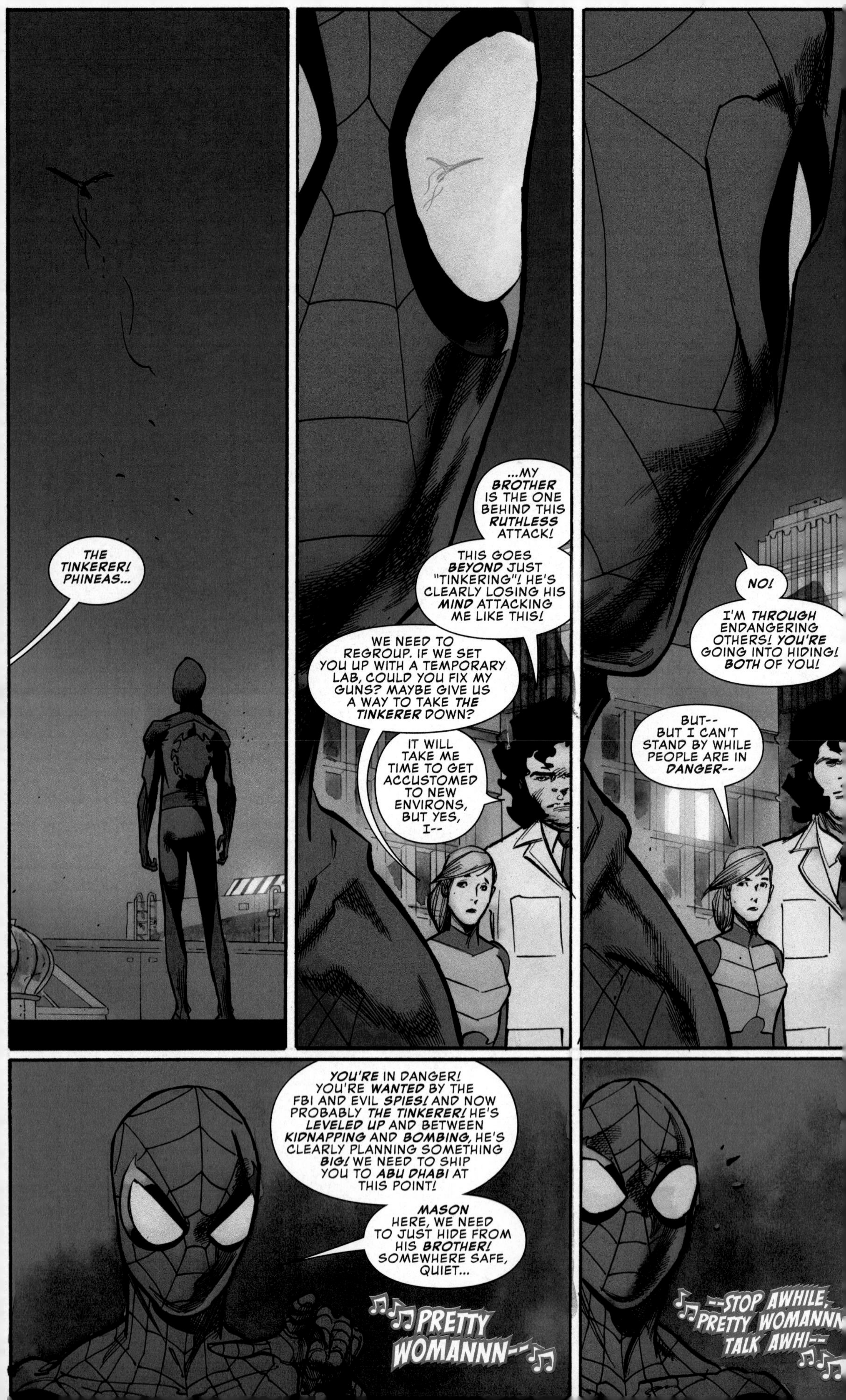
THE TINKERER! PHINEAS...
...MY BROTHER IS THE ONE BEHIND THIS RUTHLESS ATTACK!
THIS GOES BEYOND JUST "TINKERING"! HE'S CLEARLY LOSING HIS MIND ATTACKING ME LIKE THIS!
WE NEED TO REGROUP. IF WE SET YOU UP WITH A TEMPORARY LAB, COULD YOU FIX MY GUNS? MAYBE GIVE US A WAY TO TAKE THE TINKERER DOWN?
IT WILL TAKE ME TIME TO GET ACCUSTOMED TO NEW ENVIRONS, BUT YES, I--
NO!
I'M THROUGH ENDANGERING OTHERS! YOU'RE GOING INTO HIDING! BOTH OF YOU!
BUT-- BUT I CAN'T STAND BY WHILE PEOPLE ARE IN DANGER--
YOU'RE IN DANGER! YOU'RE WANTED BY THE FBI AND EVIL SPIES! AND NOW PROBABLY THE TINKERER! HE'S LEVELED UP AND BETWEEN KIDNAPPING AND BOMBING, HE'S CLEARLY PLANNING SOMETHING BIG! WE NEED TO SHIP YOU TO ABU DHABI AT THIS POINT!
MASON HERE, WE NEED TO JUST HIDE FROM HIS BROTHER! SOMEWHERE SAFE, QUIET...
PRETTY WOMANNN--
--STOP AWHILE, PRETTY WOMANNN TALK AWHI--

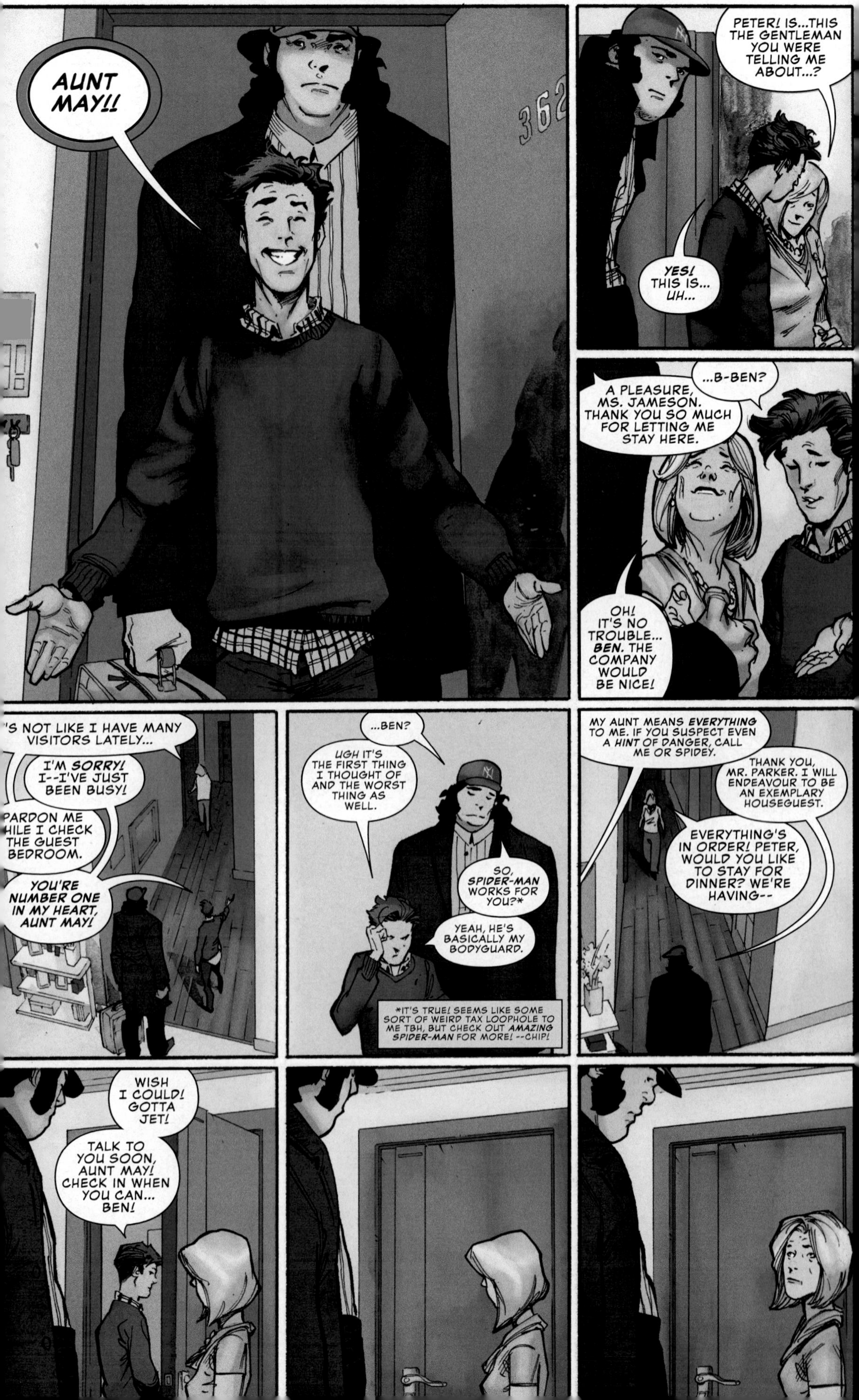
AUNT MAY!!
362
PETER! IS...THIS THE GENTLEMAN YOU WERE TELLING ME ABOUT...?
YES! THIS IS... UH...
...B-BEN?
A PLEASURE, MS. JAMESON. THANK YOU SO MUCH FOR LETTING ME STAY HERE.
OH! IT'S NO TROUBLE... BEN. THE COMPANY WOULD BE NICE!
'S NOT LIKE I HAVE MANY VISITORS LATELY...
I'M SORRY! I--I'VE JUST BEEN BUSY!
PARDON ME HILE I CHECK THE GUEST BEDROOM.
YOU'RE NUMBER ONE IN MY HEART, AUNT MAY!
...BEN?
UGH IT'S THE FIRST THING I THOUGHT OF AND THE WORST THING AS WELL.
SO, SPIDER-MAN WORKS FOR YOU?*
YEAH, HE'S BASICALLY MY BODYGUARD.
*IT'S TRUE! SEEMS LIKE SOME SORT OF WEIRD TAX LOOPHOLE TO ME TBH, BUT CHECK OUT AMAZING SPIDER-MAN FOR MORE! --CHIP!
MY AUNT MEANS EVERYTHING TO ME. IF YOU SUSPECT EVEN A HINT OF DANGER, CALL ME OR SPIDEY.
THANK YOU, MR. PARKER. I WILL ENDEAVOUR TO BE AN EXEMPLARY HOUSEGUEST.
EVERYTHING'S IN ORDER! PETER, WOULD YOU LIKE TO STAY FOR DINNER? WE'RE HAVING--
WISH I COULD! GOTTA JET!
TALK TO YOU SOON, AUNT MAY! CHECK IN WHEN YOU CAN... BEN!

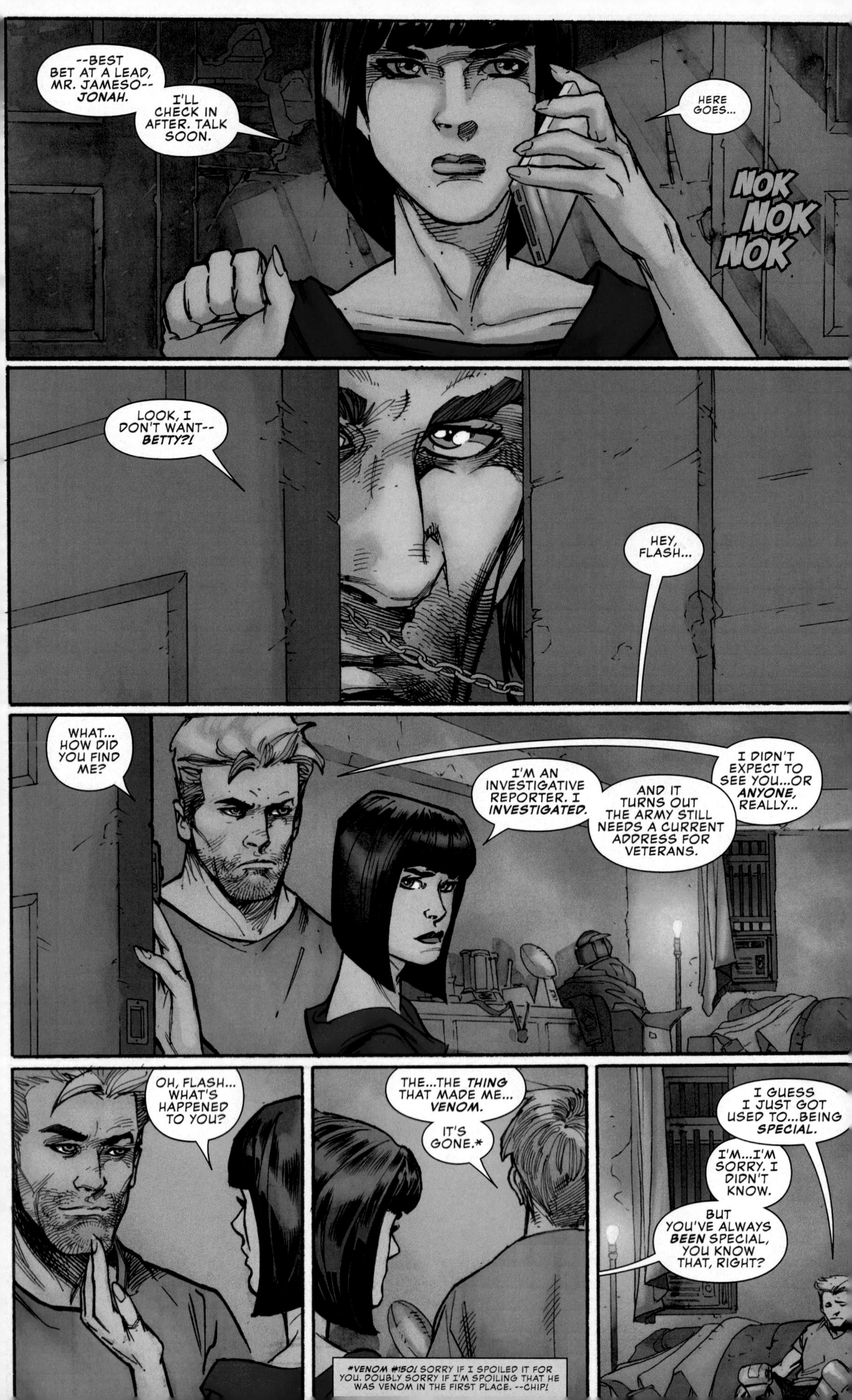
--BEST BET AT A LEAD, MR. JAMESO-- JONAH.
I'LL CHECK IN AFTER. TALK SOON.
HERE GOES...
NOK NOK NOK
LOOK, I DON'T WANT-- BETTY?!
HEY, FLASH...
WHAT... HOW DID YOU FIND ME?
I DIDN'T EXPECT TO SEE YOU...OR ANYONE, REALLY...
I'M AN INVESTIGATIVE REPORTER. I INVESTIGATED.
AND IT TURNS OUT THE ARMY STILL NEEDS A CURRENT ADDRESS FOR VETERANS.
OH, FLASH... WHAT'S HAPPENED TO YOU?
THE...THE THING THAT MADE ME... VENOM.
IT'S GONE.*
*VENOM #150! SORRY IF I SPOILED IT FOR YOU. DOUBLY SORRY IF I'M SPOILING THAT HE WAS VENOM IN THE FIRST PLACE. --CHIP!
I GUESS I JUST GOT USED TO...BEING SPECIAL.
I'M...I'M SORRY. I DIDN'T KNOW.
BUT YOU'VE ALWAYS BEEN SPECIAL, YOU KNOW THAT, RIGHT?

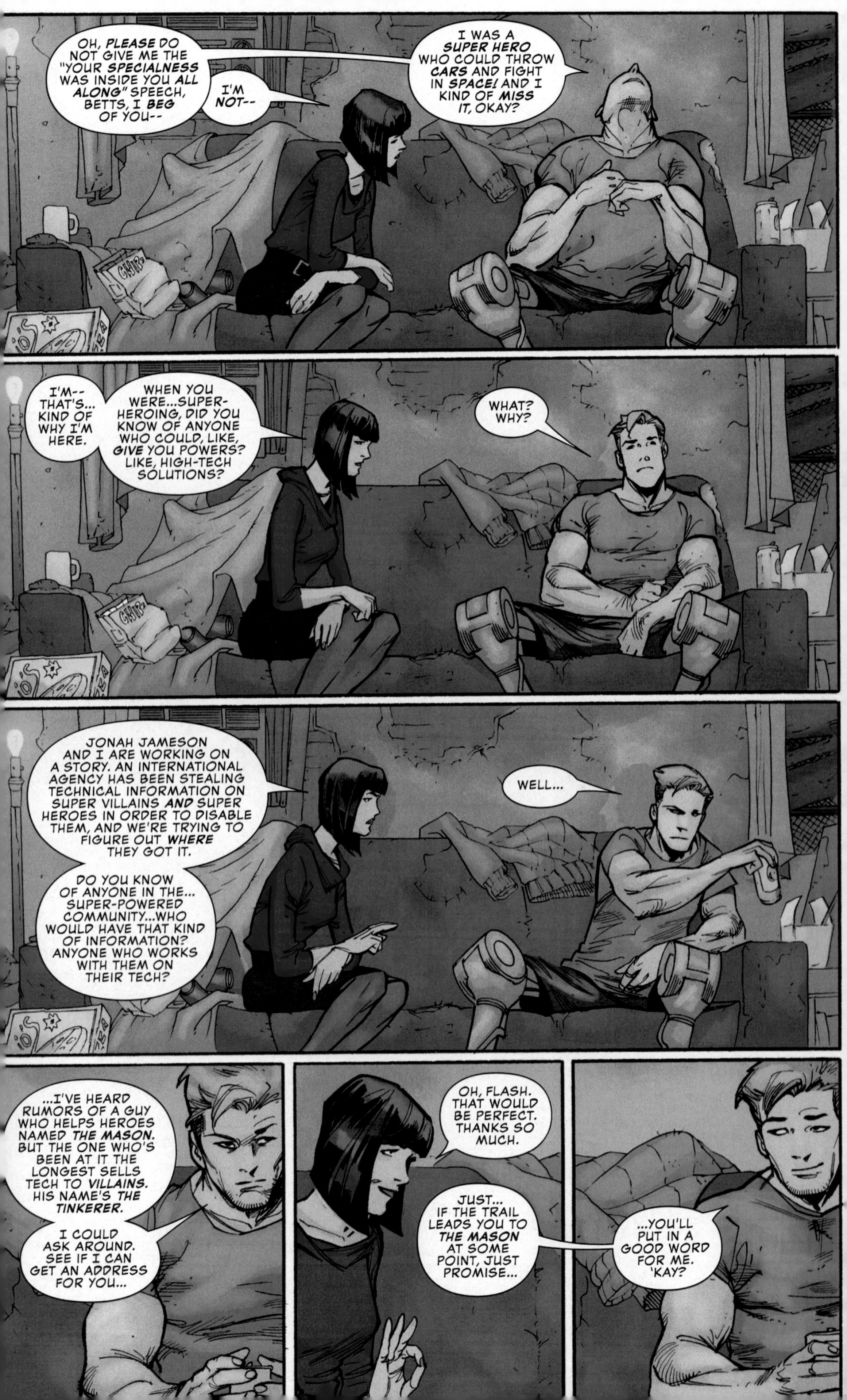

OH, PLEASE DO NOT GIVE ME THE "YOUR SPECIALNESS WAS INSIDE YOU ALL ALONG" SPEECH, BETTS, I BEG OF YOU--
I'M NOT--
I WAS A SUPER HERO WHO COULD THROW CARS AND FIGHT IN SPACE! AND I KIND OF MISS IT, OKAY?
I'M-- THAT'S... KIND OF WHY I'M HERE.
WHEN YOU WERE...SUPER-HEROING, DID YOU KNOW OF ANYONE WHO COULD, LIKE, GIVE YOU POWERS? LIKE, HIGH-TECH SOLUTIONS?
WHAT? WHY?
JONAH JAMESON AND I ARE WORKING ON A STORY. AN INTERNATIONAL AGENCY HAS BEEN STEALING TECHNICAL INFORMATION ON SUPER VILLAINS AND SUPER HEROES IN ORDER TO DISABLE THEM, AND WE'RE TRYING TO FIGURE OUT WHERE THEY GOT IT.
DO YOU KNOW OF ANYONE IN THE... SUPER-POWERED COMMUNITY...WHO WOULD HAVE THAT KIND OF INFORMATION? ANYONE WHO WORKS WITH THEM ON THEIR TECH?
WELL...
...I'VE HEARD RUMORS OF A GUY WHO HELPS HEROES NAMED THE MASON. BUT THE ONE WHO'S BEEN AT IT THE LONGEST SELLS TECH TO VILLAINS. HIS NAME'S THE TINKERER.
I COULD ASK AROUND. SEE IF I CAN GET AN ADDRESS FOR YOU...
OH, FLASH. THAT WOULD BE PERFECT. THANKS SO MUCH.
JUST... IF THE TRAIL LEADS YOU TO THE MASON AT SOME POINT, JUST PROMISE...
...YOU'LL PUT IN A GOOD WORD FOR ME. 'KAY?

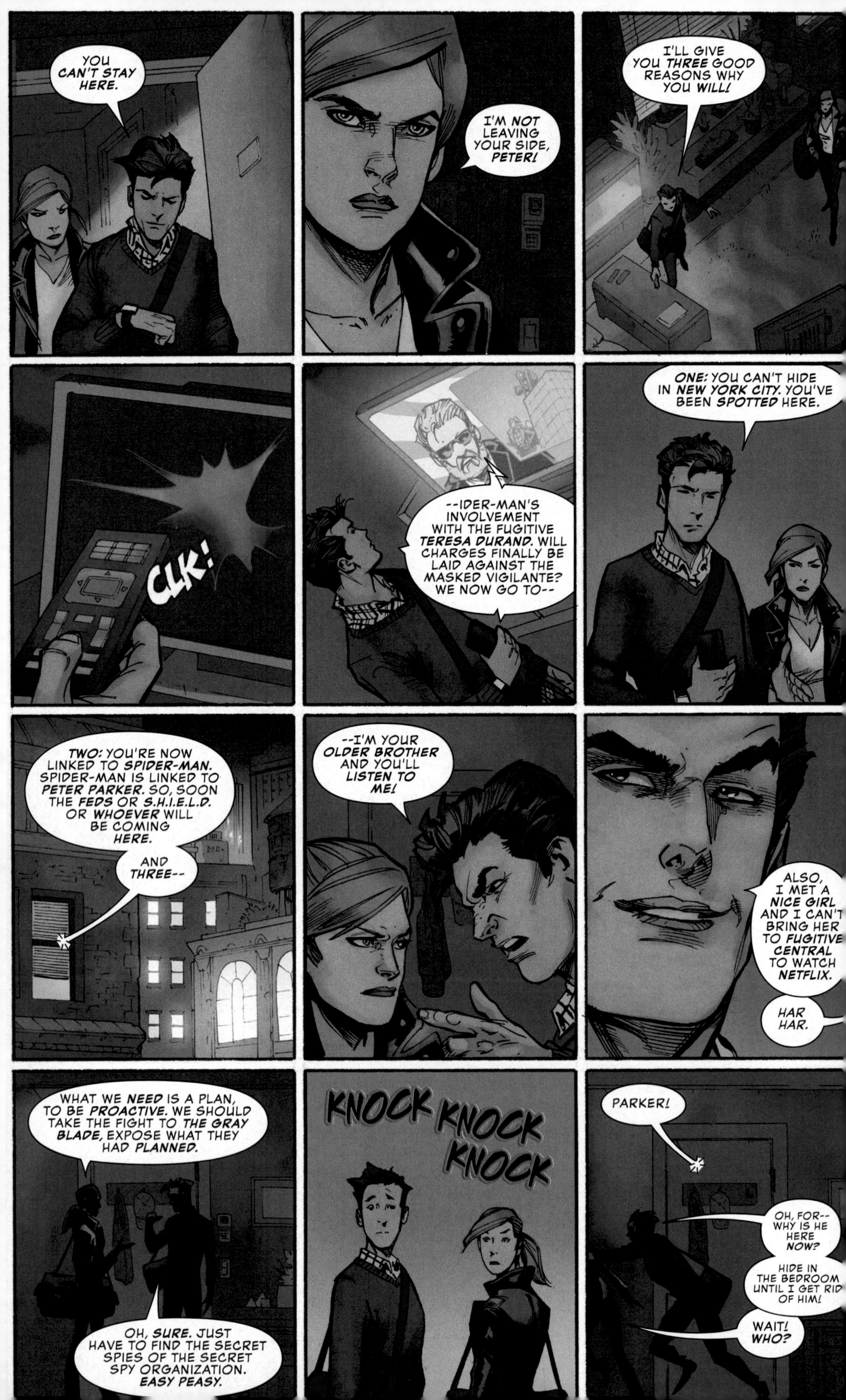
YOU CAN'T STAY HERE.
I'M NOT LEAVING YOUR SIDE, PETER!
I'LL GIVE YOU THREE GOOD REASONS WHY YOU WILL!
CLK!
--IDER-MAN'S INVOLVEMENT WITH THE FUGITIVE TERESA DURAND. WILL CHARGES FINALLY BE LAID AGAINST THE MASKED VIGILANTE? WE NOW GO TO--
ONE: YOU CAN'T HIDE IN NEW YORK CITY. YOU'VE BEEN SPOTTED HERE.
TWO: YOU'RE NOW LINKED TO SPIDER-MAN. SPIDER-MAN IS LINKED TO PETER PARKER. SO, SOON THE FEDS OR S.H.I.E.L.D. OR WHOEVER WILL BE COMING HERE.
AND THREE--
--I'M YOUR OLDER BROTHER AND YOU'LL LISTEN TO ME!
ALSO, I MET A NICE GIRL AND I CAN'T BRING HER TO FUGITIVE CENTRAL TO WATCH NETFLIX.
HAR HAR.
WHAT WE NEED IS A PLAN, TO BE PROACTIVE. WE SHOULD TAKE THE FIGHT TO THE GRAY BLADE, EXPOSE WHAT THEY HAD PLANNED.
OH, SURE. JUST HAVE TO FIND THE SECRET SPIES OF THE SECRET SPY ORGANIZATION. EASY PEASY.
KNOCK KNOCK KNOCK
PARKER!
OH, FOR-- WHY IS HE HERE NOW?
HIDE IN THE BEDROOM UNTIL I GET RID OF HIM!
WAIT! WHO?

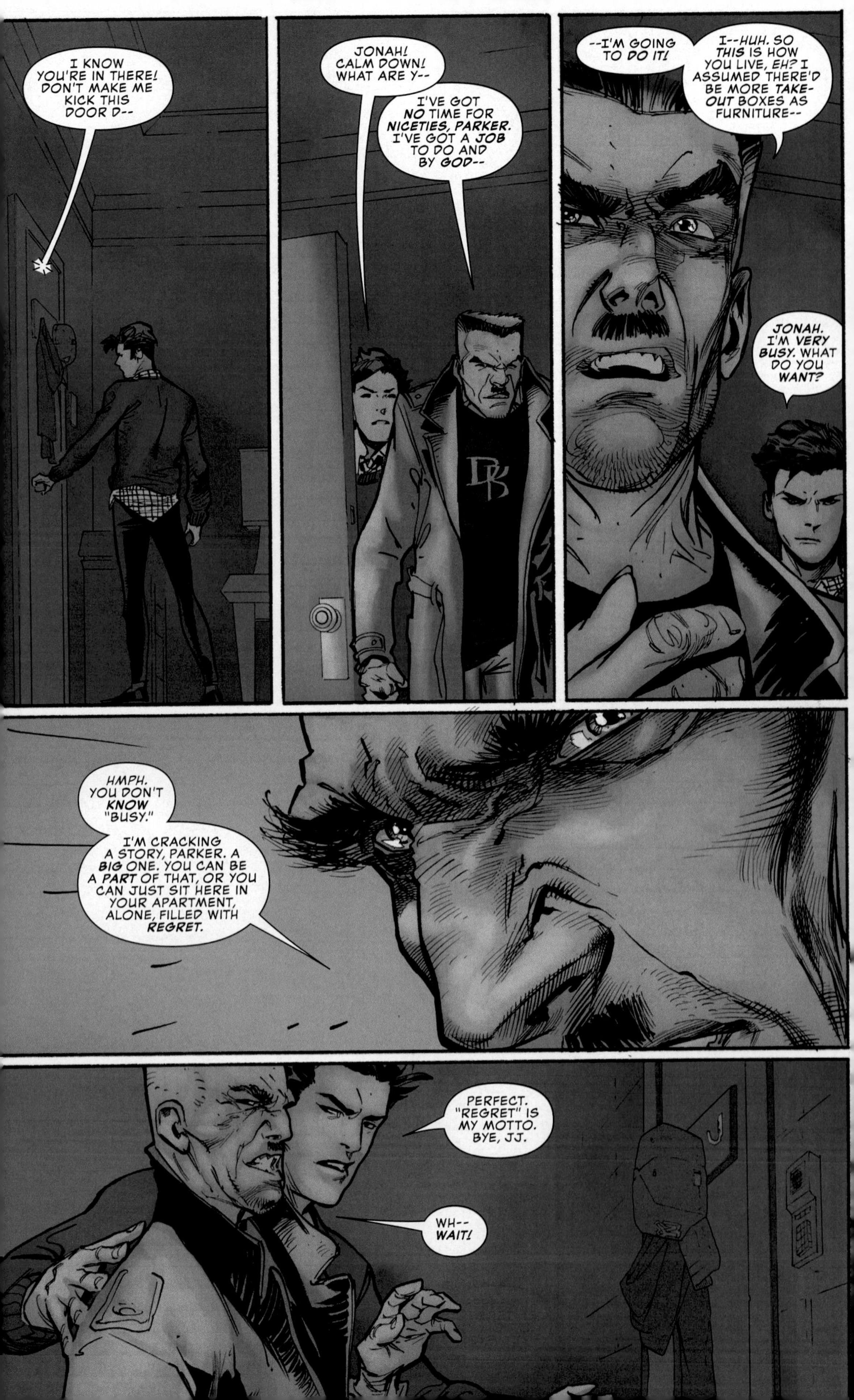

I KNOW YOU'RE IN THERE! DON'T MAKE ME KICK THIS DOOR D--
JONAH! CALM DOWN! WHAT ARE Y--
I'VE GOT NO TIME FOR NICETIES, PARKER. I'VE GOT A JOB TO DO AND BY GOD--
--I'M GOING TO DO IT!
I--HUH. SO THIS IS HOW YOU LIVE, EH? I ASSUMED THERE'D BE MORE TAKE-OUT BOXES AS FURNITURE--
JONAH. I'M VERY BUSY. WHAT DO YOU WANT?
HMPH. YOU DON'T KNOW "BUSY."
I'M CRACKING A STORY, PARKER. A BIG ONE. YOU CAN BE A PART OF THAT, OR YOU CAN JUST SIT HERE IN YOUR APARTMENT, ALONE, FILLED WITH REGRET.
PERFECT. "REGRET" IS MY MOTTO. BYE, JJ.
WH-- WAIT!

PARKER! SON...I KNOW WE'VE HAD OUR DIFFERENCES... BUT I NEED YOUR *HELP*. I NEED...

I NEED TO TALK TO SPIDER-MAN.

WAIT, WHAT?

WHY ON *EARTH* WOULD SPIDER-MAN WANT TO TALK TO *YOU?* YOU'RE RUNNING A *BLOG* DEDICATED TO *SLAGGING* HIM!

I NEED TO *INTERVIEW* HIM! IT'S *IMPORTANT!* IT'S...IT'S ABOUT THE *WOMAN* HE WAS WITH! THE ONE WITH THE STOLEN FILES! I'M *SURE* YOU DON'T WATCH THE *NEWS,* BUT YOUR *BODYGUARD* HAS BEEN HELPING A *KNOWN FUGITIVE!*

...GO ON.

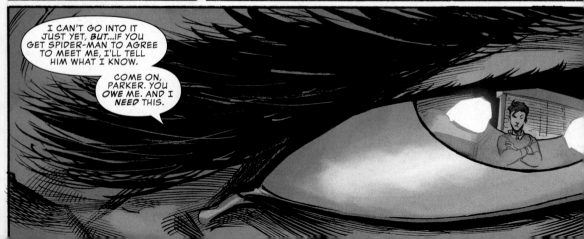

I CAN'T GO INTO IT JUST YET, *BUT...*IF YOU GET SPIDER-MAN TO AGREE TO MEET ME, I'LL TELL HIM WHAT I KNOW.

COME ON, PARKER. YOU *OWE* ME. AND I *NEED* THIS.

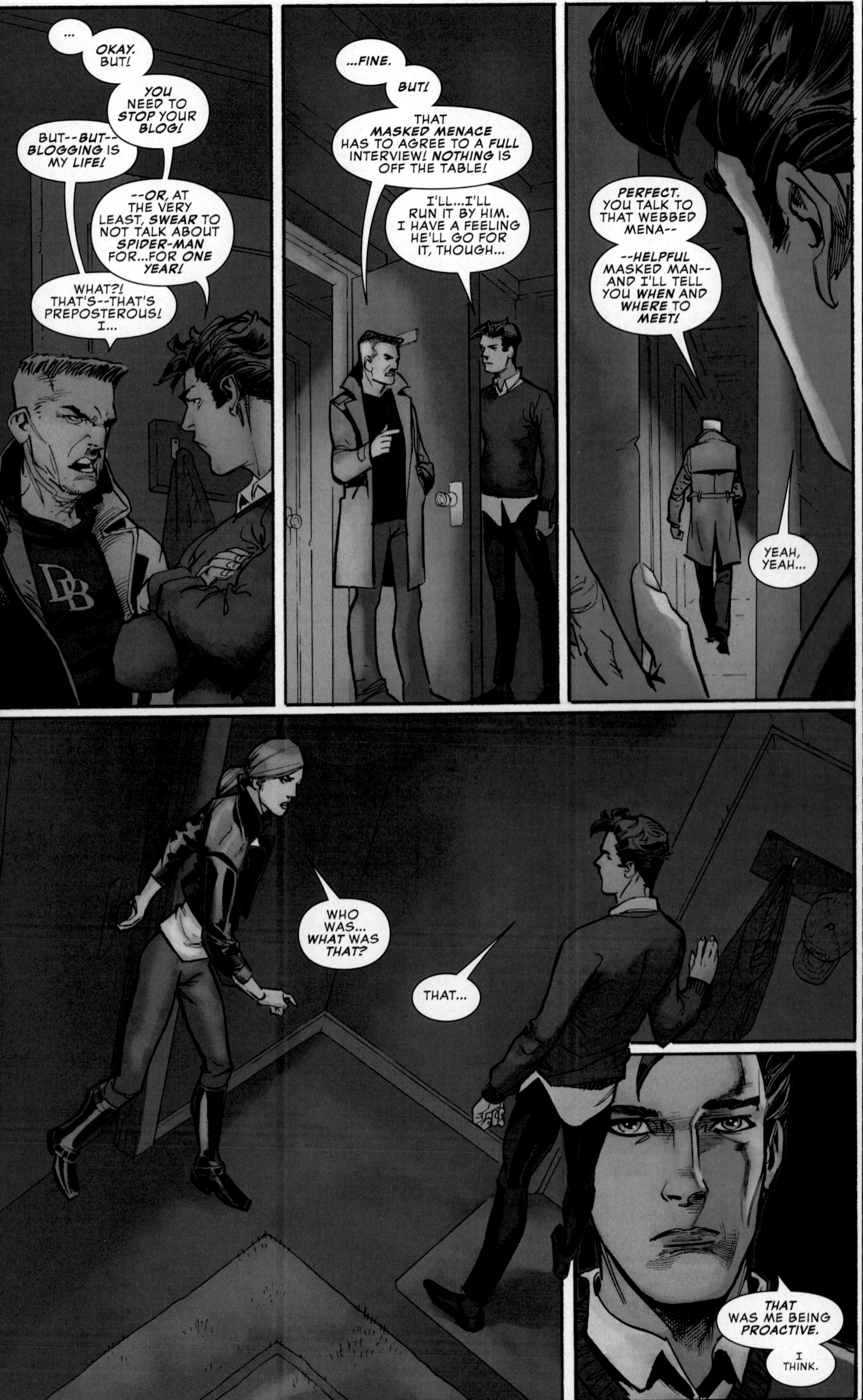
...
OKAY. BUT!
YOU NEED TO STOP YOUR BLOG!
BUT--BUT--BLOGGING IS MY LIFE!
--OR, AT THE VERY LEAST, SWEAR TO NOT TALK ABOUT SPIDER-MAN FOR...FOR ONE YEAR!
WHAT?! THAT'S--THAT'S PREPOSTEROUS! I...
...FINE.
BUT!
THAT MASKED MENACE HAS TO AGREE TO A FULL INTERVIEW! NOTHING IS OFF THE TABLE!
I'LL...I'LL RUN IT BY HIM. I HAVE A FEELING HE'LL GO FOR IT, THOUGH...
PERFECT. YOU TALK TO THAT WEBBED MENA--
--HELPFUL MASKED MAN--AND I'LL TELL YOU WHEN AND WHERE TO MEET!
YEAH, YEAH...
WHO WAS... WHAT WAS THAT?
THAT...
THAT WAS ME BEING PROACTIVE.
I THINK.

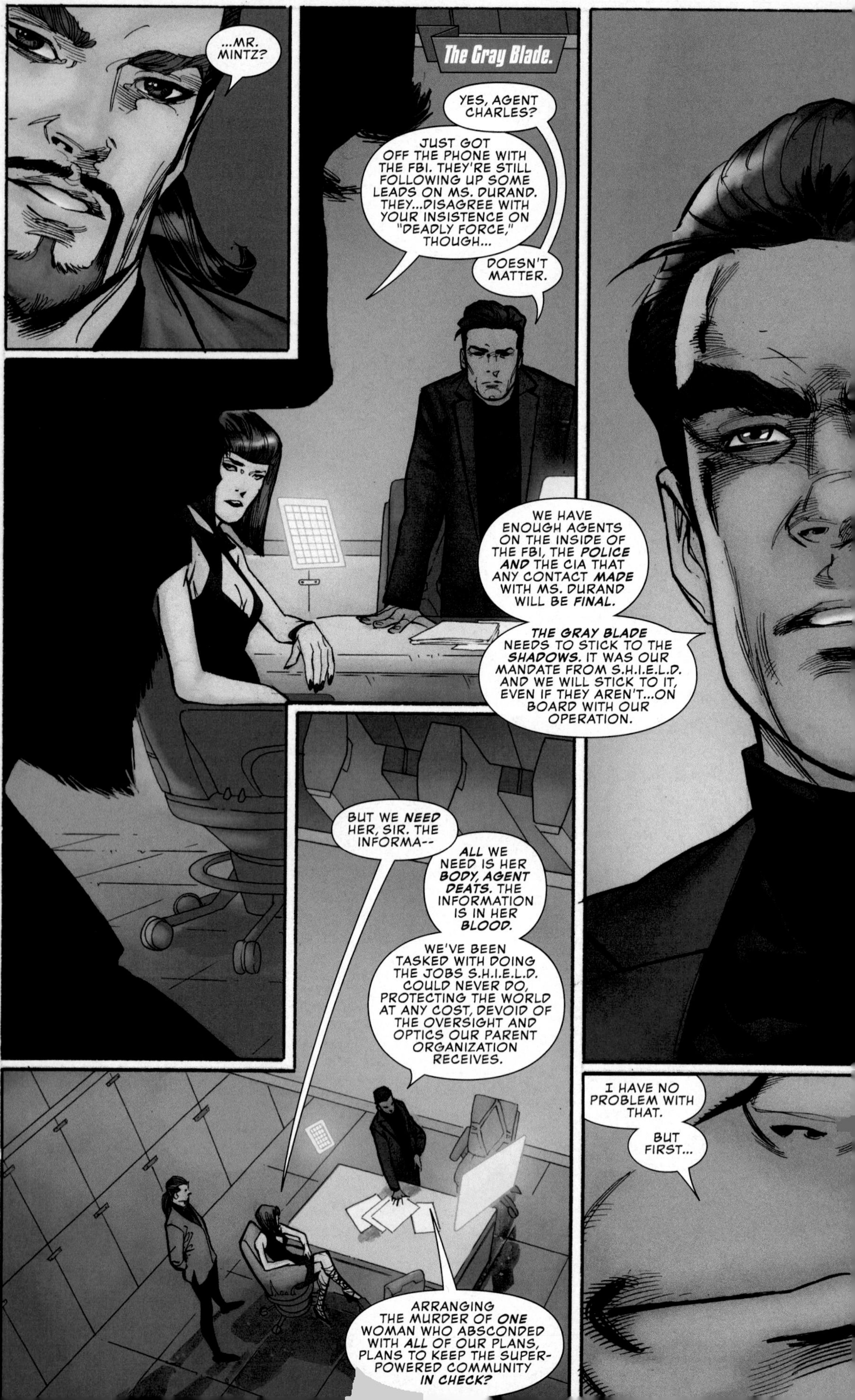
...MR. MINTZ?
The Gray Blade.
YES, AGENT CHARLES?
JUST GOT OFF THE PHONE WITH THE FBI. THEY'RE STILL FOLLOWING UP SOME LEADS ON MS. DURAND. THEY...DISAGREE WITH YOUR INSISTENCE ON "DEADLY FORCE," THOUGH...
DOESN'T MATTER.
WE HAVE ENOUGH AGENTS ON THE INSIDE OF THE FBI, THE POLICE AND THE CIA THAT ANY CONTACT MADE WITH MS. DURAND WILL BE FINAL.
THE GRAY BLADE NEEDS TO STICK TO THE SHADOWS. IT WAS OUR MANDATE FROM S.H.I.E.L.D. AND WE WILL STICK TO IT, EVEN IF THEY AREN'T...ON BOARD WITH OUR OPERATION.
BUT WE NEED HER, SIR. THE INFORMA--
ALL WE NEED IS HER BODY, AGENT DEATS. THE INFORMATION IS IN HER BLOOD.
WE'VE BEEN TASKED WITH DOING THE JOBS S.H.I.E.L.D. COULD NEVER DO, PROTECTING THE WORLD AT ANY COST, DEVOID OF THE OVERSIGHT AND OPTICS OUR PARENT ORGANIZATION RECEIVES.
ARRANGING THE MURDER OF ONE WOMAN WHO ABSCONDED WITH ALL OF OUR PLANS, PLANS TO KEEP THE SUPER-POWERED COMMUNITY IN CHECK?
I HAVE NO PROBLEM WITH THAT.
BUT FIRST...

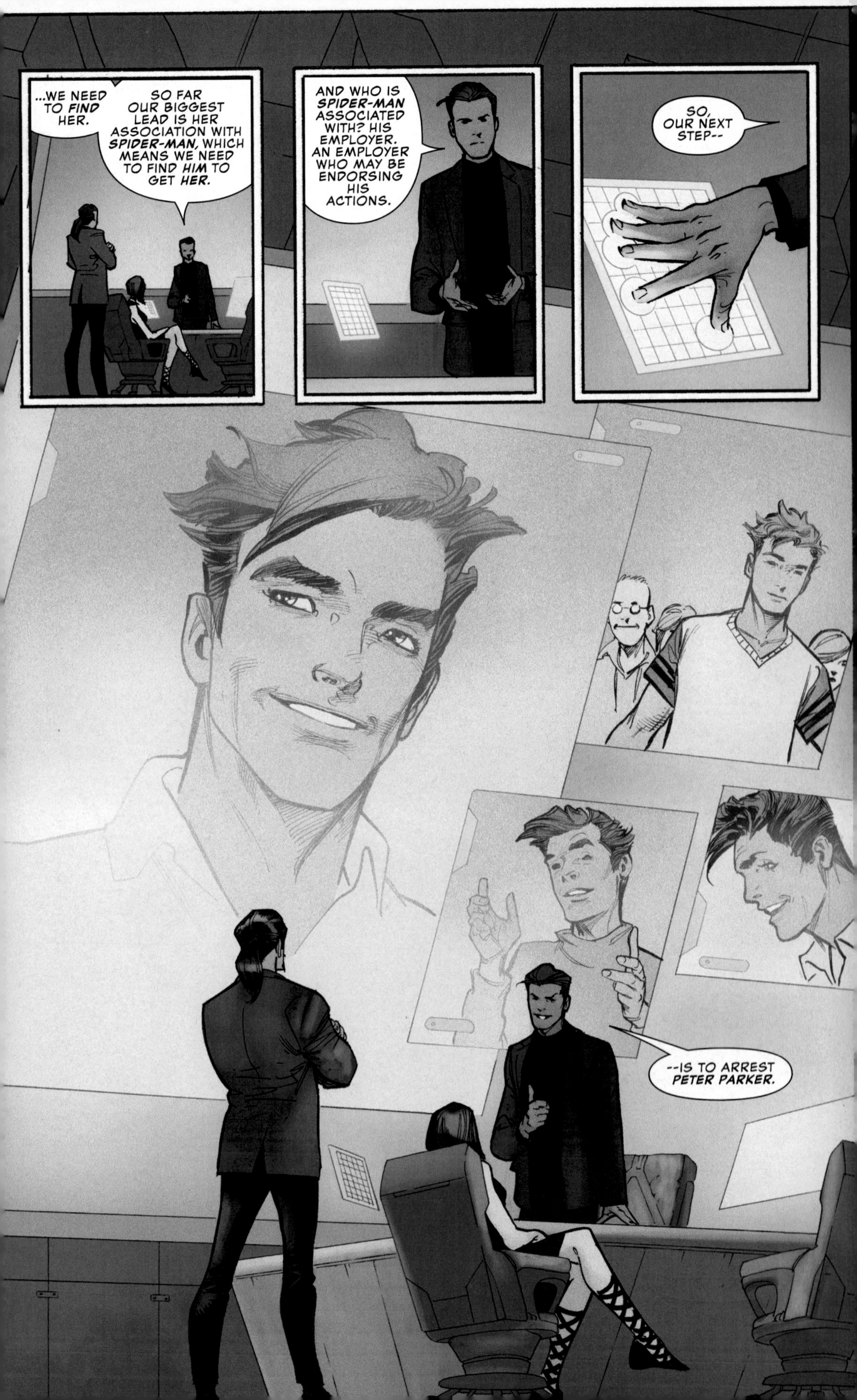
...WE NEED TO *FIND* HER.
SO FAR OUR BIGGEST LEAD IS HER ASSOCIATION WITH *SPIDER-MAN,* WHICH MEANS WE NEED TO FIND *HIM* TO GET *HER.*
AND WHO IS *SPIDER-MAN* ASSOCIATED WITH? HIS EMPLOYER. AN EMPLOYER WHO MAY BE ENDORSING HIS ACTIONS.
SO, OUR NEXT STEP--
--IS TO ARREST *PETER PARKER.*

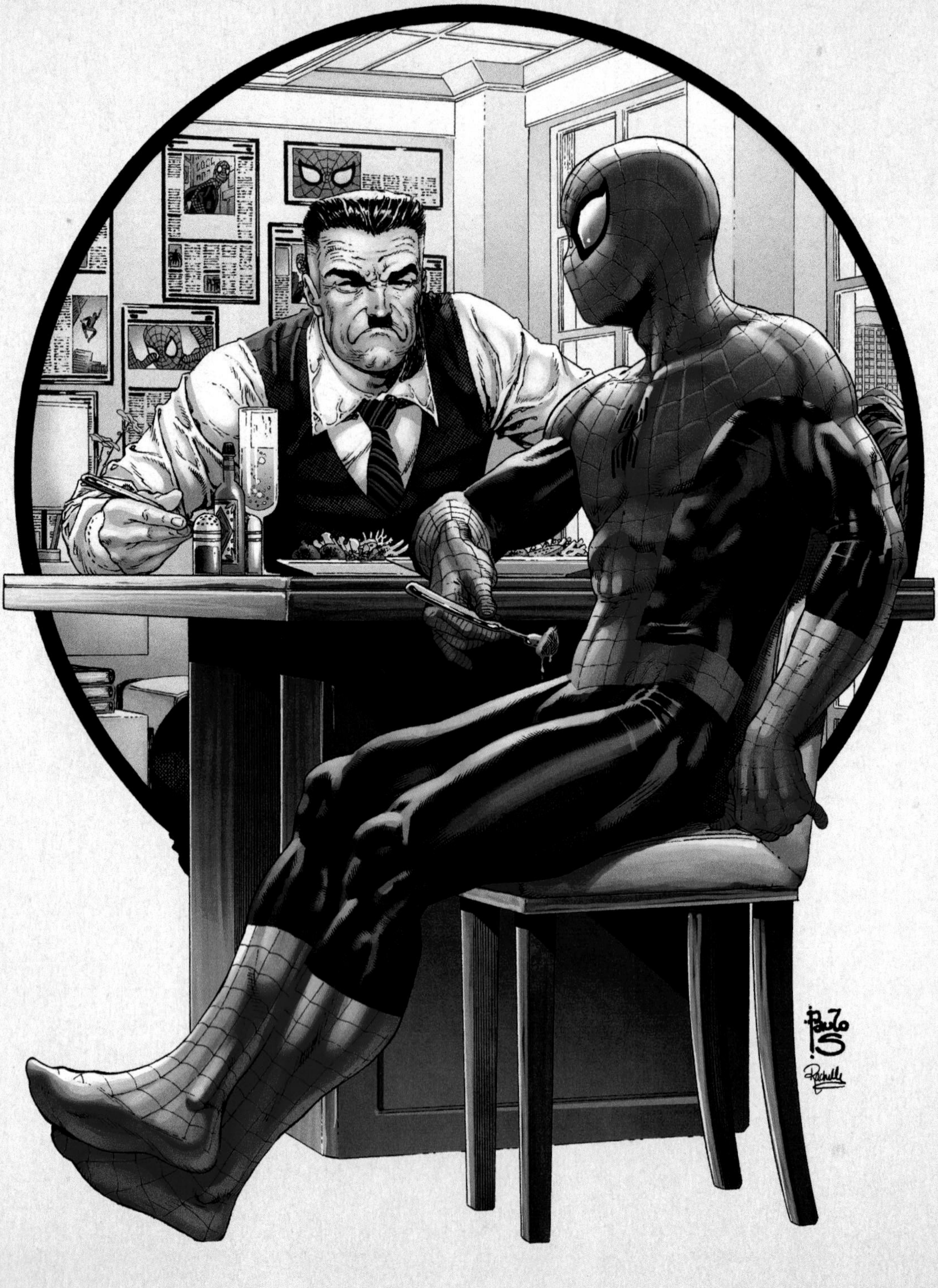

6

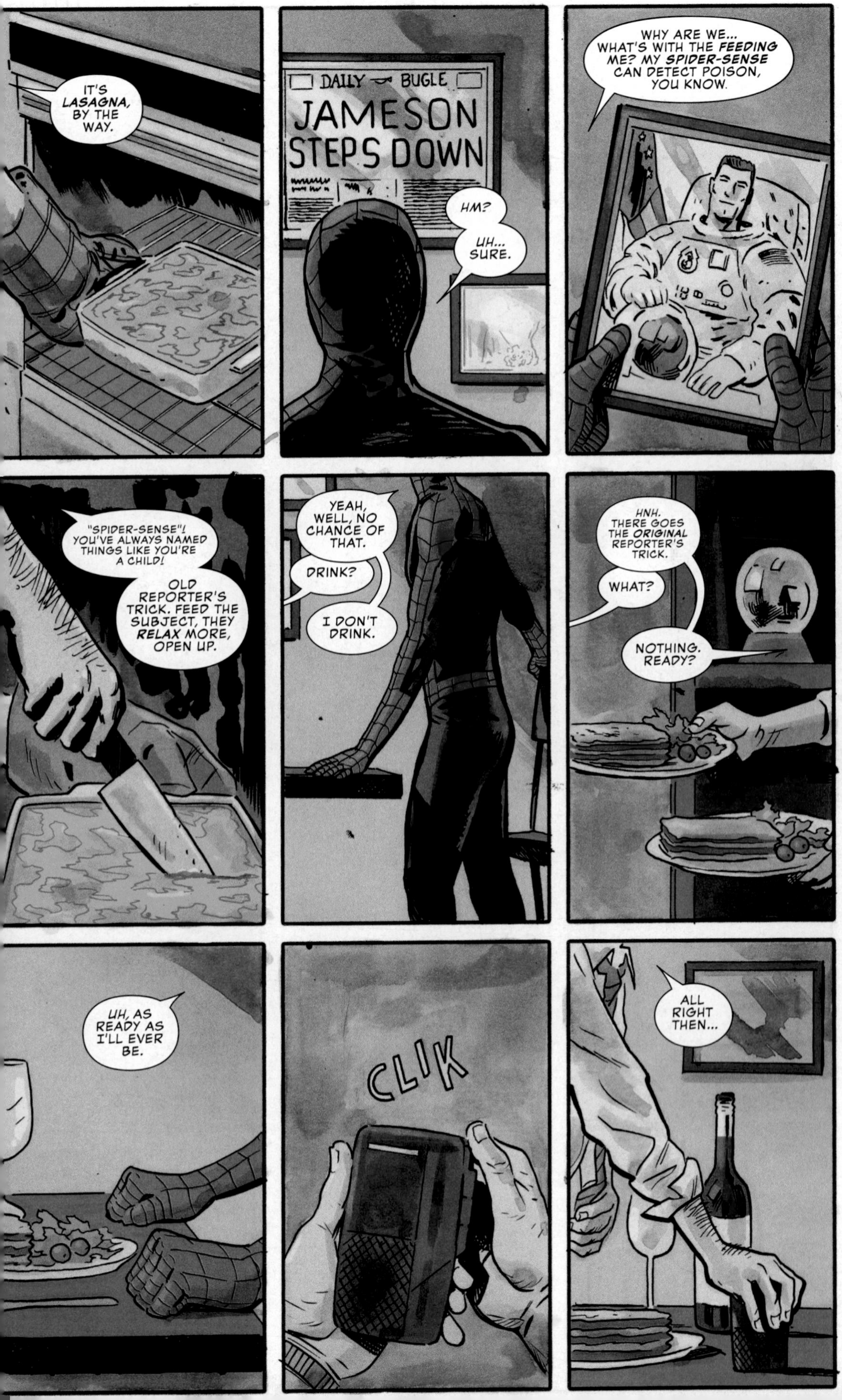
IT'S LASAGNA, BY THE WAY.
DAILY BUGLE
JAMESON STEPS DOWN
HM?
UH... SURE.
WHY ARE WE... WHAT'S WITH THE FEEDING ME? MY SPIDER-SENSE CAN DETECT POISON, YOU KNOW.
"SPIDER-SENSE"! YOU'VE ALWAYS NAMED THINGS LIKE YOU'RE A CHILD!
OLD REPORTER'S TRICK. FEED THE SUBJECT, THEY RELAX MORE, OPEN UP.
YEAH, WELL, NO CHANCE OF THAT.
DRINK?
I DON'T DRINK.
HNH. THERE GOES THE ORIGINAL REPORTER'S TRICK.
WHAT?
NOTHING. READY?
UH, AS READY AS I'LL EVER BE.
CLIK
ALL RIGHT THEN...

MARVEL COMICS PRESENTS

MY DINNER WITH JONAH

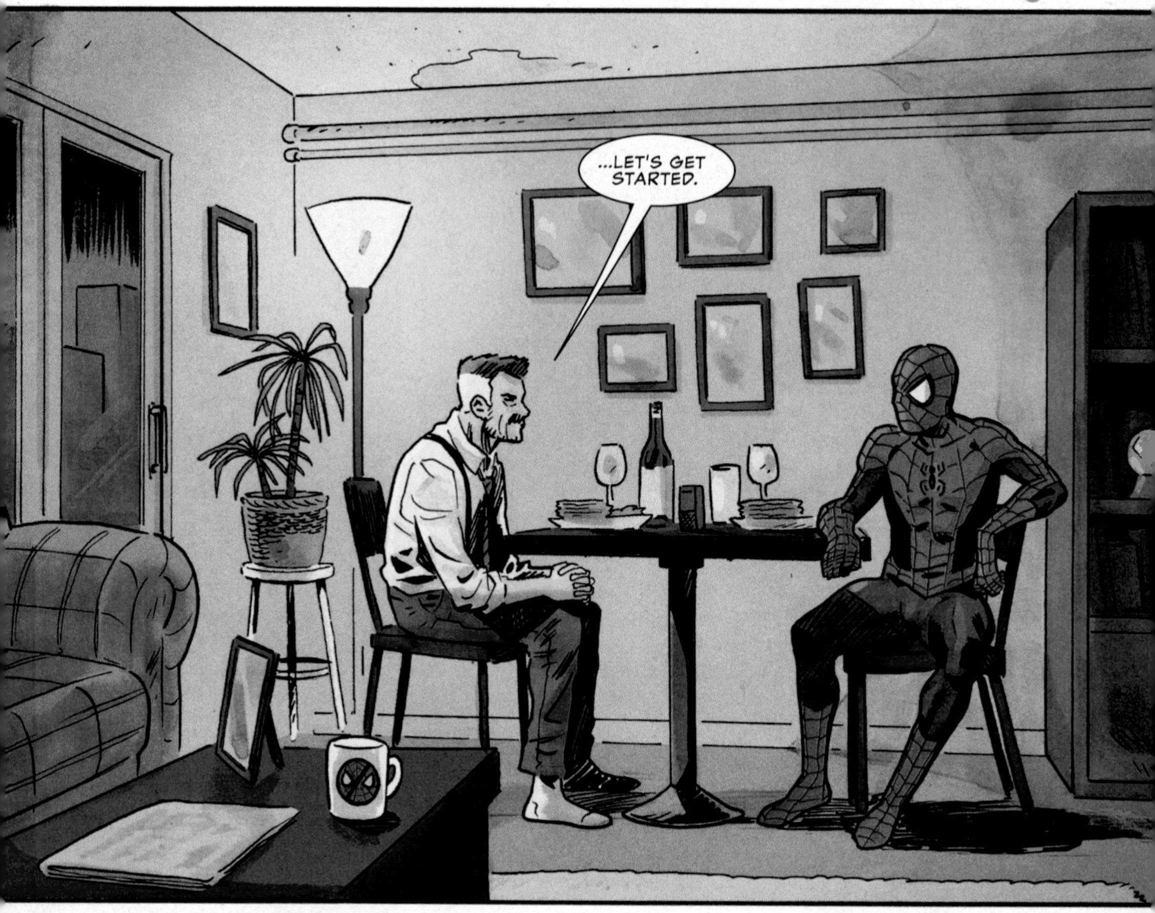
...LET'S GET STARTED.

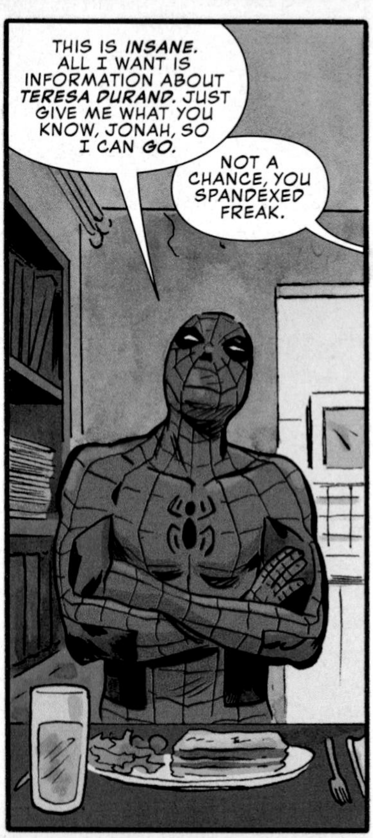
THIS IS INSANE. ALL I WANT IS INFORMATION ABOUT TERESA DURAND. JUST GIVE ME WHAT YOU KNOW, JONAH, SO I CAN GO.
NOT A CHANCE, YOU SPANDEXED FREAK.

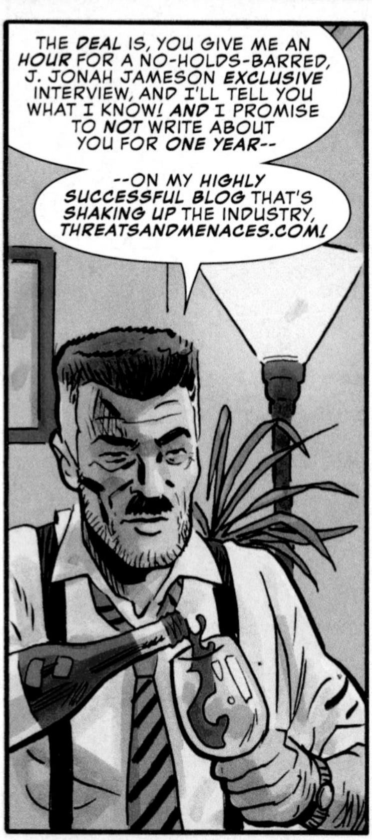
THE DEAL IS, YOU GIVE ME AN HOUR FOR A NO-HOLDS-BARRED, J. JONAH JAMESON EXCLUSIVE INTERVIEW, AND I'LL TELL YOU WHAT I KNOW! AND I PROMISE TO NOT WRITE ABOUT YOU FOR ONE YEAR--
--ON MY HIGHLY SUCCESSFUL BLOG THAT'S SHAKING UP THE INDUSTRY, THREATSANDMENACES.COM!

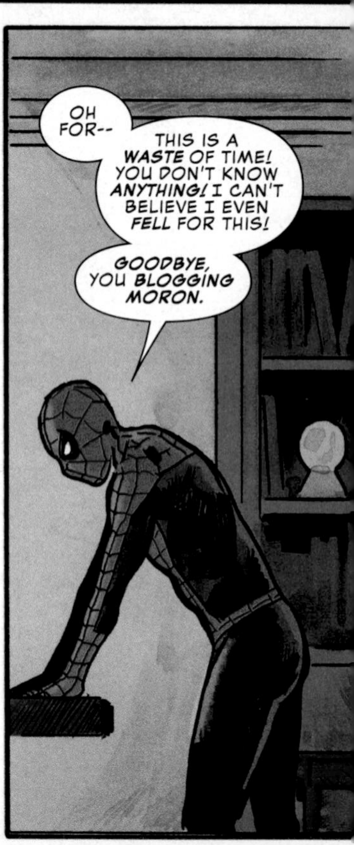
OH FOR--
THIS IS A WASTE OF TIME! YOU DON'T KNOW ANYTHING! I CAN'T BELIEVE I EVEN FELL FOR THIS!
GOODBYE, YOU BLOGGING MORON.

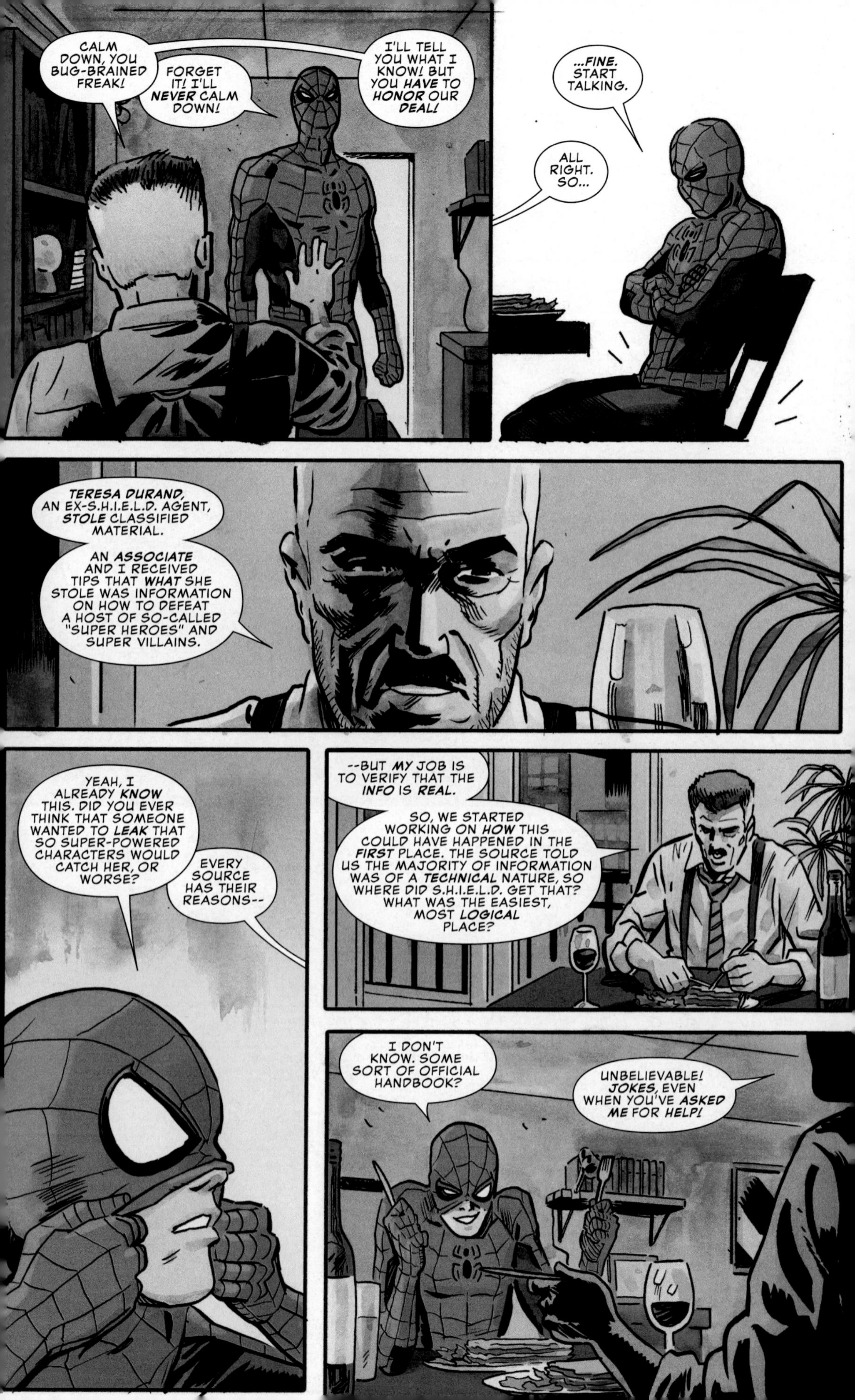
CALM DOWN, YOU BUG-BRAINED FREAK!
I'LL TELL YOU WHAT I KNOW! BUT YOU HAVE TO HONOR OUR DEAL!
FORGET IT! I'LL NEVER CALM DOWN!
...FINE. START TALKING.
ALL RIGHT. SO...
TERESA DURAND, AN EX-S.H.I.E.L.D. AGENT, STOLE CLASSIFIED MATERIAL.
AN ASSOCIATE AND I RECEIVED TIPS THAT WHAT SHE STOLE WAS INFORMATION ON HOW TO DEFEAT A HOST OF SO-CALLED "SUPER HEROES" AND SUPER VILLAINS.
YEAH, I ALREADY KNOW THIS. DID YOU EVER THINK THAT SOMEONE WANTED TO LEAK THAT SO SUPER-POWERED CHARACTERS WOULD CATCH HER, OR WORSE?
EVERY SOURCE HAS THEIR REASONS--
--BUT MY JOB IS TO VERIFY THAT THE INFO IS REAL.
SO, WE STARTED WORKING ON HOW THIS COULD HAVE HAPPENED IN THE FIRST PLACE. THE SOURCE TOLD US THE MAJORITY OF INFORMATION WAS OF A TECHNICAL NATURE, SO WHERE DID S.H.I.E.L.D. GET THAT? WHAT WAS THE EASIEST, MOST LOGICAL PLACE?
I DON'T KNOW. SOME SORT OF OFFICIAL HANDBOOK?
UNBELIEVABLE! JOKES, EVEN WHEN YOU'VE ASKED ME FOR HELP!

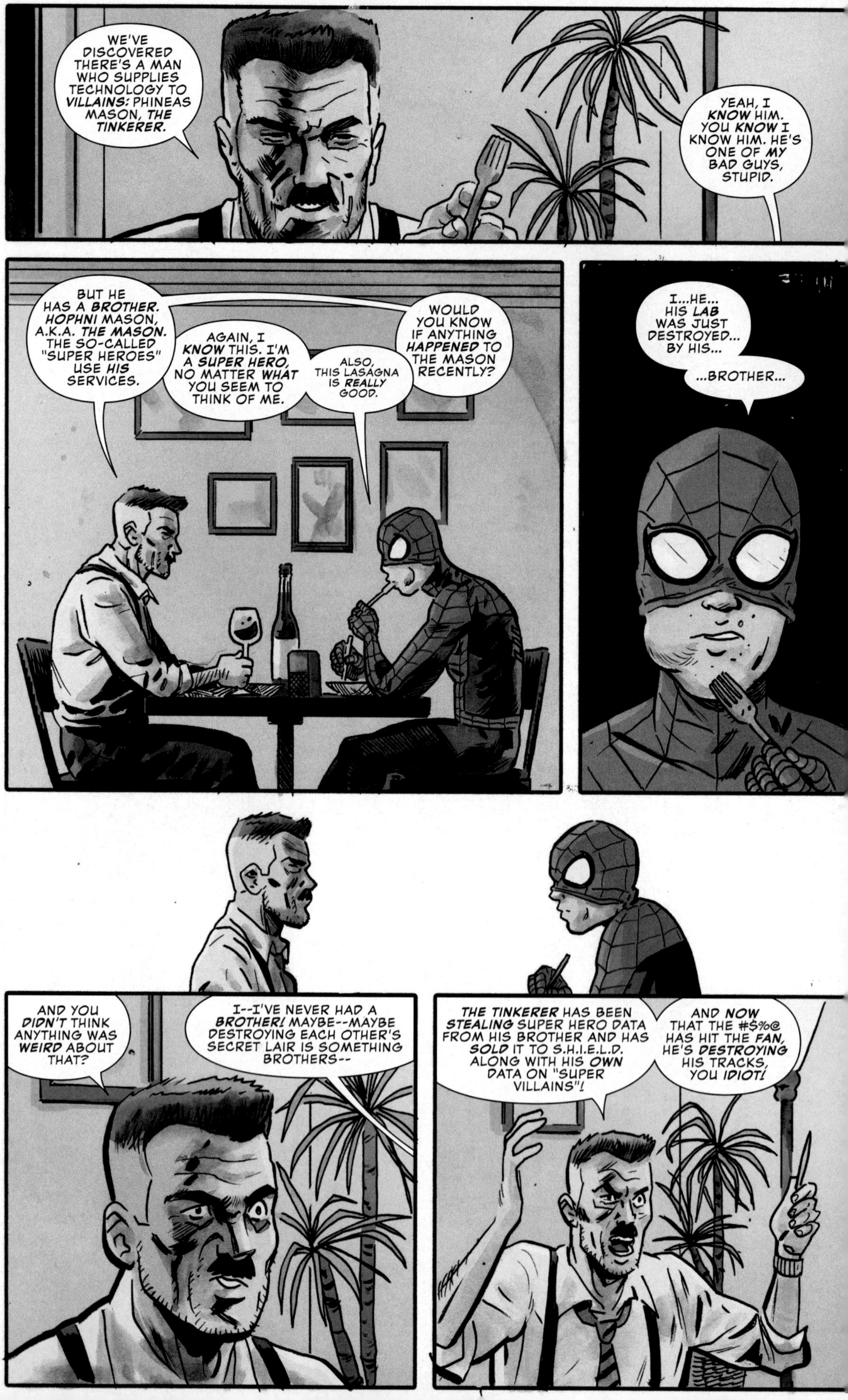
WE'VE DISCOVERED THERE'S A MAN WHO SUPPLIES TECHNOLOGY TO VILLAINS: PHINEAS MASON, THE TINKERER.
YEAH, I KNOW HIM. YOU KNOW I KNOW HIM. HE'S ONE OF MY BAD GUYS, STUPID.
BUT HE HAS A BROTHER. HOPHNI MASON, A.K.A. THE MASON. THE SO-CALLED "SUPER HEROES" USE HIS SERVICES.
AGAIN, I KNOW THIS. I'M A SUPER HERO, NO MATTER WHAT YOU SEEM TO THINK OF ME.
ALSO, THIS LASAGNA IS REALLY GOOD.
WOULD YOU KNOW IF ANYTHING HAPPENED TO THE MASON RECENTLY?
I...HE... HIS LAB WAS JUST DESTROYED... BY HIS...
...BROTHER...
AND YOU DIDN'T THINK ANYTHING WAS WEIRD ABOUT THAT?
I--I'VE NEVER HAD A BROTHER! MAYBE--MAYBE DESTROYING EACH OTHER'S SECRET LAIR IS SOMETHING BROTHERS--
THE TINKERER HAS BEEN STEALING SUPER HERO DATA FROM HIS BROTHER AND HAS SOLD IT TO S.H.I.E.L.D. ALONG WITH HIS OWN DATA ON "SUPER VILLAINS"!
AND NOW THAT THE #$%@ HAS HIT THE FAN, HE'S DESTROYING HIS TRACKS, YOU IDIOT!

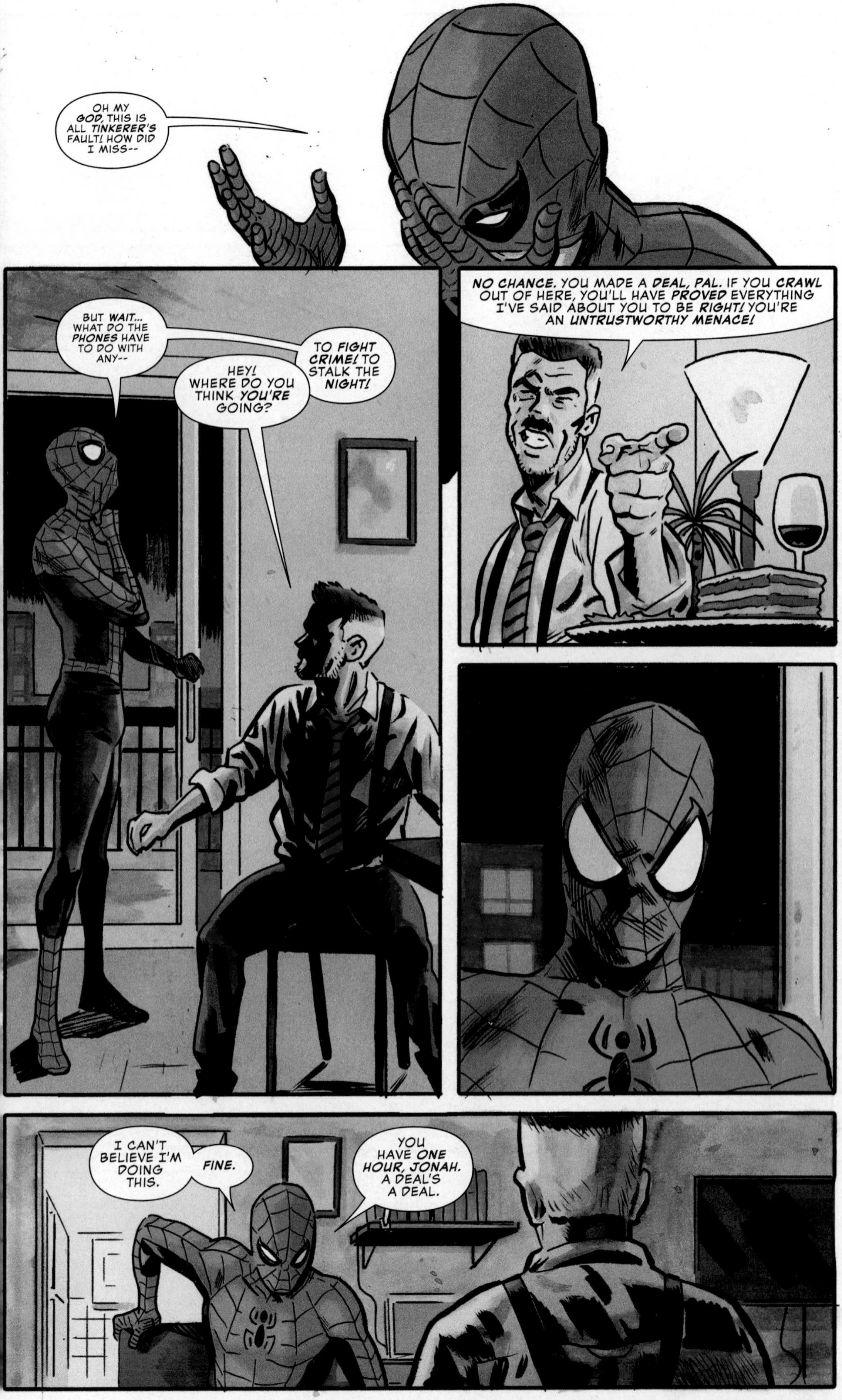
OH MY GOD, THIS IS ALL TINKERER'S FAULT! HOW DID I MISS--
BUT WAIT... WHAT DO THE PHONES HAVE TO DO WITH ANY--
TO FIGHT CRIME! TO STALK THE NIGHT!
HEY! WHERE DO YOU THINK YOU'RE GOING?
NO CHANCE. YOU MADE A DEAL, PAL. IF YOU CRAWL OUT OF HERE, YOU'LL HAVE PROVED EVERYTHING I'VE SAID ABOUT YOU TO BE RIGHT! YOU'RE AN UNTRUSTWORTHY MENACE!
I CAN'T BELIEVE I'M DOING THIS.
FINE.
YOU HAVE ONE HOUR, JONAH. A DEAL'S A DEAL.

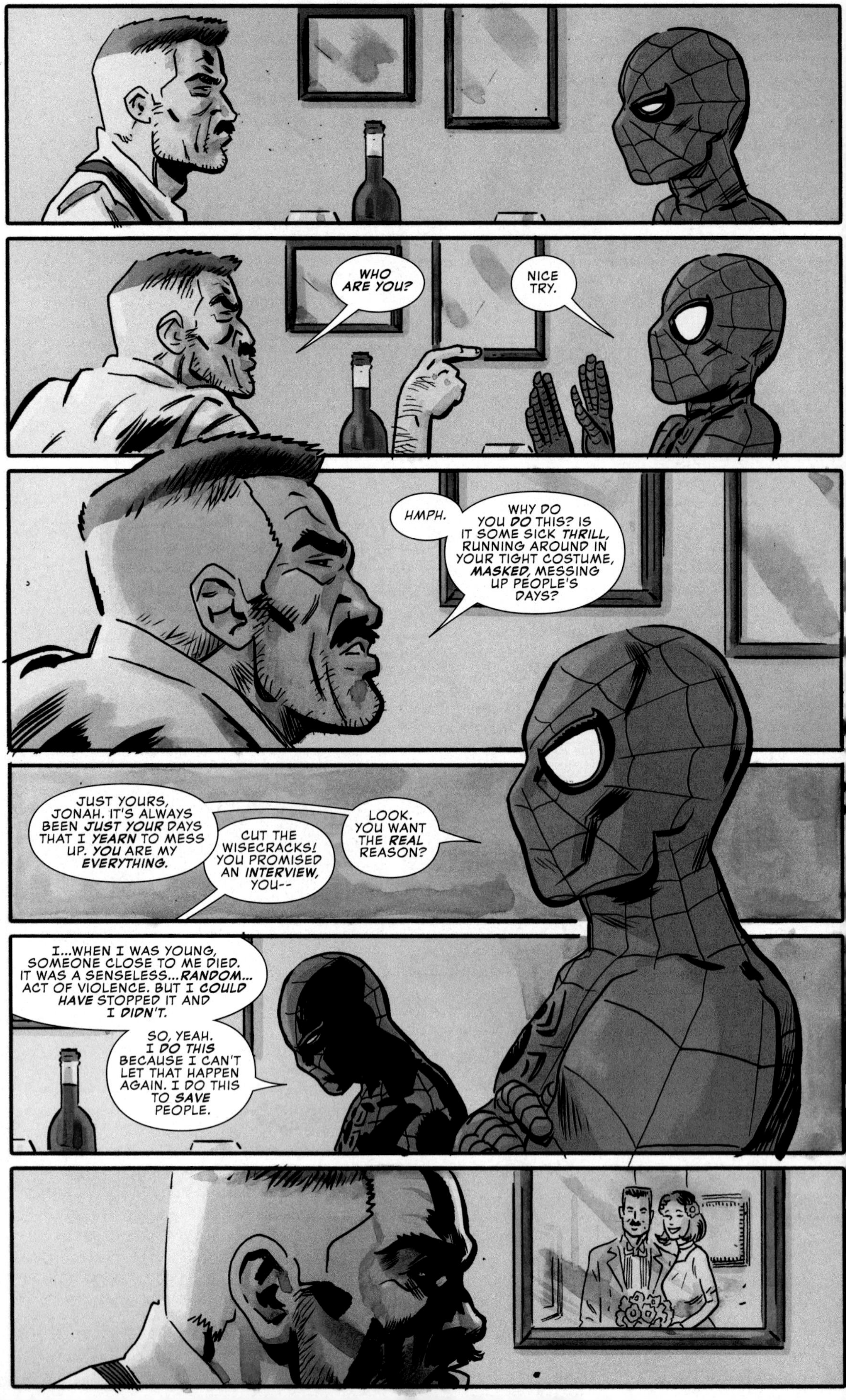
WHO ARE YOU?
NICE TRY.
HMPH.
WHY DO YOU DO THIS? IS IT SOME SICK THRILL, RUNNING AROUND IN YOUR TIGHT COSTUME, MASKED, MESSING UP PEOPLE'S DAYS?
JUST YOURS, JONAH. IT'S ALWAYS BEEN JUST YOUR DAYS THAT I YEARN TO MESS UP. YOU ARE MY EVERYTHING.
CUT THE WISECRACKS! YOU PROMISED AN INTERVIEW, YOU--
LOOK. YOU WANT THE REAL REASON?
I...WHEN I WAS YOUNG, SOMEONE CLOSE TO ME DIED. IT WAS A SENSELESS...RANDOM... ACT OF VIOLENCE. BUT I COULD HAVE STOPPED IT AND I DIDN'T.
SO, YEAH. I DO THIS BECAUSE I CAN'T LET THAT HAPPEN AGAIN. I DO THIS TO SAVE PEOPLE.

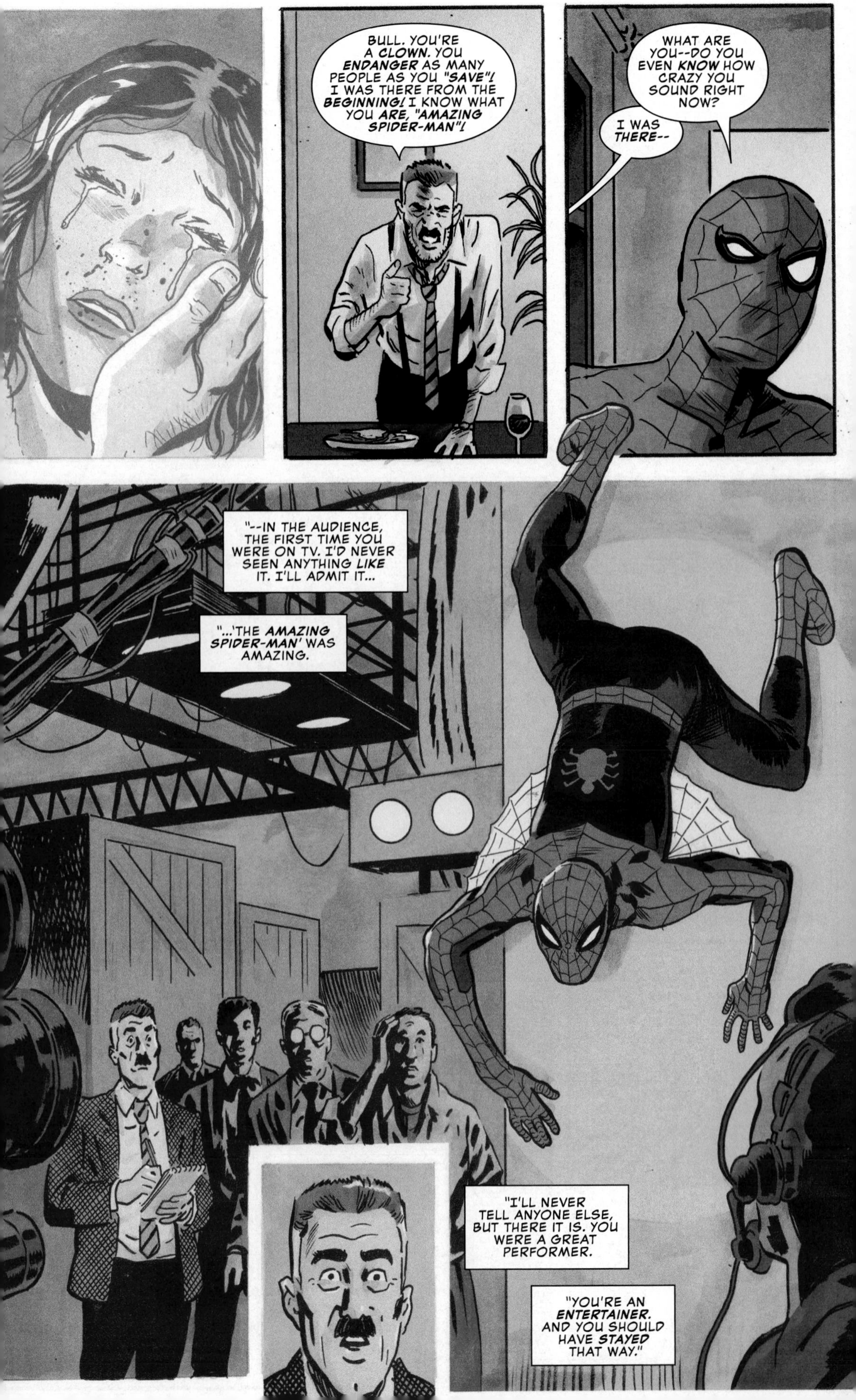

BULL. YOU'RE A CLOWN. YOU ENDANGER AS MANY PEOPLE AS YOU "SAVE"! I WAS THERE FROM THE BEGINNING! I KNOW WHAT YOU ARE, "AMAZING SPIDER-MAN"!
WHAT ARE YOU--DO YOU EVEN KNOW HOW CRAZY YOU SOUND RIGHT NOW?
I WAS THERE--
"--IN THE AUDIENCE, THE FIRST TIME YOU WERE ON TV. I'D NEVER SEEN ANYTHING LIKE IT. I'LL ADMIT IT...
"...'THE AMAZING SPIDER-MAN' WAS AMAZING.
"I'LL NEVER TELL ANYONE ELSE, BUT THERE IT IS. YOU WERE A GREAT PERFORMER.
"YOU'RE AN ENTERTAINER. AND YOU SHOULD HAVE STAYED THAT WAY."

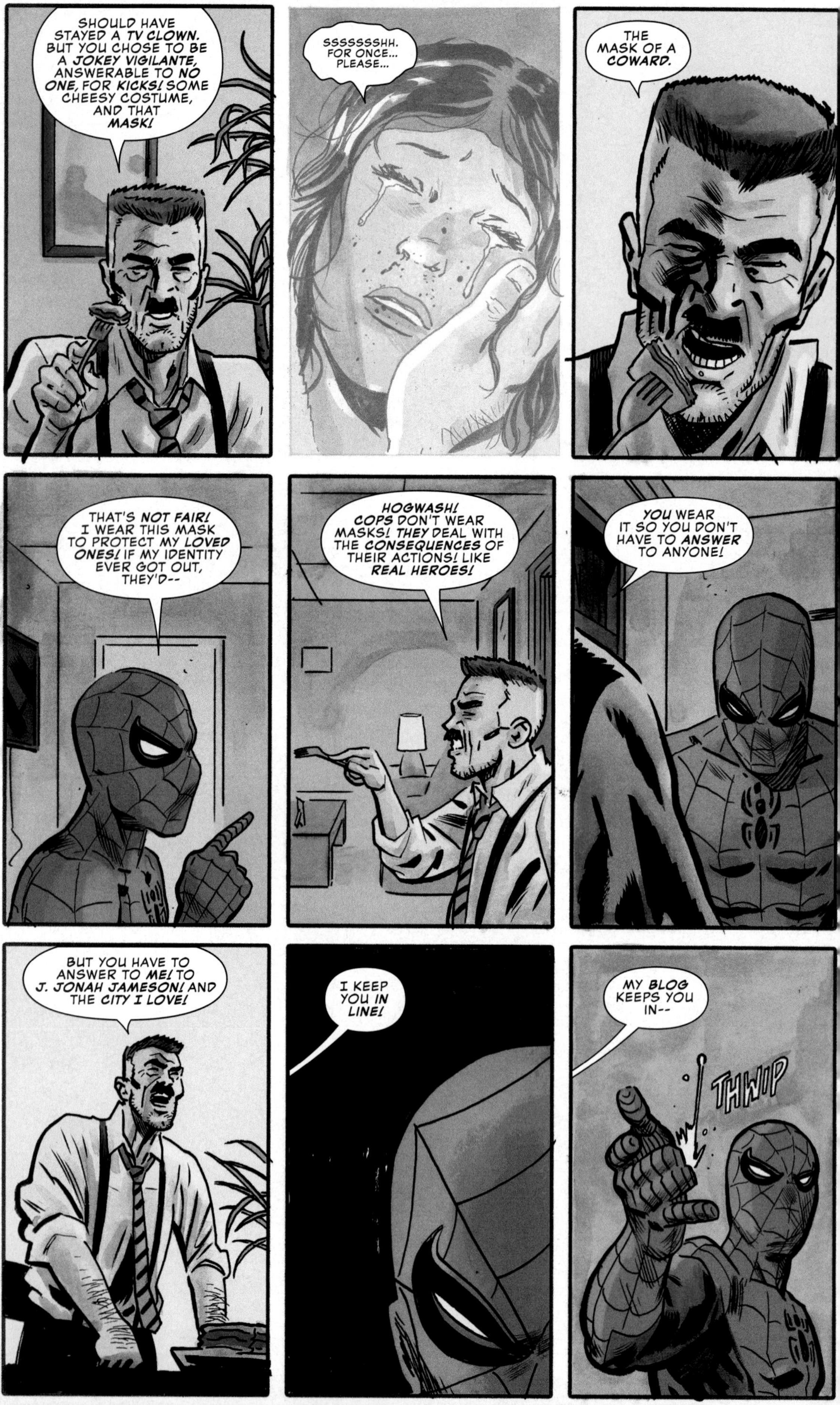

SHOULD HAVE STAYED A TV CLOWN. BUT YOU CHOSE TO BE A JOKEY VIGILANTE, ANSWERABLE TO NO ONE, FOR KICKS! SOME CHEESY COSTUME, AND THAT MASK!
SSSSSSSHH. FOR ONCE... PLEASE...
THE MASK OF A COWARD.
THAT'S NOT FAIR! I WEAR THIS MASK TO PROTECT MY LOVED ONES! IF MY IDENTITY EVER GOT OUT, THEY'D--
HOGWASH! COPS DON'T WEAR MASKS! THEY DEAL WITH THE CONSEQUENCES OF THEIR ACTIONS! LIKE REAL HEROES!
YOU WEAR IT SO YOU DON'T HAVE TO ANSWER TO ANYONE!
BUT YOU HAVE TO ANSWER TO ME! TO J. JONAH JAMESON! AND THE CITY I LOVE!
I KEEP YOU IN LINE!
MY BLOG KEEPS YOU IN--
THWIP

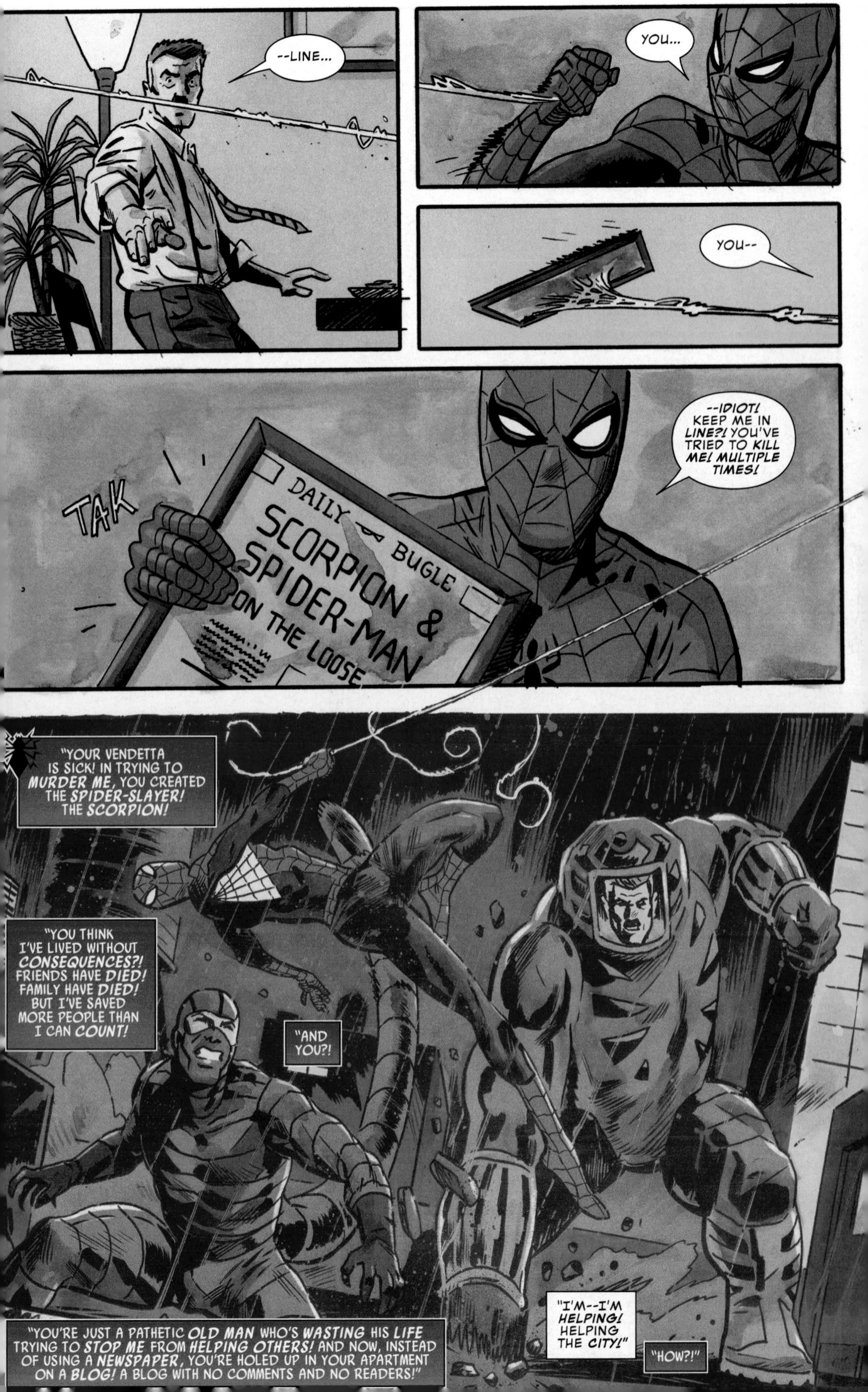
--LINE...
YOU...
YOU--
TAK
DAILY BUGLE
SCORPION & SPIDER-MAN ON THE LOOSE
--IDIOT! KEEP ME IN LINE?! YOU'VE TRIED TO KILL ME! MULTIPLE TIMES!
"YOUR VENDETTA IS SICK! IN TRYING TO MURDER ME, YOU CREATED THE SPIDER-SLAYER! THE SCORPION!
"YOU THINK I'VE LIVED WITHOUT CONSEQUENCES?! FRIENDS HAVE DIED! FAMILY HAVE DIED! BUT I'VE SAVED MORE PEOPLE THAN I CAN COUNT!
"AND YOU?!
"YOU'RE JUST A PATHETIC OLD MAN WHO'S WASTING HIS LIFE TRYING TO STOP ME FROM HELPING OTHERS! AND NOW, INSTEAD OF USING A NEWSPAPER, YOU'RE HOLED UP IN YOUR APARTMENT ON A BLOG! A BLOG WITH NO COMMENTS AND NO READERS!"
"I'M--I'M HELPING! HELPING THE CITY!"
"HOW?!"

BY HOLDING YOU ACCOUNTABLE!!! BY TAKING OFF THAT #$@%#& MASK!!!

...

WHAT DOES IT EVEN MATTER TO YOU?

I'M NOT THE ONE BEING INTERVIEWED, YOU CRETIN.

I DON'T CARE. THIS...THING BETWEEN US HAS GONE ON LONG ENOUGH, JONAH. WHY, OF EVERYTHING IN THE WORLD, IS THIS YOUR MISSION?

...YOU KNOW, YEARS AGO-- DECADES, REALLY--I WAS MUGGED.

I WAS GOING TO FIGHT BACK, BUT THE GIRL I WAS DATING AT THE TIME SAID NOT TO.

SHE WAS RIGHT, BUT STILL. I SURE WOULD'VE LIKED TO. HE--

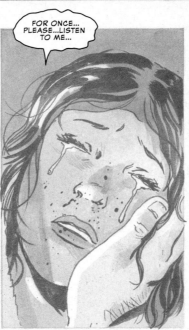

FOR ONCE... PLEASE...LISTEN TO ME...

--HE WORE A MASK. I ALWAYS REMEMBER WHAT WAS GOING THROUGH MY HEAD, SEEING THAT.

"YOU COWARD.

"YOU DAMN COWARD."

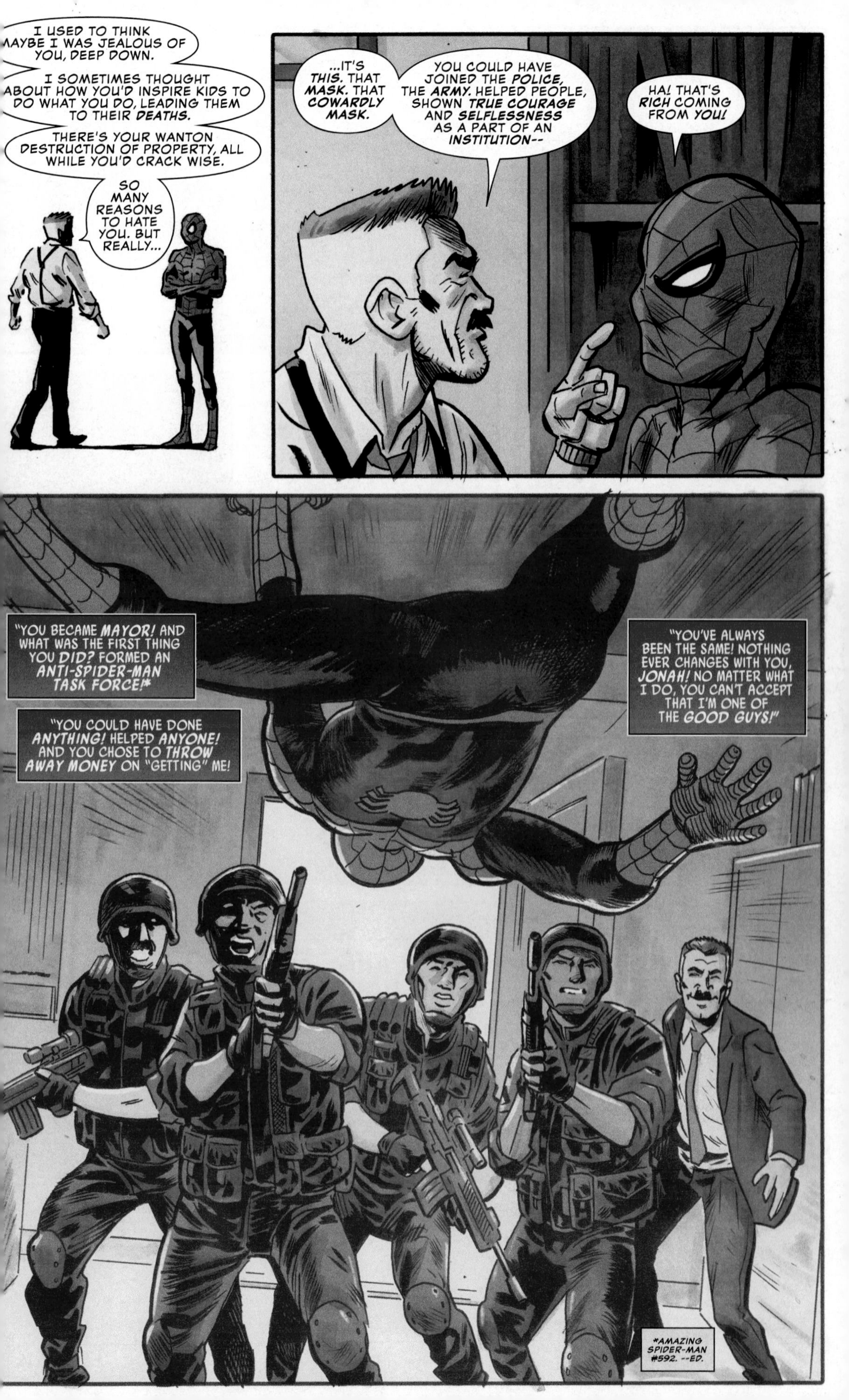
I USED TO THINK MAYBE I WAS JEALOUS OF YOU, DEEP DOWN.
I SOMETIMES THOUGHT ABOUT HOW YOU'D INSPIRE KIDS TO DO WHAT YOU DO, LEADING THEM TO THEIR DEATHS.
THERE'S YOUR WANTON DESTRUCTION OF PROPERTY, ALL WHILE YOU'D CRACK WISE.
SO MANY REASONS TO HATE YOU. BUT REALLY...
...IT'S THIS. THAT MASK. THAT COWARDLY MASK.
YOU COULD HAVE JOINED THE POLICE, THE ARMY. HELPED PEOPLE, SHOWN TRUE COURAGE AND SELFLESSNESS AS A PART OF AN INSTITUTION--
HA! THAT'S RICH COMING FROM YOU!
"YOU BECAME MAYOR! AND WHAT WAS THE FIRST THING YOU DID? FORMED AN ANTI-SPIDER-MAN TASK FORCE!*
"YOU COULD HAVE DONE ANYTHING! HELPED ANYONE! AND YOU CHOSE TO THROW AWAY MONEY ON "GETTING" ME!
"YOU'VE ALWAYS BEEN THE SAME! NOTHING EVER CHANGES WITH YOU, JONAH! NO MATTER WHAT I DO, YOU CAN'T ACCEPT THAT I'M ONE OF THE GOOD GUYS!"
*AMAZING SPIDER-MAN #592. --ED.

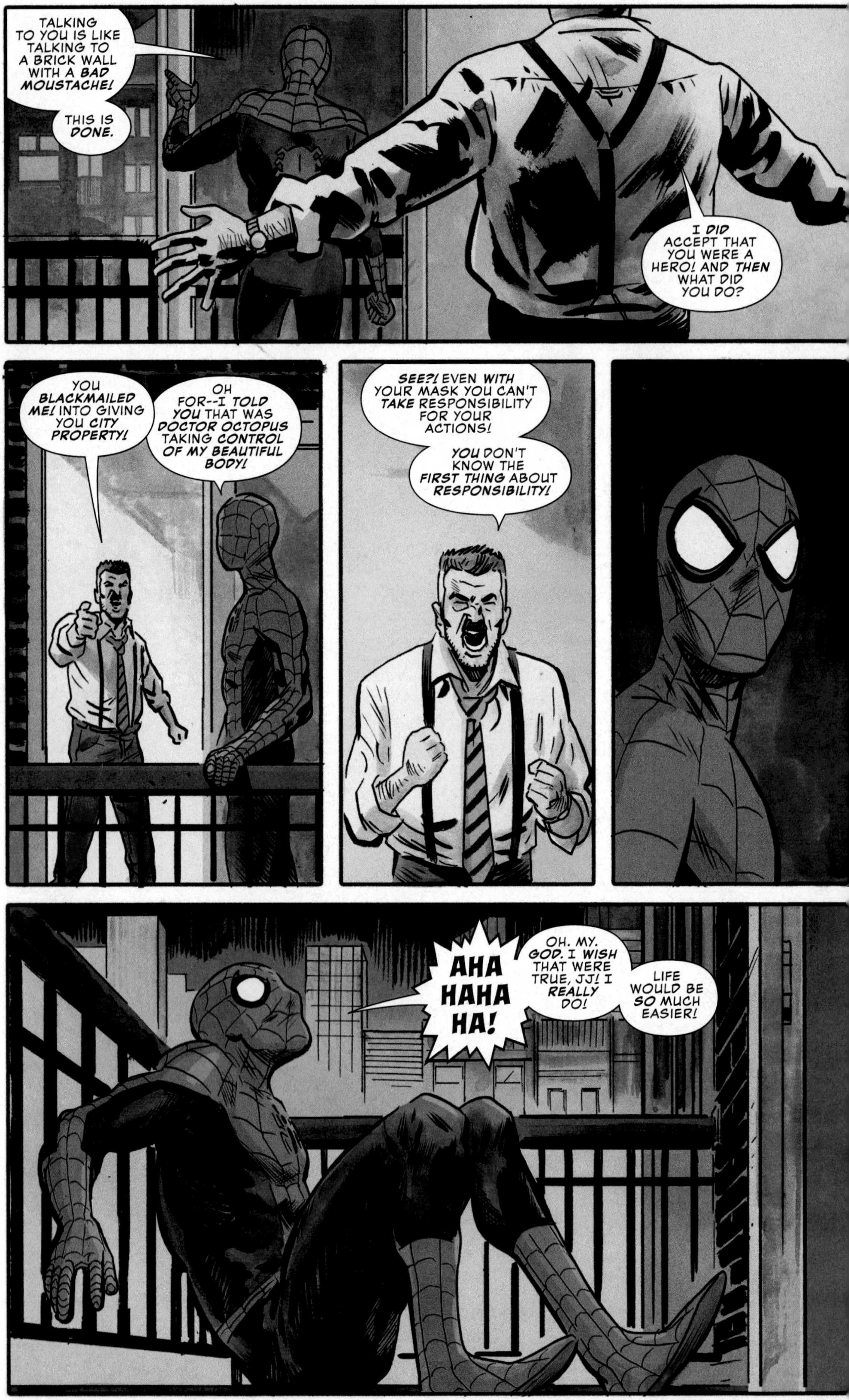
TALKING TO YOU IS LIKE TALKING TO A BRICK WALL WITH A BAD MOUSTACHE!
THIS IS DONE.
I DID ACCEPT THAT YOU WERE A HERO! AND THEN WHAT DID YOU DO?
YOU BLACKMAILED ME! INTO GIVING YOU CITY PROPERTY!
OH FOR--I TOLD YOU THAT WAS DOCTOR OCTOPUS TAKING CONTROL OF MY BEAUTIFUL BODY!
SEE?! EVEN WITH YOUR MASK YOU CAN'T TAKE RESPONSIBILITY FOR YOUR ACTIONS!
YOU DON'T KNOW THE FIRST THING ABOUT RESPONSIBILITY!
AHA HAHA HA!
OH. MY. GOD. I WISH THAT WERE TRUE, JJ! I REALLY DO!
LIFE WOULD BE SO MUCH EASIER!

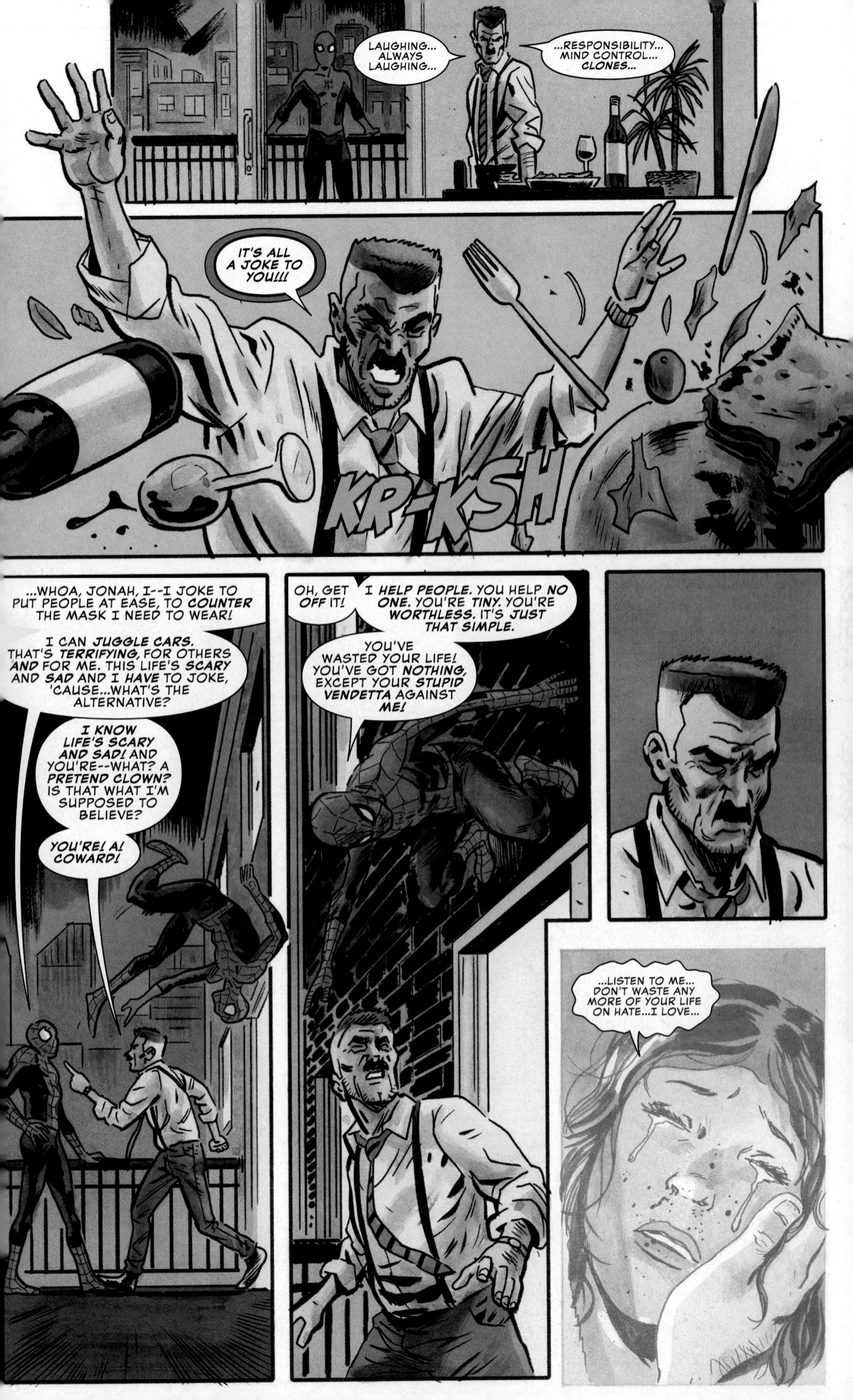
LAUGHING... ALWAYS LAUGHING...
...RESPONSIBILITY... MIND CONTROL... CLONES...
IT'S ALL A JOKE TO YOU!!!
KR-KSH
...WHOA, JONAH, I--I JOKE TO PUT PEOPLE AT EASE, TO COUNTER THE MASK I NEED TO WEAR!
I CAN JUGGLE CARS. THAT'S TERRIFYING, FOR OTHERS AND FOR ME. THIS LIFE'S SCARY AND SAD AND I HAVE TO JOKE, 'CAUSE...WHAT'S THE ALTERNATIVE?
I KNOW LIFE'S SCARY AND SAD! AND YOU'RE--WHAT? A PRETEND CLOWN? IS THAT WHAT I'M SUPPOSED TO BELIEVE?
YOU'RE! A! COWARD!
OH, GET OFF IT!
I HELP PEOPLE. YOU HELP NO ONE. YOU'RE TINY. YOU'RE WORTHLESS. IT'S JUST THAT SIMPLE.
YOU'VE WASTED YOUR LIFE! YOU'VE GOT NOTHING, EXCEPT YOUR STUPID VENDETTA AGAINST ME!
...LISTEN TO ME... DON'T WASTE ANY MORE OF YOUR LIFE ON HATE...I LOVE...

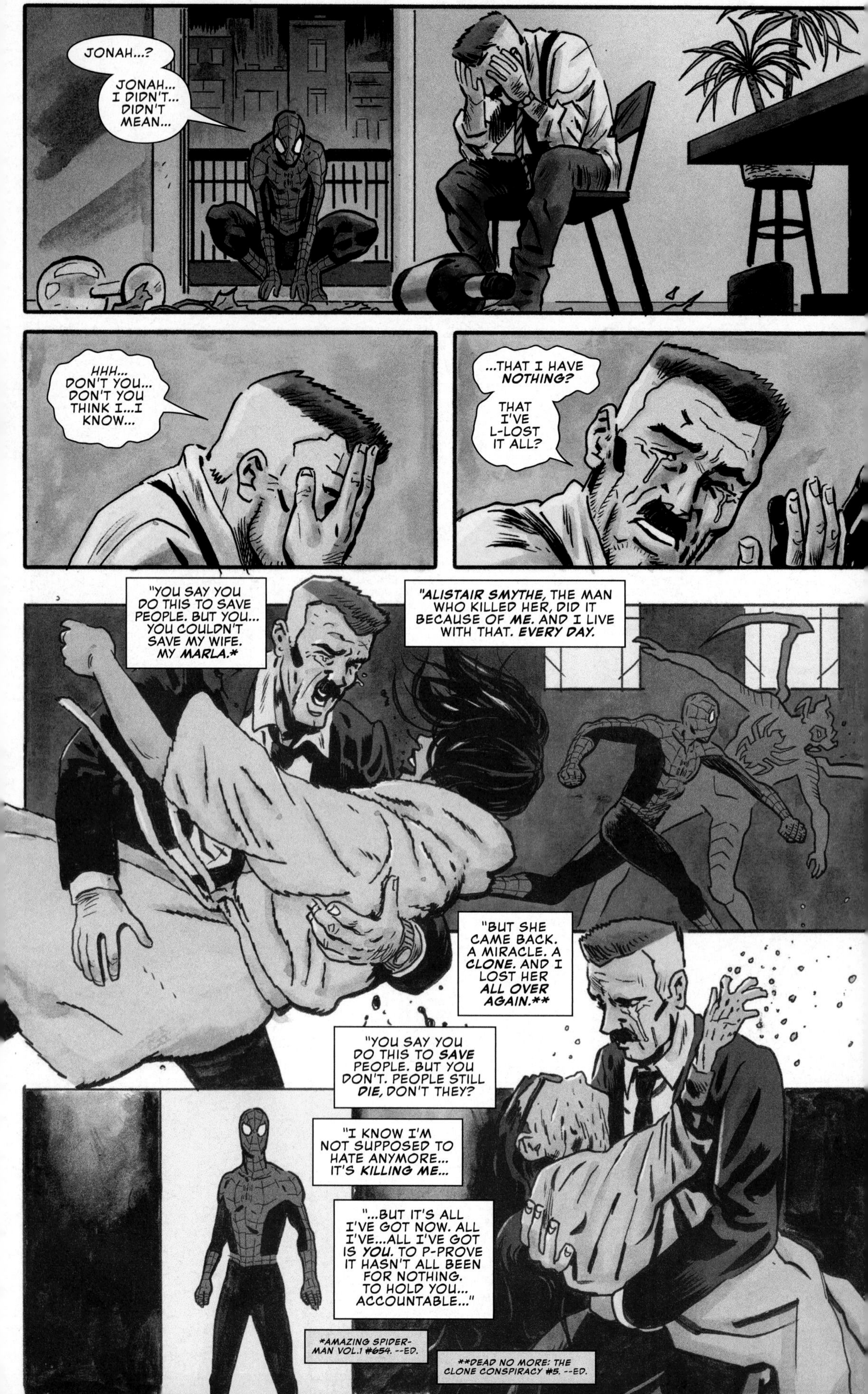
JONAH...?
JONAH... I DIDN'T... DIDN'T MEAN...
HHH... DON'T YOU... DON'T YOU THINK I...I KNOW...
...THAT I HAVE NOTHING?
THAT I'VE L-LOST IT ALL?
"YOU SAY YOU DO THIS TO SAVE PEOPLE. BUT YOU... YOU COULDN'T SAVE MY WIFE. MY MARLA.*
"ALISTAIR SMYTHE, THE MAN WHO KILLED HER, DID IT BECAUSE OF ME. AND I LIVE WITH THAT. EVERY DAY.
"BUT SHE CAME BACK. A MIRACLE. A CLONE. AND I LOST HER ALL OVER AGAIN.**
"YOU SAY YOU DO THIS TO SAVE PEOPLE. BUT YOU DON'T. PEOPLE STILL DIE, DON'T THEY?
"I KNOW I'M NOT SUPPOSED TO HATE ANYMORE... IT'S KILLING ME...
"...BUT IT'S ALL I'VE GOT NOW. ALL I'VE...ALL I'VE GOT IS YOU. TO P-PROVE IT HASN'T ALL BEEN FOR NOTHING. TO HOLD YOU... ACCOUNTABLE..."
*AMAZING SPIDER-MAN VOL.1 #654. --ED.
**DEAD NO MORE: THE CLONE CONSPIRACY #5. --ED.

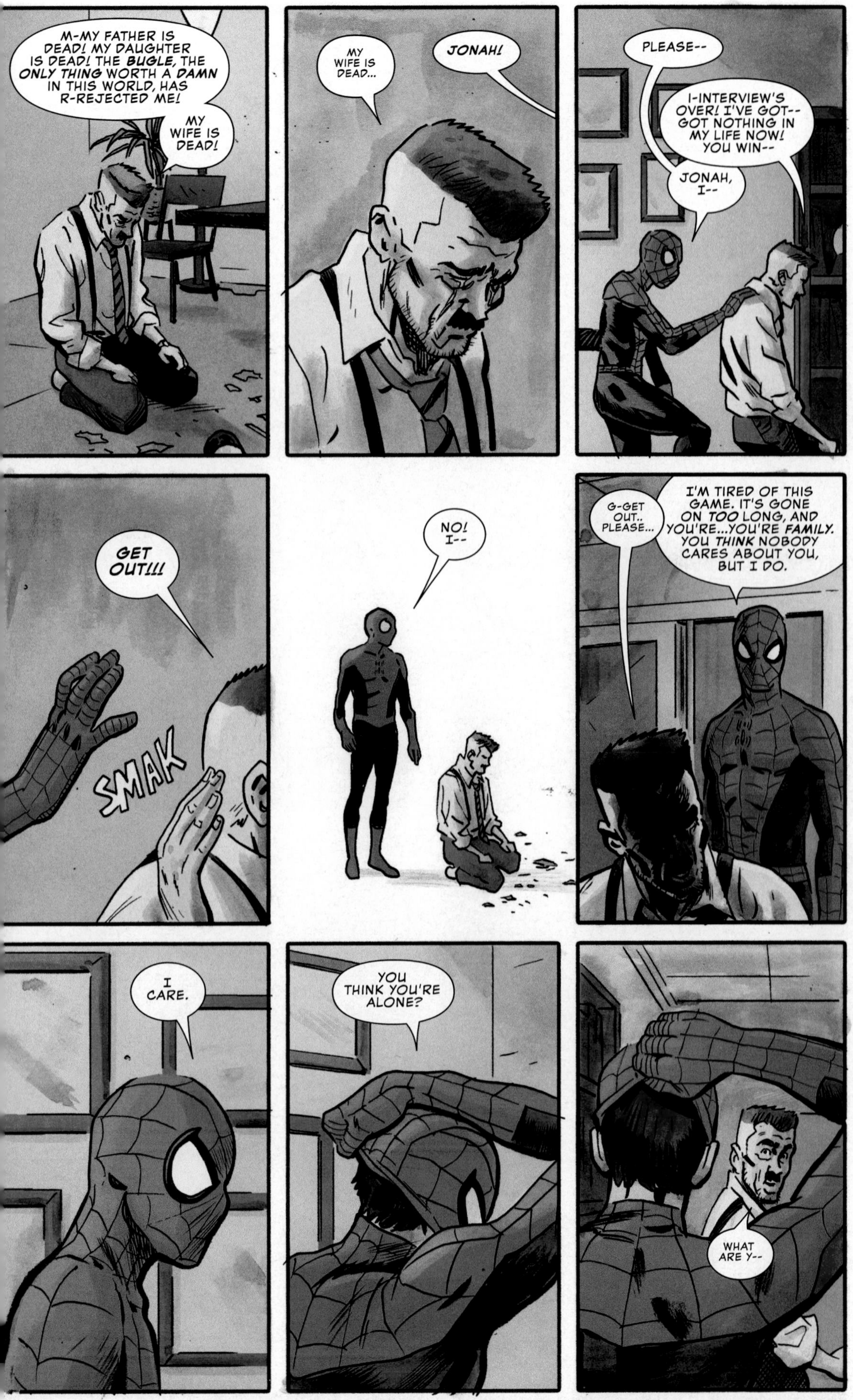
M-MY FATHER IS DEAD! MY DAUGHTER IS DEAD! THE BUGLE, THE ONLY THING WORTH A DAMN IN THIS WORLD, HAS R-REJECTED ME!
MY WIFE IS DEAD!
MY WIFE IS DEAD...
JONAH!
PLEASE--
I-INTERVIEW'S OVER! I'VE GOT-- GOT NOTHING IN MY LIFE NOW! YOU WIN--
JONAH, I--
GET OUT!!!
SMAK
NO! I--
G-GET OUT.. PLEASE...
I'M TIRED OF THIS GAME. IT'S GONE ON TOO LONG, AND YOU'RE...YOU'RE FAMILY. YOU THINK NOBODY CARES ABOUT YOU, BUT I DO.
I CARE.
YOU THINK YOU'RE ALONE?
WHAT ARE Y--

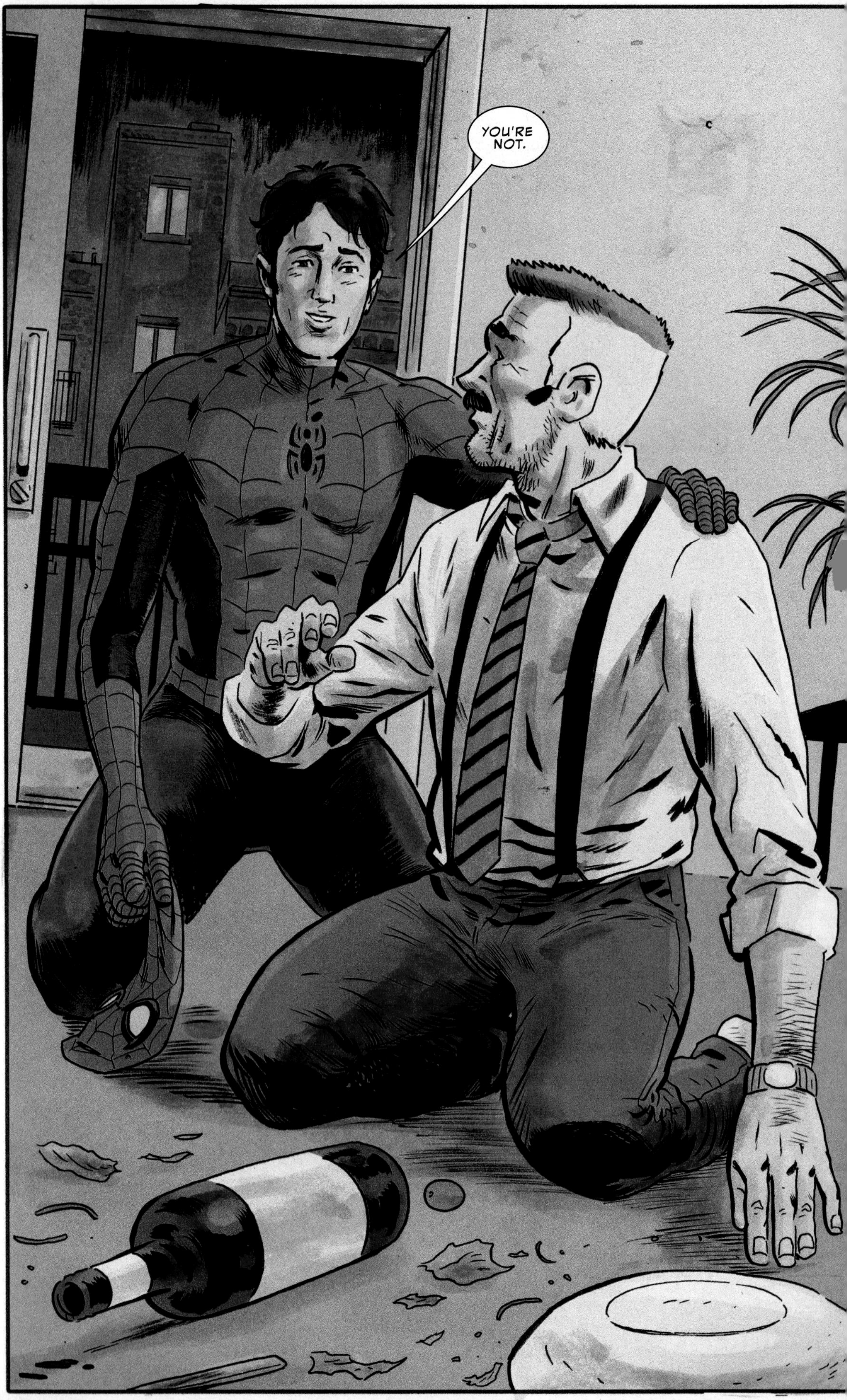
YOU'RE NOT.

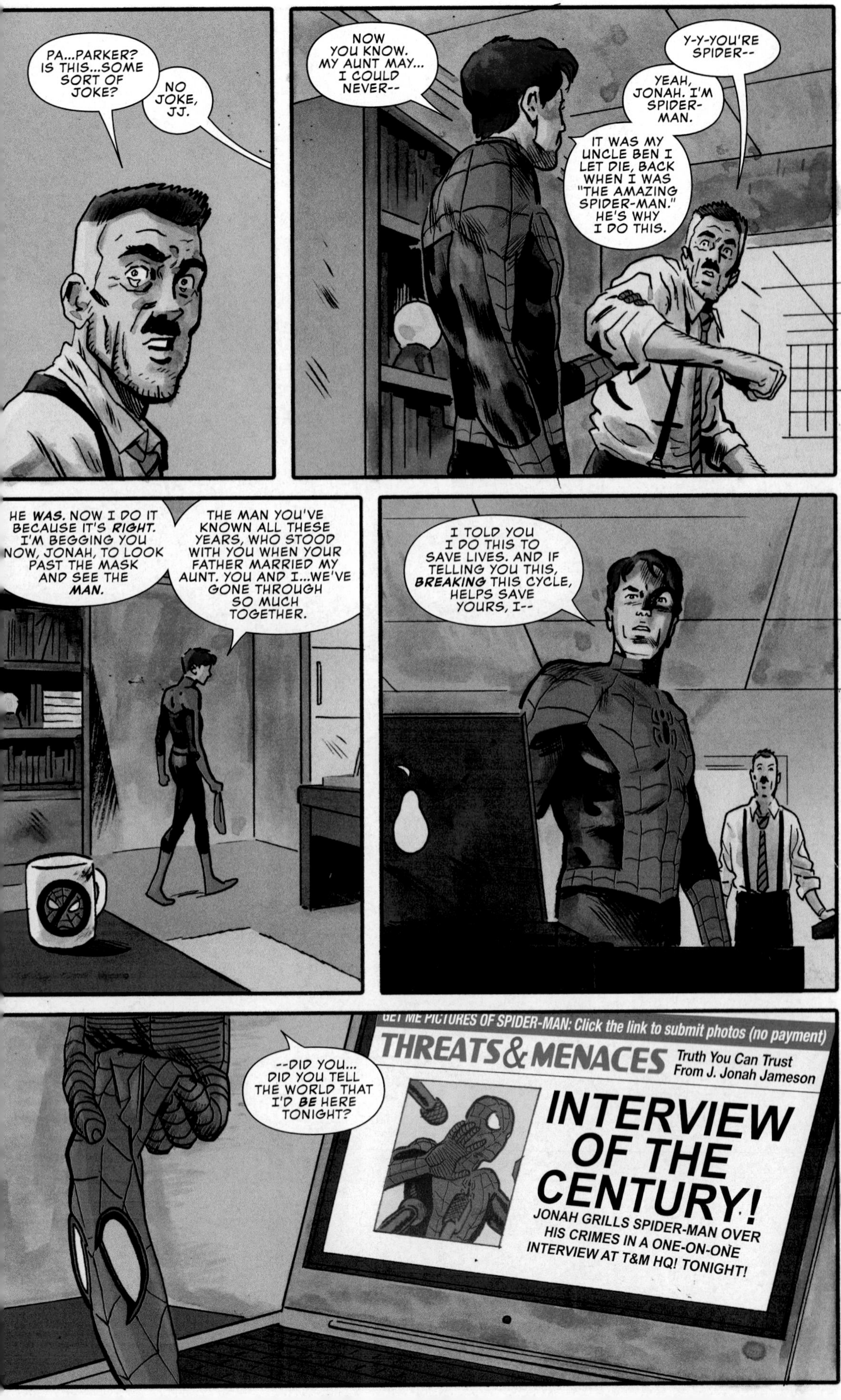
PA...PARKER? IS THIS...SOME SORT OF JOKE?
NO JOKE, JJ.
NOW YOU KNOW. MY AUNT MAY... I COULD NEVER--
Y-Y-YOU'RE SPIDER--
YEAH, JONAH. I'M SPIDER-MAN.
IT WAS MY UNCLE BEN I LET DIE, BACK WHEN I WAS "THE AMAZING SPIDER-MAN." HE'S WHY I DO THIS.
HE *WAS.* NOW I DO IT BECAUSE IT'S *RIGHT.* I'M BEGGING YOU NOW, JONAH, TO LOOK PAST THE MASK AND SEE THE *MAN.*
THE MAN YOU'VE KNOWN ALL THESE YEARS, WHO STOOD WITH YOU WHEN YOUR FATHER MARRIED MY AUNT. YOU AND I...WE'VE GONE THROUGH SO MUCH TOGETHER.
I TOLD YOU I DO THIS TO SAVE LIVES. AND IF TELLING YOU THIS, *BREAKING* THIS CYCLE, HELPS SAVE YOURS, I--
--DID YOU... DID YOU TELL THE WORLD THAT I'D *BE* HERE TONIGHT?
GET ME PICTURES OF SPIDER-MAN: Click the link to submit photos (no payment)
THREATS & MENACES
Truth You Can Trust From J. Jonah Jameson
INTERVIEW OF THE CENTURY!
JONAH GRILLS SPIDER-MAN OVER HIS CRIMES IN A ONE-ON-ONE INTERVIEW AT T&M HQ! TONIGHT!

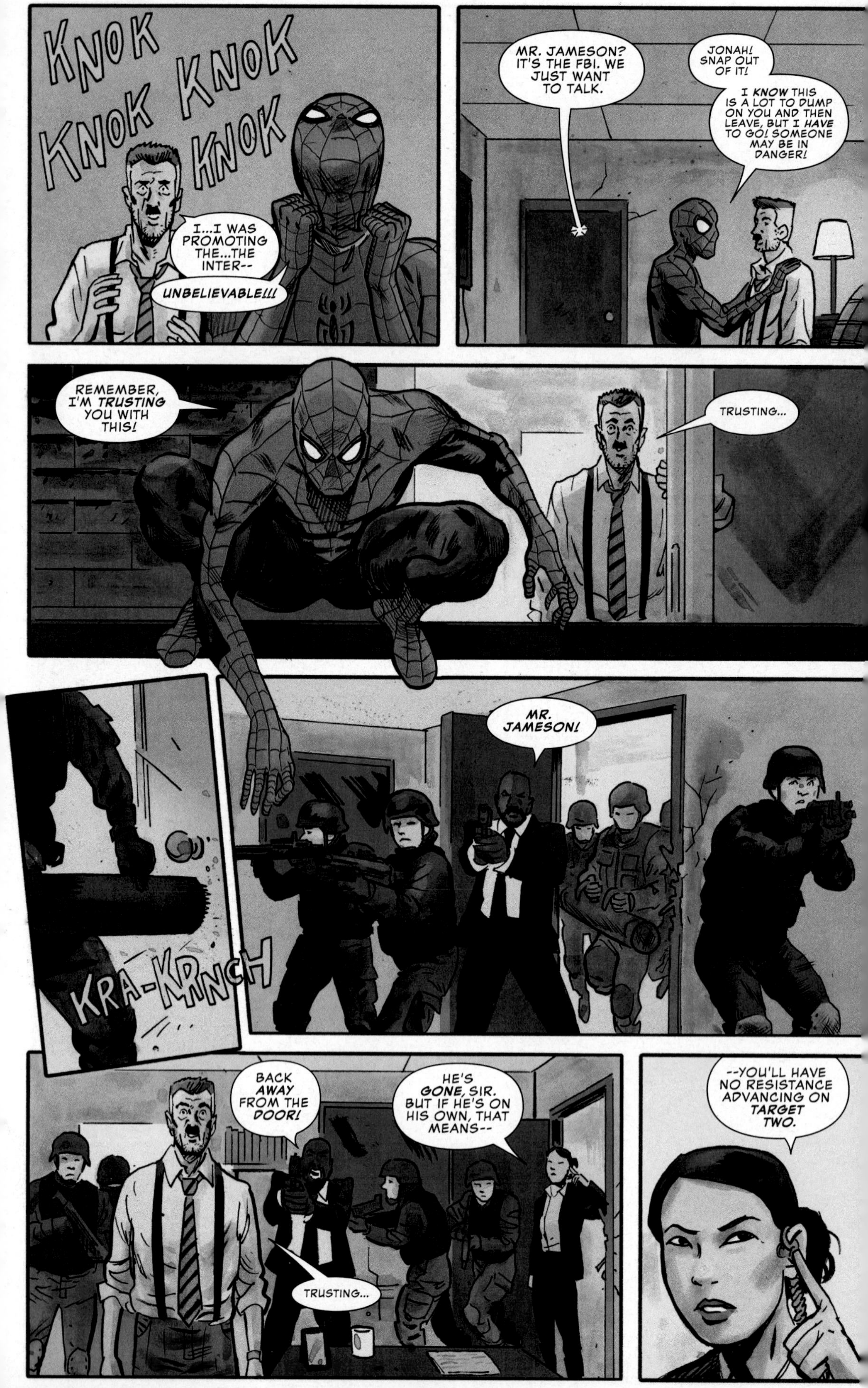
KNOK KNOK KNOK KNOK KNOK
I...I WAS PROMOTING THE...THE INTER--
UNBELIEVABLE!!!
MR. JAMESON? IT'S THE FBI. WE JUST WANT TO TALK.
JONAH! SNAP OUT OF IT!
I KNOW THIS IS A LOT TO DUMP ON YOU AND THEN LEAVE, BUT I HAVE TO GO! SOMEONE MAY BE IN DANGER!
REMEMBER, I'M TRUSTING YOU WITH THIS!
TRUSTING...
KRA-KRNCH
MR. JAMESON!
BACK AWAY FROM THE DOOR!
TRUSTING...
HE'S GONE, SIR. BUT IF HE'S ON HIS OWN, THAT MEANS--
--YOU'LL HAVE NO RESISTANCE ADVANCING ON TARGET TWO.

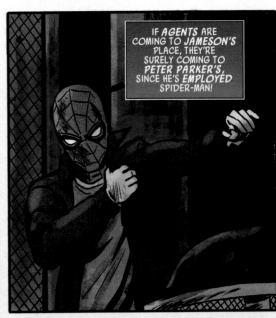

IF *AGENTS* ARE COMING TO *JAMESON'S* PLACE, THEY'RE SURELY COMING TO *PETER PARKER'S*, SINCE HE'S *EMPLOYED* SPIDER-MAN!

MAN, I DON'T KNOW WHAT CAME OVER ME. I'VE *NEVER* SEEN JJ LIKE THAT BEFORE. HE JUST SEEMED SO... *BROKEN.*

I JUST WANTED HIM TO FEEL LIKE HE DIDN'T HAVE TO *HATE* ANYMORE...

HAVE TO DEAL WITH HIM *LATER.* FOR NOW, I BETTER CHECK IN ON *TERESA.*

AND IF THEY *BUST IN* LIKE THEY DID AT *JONAH'S,* I BETTER NOT HAVE MY *SPIDEY* STUFF IN THERE AT THE TIME!

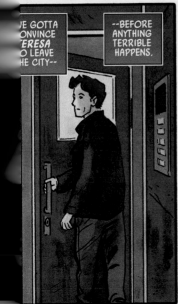

VE GOTTA ONVINCE *TERESA* O LEAVE HE CITY--

--BEFORE ANYTHING TERRIBLE HAPPENS.

CLIK

--JUST ARRIVED, SIR...

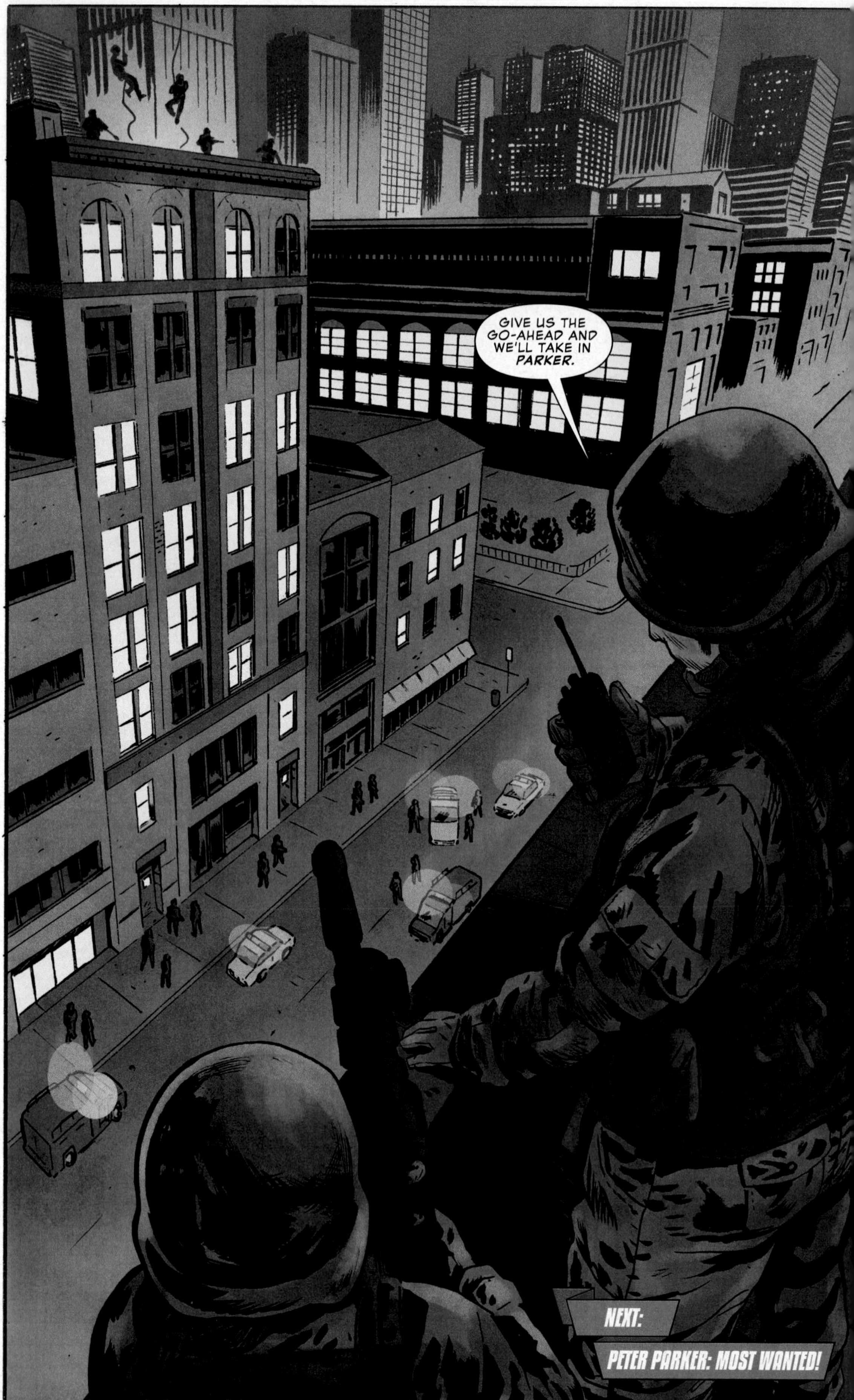
GIVE US THE GO-AHEAD AND WE'LL TAKE IN PARKER.
NEXT:
PETER PARKER: MOST WANTED!

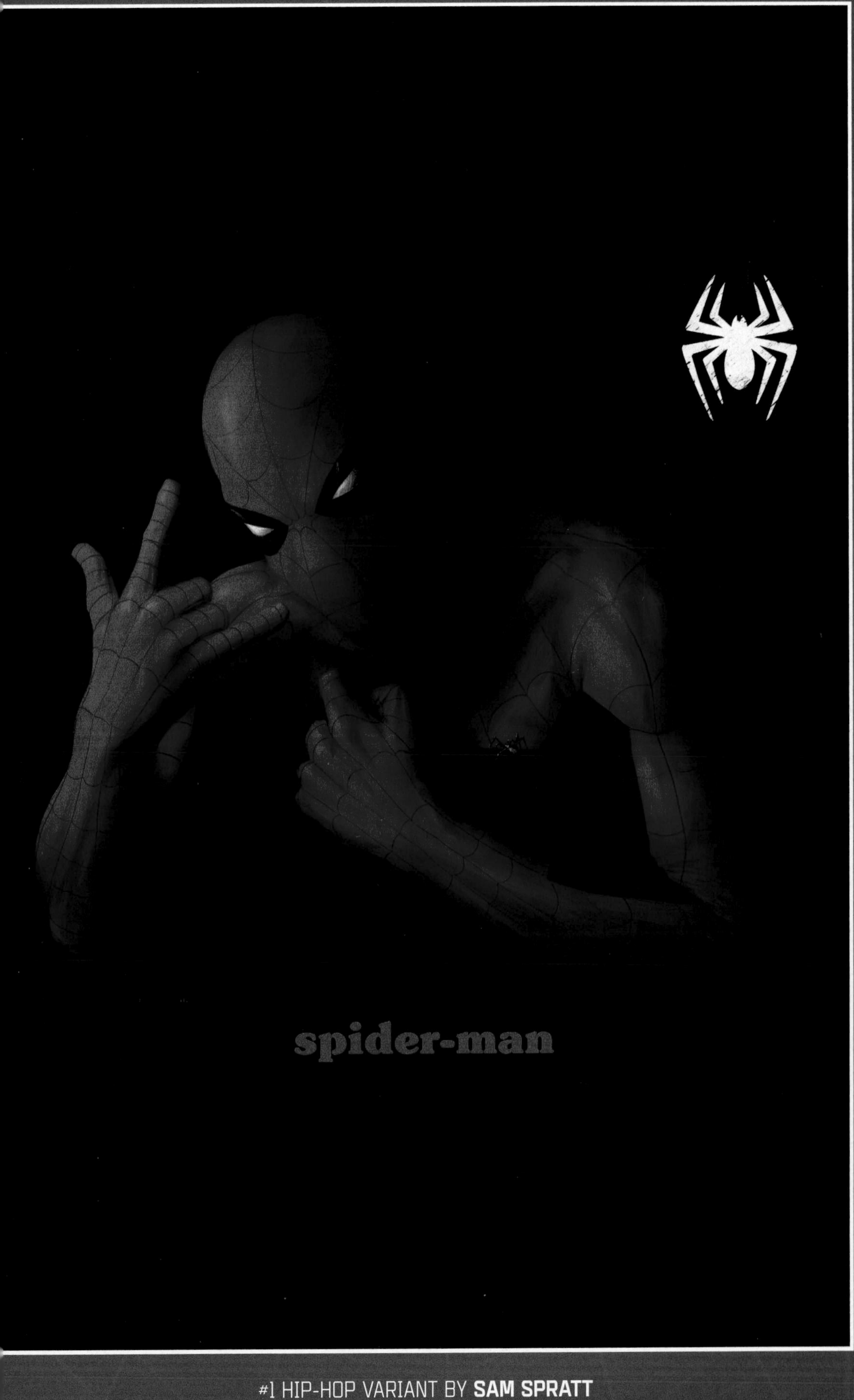
spider-man

#1 HIP-HOP VARIANT BY **SAM SPRATT**

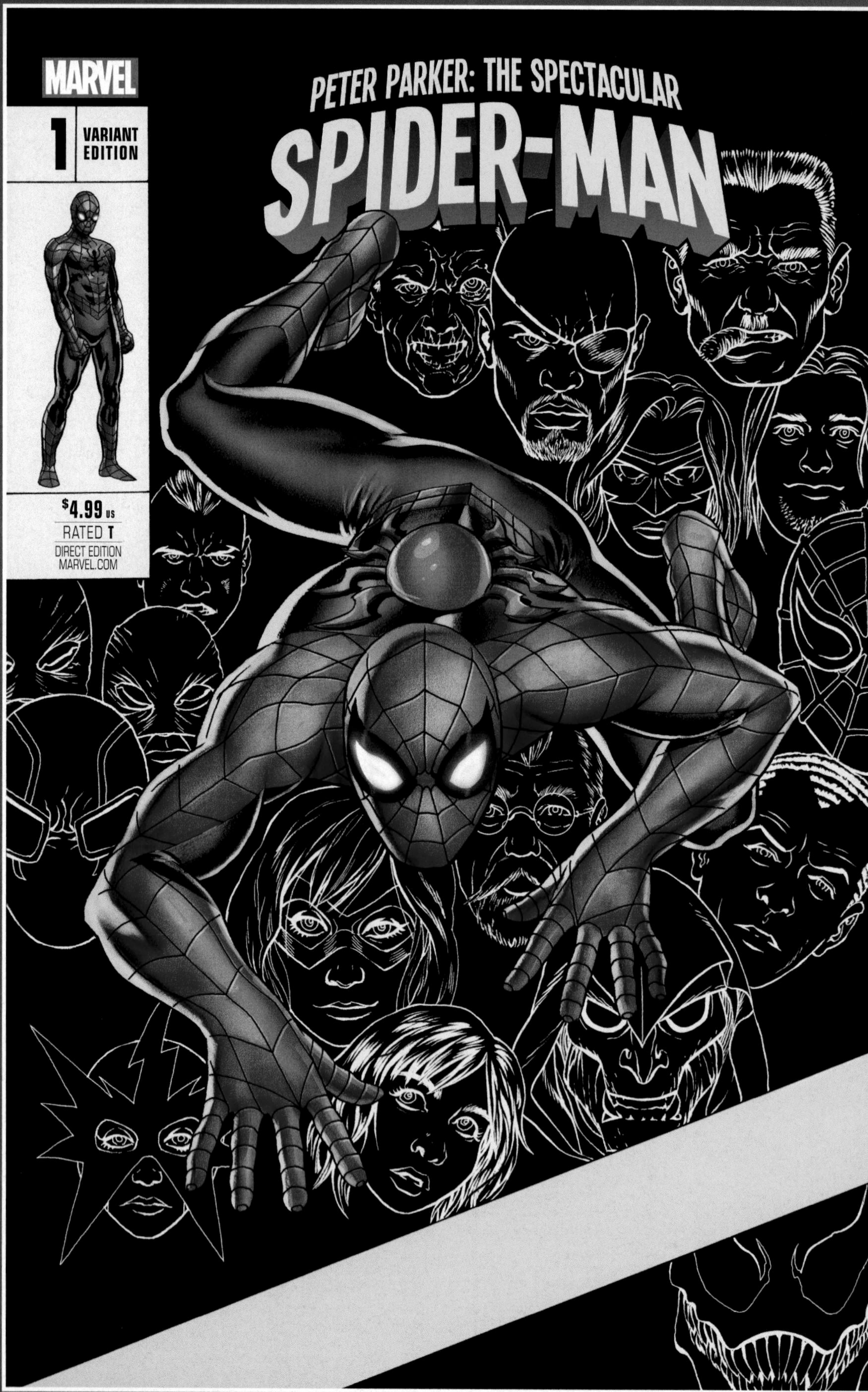
MARVEL
1 VARIANT EDITION
PETER PARKER: THE SPECTACULAR
SPIDER-MAN
$4.99 US
RATED T
DIRECT EDITION
MARVEL.COM

#1 VARIANT BY **JOHN CASSADAY** & **PAUL MOUNTS**

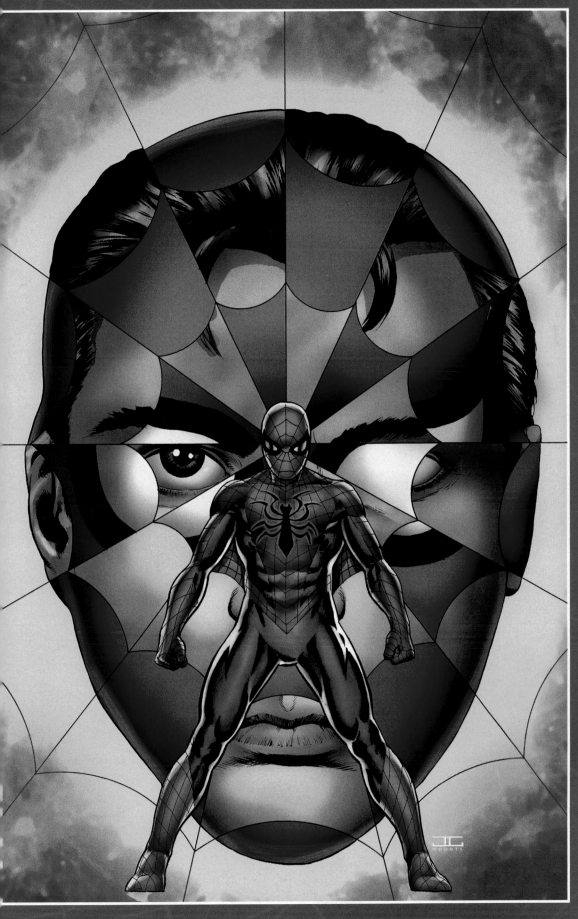

#1 VARIANT BY **JOHN CASSADAY** & **PAUL MOUNTS**

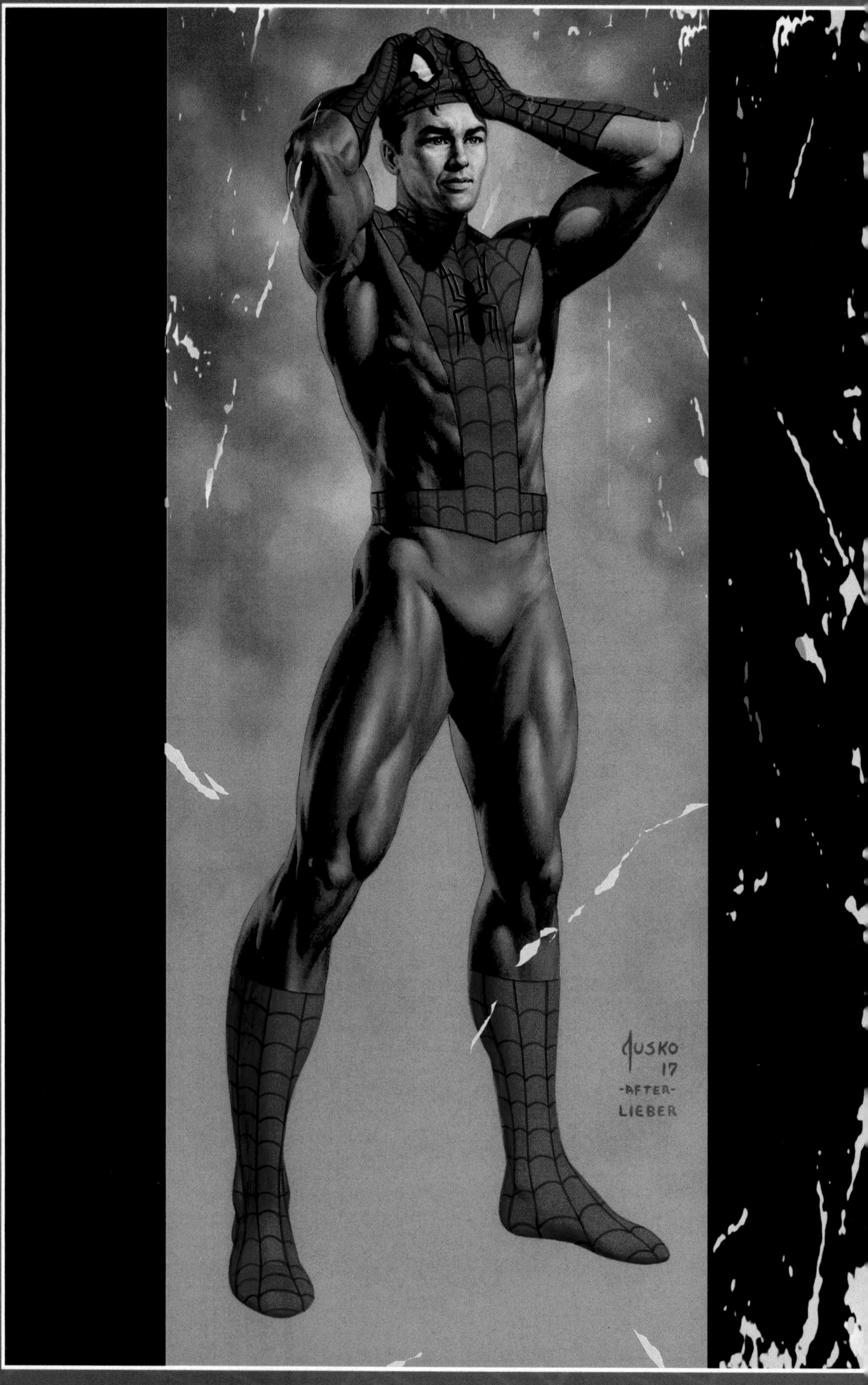
JUSKO
17
-AFTER-
LIEBER

#1 CORNER BOX VARIANT BY **JOE JUSKO**

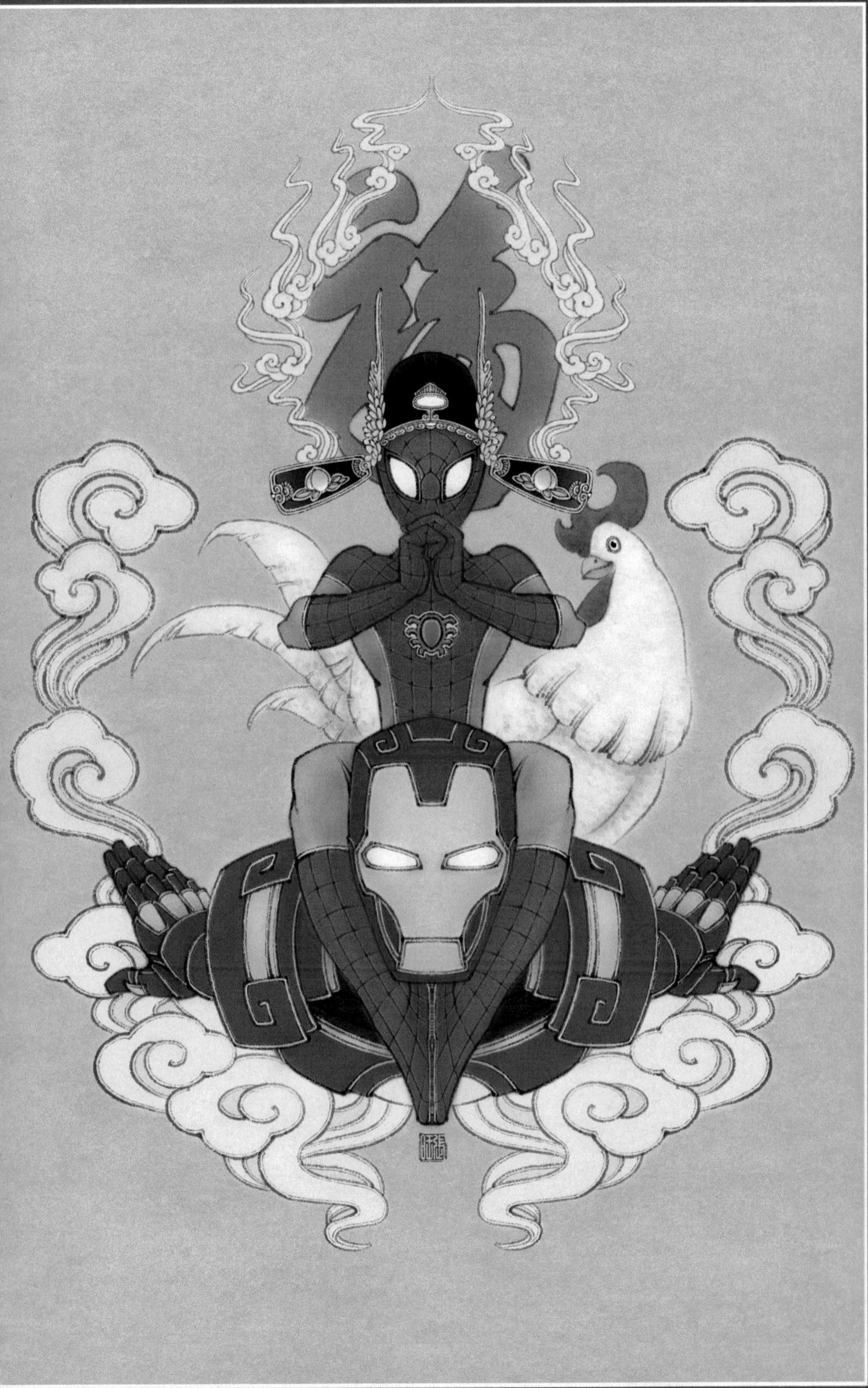

#1 YEAR OF THE ROOSTER VARIANT BY **ZHANG WANG**

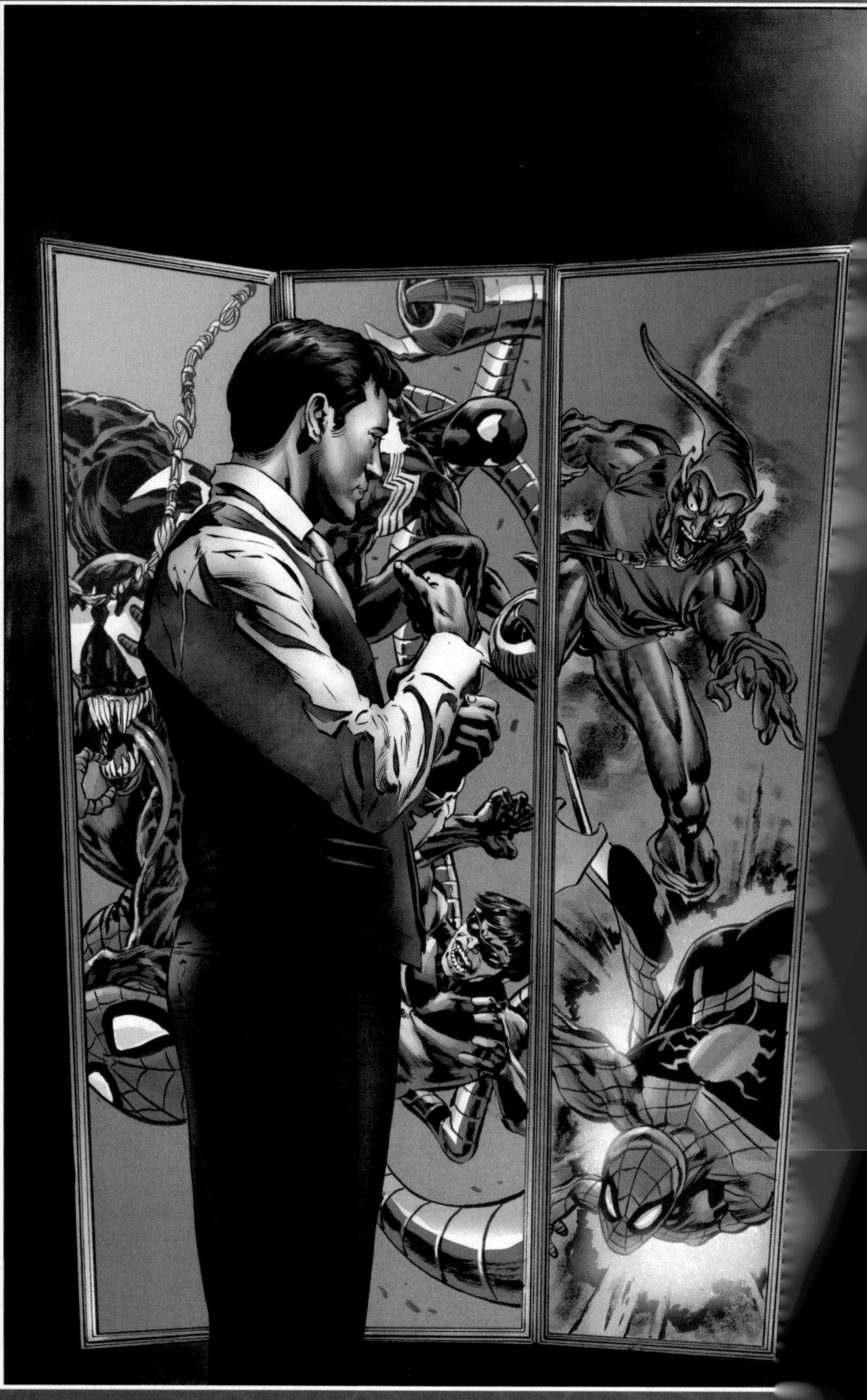

#1 VARIANT BY **MIKE PERKINS** & **ANDY TROY**

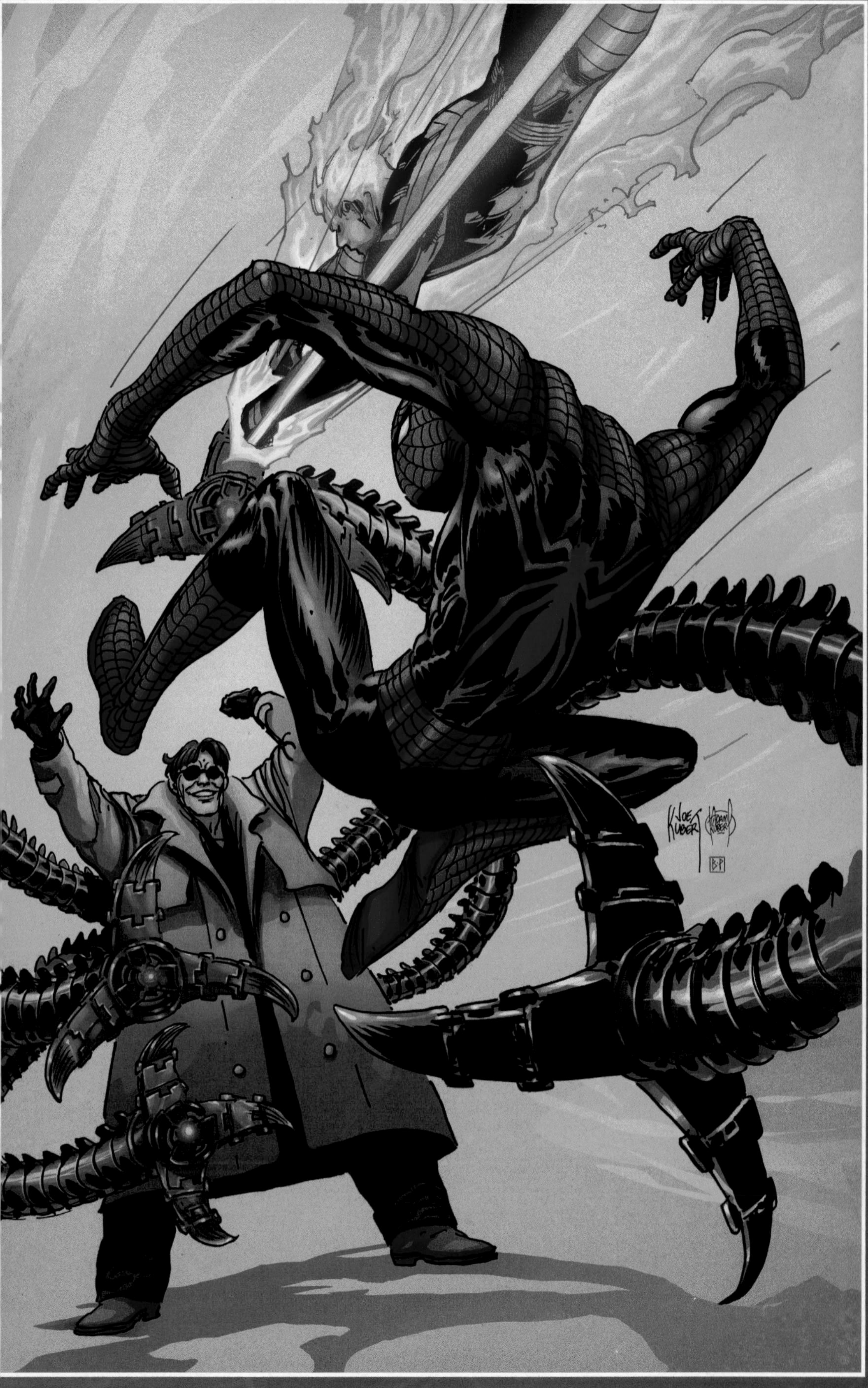

#1 VARIANT BY **JOE KUBERT, ADAM KUBERT & BRITTANY PEZZILLO**

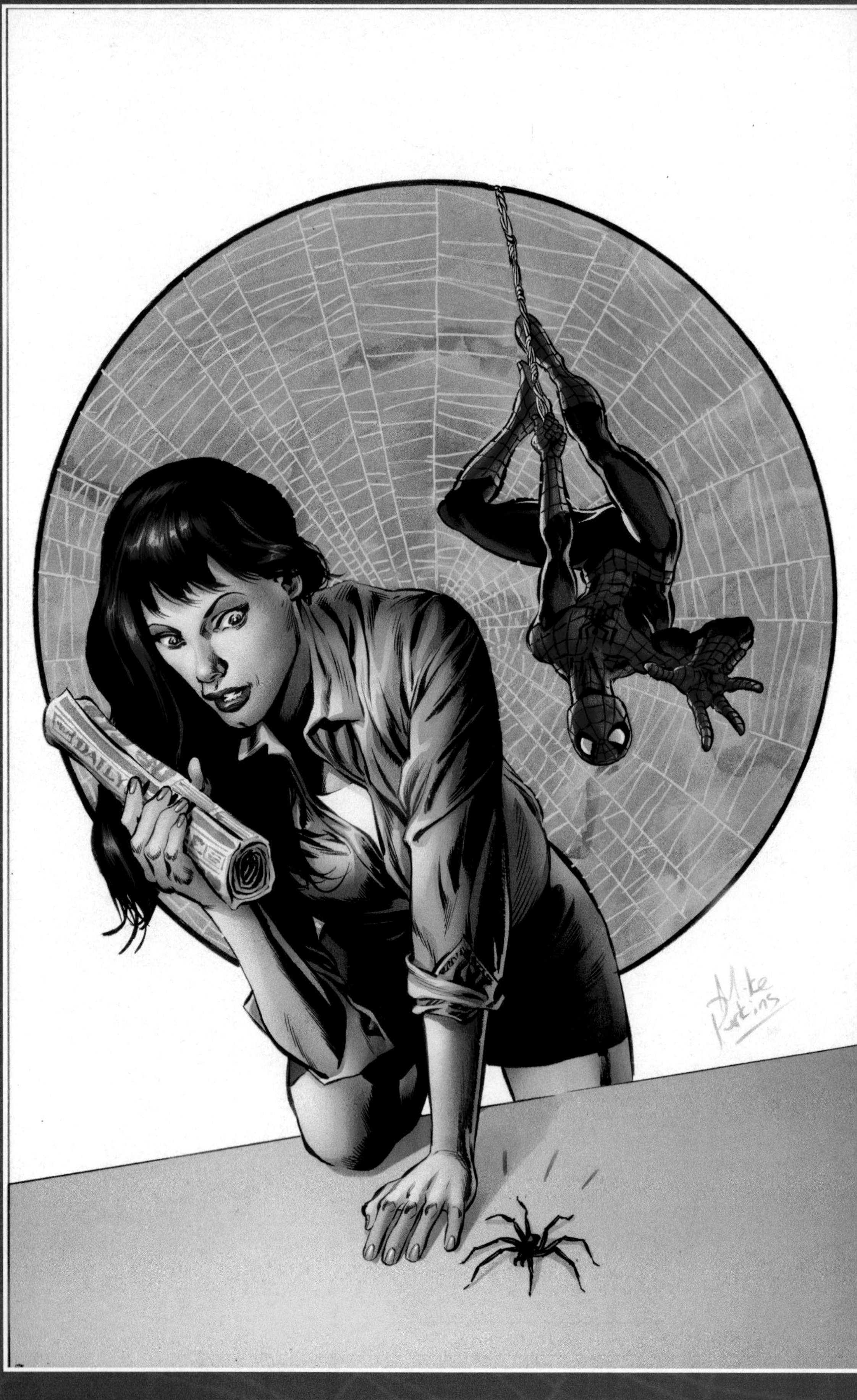
DAILY
Mike Perkins
#1 VARIANT BY **MIKE PERKINS** & **ANDY TROY**

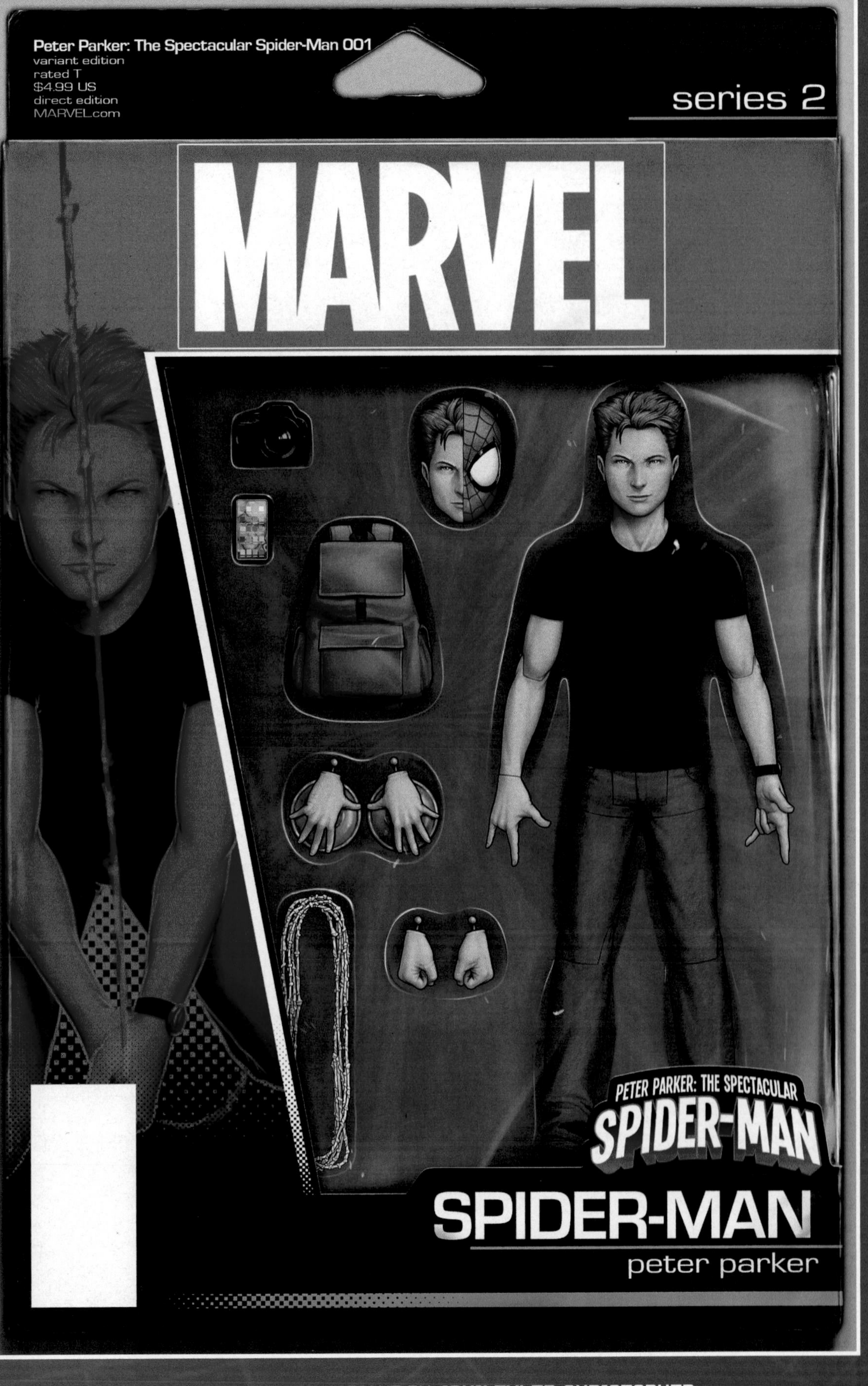
Peter Parker: The Spectacular Spider-Man 001
variant edition
rated T
$4.99 US
direct edition
MARVEL.com
series 2
MARVEL
PETER PARKER: THE SPECTACULAR
SPIDER-MAN
SPIDER-MAN
peter parker

#1 ACTION FIGURE VARIANT BY **JOHN TYLER CHRISTOPHER**

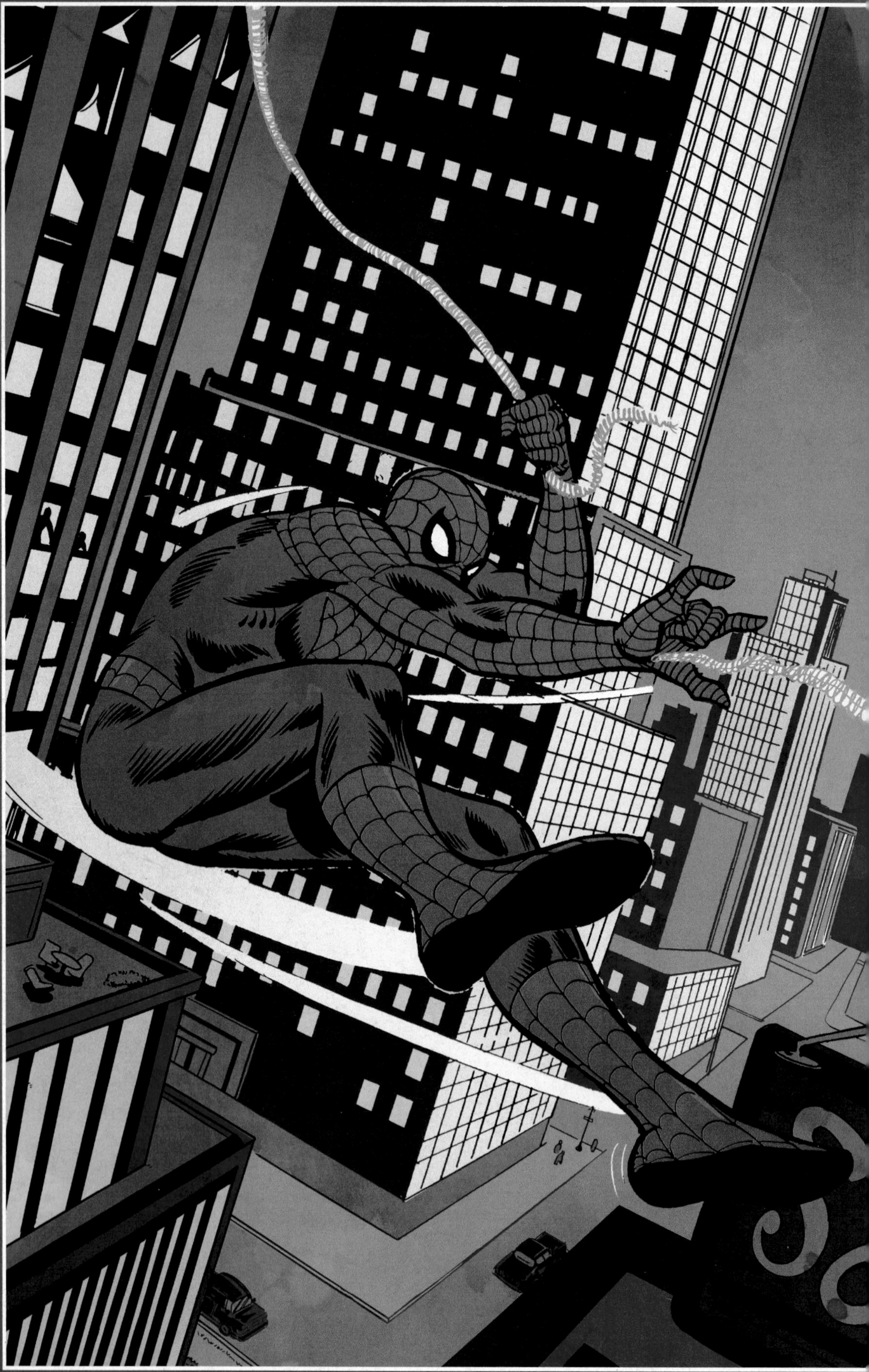

#1 REMASTERED VARIANT BY **ROSS ANDRU** & **RACHELLE ROSENBERG**

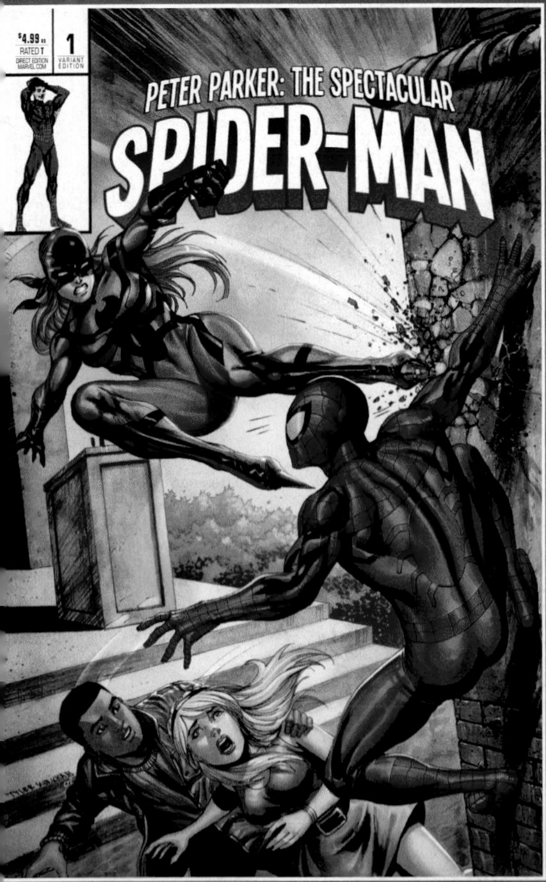
$4.99 US
RATED T
DIRECT EDITION
MARVEL.COM
1
VARIANT EDITION
PETER PARKER: THE SPECTACULAR
SPIDER-MAN

#1 VARIANT BY **TYLER KIRKHAM** & **ARIF PRIANTO**

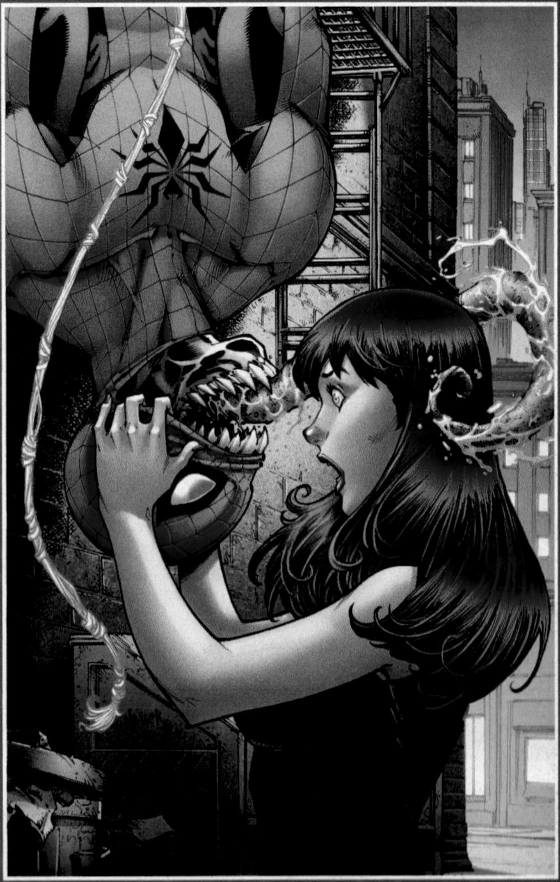

#1 VARIANT BY **TODD NAUCK** & **RACHELLE ROSENBERG**

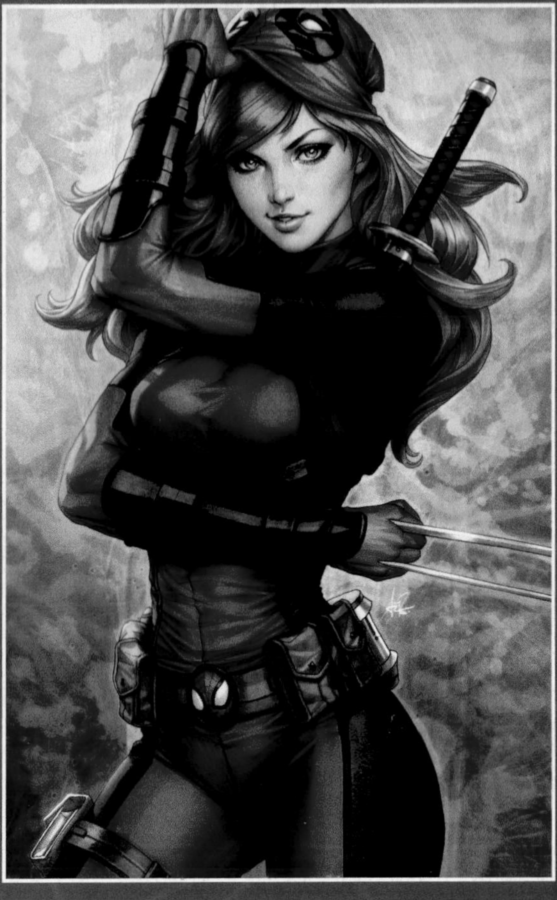

#1 VARIANT BY **ARTGERM**

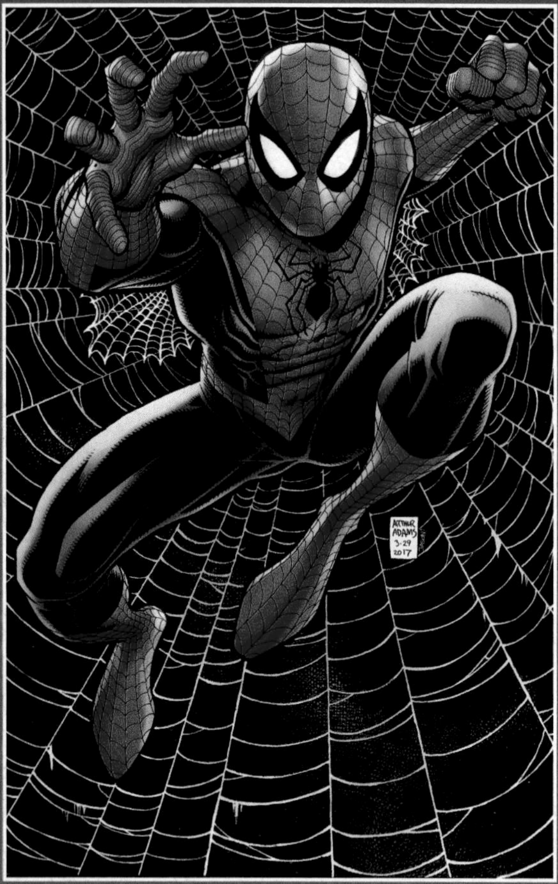
ARTHUR ADAMS 3-29 2017

#2 VARIANT BY **ARTHUR ADAMS** & **JASON KEITH**

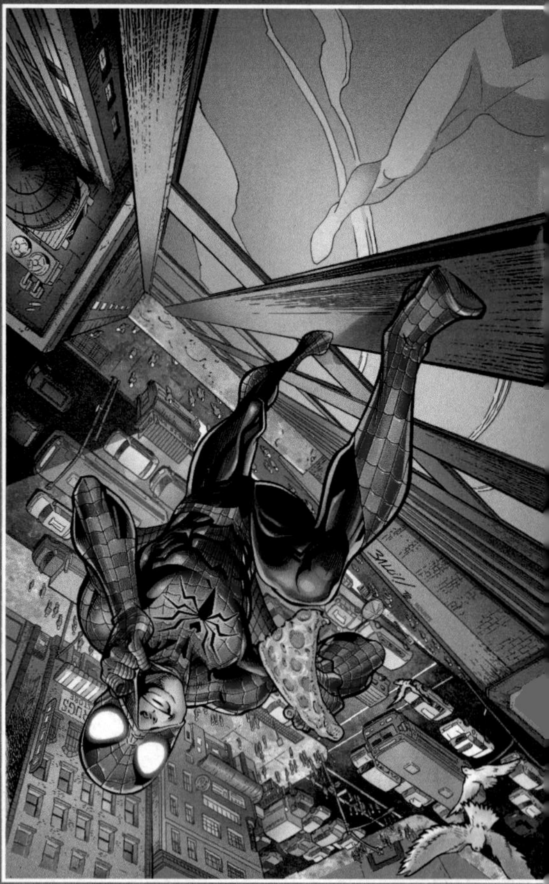

#3 VARIANT BY **MARK BAGLEY**, **TERRY PALLOT** & **PAUL MOUNT**

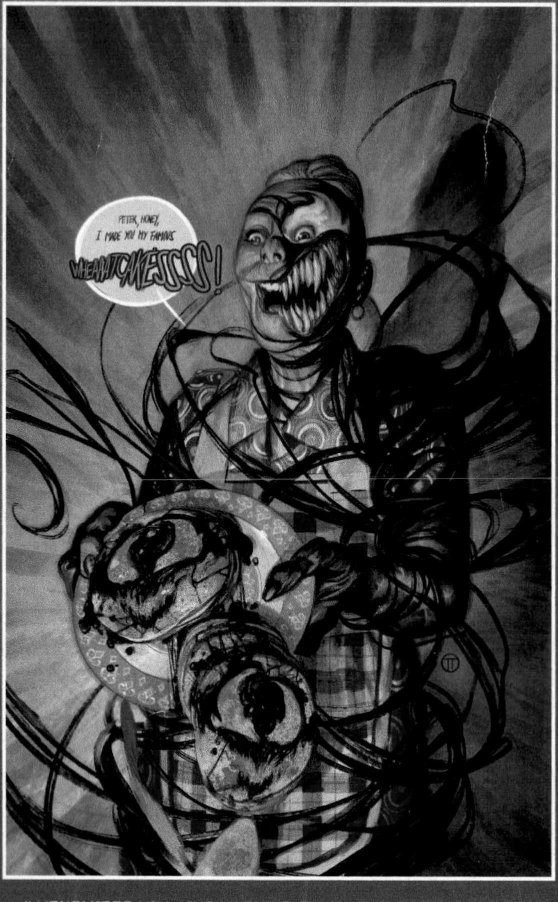
PETER, HONEY, I MADE YOU MY FAMOUS
WHEAAATCAKESSSS!

#4 VENOMIZED VILLAINS VARIANT BY **JULIAN TOTINO TEDESCO**